Commercial Flower Forcing

McGraw-Hill Book Company

New York   St. Louis   San Francisco
Auckland   Bogotá   Düsseldorf
Johannesburg   London   Madrid   Mexico
Montreal   New Delhi   Panama
Paris   São Paulo   Singapore
Sydney   Tokyo   Toronto

Alex Laurie, B.S., M.S.
Professor Emeritus of Floriculture
The Ohio State University

D. C. Kiplinger, B.S., M.S., Ph.D.
Late Professor of Floriculture
The Ohio State University

Kennard S. Nelson, B.A., M.S., Ph.D.
Consultant, Florconsult
Columbus, Ohio
Formerly Extension Specialist in Floriculture
The Ohio State University

Eighth Edition

COMMERCIAL FLOWER FORCING

The Fundamentals
and Their Practical
Application to
the Culture of
Greenhouse Crops

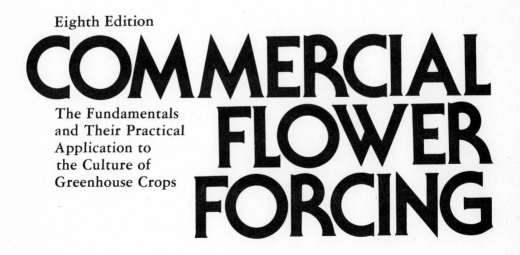

Commercial Flower Forcing

1234567890 DODO 7832109

This book was set in Garamond by Black Dot, Inc. (ECU).
The editors were C. Robert Zappa and James W. Bradley;
the designer was Nicholas Krenitsky;
the production supervisor was Leroy A. Young.
The cover photograph was taken by Martin Bough.
R. R. Donnelley & Sons Company was printer and binder.

Library of Congress Cataloging in Publication Data

Laurie, Alexander, date
    Commercial flower forcing.

    Includes index.
    1. Floriculture. 2. Greenhouse management.
3. Forcing (Plants) I. Kiplinger, Donald Carl,
date   joint author. II. Nelson, Kennard S., joint
author. III. Title.
SB415.L3   1979   635.9'82   78-17130
ISBN 0-07-036633-0

Contents

Preface

Plants. Cutting and Grading Cut-Flower Crops.
Transportation of Cut Flowers. Pest and Pathogen Control
for Cut-Flower Crops. Rotations for Cut-Flower Crops.
Cut-Flower Crops. *Aster. Baby's Breath. Bachelor's Button.
Calla. Candytuft. Carnation. Celosia. Chrysanthemum.
Daffodil. Delphinium. Forget-Me-Not. Freesia. Gladiolus.
Iris. Larkspur. Orchid. Rose. Schizanthus. Snapdragon.
Statice. Stephanotis. Stock. Transvaal Daisy. Zinnia.*

6. Pot-Plant Crop Production 279

The Pot-Plant Crops. Land for Pot-Plant Production.
Structures for Pot-Plant Crops. Pots. *Containers.* Soil
Preparation for Pot-Plant Crops. Sowing, Sticking, Pot-
ting, and Transplanting. Irrigation of Pot-Plant Crops.
Fertilizer Application for Pot-Plant Crops. Transportation
of Pot Plants. Assembling and Wrapping Pot Plants for
Shipping. Pest and Pathogen Control for Pot
Plants. Pot-Plant Rotations. Flowering Pot Plants.
*African Violet. Azalea. Elatior Begonia. Calceolaria.
Cherry. Christmas Cactus. Chrysanthemum. Cineraria.
Clerodendrum. Crocus. Cyclamen. Daffodil. Exacum.
Fuchsia. Gloxinia. Hyacinth. Hydrangea. Kalanchoe.
Lily. Pepper. Poinsettia. Primula. Rose. Schizanthus.
Streptocarpus. Tulip. Zinnia.* Foliage Plants. *Foliage-
Plant Production Areas. Foliage-Plant Marketing. Foliage-
Plant Growing Environments and Holding Environments. Foliage
Plants Listed by Genus.* Bedding Plants. *Acalypha.
Ageratum. Alternanthera. Alyssum. Asparagus. Begonia.
Browallia. Caladium. Canna. Celosia. Chrysanthemum.
Coleus. Cordyline. Croton. Dahlia. Dianthus. Dusty
Miller. Echeveria. Flowering Maple. Fuchsia. Geranium.
Globe Amaranth. Impatiens. Iresine. Lantana.
Lobelia. Marigold. Nicotiana. Pansy. Petunia. Phlox.
Salvia. Santolina. Snapdragon. Verbena. Vinca. Zinnia.*

7. Marketing 403

Marketing through Wholesale Commission Houses.
Selling Directly from the Wholesale Greenhouse to the
Retail Shop. Preparation of Flowers for Market.
Keeping Qualities of Cut Flowers.

8. Costs of Production 417

Costs Vary with the Expenditures and the Quantity
Produced. Labor Is the Largest Item in Cost of
Production. Means of Reducing Costs of Production.

Index 423

Preface

It is believed that *Commercial Flower Forcing* is used mainly by college students taking courses in preparation for commercial, educational, or sales work in floriculture, and by operators and workers in the floriculture industry who may or may not have had formal training in floriculture. The intent is that the summary and conceptual treatment used here in the presentation of basic information on plants, soils, pathogens, pests, engineering, and marketing is compatible with the more detailed information the students have in these specific subjects, and that it also will be understood easily by those who have not had the background subjects.

Wherever possible, metric units are used and comparisons with customary units are presented. It is believed that in most instances in the change commercially to metric units, the closest metric whole value to the customary value will be used.

There is considerable reorganization in this edition. Chapter 2 has been enlarged to include all types of facilities that are required in the floriculture production business. Chapter 3 presents all aspects of plant growth and development that typically are encountered in commercial flower forcing. The attempt in Chapter 4 is to describe the effects of the total environment—above ground and below ground—on greenhouse crop plants. Chapter 5 and 6 have introductions to the general procedures used for these crops. Some crops have been added and a few have been removed. The chapter on pot-plant crops now includes flowering pot plants, foliage plants, and bedding plants.

Several changes in plant names have been made. *Hortus Third* was used as the standard guide in making these changes, and further reference was made to *Exotic Plant Manual* and *Manual of Cultivated Plants.*

During this work, the authors used information and suggestions from many colleagues in education, research, and the industry. Their help is appreciated and gratefully acknowledged.

Alex Laurie
Kennard S. Nelson

The Floriculture Industry

1

Commercial flower forcing is an important segment of the floriculture industry. It is a production or manufacturing business. The products are flowers and ornamental plants, and they are produced in closely controlled conditions—to a great extent in greenhouses.

RELATED INDUSTRIES

Floriculture is one of the branches of agriculture. The agricultural industry generally is understood to be involved in the production of various plant crops and livestock, and sometimes the term is restricted to farming or crops produced on farms—food and fiber. But agriculture does include the production of fruit crops (pomology), vegetable crops (olericulture), landscape ornamental plants (ornamental horticulture), and flowers and ornamental plants (floriculture). These specialized food and ornamental-plant production businesses are grouped together in the section of agriculture that is known as horticulture.

The individuals who work in the floriculture industry could be called floriculturists, horticulturists, or agriculturists, but frequently they are known as flower and plant producers or florists.

The plant producers in the various branches of agriculture have several common bonds. The basics of plant growth and development (botany, plant physiology, taxonomy, morphology) are essentially the same for any of the crops, and the understanding and concepts of plant diseases (plant pathology), plant pests (entomology), and soils (soil science and agronomy) are vital for the good conduct of all these agricultural plant production businesses.

There are many special applications of information to specific crops, and these details are learned by the flower and plant producer either by formal schooling in floriculture or by practical experience in the floriculture production industry—or, better yet, by a combination of them.

FLORICULTURE PRODUCTION AND MARKETING BUSINESSES

The flower and plant producers may have either retail or wholesale businesses depending on how their products are marketed. Retail producers usually try to grow the crops that can be sold in their own retail outlet or outlets. If any of the crops cannot be sold through their retail stores, they will attempt to sell the merchandise through the wholesale market. Because the primary objective is to supply only the needs for a retail market, the production area usually is comparatively small, and the crops are varied.

Some flower and plant producers purposely develop combination retail and wholesale production businesses. In some instances all of the crops that are grown may be sold either retail or wholesale, but more often most of the crops are sold retail and a specialty crop or two is sold both retail and wholesale.

It probably would be best to operate most flower and plant production greenhouses as wholesale businesses. An individual who operates the greenhouse and has one or more retail stores is then the operator of two businesses—a wholesale production business and a retail marketing business. In these situations, it just happens that the same individual owns and operates both concerns. When this separation of businesses is used, it is possible to determine the degree of financial success of each phase of the business. It does take a dedicated and hard-headed business manager, however, to separate the two sufficiently so that reliable accounting can be done for the production business and the marketing business.

With this rationale, it can be accepted that all flower and plant production businesses are (or should be) classed as wholesale businesses, but because of size of operation or ownership situations in some instances all (or most) of the produce will be sold to a single firm.

Some greenhouse operators sell some or all of their product directly to firms that are in the retail business. These retailers may handle flowers and plants as their primary products for sale, or this may be only a portion of the merchandise that they have for their customers. Some of the retail firms sell services of various kinds in conjunction with their flower and plant sales, and they commonly are referred to as flower shops, flower stores, or retail florists. Commonly the retail florists are members of services that provide for handling of flower and plant orders at any location. The customer places the order with a local florist; the local florist places the order by wire or telephone with a fellow member florist at the out-of-town location; both florists report the transaction to the service headquarters; the local florist collects from the customer; and member debits and credits are adjusted periodically through the service headquarters. Some of the service organizations also provide schooling, literature, and national advertising for their members.

The greenhouse operator may be involved in local marketing and may deliver to the retailer, or the retailer in some instances may make pickup at the greenhouse. It may be long-distance marketing in which the greenhouse operator ships via air freight or special truck carriers directly to the retail outlet. In some situations, the shipment is made to the retail firms' warehouses for distribution to their stores from that point.

Flower and plant producers may sell some or all of their products through middlemen or wholesalers. The traditional wholesalers in the floriculture industry have been known as wholesale commission florists. They accept the produce on consignment and deduct a commission when they sell the merchandise. Many of these wholesale firms purchase all or a portion of the flowers and plants that they handle for resale. Greenhouse operators try to use local or nearby wholesale firms for handling their products, but frequently long-distance shipping is involved.

There are some floriculture businesses that are vertically integrated to a degree. Many greenhouse operators sell all or most of their product through their own retail stores. Some of the operators of larger production areas have their own wholesale stores and attempt to sell all of their product as well as other produce that is consigned to them or bought for resale.

In several areas of the country, flower and plant producers have formed cooperatives of some type primarily for marketing their crops, but they also may function in purchasing supplies for the members. The cooperatives may sell through wholesale houses or they may sell to retailers—or both.

Some of the largest floriculture industry businesses are those that produce plants for other segments of the industry. These are specialists that produce seeds, bulbs, cuttings, small plants, and dormant plants that flower and plant producers use to start their crops. These firms produce such things as mum cuttings, budded rose plants, bedding plant and other types of seed, foliage plants, azaleas, carnation cuttings, poinsettias, begonias, kalanchoes, geraniums, and bulbs of various kinds. These plant production businesses may sell directly to the flower and plant producer, or they may use wholesalers to sell their products. Much of this plant material is sold by firms on a brokerage basis—sales representatives for the firm take orders from greenhouse operator customers, and the product is shipped directly from the producer to the customer.

THE CUSTOMERS' NEEDS FOR FLOWERS AND ORNAMENTAL PLANTS

Regardless of the product, purchases are made to satisfy needs and wants. These needs and wants may be classed as either emotional or physical, and the decision to make the purchase may be made on emotional or economic bases.

Flowers and ornamental plants are purchased to satisfy emotional needs. To some individuals emotions, often described as feelings, are a condition in another person caused by imagination. This view, however, is inaccurate. The emotional needs of human beings are just as real as their physical needs, and each is affected by the other. Flower and plant producers should understand the effect that the purchase of their products can have on customers and evaluate their products on that basis. Customers want to improve their own and/or someone else's emotional well-being, and in this instance accomplish it by the purchase of flowers or ornamental plants. The flower and plant grower who can sense the real emotional needs of the customer will do a much better job of supplying the right product.

Just a flower or a plant is not enough. The product must have the most satisfying effect. The flower and plant growers' end product has to be emotional betterment. Growers should not get very involved in growing flowers and plants that meet high professional standards but lose sight of the fact that the real evaluation has to be based on the effect the product has on the customers' emotions.

Some industry people have recognized the need, and better foliage plants for use indoors have been developed. There have been many improvements in bedding plants that better satisfy customer needs in outdoor landscaping. New rose, poinsettia, and begonia cultivars are more acceptable to customers. They are more satisfied—they feel better from using these products.

There was a time when the manufacturers of plastic flowers and plants were able to satisfy customer needs with their products. Eventually, however, the customers found that these lifeless products had very little value in their emotional betterment, and they returned to purchasing live flowers and plants.

Flower and plant products do have much competition in the marketplace from inanimate products. These competing products may be clothing, jewelry, cosmetics, candy, food, appliances, and various other items, and this does need to be recognized. Although some of these products have direct physical effects, they also have emotional values. The customer may put more value on the combined physical and emotional effect of a steak dinner than he would on the emotional effect of a vase of flowers or a potted plant. The economic factor enters here, too. A $10.00 piece of jewelry may be equated as having similar emotional value for a Valentine gift as a $25.00 vase of roses.

The floriculture industry should be affected less by generally depressed markets than some other industries because the emotional value of flowers or plants is greater than more expensive appliances or clothing.

FLORICULTURE BUSINESS COMPETITION

The flower and plant manufacturer does have competition from many other types of businesses that make products which can provide emotional betterment in human beings. These competing fields may be entertainment, literature, welfare, cosmetics, memorials, appliances, jewelry, foods, and several others. This is a big field, but the grower should look on it not as a business threat but as an opportunity to participate in the obviously large market for emotional improvement. There are a large number of potential customers that need the help that flowers or plants could give them.

The flower and plant producer can have competition from business peers within and outside of the United States. These competitors may be able to produce a better product or sell the same product more reasonably because of climatic or business advantages at their locations. Sometimes the local grower can meet the competition successfully, but in other situations must change crops or methods in order to keep the business viable. Distant producers always do have the disadvantage of shipping costs and shipping time, but in spite of this they may be difficult to compete with.

The highly competitive areas within the United States have been California, Colorado, and Florida, primarily because of some climatic advantages over some other areas. Most of the competition is in some of the cut-flower crops, but there are some highly competitive situations in pot-plant crops also.

More recently there has been increased competition from outside the country. With continued improvements in transportation, competition from flower and plant producers in any part of the world could be expected. The effects of this competition varies considerably with location and air transport facilities. The competitive advantage that these growers have is favorable climatic conditions or some economic advantages. Some of the countries and regions that ship flowers or plants into the United States are Canada, Mexico, Central America, South America, Holland, Belgium, Israel, and Australia. In some instances the imports into the United States have had such great effects on the market that some domestic producers have either discontinued business or changed their crop production.

SOURCES OF SUPPLY FOR COMMERCIAL FLOWER FORCERS

Some supplies can be obtained locally: general industrial or agricultural kinds of things such as plumbing and pipe-fitting, electrical, automotive, heating, and general construction materials; farm fertilizers; and some pesticides.

Many of the items needed are specific to the business and cannot be obtained locally. Greenhouse structures and some of the related equipment are available from a few (less than six) firms in the United States that specialize in that work. Greenhouse structures that can be erected by growers and their workers are available in several types from various firms that specialize in that equipment.

Other specific items that are required, such as nozzles, timers, fertilizers, growth regulators, pesticides, and conveyors, can be obtained from specialty supply firms (possibly fewer than 24) in various parts of the country. Some of these suppliers (approximately 12) also handle plants that are needed by the growers. The plants are handled as a brokerage item—they are shipped directly to the customer by the plant producer. These plant sellers, however, do provide scheduling and advisory services for their customers.

Some plant suppliers sell their own plants, and they may have one or more sales representatives traveling in the United States who call on their greenhouse customers once or more times a year.

Most of these firms that handle plants or supplies for commercial greenhouse operations advertise regularly in the trade papers.

TRADE ORGANIZATIONS

The national trade organization is the Society of American Florists (SAF). It represents the floriculture industry and has divisions for producers, retail marketers, and wholesale marketers. The SAF is involved in an advisory capacity with the federal legislative bodies. It disseminates pertinent information to the membership, and it sponsors programs and advertising for the promotion of the floriculture industry.

Other national trade organizations are Roses, Inc., which represents the greenhouse rose producers, and Wholesale Florists and Florist Suppliers of America (WF&FSA), which represents the wholesale marketers.

In most states, members of the industry have banded together in organizations that may include the producers or the retailers or both groups. Some of these state organizations are very active. In addition to sponsoring meetings, they may represent their members in legislative or other matters. Some of the state organizations publish bulletins regularly. Frequently the state extension service works closely with the organization in organizing and conducting meetings.

Most metropolitan areas have organizations called allieds that represent producers, retailers, and wholesalers in the promotion of industry business in the area. In many localities they have effectively increased business.

EDUCATION AND RESEARCH IN FLORICULTURE

Because of federal encouragement and monetary grants, vocational high schools have been established in most cities in the United States. Some of these schools offer courses in horticulture. The results of this instruction have been variable because of several factors. Some of the schools have graduated individuals who are interested in and well-qualified for employment in the greenhouse. If the local school is not making good progress in development of vocational students, possibly the administrators and educators would welcome suggestions from industry members.

Some states have post-high schools that offer 2-year courses in commercial floriculture instruction. A good source of information on these schools and the courses of study that they offer should be available in most high school principals' offices. College registrars' offices also should have this information.

Many states have colleges that offer degree work in floriculture. This is academic rather than vocational education, but in spite of this some educators do an excellent job of acquainting the students with the realities in commercial floriculture production. The strictly academic courses of study are more suitable for the instruction of teachers and research workers. The individuals who are most interested in thorough understanding of commercial procedures will get part-time employment in the industry before or while they attend college.

Usually the state-supported university that offers a course of study in floriculture also will have a research program in floriculture. This work may be done right at the university or it may be conducted at another site in the state. Some of the work will have federal as well as state funding.

The United States Department of Agriculture (USDA) conducts some research in floriculture at Beltsville, Maryland, and at other locations in the country. The results of this work are published in the trade papers. They have 1-day meetings at Beltsville periodically in which the current research work is displayed and discussed.

State universities have an extension staff that is responsible for disseminating pertinent information and advice on technical matters to agriculturists in the state. Each county also has extension personnel. The extension program has federal funding. The size of the extension staff is determined by the amount of agriculture industry in the state, and the specialties of the staff members correspond to the kind of agriculture business that is predominant in the state. If there is a significant amount of floriculture production business in the state, there will be one or more floriculture specialists on the state extension staff. The extension specialists organize and conduct meetings for trade members, and they may make visits to a place of business if assistance is requested.

PUBLICATIONS

The trade papers are published weekly, and they include reports on trade meetings, editorials, all types of advertising, calendar of coming events, and reports on research work. The *Florists' Review,* 310 S. Michigan Ave., Chicago, Illinois 60604, gives coverage throughout the United States. The *Canadian Florist,* Box 697, Streetsville, Ontario, Canada, serves the industry to the North and *Southern Florist and Nurseryman,* Box 1868, Fort Worth, Texas 76101, gives particular coverage to industry events in the South and West.

The larger firms, which sell plants and supplies to the industry, publish catalogs that include much helpful information as well as the listings of the products that they handle. Some of these firms also publish newsletters or bulletins. Industry members may request to be placed on their mailing lists.

Several of the state trade organizations publish bulletins regularly that contain articles of worth to industry members in any part of the country. These bulletins may be obtained by membership in the organization. The fee for out-of-state membership usually is less than it is for the in-state members.

Several of the state extension services publish bulletins regularly or distribute reports when they are available. There is no fee for this service, and it is possible to get on their mailing lists by making the request. The extension service office will be at the state university. The county extension office also can supply the information on bulletins and other literature that is available.

Facilities for Commercial Flower Forcing

2

There are several different kinds of facilities that are needed in the commercial production of flowers and plants. Some of these are obvious, some are overlooked, and others are taken for granted. Probably the most obvious of the facilities are the structures and the equipment. These are quite visible, and it is apparent that they are involved in the development of the product.

Some of the essential facilities that may be taken for granted are a market, personnel, site, and utilities.

A facility that often is overlooked is funds.

All these facilities are vital in the conduct of commercial flower forcing. Some will be easier to obtain than others, and the prospective greenhouse operator will have to put them in their proper order of importance so that the most critical situations are handled first. The order in which the individual starting in business usually will need to be concerned with facilities is market, funds, personnel, site, utilities, structures, and equipment.

It is true that when a business is inherited many of these facilities come with the business. The facilities most frequently lacking are personnel and funds. Usually some of the other facilities will need evaluation for their effectiveness in present conditions.

The importance of some personal considerations in making business decisions must be acknowledged. There may be medical, family, personal capability, or geographical situations that would affect the judgments that are made, but the effects of any compromise need to be admitted.

MARKET EVALUATION

If the business is inherited or purchased it should be relatively routine to get an accurate account of the market experience in the past. It then should be possible to project an estimate of the market of the future based on present conditions.

Before a new production business is started it must be established where the market is, what the market needs are, and what the market prices are. It is not too difficult to locate marketplaces, but it is very difficult to get reliable information on market needs and prices. It is wise to consider what the alternative markets would be if the original market develops less favorably than anticipated

The flower and plant production facilities need to be planned and operated to satisfy a market demand at a price that gives the producer an adequate return on costs and investment.

Yes, it is true that a market demand at an adequate product price can be created, but before the production facilities are established, sound plans for the development of such a market need to be made.

FUNDS FOR THE PRODUCTION FACILITY

Funds are required for the establishment and operation of any business. The amount of money needed will depend on the size of the business, the kind of acquisition, the facilities provided, the method of doing business, and production and marketing results.

Some of the funds will be used for capital investments in land, structures, some utilities, and some equipment. Funds also will be needed for operating the business. The operating funds are needed for such items as payroll, fuel, interest, taxes, purchases (including plants), shipping costs, and marketing costs. These operating expenditures always precede the marketing receipts, and funds are needed for this purpose. The individual just starting in business must anticipate a considerable time lag between expenditures and receipts and will need enough funds to tide the business over a period of a few months when there will be no product ready for sale—and no income.

The requirement for funds is quite different for a retail greenhouse operation than it is for a greenhouse that produces crops for the wholesale market. Usually, retail greenhouses are smaller. Retailers can buy on the wholesale market and have a very active retail trade regardless of the amount produced in their own greenhouses. The potential gross income from the wholesale greenhouse is related directly to size. Within limits, the only way wholesale growers can increase their income is by expanding their growing area. Retail growers will have the time delay in income from their greenhouses that wholesale growers have, but the income in their flower shops will start almost immediately because of the buying and selling procedure.

Retail growers may require less land for their ventures, but it may be more expensive land because of the necessity of being in preferred retail marketing areas, whereas wholesale growers may locate on less costly rural land.

Availability of Money for Financing a Greenhouse Business

Most individuals do not have enough funds of their own to finance a greenhouse operation. They have to get funds from an outside source, of which there are several different possibilities. The business frequently is started as a proprietorship because that is the easiest form of business to start—and terminate. The responsibilities and benefits are solely those of the proprietor. There is no real distinction between personal and business affairs. One of the first sources of funds for a proprietorship is from relatives. This may have either good or bad features. On any basis such loans need to be arranged on a business basis so that the parties involved know the exact terms of the loan. These loans usually are made without specification of collateral, but it probably would be better if collateral were used.

If the form of business is a partnership, there are two or more sources of personal funds that may be used in operating the business—and two or more sets of relatives who could possibly become involved in loans. Most partnerships are established on the basis of equal sharing of responsibilities and benefits. The personal and business relationship is much the same as it is in a proprietorship, but in a partnership either individual can be held totally responsible for the obligations of the business. In addition to the effects that a partnership has on the source of funds, there will be a division of income. If both partners are active in the business (sometimes a partner's involvement will be solely financial), there also will be a division of responsibilities. On any basis there must be a thorough and workable understanding of each partner's function in the business.

The business may be formed as a corporation. The funds for this business may originate from one individual or from several. In this form of business there is separation of personal and business affairs. It is a more formal and involved way of conducting a business. The corporation operates under laws in the state where it is located. It is governed by a board of directors, and there may be two or more officers named to executive positions in the corporation. Many of the corporations meet the formal requirements of law as simply as possible, and the direction of the corporation is by the individual who has the controlling financial interest in the business. Most commonly in small corporations (closely held corporations) the individual with the majority financial interest is "elected" to the position of chairman of the board, or president, or general manager, or whatever term is used for the head of the business. Corporations frequently get their initial funds from relatives, who are issued stock in the company accordingly.

Regardless of the form of business some additional funding is often required, and this may be obtained from banks or other kinds of loaning agencies. It generally is found that most businesses underestimate their needs for funds, and for that reason they cannot be operated efficiently and profitably. Most loans must be secured with collateral. This may be by real estate, mortgage, insurance, stocks, equipment, or inventory. On any basis the loaning firm will need to have complete information on the individuals responsible for the business, past business experiences, and plans and projections for the future. There is a tendency to consider that short-term loans will suffice. This involves higher interest rates and also refinancing when the money is needed for longer periods of time. Usually there is a need for some long-term, as well as short-term, financing.

It is not unusual that a portion of the funds needed is obtained by trade credit. A major supplier or two of the business may agree to extend credit for a longer period of time. Frequently this degenerates into a situation in which the greenhouse operator is continually indebted to the supplier for a sum of money and never does bring the account up to date. If the supplier makes a handling charge, it probably is at the rate of 18 percent per annum. This is expensive money. It is even more costly when it is considered that many suppliers give a discount for prompt payment of invoices. In most cases, the greenhouse operator would save money by borrowing from traditional loaning agencies and then discounting the bills in paying suppliers.

PERSONNEL FOR COMMERCIAL FLOWER FORCING

Management personnel must be given first consideration. If the business is large enough to have more management personnel than just the owner of the business, the decisions will need to be made as to what kind of managers are needed, the number required, and how they can be obtained.

Regardless of the size of the business, the various management specialties that are needed could be production, marketing, engineering, and business office. For the small place of business, the owner and/or family members may function in all capacities of management as well as doing all the other work. For larger businesses, the managers that are needed are either recruited from schools and competitors or are brought up through the ranks. There are some advantages in each method. Although the intent may be to develop managers within the work crew, eventually this will not be possible and someone will have to be brought in from outside.

Someone from management needs to live on the greenhouse property or adjacent to it. There are too many after-hours emergencies in greenhouses that cannot be handled by commuters.

The greenhouse workers will need to be recruited from the immediate community. In most instances these workers can be trained on the job if the manager is a capable one. The workers may be male or female and on part-time or full-time employment. Usually there is more flexibility when there are some workers from each category.

Many greenhouse businesses are small-sized when started—2,000 square meters or less—with the owner and spouse wedded to the venture 24 hours a day, month in and month out. This size of business may be just about large enough to supply the income needed for one family. Some workers may be employed, but probably no one is qualified to accept the responsibility of operating the place for a few days or for a week or two while the owner is away. To be able to justify the expenditure of funds for a responsible manager, the business may need to be twice as large.

Once personnel are employed, the owner then should have operating procedures that ensure the retention of the good employee and the separation of the inept one. Without such a policy, the good workers move on and the bad ones stay. The first assessment of the worker's fit on the job should be made about 1 month after hiring. At that time the worker should be given further encouragement to remain on the job or should be fired. Subsequent evaluations of the worker's effectiveness should be made periodically—and some action taken by management to retain or release him or her.

THE GREENHOUSE SITE

There are a multitude of considerations in selecting the site for the greenhouse. The geographical location may be chosen because of the favorable effects of that climate for plant growth or proximity to the market. Some other business considerations are availability and price of fuel, utilities, water, and labor. Taxes for comparable areas need to be evaluated.

Sometimes considerations other than strictly business ones are important and will influence the decision. Some of these are the suitability of living conditions, schools, places of worship, stores, cultural and athletic events, and recreational areas. Family ties may be strong on either or both sides, and the owner may want to retain these, with business adjusted in the best possible way.

When the geographical location has been selected, the items to consider in addition to the above are topography of the land, price, transportation, and present and future effects of adjacent properties.

A few years ago one of the requirements for location of a greenhouse site was proximity to railroad service so that a spur could be constructed and coal brought in by rail. That became of no importance when coal was replaced by oil or gas as fuels. However, as fuel shortages develop there may be a return to the use of coal. Regardless of the kind of fuel, it must be determined that for the present time and foreseeable future the greenhouse site is easily accessible for fuel delivery.

There have been some investigations into the use of heat generated as a by-product by electricity-generating plants. When this is done the greenhouse site must necessarily be adjacent to the generating facility.

Topography of the land determines the amount of work and expense that will be required to provide good surface drainage and efficient transportation. Water drainage problems are compounded when any buildings are constructed because the area covered contributes to the surface drainage water that has to be handled in adjacent areas. Before structure construction starts, the land must be worked so that there will be adequate water drainage away from the site after the present construction or any future construction.

Transportation in and around the greenhouse will be most efficient on land that is essentially level. If the proposed site is hilly, it should be anticipated that considerable land preparation will be required. Access roads to the property will need to be large enough and surfaced to handle large motor freight equipment. A parking lot will need to be provided that is large enough to handle customers' and workers' cars.

It is possible that neighboring properties may have several different effects on the greenhouse business. If it is an industrial area—or becomes one—there could be damage to crops from some kinds of air pollution. Some federal or state agencies should be able to evaluate current situations. The problems that might develop in the future are a matter of estimation.

If adjacent land becomes developed for residential use, new zoning restrictions may affect operation, maintenance, or additions to the greenhouse property.

Changes in land valuation affect the cost of doing business. Greenhouses that were built outside of cities become surrounded by urban development with increased taxation to support all phases of this growth—streets, schools, water and sewerage, and politicians. It is true that the land could be sold for much more than was paid for it, but it is not likely that it would cover the cost of relocation to another site.

UTILITIES

Some sites will have better utility service than others. Greenhouse businesses cannot have interruption of electrical service for more than a few minutes without serious consequences. What has the experience been in the area in question—and what guarantees of continuous service will the utility make? Electrical shutdowns that are a nuisance for a machine shop could be a disaster for a greenhouse.

The quality of telephone service varies from area to area. The effectiveness of this utility for the greenhouse site needs to be determined primarily because of its effect on the marketing of a perishable product.

The quality and quantity of water that is available to the site must be determined. If municipal water is available, usually it is acceptable for irrigation and for use in boilers with some treatment. When water has to be supplied by well or pond on the site, there are some potential problems. The quantity might not be great enough. There might be some quality problems. Well water typically has dissolved minerals that give it the quality referred to as hardness. Most greenhouse operations will not be able to establish water-treatment facilities to remove these minerals from the irrigation water. As a result there may be an undue amount of nozzle or valve clogging and residue deposits on leaves or flowers. Extensive treatment may be needed for boiler make-up water. It is possible, too, that sand or silt may be pumped along with the water from the well, and this may clog some equipment or cause abrasion and damage to other equipment.

Pond water can be expected to have qualities characteristic of the watershed, so, before the pond is constructed, the potential effects of

Table 2-1 Total Salts Content of Water as Determined by a Solu Bridge

Solu Bridge reading of water	Interpretation
0–0.25	Excellent
0.25–0.75	Good
0.75–1.50	Fair
1.50–2.00	Permissible
2.00 plus	Excessive (too salty)

watershed on quality of water should be analyzed. If the greenhouse drainage water contributes to the pond, it can be expected that the residues from fertilizers may be rather high. Also it is possible that some isolated infestation of pest or pathogen may be distributed throughout the greenhouse by this means.

Because of the widespread use of herbicides on farm lands, this effect on the pond water needs to be established. Herbicides that may be safe for use on corn or soybeans may be harmful to some greenhouse crops. Is it possible that the watershed will contribute herbicides to the pond water?

It can be expected that some sand or silt may be pumped with the pond water with the same problems that were outlined for that occurrence in well water.

Usually some pond maintenance is required. The most persistent problem may be the control of weeds. Weeds may be controlled with geese or some kinds of fish, or it is possible to use certain kinds of herbicides. But it must be determined that the herbicide will be completely harmless to all the greenhouse crops.

Sewerage will be needed for the business, and if it is not available on the site, the greenhouse operator will have to supply it. This is sanitary sewerage for disposal of sewage, and storm sewerage to handle surface-water drainage. If the sewerage system is not on the property or it is not adequate for this new business, the costs for supplying this service need to be evaluated.

It should be determined if fuel gas is available at the site and on what basis the fuel can be used. If there is no fuel gas service there at this time, what are the plans for the future for supplying it?

Trash disposal has become more of a problem. If the site is urban, there may be a routine and adequate trash disposal service. If the site is rural, greenhouse operators may have to devise their own service. If this is necessary, what methods are authorized for the area?

Are bus or other public transportation services available to the site? In some instances this will be a consideration in obtaining workers.

GREENHOUSE STRUCTURES

The most obvious difference between greenhouses and other production structures is that greenhouses are covered with material that transmits light. Glass covering has been used for years and still is used effectively. In some places other than the United States these structures quite properly are referred to as glasshouses.

The supporting framework may be wood, steel, or aluminum, although the use of wood is no longer common practice.

Greenhouses may be constructed either as permanent or temporary structures. Most installations are permanent ones, but temporary structures may be used for seasonal crops, when the land needs to be vacated shortly, or to comply with current building codes.

Greenhouse businesses will have other structures that have opaque coverings. These may be for heat-generating equipment, retail sales, potting or shipping, storage, and cool storage.

Size and Arrangement of Houses

The requirements of the crops should be considered first. Pot-plant crops are grown more easily in smaller houses that have easy access to a central headhouse and shipping room. In such a situation the varied

Figure 2-1 Various arrangements of greenhouses are used depending on the crops to be grown and the land available. Separate greenhouses require more land than gutter-connected (ridge and furrow) ones, but they can provide better light, ventilation, and temperature control. *(Lord & Burnham drawing.)*

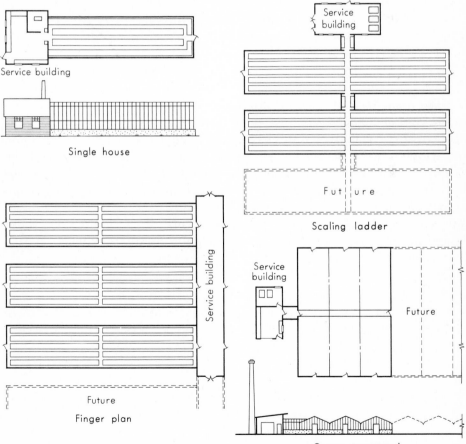

temperatures can be provided that are needed for pot-plant crops; and movement to and from the potting area, greenhouses, and the shipping room is direct and convenient. Cut-flower crops are often grown better in larger houses; however, with crops such as mums there is an advantage in having units that can be handled separately.

Economy of construction is important. Ridge and furrow type construction is usually more economical, and it does require less land area. Some disadvantages are excessive shade from the gutters, lack of temperature control of individual houses, and no side ventilation. If forced-air ventilation is used, the lack of side ventilators may be no problem.

The houses should be arranged so that labor is conserved and the crop is handled most efficiently. Consideration should be given to the ease with which flowers can be cut and moved to the grading area, and pot plants moved from area to area or to the shipping room.

The benching arrangement as well as the heating and cooling system should be planned while the general layout for the greenhouse is being made. This is much easier than trying to fit them into the established range after it is up, and it may very easily change preconceived ideas on the best arrangement of houses.

Types of Greenhouse Framework

The framework of the greenhouse consists of side posts—or gutter posts in the case of connected houses—at about 3-meter intervals, to support the roof trusses. The eave or gutter extends from post to post at the point where the truss joins the side post. The ridge extends from truss to truss at the peak of the house. Midway between the ridge and eave a purlin extends from truss to truss. If the house is wide, two or more purlins may be spaced equidistant between ridge and eave. For narrow houses or houses with adequate trusswork that is the basic framework of the house. For wider houses or for trusses that need additional support, posts are provided at each truss from the purlin to the ground.

Comparison of Customary and Metric Units of Length

Customary	Metric (approximate)
1 inch	2.5 centimeters
1 foot	30.0 centimeters
1 yard	1.0 meter
100 feet	30.5 meters
1 mile	1.6 kilometers

Figure 2-2 Connected (ridge and furrow) greenhouses in the process of construction. These are clear-span greenhouses—the roof is supported solely by the trusses which extend from side post to opposing gutter post. *(Lord & Burnham photograph.)*

Usually a curtain wall of concrete or transite is used for about 1 meter at the base of the sidewalls of the greenhouse. For glass houses, roof bars are installed approximately 60 centimeters apart from ridge to purlin to eave, and wall bars are placed from the eave to the sill of the sidewall. These bars provide the base for the glass. Houses that are to be covered with film plastic may have bars or rafters spaced about 120 centimeters apart with wire fabric installed beneath the plastic film to support it. Corrugated plastics should be applied to framework members that run lengthwise to the house (purlins). These should be installed about every 90 centimeters across the width of the roof depending on the weight of the corrugated plastic and the pitch of the roof.

The post and truss designs for greenhouses may be the same whether they are to be covered with glass, film plastic, or rigid plastic; but the purlin and bar arrangement should be made specifically for the type of material that will be used to cover the structure. Usually it is not possible to switch from one type of covering to another without making the necessary changes in bars or purlins first. However, in replacing glass with corrugated plastic in old, wooden bar houses, it is possible to remove the glass, clean and paint the bars, and then apply the corrugated plastic directly to the bars at a slight angle.

The choice of materials for the framework of a greenhouse is based on structural strength, durability, initial cost, and maintenance costs. Wooden framework is used primarily for temporary or semipermanent structures. The most durable wood with the least maintenance cost is redwood. Steel framework has been used widely. This does require frequent painting to prevent rust, but it is very satisfactory in other respects. Steel frame houses may have redwood or aluminum roof and wall bars as well as ventilator sash.

Aluminum has become increasingly popular for the greenhouse framework. The roof and wall bars and ventilating sash all are made of aluminum. The corrosion problem with aluminum is slight, and the structure does not require painting. It should be kept in mind, however, that the glazing procedure and maintenance are approximately the same for wood, steel, or aluminum.

The greenhouse framework that has just been described has plane

Figure 2-3 The supporting framework for greenhouses is side or gutter posts with trusses extending across the house between opposite posts. The trusses join with the ridge at the peak, the eave or gutter at the side, and one or more purlins spaced equidistant between ridge and gutter. The roof bars which hold the glass extend from ridge or ventilator header to purlins to gutter or eave. *(Lord & Burnham photograph.)*

surfaces, and it is suitable for being covered by material that is rigid and has plane configuration. Glass panes most commonly have those characteristics. Greenhouses require coverings that transmit light, and because of the excellent light-transmission properties of glass, greenhouse structures were constructed with plane surfaces so they could be covered with glass.

Greenhouse roofs must shed moisture—rain and snow—and with a structure of plane surfaces, the pitched roof provides that property.

Greenhouses require a venting system of some kind. A gravity type of ventilation system needs a ventilator at the highest point in the structure, and the pitched-roof design of greenhouses provides that highest point at the ridge. Thus greenhouse structural design includes ventilators at the ridge.

Two developments have given some flexibility in the structural design of greenhouses—the use of plastic coverings and fans. The plastic coverings can be and are used on structures of pitched-roof design, but they also can be used on structures of arc-roof design when fans are included to handle ventilation. Regardless of kind of covering material, greenhouses of pitched-roof design may be constructed without ridge ventilators if the fan system that is installed is able to handle the total ventilation needs.

Most new greenhouse construction does include total ventilation by means of fans, but there are differences of opinion about the suitability of covering materials. The greenhouse operators who desire glass as a covering must have pitched-roof structures. Those who prefer plastic of some type as a greenhouse covering may use either pitched- or arc-roof design or both.

The use of plastic-film covering for greenhouses led to many innovations in greenhouse structures. Many acres of land were covered in moderate climates such as California with wooden structures in which the windward roof surface is elevated higher than the leeward surface, and the difference in elevations provides an open ventilator. In cooler climates many different types of structures have been designed for covering with plastic film. These, however, must have functional ventilation systems. Unfortunately many individuals rush into the construction of seemingly inexpensive, plastic-film-covered structures without proper evaluation of the means or costs of providing ventilation, heating, irrigation, and benching.

For a structure of the same durability, the greenhouse framework to be covered by plastic must be as sound as the one that will be covered by glass. The design of the structure might be different, but the quality of materials and the strength of the framework must be the same.

The basic difference in framework for greenhouses to be covered with plastic rather than glass is that no roof bars are provided. The plastic is supported and/or attached to purlins that are installed from truss to truss or arc to arc for the length of the greenhouse. Because of this there are a greater number of purlins in the framework of a house to be covered with plastic than one that will be covered with glass.

Types of Greenhouse Covering Materials

The greenhouse must be covered with as clear a material as possible to provide the maximum amount of sunlight for the plants. This is the primary requisite of the structure. The durability of the covering material, the initial cost, and the maintenance costs then determine the desirability of the material.

Light transmission through glass is excellent, and for that reason it has been the primary covering material used through the years. Applying a glass covering is called glazing. The initial cost of glass is reasonable, but it is difficult to install and the periodic reglazing that is required is costly. It is subject to considerable breakage in areas subject to hail storms. In fact, hail damage is such a threat in certain locations that wire netting is installed above the glass to protect it from the hail.

Glass is placed on the greenhouse in much the same manner as shingles on a home—except that the panes are not lapped as much, and they are held in place by glazing points placed at the bottom of each pane, on each side, and also at the top surface at each side. To make the house watertight the glass is set in bedding compound on the bars, and after the glass is in place glazing compound is run along each side of the bar and then painted to complete the seal. The exterior of a glass house needs repainting every 2 to 4

Figure 2-4 Roof bars are designed so that the glass can be placed in bedding compound on each side, and there are drip grooves toward the bottom to conduct the condensation to the sidewall. The bar cap covers the bar to preserve the glazing. (*Lord & Burnham photograph.*)

years to maintain a good seal between bar and glass. Occasionally, loose glazing compound will need to be replaced before repainting. If the seal between bars and glass becomes loose, it is then necessary to reglaze the house. In reglazing, all the glass is removed from the house, the bars are cleaned, and the glass is relaid. This is an expensive procedure but a necessary one if the best growing conditions are to be maintained in the greenhouse. This glazing procedure is virtually the same whether the bars are wooden, steel, or aluminum, but wooden or steel bars must be painted before the bedding compound is applied.

To reduce the frequency of painting and reglazing that is necessary, aluminum bar caps are used. As the name indicates they are aluminum caps or strips that are installed over the bar. They protect the seal from the weather and reduce the amount of maintenance that is needed.

Through the years there has been much interest in the use of materials other than glass for covering greenhouses. The search has been for a material that transmits light as well as glass but has improvements in other properties such as breakage, tightness of seal, and covering and recovering costs. The hope seems to be with plastic of some type, and the various plastics have been tried as they have been developed. Some plastic materials can be used with certain success, and it is possible that other materials will be developed that are even more suitable.

The plastic greenhouse coverings in most common usage are polyethylene film and fiberglass. Many improvements have been made in these materials since they were introduced, and it should be expected that further improvements will evolve. Degradation of both types of materials in ultraviolet (UV) light has limited their usefulness in the past, but the incorporation of UV stabilizers in the products has decreased the rate of degradation.

Fiberglass is a product that has glass fibers imbedded in plastic. The glass fibers provide reinforcement, and the fiberglass panels are flexible but somewhat rigid. Fiberglass can be made in various configurations, but the most common one used for greenhouse covering is corrugated. A form such as this increases the rigidity of the product and does not require as much support as a plane (flat) form would need. Fiberglass is manufactured in panels about 134 centimeters wide and in the length needed for the job. The panels are lapped when they are installed and the effective coverage in width is 120 centimeters per panel. With greenhouse roofs that do not have ridge ventilators, the fiberglass panels are continuous from ridge to eave or gutter. Closure with the plane surfaces of ridge and eave or gutter are made with strips that are plane on one side and corrugated on the other and are placed between the panels and ridge and eave or gutter. The ridges and furrows of

Figure 2-5 Connected Quonset structures covered with clear, corrugated fiberglass. There are no ventilators. Ventilation and cooling are by exhaust fans in one end wall and wet pads in the opposite end. Note the steam mains which service these and other houses. They are sufficiently elevated to give adequate clearance for trucks, and they are insulated to conserve heat. *(Jos. W. Vestal and Sons, Inc. photograph.)*

the corrugations extend the length of the panel, and the attachment of the panel to the framework should be through the ridge because that minimizes leakage. For the attachment at purlins, spacers should be used between panel and purlin so that the panel does not contact the purlin. The moisture that condenses on the inner surface of the panel then can flow uninhibited to the sidewall.

Fiberglass is manufactured in several colors, but it is the clear kind that is used in greenhouse construction. It is a translucent substance that transmits about 90 percent as much light as glass does, but plant growth under fiberglass that is in good condition can be as good as it is under glass. Fiberglass does degrade in time, causing two noticeable effects. The plastic may change color gradually to tan or brown. The rate of this color change has been decreased by the addition of UV stabilizers in the plastic. Also the exterior surface erodes, causing the exposure of glass fibers. This rough surface causes the collection of dirt with the resultant reduction in light transmission. When this occurs, the outer surface can be cleaned with forceful streams of water.

Fiberglass is available with Tedlar film bonded to the exterior surface, and the light transmission of this product remains good for many years with only minimum maintenance of the outer surface of the panels.

The fiberglass manufacturers sell their products under limited warranty of either 10 or 20 years depending on the grade. The actual useful life of fiberglass can be expected to be something less than the full warranted time.

Fiberglass has a rather low flash point as compared to other greenhouse covering materials, and the rate of combustion is fast when the flash point is reached. Special precautions need to be taken to keep fires from any source away from fiberglass-covered greenhouses.

Polyethylene (poly) film is by far the least expensive of the greenhouse covering materials. It also needs to be replaced most often. Ordinary grades of poly film degrade rapidly in high-intensity sunlight, and the film disintegrates. In the northern United States, poly film installed on greenhouses in October usually gives satisfactory service until May. The same grade film installed in May could start to deteriorate by September. However, the newer kinds of poly film that are resistant to ultraviolet deterioration may be used for 2 years before replacement.

It is the clear polyethylene film that is used for greenhouse covering and usually in the 6-mil grade. It is a translucent substance that can transmit 80 to 90 percent as much light as glass does. Plant growth can be as good under poly film as it is under glass.

Poly film is made in widths to 12.2 meters, and the common length of a roll is 30.5 meters. This is large enough to completely cover some greenhouses. Because of the continuous covering, the poly-film-covered houses have less leakage than houses covered with any other material. They are called tight houses. This has some good and some bad features. There is less heat lost by infiltration, but the relative humidity may be too high at times. Also the gas exchange with the outdoors can be so limited that there will be a shortage of oxygen or carbon dioxide or both in the plastic house. If unit heaters or carbon dioxide generators are used in plastic houses, adequate air inlet from outdoors must be provided to sustain the combustion. The manufacturers of the heating or generating equipment can supply the information on the size of air inlet that is needed.

Moisture that condenses on the inner surface of the poly-film covering of greenhouses can be a problem. Typically this moisture showers downward when the film ripples with the wind. The film of moisture on the polyethylene reduces the amount of light transmitted into the greenhouse, and the periodic showers can cause some plant diseases. Individuals in the plastic-covered houses might object to the showers also. These problems, however, can be eased by spraying the inner surface of the plastic with a product called Sun Clear. It causes the condensed moisture to flow on the surface of the film until it reaches the base. Sun Clear also can be used on fiberglass if there is a moisture-flow problem on it.

Primarily in an effort to save heat energy, some greenhouses are covered with a double layer of poly film and inflated so there is an air space between the two layers. This does cause a further reduction in light intensity in the greenhouse, and that effect needs to be evaluated together with the heat factor.

Conservation of Heat Energy

There is considerable interest in the conservation of heat energy in greenhouses primarily because of dwindling fuel supplies, but also because of greatly increased costs of fuels. Because of the need for a light-transparent covering on greenhouses, it is not possible to install convention-al types of heat insulation material in greenhouse structures. The insulation either must be transparent or there needs to be a way to install and remove the insulation daily.

The greatest heat loss in greenhouses is through the roof because this is the largest exposed area and the temperature differential between indoors and outdoors is greatest at the roof. There have been mainly two approaches to insulation of greenhouse roofs—the installation of a second, translucent covering over the roof with inflation to maintain an air space between the two coverings or the installation of a removable covering from eave to eave or gutter to gutter. Either system can effectively conserve heat. It generally is esimated that 50 percent savings in fuel is possible with either method of insulation. It must be understood, however, that in northern climates heat does need to be expended sometimes to remove snow and ice from the roof, and the roof-insulation system must be adaptable enough so that the roof can be heated for this purpose when necessary. Whatever method is employed needs to be approved by the firm that carries insurance on the structure.

Frequently the greenhouses covered with polyethylene film do have two layers of the plastic film with inflation equipment to keep the layers separated. If the structure is Quonset-type, the entire structure is double-covered. With structures that have walls and roofs, the double covering may be only on the roofs.

Structures that are covered with glass may be insulated by placing a double layer of polyethylene film over the glass and keeping it inflated.

The double-roof coverings are a fixed installation, but the polyethylene film will need to be replaced every 2 years. The double covering reduces the light intensity in the greenhouse and during the winter this has some adverse effect on plant growth.

The movable insulation that is placed from eave to eave or gutter to gutter may be polyethylene film, or more likely it is other types of material that are considered to be more effective insulators. This type of insulation requires movement, and this may be done either manually or mechanically. The most efficient systems use tracks and rollers for suspension and movement of the insulator.

Various other procedures are used to conserve heat energy. Some of these are installation of conventional insulation on north walls, double covering of walls on other sides with translucent material, replacement of heating lines toward the base of the structure, improved maintenance programs to minimize leakage in coverings, improved programs to maximize the conversion of chemical energy of the fuel to usable heat energy in the greenhouse, the installation of windbreaks outside the greenhouse, and the use of air-circulation fans in the greenhouse to return the warm, upper air toward the base.

Ventilating and Air-Movement Equipment

A means of exchanging air with the outside is needed to regulate the temperature and humidity in the greenhouse. Recently there has been concern with ventilation in relation to the carbon dioxide content of the air in the greenhouse.

Figure 2-6 Ridge ventilators for the control of temperature, air circulation, and humidity in the greenhouse. *(Lord & Burnham photograph.)*

Usually the greenhouse has had ventilator sash located at the ridge. In separate houses ventilator sash may be located also just below the eave of the sidewall. The principle involved is that the hot air, being lighter, rises and passes through the ventilator. The cold air from the exterior, being heavier, flows toward the base of the greenhouse after it enters the ventilator. This provides air movement as well as temperature adjustment in the greenhouse. Usually the ventilators are operated manually by crank-type units located approximately every 30 meters in the greenhouse. The object is to coordinate the ventilator operation with the amount of heat that is used so that the greenhouses are maintained at the correct temperature and, at least in some instances, at the best humidity. In recent years motor-driven units have been designed for automated ventilator operation. These are controlled by thermostats, and with proper installation it is possible to have automatic ventilator operation and good temperature control in the greenhouse without personal supervision.

Early in the 1950s the fan and pad method of ventilating and cooling

Figure 2-7 Sidewall ventilator with operating equipment. One of the advantages of separate houses is increased ventilation because of sidewall ventilators. *(Lord & Burnham photograph.)*

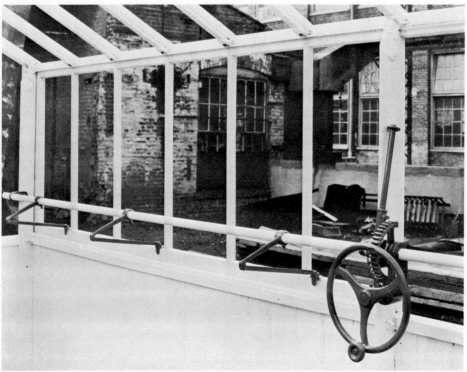

Figure 2-8 A greenhouse without ridge ventilators. Hot-weather ventilation and cooling are provided by a fan and pad cooling system. Cool-weather ventilation is supplied by the perforated, plastic ventilation tube and exhaust fans. The primary source of heat in these houses is from the overhead heating lines hung by chains from the trusses. Note that the supporting members for the networks that keep the plants erect are perforated metal straps hung from the trusses. *(Lord & Burnham photograph.)*

greenhouses was developed in the southwestern United States. Since that time these systems have been used widely throughout the country. They involve the installation of moistened pads on one wall of the greenhouse and exhaust fans in the opposite wall. During warm weather the ventilators are closed, the exhaust fans are operated, and air enters the greenhouse through the moistened pads. The temperature of the air that is introduced into the greenhouse is reduced by this method.

Initially fan and pad systems were installed on existing structures by making necessary minimum modifications. Subsequently attempts have been made to alter the greenhouse design to allow for the most efficient fan and pad installation.

The exhaust fans are permanently mounted, but the pads must be installed each season in order to provide for maximum air entry during hot weather and a tightly closed greenhouse during the cold season. There is an advantage, particularly during spring and fall, in providing an option in the structure for pad operation or an entirely closed greenhouse from day to day depending on the weather. This can be done by installing the pad on the inside of the side or end ventilators.

A very important development in greenhouse-ventilation equipment was the introduction of the plastic ventilation tube. It is used in conjunction with exhaust fans. Many greenhouse operators ventilate the houses by means of ventilation tubes from fall to spring, and from spring to fall the fan and pad system is used. They may not use traditional greenhouse ventilators at all.

It was the ventilation tube that made fall to spring ventilation practical in arc-roof greenhouses. And it is because of the ventilation tube plus fan and pad cooling that greenhouses of any design may be constructed without traditional greenhouse ventilators.

Three sizes of ventilation tube are used depending on the size of the greenhouse. The inflated diameters of these tubes are 45, 60, and 75 centimeters. The tubes are perforated along each side, and the hole size and spacing are determined by the length of the tube that is used.

The ventilation tubes are installed the length of the house above the bottom member of the trusses. One end of the tube is tied closed, and the other, open end is attached to a shutter in the sidewall. When the shutter is open and exhaust fans are operating, air from the exterior enters the tube and then distributes into the greenhouse through the holes. One tube is used in small greenhouses and two or more tubes are installed in wider greenhouses.

The fan and tube system can be a very effective method for handling ventilation in greenhouses from fall to spring. Also shutters can be motorized and fans and shutters activated by thermostats.

Another development with the fan and tube system was the addition of a tube fan. The tube fan can be operated when the shutter is open to aid in the introduction of air into the greenhouse, or it can be operated while the shutter is closed, providing circulation of air within the greenhouse.

The air in the greenhouse should be in constant motion, to assure even temperature and humidity throughout the air mass, reduce the incidence of disease, and distribute carbon dioxide equally. Air circulation occurred in greenhouses in the past only if there was a temperature differential. It has been good, common practice to provide some ventilation even while operating heating lines. This assures air circulation because the heated air rises and the cool air from the exterior flows toward the bottom. This method can be used during a considerable period of the year. However, in extremely cold weather it may not be possible to open the ventilators, and during the summer there may be many occasions when there is no temperature differential between outdoors and within the greenhouse. A mechanical means for circulating the air at those times especially is needed.

The best means of circulating the air in the greenhouse is the tube-fan system, or the Nivola fan which is designed to recirculate the air from the upper part of the greenhouse toward the base. These air-circulation devices should be kept in constant operation except when the fan and pad system is being used.

Carbon Dioxide Generation Equipment

Particularly with some kinds of plants there is promotion in growth and development if the amount of carbon dioxide in the greenhouse atmosphere is increased. In the portions of the country that have cool weather from fall to spring, when venting is reduced, it is possible to increase the concentration of carbon dioxide in the air. Various means have been used, but the most common method is by combusion of gas or oil in burners spaced throughout the greenhouse. These units are called carbon dioxide generators, but most of them are adaptations of heating units. The products of the combustion are heat, carbon dioxide, and water vapor.

The natural carbon dioxide concentration in the atmosphere is 300 ppm. The generators are used to increase the amount to 1,000 ppm or more.

The effective time for the increased amount of carbon dioxide is during the daylight hours when food manufacturing is taking place in the plants and carbon dioxide is being used in this process.

Figure 2-9 This is a gas-fired carbon dioxide generator. In addition to carbon dioxide, heat and water vapor also are produced.

The general effects of the increased quantities of carbon dioxide are an increased rate of growth and development (crop production time is shorter) and larger stems, leaves, and flowers. Some of the greenhouse crop plants that benefit from increased amounts of carbon dioxide are geranium, snapdragon, chrysanthemum, and rose.

Greenhouse Benches

There are two reasons why benches are used in the greenhouse. They make it possible for better control of the environment around the plants, and they allow the work to proceed more efficiently.

The greenhouse bench for cut flowers needs to be level or very nearly level and deep enough to hold at least 15 centimeters of soil. It should provide excellent water drainage and isolation from disease or insect infestation. If the bench is constructed on the ground, the bottom and sides must be a solid piece. Concrete is the only material suitable for such a bench. To assure good drainage a V-bottom is used, with the bottom of the V at least 4 centimeters below the side. A half tile is placed over the bottom of the V, and the bottom is then filled level with coarse gravel. Lengthwise the bottom of the bench must fall 3 centimeters per 30 meters.

Raised benches may be constructed from wood, concrete, steel, or transite. Regardless of the material, water drainage must be perfect. The

Figure 2-10 Wooden benches for cut flowers. These are elevated enough to assure isolation from pests and pathogens as well as to provide good drainage. Benches for pot plants should be higher for ease in handling plants. *(Yoder Bros., Inc. photograph.)*

Figure 2-11 The boards in the bench bottom must be well spaced as illustrated to assure complete and immediate drainage of water from the bench. *(Yoder Bros., Inc. photograph.)*

reasons for using raised benches are better drainage, isolation from pests and pathogens without solid construction, and easier and more efficient height for work. For most cut-flower crops it is considered now that the bench should be close to the ground. There was a time when it was thought necessary to have heating lines under each bench. This is no longer desired, and underbench space is not needed for this reason. Many crops are grown tall, and sufficient head room is an advantage. The width of a concrete block makes about the right elevation for a raised cut-flower bench. The bench width is usually 105 or 120 centimeters.

Cut-flower benches are steamed often. For steaming it is best to have benches without posts so that they can be covered easily, and concrete benches must be constructed carefully to prevent cracking. Most cut-flower crops require some overbench structure to support cloth or wires. The method for attaching such support should be considered when the bench material is selected.

The requirements for pot-plant benches are quite different. They should be raised to about 75 centimeters for convenience in working. If they are going to be worked from both sides, the most efficient width is about 2 meters. Ideal drainage is needed, and there is interest in perfect air circulation around pot plants. Pot-plant benches are often constructed

Figure 2-12 Concrete, ground benches for cut flowers. Benches of this type have sides and bottoms poured in one piece for good control of pests and pathogens. The bench bottom is V-shaped for adequate water drainage.

without sideboards and with their bottoms as open as possible. A very good pot-plant bench bottom is either 14-gauge, 2.5- by 2.5-centimeter welded-wire fabric or expanded metal. This allows the ideal air circulation around pot plants that is needed.

The arrangement of the benches can affect working conditions in the house considerably. In building a new structure it would really be best to plan the work area and bench arrangement, and then choose the structure to properly enclose it. Too often the greenhouse is all erected before thought is given to how the benches fit.

Figure 2-13 Transite bench construction. Corrugated transite must be used on the bottom for strength. To provide good drainage, the bottom should be pitched from one side to the other. If this cannot be done, drainage holes must be drilled in each valley. *(Lord & Burnham photograph.)*

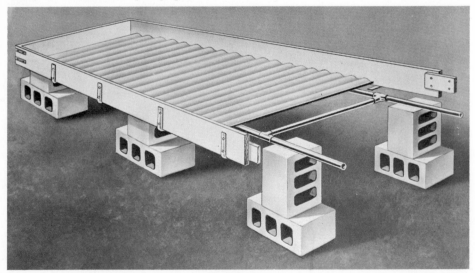

Figure 2-14 Welded-wire fabric can be used as bottoms for pot-plant benches. This provides maximum drainage and air circulation. The 14-gauge wire has 2.5 centimeter spacing.

Traditionally benches have been installed lengthwise in the greenhouse. This has been based to some extent on convenience and efficiency of working, but another reason for it is that this orientation has seemed to be the best solution for supporting bench heating lines and water lines without interference to walking. Long benches, however, are not always the most efficient size. With some crops, cut flowers for example, long benches necessitate frequent trips through narrow walks, and long benches can be even more of a problem with pot plants. There also is an advantage in having crop-size benches, which often means that the unit should be shorter than the length of the house.

Figure 2-15 Cross-benching in a greenhouse. The principal advantages are crop-size benches and the use of wheeled carts in the wide walk to service all benches. Note that the primary source of heat is overhead unit heaters but that heating lines are provided on the sidewalls as well. *(Lord & Burnham photograph.)*

There is a trend away from installation of heating lines on the bench. Overhead heating systems do perform satisfactorily, and they are not nearly as costly to maintain as bench lines. With the heating lines overhead, the ground area can be benched for the most efficient use. One such arrangement is peninsular benching or cross-benching. A walk wide enough to accommodate wheeled carts is provided the length of the house, either at the side or in the middle, depending on the width of the house. The benches are installed across the width of the house and butt on the wide walk. Such an arrangement can increase the efficiency of a pot-plant house, and it may be an advantage in some cut-flower houses, depending on the situation.

Greenhouse walks are usually minimum width and for good reason. Production space in the greenhouse should be utilized to the best advantage, and it is apparent that no flowers can be grown in the walks. It is possible to use 45- to 60-centimeter walks; however, at least one walk in the house should be wide enough to handle wheelbarrows, sprayers, or wheeled carts. Walks should be level and should have a satisfactory surface in order to promote the best movement of workers or vehicles.

Some pot-plant growers have eliminated some walks in greenhouses by using rollers between the legs and the floor of the bench so the entire bench top can be rolled a short distance to either side. Such an arrangement allows for one or two walks in the greenhouse and the position of the walk will depend on the direction in which the bench tops are moved.

In the typical greenhouse arrangement with fixed benches, approximately two-thirds of the area is benches and one-third walks. With movable bench tops it is possible to increase the production area up to eleven-twelfths of the total area.

Workroom

The workroom should be located, if possible, at the north end of the greenhouse, in order to provide some protection from cold prevailing winds. Its size and design are largely dependent on the size and number of greenhouses it is to serve and the type of crops being grown. If separate from the greenhouse, the workroom should be near enough to minimize walking and make transportation of plants between the two structures simple and convenient.

The workroom should be heated, well lighted, and equipped with tables and storage bins for soil, sand, peat, and other similar materials. A cooler is necessary for the storage of cut flowers. Storage for cut-flower boxes, flats, tools, insecticides, fungicides, fertilizers, and other items necessary for the production of plants should be provided. A steam-treatment box or unit in the workroom is a desirable asset.

The table space for grading, bunching, and wrapping of cut flowers and space for pot plants should be ample for all occasions such as holiday periods when a large volume of stock is handled. Substantial potting benches at the proper height for ease in working are necessary. Potting benches on wheels can be rolled to the desired location, which eliminates moving of pots in the workrooms.

The workroom is often a part of the building where cut flowers, plants, pots, and other materials are received or loaded for shipping out. If such is the case, the room should be wide and long enough to accommodate one or more large trucks. Cut flowers and plants for holiday delivery may be loaded inside the warm workroom, which somewhat reduces the wrapping and insulation necessary for protection from cold. Doors should be high and wide to accommodate trucks.

Conveyors

The use of some type of conveyor is widespread in industrial plants where mass-production methods are in vogue. The florist industry, with some exceptions, has been slow to recognize the advantages of such labor-saving devices. This is partially due to the lack of knowledge of the costs of various operations, and also to the reluctance of many growers to change with the times. Conveyor systems are probably most useful where pot plants are grown. The use of conveyors to move plants for the purpose of potting, shifting from one house to another, or moving finished plants out of the houses for delivery eliminates hours of drudgery. Trolley systems are reasonably priced and save time and money in addition to increasing the efficiency of every employee.

Cloth Houses

The purpose of a cloth house is to expand production area for the period when weather conditions are favorable for culture of plants without benefit of a greenhouse. Although cloth houses are no longer as popular as they once were, good-quality asters and mums can be produced under cloth.

The side posts may be of wood, 8-centimeter pipe, or old boiler tubes and should be set deep enough in the ground so that they will not be heaved out by freezing and thawing. Because of the weight of the cloth, guy wires should be attached to a "dead man" support. Usually No. 9 galvanized wire is fastened to the tops of the posts, and the cloth is sewn to it. Posts within the cloth house need not be very heavy since they are subject to far less strain. The cloth covering is generally plastic screen rather than cotton.

Figure 2-16 Cloth house to provide partial shade and protection from pests for crops grown outdoors during the summer in the North and the year-round in the South. This house is covered with cotton tobacco cloth, but plastic screen commonly is used.

Lath Houses

The precision growing of such plants as azaleas and hydrangeas may require the use of lath shade during the summer months in many localities. Cold frames with lath covering in place of glass sash are useful, although the inconvenience of frames often limits their use for this purpose. Snow fence is commonly used by supporting it 1 meter above 120-centimeter beds.

In the South, slat sheds are used for growing foliage plants. The 4-meter posts of 10- by 10-centimeter pine, pressure treated with copper naphthenate, are spaced 4 meters apart with 1 meter buried in concrete in the soil. The stringers are 60- by 180-centimeter pressure-treated pine boards, nailed on alternate sides of the posts at the top. The slats on the roof are 1- by 5- by 7.5 centimeter rough cypress spaced 2 centimeters apart. Most crops are grown under 75 percent shade, but aglaonema is best under 90 percent shade while peperomia should be in 50 percent shade. Plastic screen of the proper density may be substituted for the roof slats. The south side is slatted the same as the roof, and the other sides are boarded solid.

One of the best types of structure consists of a permanent frame of pipe or wood at least 2 meters high, on top of which snow fence can be unrolled or lath sash placed when it is needed. When no longer needed, the snow fence is rolled together or the lath sash removed, and the plants are exposed to full sun. A permanent structure made by nailing 2.5- by 5-centimeter lumber 5 centimeters apart on a wooden frame is useful, but the plants must be moved in and out, which is not as satisfactory as rolling or unrolling snow fence.

Bulb Storage

Bulbs are very commonly stored outside in beds especially reserved for this purpose, but cold-storage buildings, erected for the sole purpose of storing bulbs to condition them for forcing or holding them back for late flowering, are preferred. Storage in a naturally cool structure such as a cellar or an insulated, refrigerated structure is very satisfactory. The uniform conditions that prevail in these structures are ideal. Although they are more expensive to construct than outside beds, cool storages are more convenient, can be equipped with shelves spaced about 45 centimeters apart to accommodate a large number of pots, and in general give more satisfactory results. When shelves are used, a layer of peat on the shelf reduces the danger of drying out.

Outside beds for bulb storage consist of nothing more than shallow pits

Figure 2-17 Lath house to provide partial shade for crops grown outdoors in the summer in the North and the year-round in the South. Southern structures usually are constructed to provide more shade and commonly are called slat sheds.

dug in the soil in which the pots or flats are placed. The variations in temperature in outside storages, the inconvenience during extremely cold weather or the muddy conditions in mild weather, and the difficulty of proper labeling are against the use of outside beds for bulbs, but because no special equipment is needed, they are common.

General Storage

For storage of cut flowers and potted plants that are fully developed in advance of the time they are wanted, some type of structure, either naturally or artificially cooled, is necessary. Refrigerated storages are ideal, as a uniform temperature may be maintained, but a shed or heavily shaded greenhouse may be used for this purpose.

GREENHOUSE HEATING AND COOLING

Accurate temperature control in the greenhouse is of great importance because the desired, best growth of plants occurs within a limited temperature range. The degree of temperature control must be much more precise than just keeping the plants from freezing or keeping them warm enough. For each kind of plant and the type of growth desired, the best results are obtained only at the proper temperature. Variations in this temperature may result in a complete lack of growth or extremely excessive development.

Plants grown in the greenhouse are classed by the night temperature at

Comparison of Customary and Metric Units of Temperature

Customary, degrees Fahrenheit	*Metric, degrees Celsius* (approximate)	*Customary, degrees Fahrenheit*	*Metric, degrees Celsius* (approximate)
212	100	55	13
180	82	50	10
145	63	45	7
95	35	40	4
90	32	34	1
85	29	32	0
80	27	20	−7
75	24	10	−12
70	21	0	−18
65	18	−10	−23
60	16	−20	−29

which they are grown. The day temperature provided is 3 to 6°C higher than night temperature depending on whether the day is cloudy or bright. Such crops as carnation and snapdragon are grown at 10°C, and some of the 16°C crops are rose, poinsettia, and chrysanthemum. Either of these night temperatures is suitable for many of the greenhouse crops, with the notable exception of most of the foliage plant crops, which require a 21°C night temperature. There are many specific effects of temperature on plant growth; but for a statement on growth in general, plants develop and grow slower in cooler temperatures and more rapidly in higher temperatures. There are specific variations, too, in the quality of growth, but in general the plants are shorter and heavier at lower temperatures and taller and thinner at higher temperatures.

There is merit in establishing the greenhouse in an area of the country with a suitable outdoor climate so that the least possible adjustment needs to be made in temperature. Unfortunately, outdoor temperatures vary considerably from one season to the other, and a desirable outdoor temperature for one time may be a definite problem for another season. Temperatures in Florida from fall to spring may be more suitable than those in northern states, but from spring to fall they are too warm for satisfactory growth of many kinds of plants. Even in Florida the winter temperatures are lower than desired for good plant growth. On occasion this results in the freezing and loss of some plants, and in less severe weather it results in delays and harmful effects in quality. In central Florida, foliage stock plants are grown in slat sheds or plastic screen houses, and the plants are propagated in greenhouses which are heated in the winter and may be cooled during the summer. For years the stock plant sheds were heated only by temporary means to prevent excessive damage from freezing, but after some years of loss, the structures were modified so that they could be covered by plastic film during the winter and heated more effectively. In fact, many of the growers installed steam heating systems. These changes in structures and heating systems not only prevented damage from freezing but provided better growing temperatures during the winter so that growers reported from 50 to 100 percent increase in production.

Sensing Temperatures

Thermometers must be located in the greenhouse at plant level and in sufficient numbers so that they reflect accurately the temperature for the entire house. Placing a single thermometer in a house is not sufficient to determine temperature differentials from end to end or side to side. Thermometers located at eye level are easy to read, but the readings are proper only if the plants are also at that level. For young plants in ground beds, the thermometer should be placed at the ground level.

Thermometers must be mounted so that the direct rays of the sun do not shine on the bulb. A suitable method of mounting thermometers is to attach them to a wooden board and orient them so that the thermometer is facing north. The proper location of thermostats which operate the ventilators or steam valves is even more important. For more precise temperature control, aspirated units are used in which a small fan draws a low volume of air through the thermometer or thermostat, providing a more representative sample of the air in the greenhouse.

Thermometers and thermostats sense air temperatures, and within limits it can be assumed that the plant temperatures are approximately the same as the air temperatures. If practical methods of sensing plant temperatures directly were available, they would be preferred. When a variable heat source is used, plant temperatures change more rapidly than air temperatures, and if plant temperatures could be sensed as rapidly as the changes occur, corrective action could be taken faster.

Sources of Heat

The primary source of heat in the greenhouse is the sun. Unfortunately it is not available for the entire 24 hours of a day, and even during the daytime the amount of heat transmitted from the sun to the plants in the greenhouse varies tremendously. During the summer days the sun causes too high temperatures in the greenhouse, and various methods are used to reduce the intensity of the rays entering the greenhouse, or cooling systems are used to reduce the temperature. On clear winter days even when the outdoor temperature is low, no supplementary heat may be required, and some ventilating may have to be used to reduce the heat.

There is much interest in the possibilities of storing solar energy for use when needed. Certainly there is a great need for such a procedure. Some greenhouses are being heated with stored solar energy, but it appears that there will have to be further developments in methods before the irradiance from the sun can be used economically as the sole source of heat in most greenhouses.

Coal, oil, and gas are used as supplementary sources of heat in greenhouses. The choice of fuel in each greenhouse depends on the cost per Btu of heat, the availability of the fuel, transportation costs, equipment costs, possibilities of automation, and labor costs. No single fuel is best for all greenhouses. A careful study must be made at each location to determine which fuel is best suited for that situation. In many localities coal may be the most economical fuel per Btu, but because it is more difficult to handle, more labor may be required. In considering the availability and transportation of a fuel, special scrutiny should be given to the coldest period of the year. In extremely cold weather, shutdown of the heating system for even a short period of time can be disastrous, and any fuel, regardless of its economy, is worthless if it is not available.

Methods of Distributing Heat

Most commonly the greenhouse heating systems are either steam or hot water. The fuel is burned in a boiler, and the hot water or steam is piped to the greenhouses in mains and heating lines in such a way as to distribute heat evenly throughout the entire area. The cool water and condensate from the heating lines are returned to the boiler for reheating.

Steam has been used primarily in larger ranges, and hot water in the smaller greenhouses, but it is possible to use closed-system hot water at high pressure and high temperature as efficiently as steam in large ranges.

More recently unit heaters have been used in some greenhouses. The fuel is burned in the heater located in the greenhouse, and the heat is

Figure 2-18 Various types of unit heaters are available. This is a gas unit with horizontal air movement and vented to the exterior. The Quonset-type house is covered with polyethylene film.

distributed throughout the greenhouse by a fan attached to the heater. The fuel for the unit heaters primarily is gas, but there are some that use oil fuel. The most common type of unit heater used in greenhouses is the kind used in various industrial heating situations such as warehouses and garages. These units are of several different capacities ranging from 30,000 to 400,000 Btu per hour. One or more unit is installed in a greenhouse at about the bottom level of the trusses. Usually in greenhouses more uniform distribution of heat is obtained by use of several smaller units rather than one large unit.

Some unit heaters have been designed for specific use with tube-fan systems in greenhouses. One type of heater installs directly in line with the tube—between the open end of the tube and the shutter. When the heater is in operation the fan directs the heat down the tube and it disperses through the holes to the greenhouse atmosphere. The other tube-fan heating system uses unit heaters on either side of the tube fan with the heat directed toward the tube fan which directs the heat down the tube.

Boilers for the Greenhouse Heating System

Improvements are made in boilers continuously, and it is best to seek the latest information and expert advice at the time of choosing a boiler. There are many variations, but boilers are made of either steel or cast iron. The steel boilers may be fire tube, in which the heat and flue gases pass through the tubes that are surrounded by water, or water tube, in which the heat and flue gases pass around the tubes that are filled with water. Each type has some advantages depending on the specific situation and how they will be used.

The capacity of a boiler is referred to in terms of horsepower, and 1 boiler horsepower equals a heat output of 33,475 Btu per hour. In order to know what size boiler is needed, the heat requirement of the greenhouse must be determined; it is based primarily on the area of surface of the greenhouse exposed to the outdoors, the desired temperature to be

Comparison of Customary and Metric Units of Area

Customary	Metric (approximate)
1 square foot	900.00 square centimeters
1 square foot	0.09 square meter
1 square yard	0.84 square meter
100 square feet	9.30 square meters

maintained within the greenhouse, and the lowest temperature to be expected outdoors. Without making this calculation it is impossible to know the exact boiler size needed. For general conditions a boiler rated at 200 horsepower should be adequate to maintain a 16°C temperature in a greenhouse covering 4,650 square meters of ground when the temperature outdoors is −23°C. Instead of one boiler of the maximum capacity, two boilers are often used with about that total maximum capacity; thus either boiler can be used separately to heat the entire place in mild weather or the two boilers can be used in conjunction to provide the maximum heat in the coldest periods. A two-boiler installation is an excellent safeguard as even in the most severe weather either boiler could prevent a freeze-up in the event of the failure of operation of one of them.

Operation of the Boiler

In order to have good combustion of fuel, the right amount of air must be supplied in the boiler. In some instances the air is furnished together with the fuel, and additional air is provided at the burner. Different methods are employed depending on the fuel and the boiler, but regardless of the method the amount of air must be carefully regulated. There must be a continuous draft that provides the new air supply to support combustion and to remove the smoke and products of combustion from the boiler. Natural draft can be established with a chimney or stack of adequate size and proper construction. The principle involved with the natural draft produced by a stack is that the column of hot air in the stack is lighter than a corresponding column of air outside it, and the hot air rises and is replaced by cool air, thus establishing the draft. In cold weather it takes some time to heat the stack, and this is important as a natural draft system will not operate unless the proper stack temperature is maintained. For good draft a stack temperature of about 285°C is needed. If the stack temperature is lower than that, the draft will not be enough; and at higher stack temperatures heat is wasted.

The stack is an integral part of the heating system, and it must be designed for the specific type of boiler and operating equipment. The advice of a specialist should be sought in erecting a new stack or in connecting a different boiler to an existing stack. The requirements of the stack for a boiler that has a mechanically induced draft are different from those of the stack that produces draft by natural thermal action.

The amount of draft is not only influenced by the diameter and height of the stack but also by the kind of flues and the material from which the stack is constructed. For natural thermal action a brick or concrete stack holds heat better than a metal stack, and this is an advantage at times when the boiler is not being operated continuously.

In modern boilers the induced draft system is used which consists of a fan placed on the stack side of the boiler. The size, arrangement, and temperature of the stack are of less concern with induced draft than with natural draft, as the draft is directly related to the mechanical efficiency of the fan located between boiler and stack. Since more positive draft control is possible with the induction system, and since a tall, costly stack does not have to be provided and maintained, there is increased use of the induced draft system. It should be acknowledged that the induced draft is entirely dependent on electric power, and if there is a power failure, the boiler does not operate. Since most boilers are dependent on other electrical controls, this just emphasizes the need for an adequate, emergency, standby power generator in the greenhouse boiler room.

The water that is used in the boiler must have the right properties, and it is best to seek advice from boiler water specialists about the treatment that the water may need. If the water is not right, it may cause undue scaling in the boiler or deterioration of the mains and the heating lines.

Operation of the boiler varies all the way from completely manual operation to highly sophisticated systems that are entirely automated. The choice of the method of operation of the boiler is based on the efficiency and the costs involved.

Heating Equipment for Emergencies

Every greenhouse business needs an emergency plan for providing enough heat to prevent loss of plants by freezing. The emergency plan needs to be well designed so that it can function immediately at any time—whatever the emergency.

If it is an interruption in supply of fuel, the alternate fuel would have to be on hand as well as the means for burning it. If it is an interruption in electric power, usually the best answer is the use of a standby power generator. Also it should be anticipated that there could be an interruption both in fuel and electric power.

Some greenhouse operators maintain a supply of alcohol and containers that could be used to keep the house above freezing temperatures for a few hours. Others store enough temporary oil burners and oil on the place to maintain temperature during an emergency.

Emergency, Standby Power

Several essential operations in the greenhouse are dependent on electric power; and since power failures are possible, it is necessary to provide an emergency, standby power unit of sufficient size to handle these operations.

The need for a continuous power supply is often associated only with the winter season as most boilers operate with electrical controls. An interruption in power for a few hours during cold weather can cause loss of all the stock by freezing. However, continuous power may also be essential at other times of the year, as ventilation may be dependent on exhaust fans, water may be available only from pumps operated by electric motors, and electric power may be needed for refrigeration. An emergency power unit must be large enough for all the essential operations, and in figuring the power needs, it must be remembered that more power is required to start motors than is needed to keep them operating. When there is a power failure, motors will have to be started; and the emergency power supply will have to be great enough to handle this peak load.

After an emergency power unit is obtained, a routine must be established to assure its readiness for operation in any situation. In most areas power failures seldom occur, and therefore if the generator were operated only during an emergency, there would probably be a long delay in getting the unit started. Hence it is wise to develop a routine for starting and operating the emergency power unit regularly every week in order to be sure that the equipment operates satisfactorily.

Figuring the Heat Requirement of the Greenhouse

The direction of movement of heat is from high temperature to low temperature, and the greater the temperature differential, the faster the heat movement or heat loss. During the heating season the direction of heat movement or loss is from the interior of the greenhouse through the roof and walls to the cooler air outdoors. The warmer the indoor temperature and the colder the outdoor temperature, the greater the transfer of heat will be—and the greater the heat requirement will be for the greenhouse. To determine the heat loss, it is necessary to know the total surface area exposed to the two different temperatures, the rate or coefficient of heat transfer through the material of which the exposed area is made, and the temperature differential between indoors and outdoors.

Since the exposed area of greenhouses is almost entirely glass, it is best to begin calculations by converting concrete, wood, or transite wall areas to the equivalent amount of glass area. The transmission of heat through those materials is considered to be one-half that of glass. If the length of the roof bars is known, the area of the roof is readily calculated. If the roof bar length is unknown and cannot be measured easily, it can be computed readily. The standard pitch of a greenhouse is $26\frac{1}{2}°$, which is a 15-centimeter rise for every 30 centimeters in width across the greenhouse. With such a pitch the height of the ridge above the eave or gutter will be one-fourth the width of the greenhouse. The ridge of a greenhouse 11 meters wide with a standard roof pitch will be 2.8 meters above the eave. By calculation of right triangles, the roof bar length is determined to be just over 6 meters, as the length of the roof bar is equal to the square root of the sum of the squares of one-half the width of the greenhouse (5.5 meters) and the height of the ridge above the eave or gutter (2.8 meters).

If it is desired to find the heat requirement of a greenhouse that covers a 12.2- by 61-meter ground area, is of standard pitch, and has 2-meter sidewalls consisting of 0.9 meter of concrete and 1.1 meters of glass, the size of the various exposed areas must be calculated and totaled. To find the area of the roof, the distance from eave to ridge to eave is multiplied by the length of the house. In many instances the length of the roof bar is known, and the roof area is then calculated by multiplying the length of the bar by 2 and then by the length of the greenhouse. If the length of the roof bar is not known, it is computed as described above. Since our example has a standard pitch roof, the height of the ridge above the eave is 3.1 meters (12.2 times 0.25), and the length of the roof bar is equal to the square root of the sum of 9.6 (the square of the height of the ridge above the eave) and 37.2 (the square of half the width of the greenhouse). The length of the roof bar is approximately 6.8 meters (the square root of 46.8).

829.6 square-meter area of roof (2 times 6.8 times 61)

134.2 square-meter area of glass sidewalls (2 times 1.1 times 61)

54.9 square-meter glass-equivalent area of concrete sidewalls (0.5 times 2 times 0.9 times 61)

64.7 square-meter area of glass gable end [2 times 1.1 times 12.2 plus (0.5 times 2 times 3.1 times 12.2)]

11.0 square-meter glass-equivalent area of concrete end walls (0.5 times 2 times 0.9 times 12.2)

1,094.4 square-meter total glass or glass-equivalent exposed area

Although this 12.2- by 61-meter greenhouse covers 744.2 square meters of ground area, it can be seen that the total glass and glass equivalent area exposed is considerably greater—in this instance 1.5 times as much.

Any surface of the greenhouse that is attached to another structure which is operated at the same temperature is not included in computing the exposed area because of an equal exchange of heat. If one end of the greenhouse is attached to a headhouse or one sidewall is attached to an adjoining greenhouse, these areas are not included in the exposed area totals.

The rate of transmission of heat through glass varies with the temperature, but the heat transmission coefficient commonly used is 21.9, which indicates the transmission by glass of 21.9 Btu of heat per square meter per hour per 1°C temperature differential from one side of the glass to the other.

The total heat loss by transmission through the exposed surfaces of the 12.2- by 61-meter greenhouse if it is going to be maintained at 16°C at −23°C outdoors would be 935,000 Btu per hour (1,094.4 times 21.9 times 39).

In addition to the transfer of heat from the inner surface of the exposed area to the outer surface, there is some heat loss in the greenhouse due to infiltration caused by the movement of heated air through openings, ventilators, glass laps, and doorways. Heat loss due to infiltration varies considerably with the structure and the wind velocity, and at best only an estimate is possible. During periods of high winds there is considerable leakage of air—and heat—through the glass laps, but fortunately during extremely cold weather the glass laps are often sealed closed by frost. During cold, windy weather the greenhouse operator can hasten the sealing of the laps with frost by spraying water on the heating lines in the house.

If the greenhouse structure is in poor condition or if high winds are common in the area, some allowance should be made for heat lost by infiltration; however, in most greenhouses the heat lost by infiltration is not of great enough significance to be included in the calculation of the heat requirements.

Methods of Distributing Heat in the Greenhouse

The heat must be transported from the boiler to the various greenhouses and then distributed throughout the greenhouses evenly. The steam or hot

Figure 2-19 Water can be returned to the boiler room by gravity if the boiler is lower than the return lines, or the return lines can be pitched to a tank as illustrated and from there pumped to the boiler room. With such a system, the boiler may be on the same level as the greenhouses.

water from the boiler is piped to the greenhouses in large pipes called mains, and the cool water is returned to the boiler in large pipes called returns, or return mains. Since steam or hot water is lighter than cool water, it is possible to get adequate flow in mains and returns if the boiler is at a lower level than the greenhouses. The light steam or hot water rises up to the greenhouses in overhead mains, and the cool water will flow back to the boiler in returns located at ground or just below ground level. Such a system operates because of the difference of weight between hot and cool water or the effect of gravity on less dense (steam or hot water) and denser materials (cool water). These systems are commonly called "gravity systems."

Mechanical devices—circulators or pumps—can be used to distribute steam or hot water through the mains, heating lines, and returns, and their use is increasing. This provides a more positive method of control over the movement of heat and eliminates the need for a cellar or basement. In addition, the heating system operates more efficiently. In a steam heating system the returns are pitched toward a receiving tank that is located below the greenhouse level, and a pump is used to bring the condensate from the receiving tank to the boiler.

Hot water systems may use either accelerators or circulators. An accelerator can be used with a gravity system, and it is located in the return main close to the boiler to increase the circulation of the water. It is a motor-driven impeller that causes increased circulation when in operation and does not impede normal flow created by gravity when the motor is not turned on.

The circulation of water in hot water systems can be handled completely

Figure 2-20 Better control of hot-water heating is provided with circulators in the various areas to be heated. *(Lord & Burnham drawing.)*

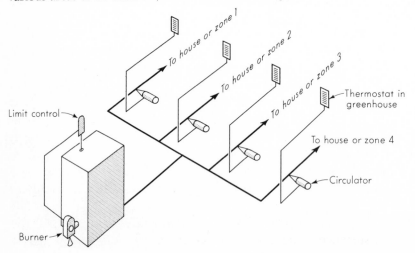

Comparison of Customary and
Metric Units of Weight

Customary	Metric (approximate)
1 ounce	28.40 grams
1 pound	450.00 grams
1 pound	0.45 kilogram

by mechanical means, using circulators. A single circulator can be used that provides circulation throughout the whole system, or circulators can be provided for individual houses or zones. When circulators are installed, the boiler may be on the same level as the greenhouse, since the flow of water is entirely independent of gravity. The water flows when the circulators are operating and does not flow when they are turned off.

Mains may be pitched up or down depending on the situation. However, steam mains must have drip pipe and traps at each low point to pass condensate to the returns, and hot water mains must have air vents installed at the high point in the main to allow the escape of trapped air.

With steam systems the steam is produced at higher pressure in the boiler and is reduced to lower pressure before circulation in the greenhouse. The pressure regulator may be located in the vicinity of the boiler so that the steam is distributed in the mains at low pressure, or pressure-regulating valves may be located at each house so that the steam is transmitted at the higher pressure in the mains. The amount of steam pressure produced depends on the type of boiler equipment and the way in which it is operated. Although terminology varies in different areas, boilers operated at 700 to 1000 grams of pressure per square centimeter are commonly known as "low-pressure systems," and those operated in excess of 1,000 grams are called "high-pressure systems." High-pressure boilers may be operated at pressures up to 63 kilograms per square centimeter and more. Regardless of the boiler operating pressure, the steam pressure is usually regulated so that it is distributed in the greenhouse at 70 to 350 grams per square centimeter.

The traditional radiators in the greenhouse are lines of black iron pipe that are installed the length of the house and distributed across the house in a way to produce even heat throughout. The heat transfer from black iron pipe is satisfactory, and the cost of material is comparatively low. If heating lines are painted, black paint should be used. Galvanized pipe or pipe painted with aluminum or light colors does not transfer heat as readily as black pipe.

In some instances finned pipe is used for heating lines, and of course the area for the transference of heat to the surrounding air is greatly increased by the addition of fins to pipe. Iron pipe is not used much for fins because it corrodes readily in the moist greenhouse atmosphere and is difficult to repair. Finned copper or aluminum pipe is used commonly in the greenhouse in unit heaters or in areas where a greater concentration of heat is needed. Transference of heat from either copper or aluminum is rapid, and there is the added advantage that these metals do not corrode as readily as iron. There is a possibility of some deterioration of copper or aluminum pipes by electrolysis when they are used in conjunction with iron pipes, but authorities differ in their opinions of the practical significance of the problem.

In steam systems 3-centimeter pipe is used, and in hot water systems 5-centimeter pipe is used most commonly; however, in high-pressure water systems smaller diameter pipe may be used. Air and the surrounding objects in the vicinity of the pipes are heated, and convection currents are established, with hot air rising and cool air descending. The air circulation that results from the hot pipelines in the greenhouse serves the double purpose of distributing heat throughout the greenhouse and giving air motion. Unless fans are used to move the air mechanically, air movement in the greenhouse is entirely dependent on the establishment of a temperature differential with the resulting convection currents. Air movement not only helps distribute heat evenly, but continuous air circulation assures uniformity of relative humidity and carbon dioxide throughout the air mass in the house.

Heat is lost in the greenhouse primarily through the surface areas of the house that are exposed to the outdoors, and the largest area is the roof, about three-fourths of the entire exposed surface in the greenhouse. Since hot air rises, the temperature differential at the roof will normally be greater than it is at the walls; and the rate of heat transfer will be faster than through the walls. The air that is cooled at the roof surface does not descend directly

Comparison of Customary and Metric Units of Pipe Diameter

Customary	*Metric* (approximate)
$\frac{3}{4}$ inch	2.0 centimeters
1 inch	2.5 centimeters
$1\frac{1}{4}$ inches	3.0 centimeters
$1\frac{1}{2}$ inches	4.0 centimeters
2 inches	5.0 centimeters
3 inches	7.5 centimeters
4 inches	10.0 centimeters

to the base of the greenhouse but flows along the inner surface of the roof. Because of the location of the cool air return along the inner surface of the greenhouse roof, it is essential to have heating lines located on the sidewalls to heat this descending, cool air before it reaches the plants and soil. The heat supplied by these lines is often referred to as "perimeter heat." Regardless of how the other heating lines in the house are located and operated, the side lines should be used whenever heat is introduced into the house. Within limits, the greater the proportion of sidewall heating lines to the total number, the better. Because of physical limitations, however, it may not be possible to place more than about one-fourth of the total heat requirement at the sidewalls, which should be sufficient.

The location of heating lines at the sidewalls is indispensable, but the balance of the heat requirement can be located in several different ways and still produce even heating. Heating lines may be located under the benches, at the sides of the benches, or above the benches; or unit heaters may be used above the benches. If handled properly, equally good results can be obtained with any of these methods. There is more interest in overhead installations, however, as they are put in more easily and do not deteriorate as rapidly. There is some objection to the possible shade caused by overhead lines or heating units. The shade is not significant with steam heating lines or unit heaters as they do not cast that much shade, but if the heating system is hot water with 5-centimeter lines, it is virtually impossible to install the pipes overhead because of extreme shade.

At a steam pressure of 70 grams per square centimeter, 3-centimeter black iron pipe will give off heat at the rate of about 590 Btu per hour per linear meter of pipe in a 16°C house, and 5-centimeter hot water pipe will transfer 525 Btu per hour per linear meter of black iron pipe when the water temperature is 118°C. The heat output of the unit heaters is listed by the manufacturers.

To satisfy the heat requirement of 935,000 Btu per hour for the 12.2- by 61-meter house discussed earlier, approximately 250,000 Btu should be furnished in sidelines. If three 3-centimeter lines with a steam heating system were located at the sides and ends of this greenhouse, there would be a total of 440 linear meters of pipe; and these side heating lines would provide approximately 260,000 Btu per hour (440 times 590). The balance of the heat to be furnished from heating lines around the benches or overhead would be 675,000 Btu (935,000 minus 260,000), which would necessitate about 1,160 meters of 3-centimeter iron pipe or 19 heating lines the length of the greenhouse. If this were an eight-bench house and heating lines were placed around each bench, there would be 16 heating lines; and the additional heat could be furnished with additional overhead lines or additional sidelines (snow-melting lines at eave or gutter). Depending on how the piping is arranged, some additional heat may be expected from mains and headers.

If the heat in addition to the sidelines is to be furnished overhead, nineteen 3-centimeter heating lines could be provided above the benches; or the overhead heat could be furnished by seven unit heaters that are rated at 100,000 Btu per hour per unit. The unit heaters would be installed about 4.5 meters from each end of the 61-meter greenhouse and then spaced equally about 9 meters apart the length of the greenhouse.

If the 12.2- by 61-meter greenhouse is to be heated with hot water at a temperature of 118°C, four 5-centimeter heating lines on each side and the ends would provide 307,650 Btu per hour (586 times 525); and the balance of the heat would need to be furnished from heating lines on the benches, from overhead units, or from a combination of the two. Placing 5-centimeter lines around each bench would provide an additional 512,400 Btu per hour (976 times 525), and the balance of 115,000 Btu could be furnished from four overhead heating lines or two additional heating lines on each side of the house.

Some 5-centimeter hot water heating lines can possibly be installed overhead, but to place all but the side heating lines overhead would cause a shade problem. It would be possible, however, to provide overhead heat with hot water unit heaters. In order to supply the additional 627,000 Btu per hour needed (935,000 minus 308,000), 10 unit heaters of 70,000 Btu capacity could be installed at about 6-meter intervals the length of the 61-meter greenhouse.

Arrangement and Placement of Heating Lines

The heating lines must be supported sufficiently so that there are no sags, but because pipe expands and contracts with changes in heat, the pipe hangers must allow for free movement of the pipe. The side heating lines are suspended from the sidewalls one pipe above the other, and the bench heating lines are hung from the sides or underneath the bench. Overhead heating lines are hung from the trusses or from purlin posts. If unit heaters are used, they are suspended from the trusses. Heating lines are more efficient if air can circulate freely around them, and for this reason the pipe should be hung so that it is not directly in contact with the bench, the wall, or the ground.

The heating lines must be arranged so that uniform and sufficient heat is furnished by using only a few lines during mild weather and most of the heating lines in cold weather. If too many heating lines are used for the existing outdoor temperature, the steam or hot water may not flow the entire length of the house before the thermostat causes the supply to be shut

Figure 2-21 Heating lines are hung by various means, but the hanger must allow for freedom of movement of the pipe as it expands and contracts with change in temperature.

off. This produces a very unsatisfactory temperature differential lengthwise in the house. If several heating lines are positioned on the sidewalls or overhead, it is best to use a continuous (trombone) coil that will produce a single pipe of heat the length of the greenhouse when steam or hot water is available for a short period of time, and heat in several pipes the length of the greenhouse if the steam or hot water remains on. If the same number of pipe lines is supplied from a common header (box coil), the steam or hot water will enter all the heating lines at the same time, but in mild weather the lines will not become heated for the full length of the greenhouse.

Steam Traps

A steam trap does just what its name implies—it traps the steam in the heating lines, but it allows water to pass on to the returns. The two types of traps that are used are thermostatic and bucket. In a thermostatic trap the bimetal element is affected by temperature; it opens the outlet when water (from condensed steam) is in the trap and closes the outlet when the higher temperature steam enters the trap. The bucket trap has an inverted float bucket that opens or closes the outlet. When water enters the trap, the bucket sinks, the outlet is opened, and the water passes to the return pipe; but when steam enters, the bucket floats and the outlet stays closed. Steam traps should have screens on the inlet side to prevent the entry of dirt or scale that would interfere with the operation of the trap.

Traps that malfunction and do not allow the passage of water to the return main cause water to be backed up in the heating line, and the line remains cool. Traps that pass steam as well as water can be identified by the hot return in the vicinity of the errant trap.

Each coil of steam heating lines in the greenhouse should be provided

Figure 2-22 Heating lines often are hung on the sides of benches. The heating line on the right is supplied from a header above, and the line on the left enters a steam trap connected to a return main.

with a trap that is large enough to take care of the water produced in the coil. Approximately 450 grams of water is produced per 1,000 Btu of heat per hour. A 3-centimeter steam pipe 61 meters long would require a trap that would handle at least 16 kilograms of water an hour (61 times 590 times 0.450). The capacity of steam traps is rated by the manufacturer, and the size of trap that will be large enough for the amount of water produced in the coil should be chosen.

Heating-Line Controls

With manual control of the heating lines, hand valves are used for regulation. By checking the thermometer regularly and activating heating lines as needed by opening valves, the greenhouse can be kept within the proper temperature range. A manual system of operation does require the presence of some dedicated workers day and night—workdays and holidays—to open or close valves as needed.

The steam heating lines in many greenhouses are either fully or partially controlled by thermostats and power-operated valves, which may be operated by electric motors, compressed air (pneumatic), or electric solenoid, or may be self-contained. The electric motor and the pneumatic valves are used more often than the other types of valves, and they are available as either two-position (open or closed) or modulating types. The modulating-type valve opens and closes gradually as it is activated by the thermostat, giving a more even control of temperature.

Temperature control in the greenhouse with a hot-water heating system is attained by regulating the temperature of the water and by the use of electric, motor-driven water circulators. In mild weather, water temperatures of approximately 98°C may be used, and in cold weather the water temperature may be increased to 118°C in an open system or higher temperatures in a closed system. The water circulators are activated by thermostats, and when heat is required in a given area, the circulator pumps the hot water through the pipes in that area.

The control of the heating system must be carefully coordinated. The boiler must be operated so that there is a sufficient supply of steam or hot water when needed but no great excess at any time. This is a problem when the weather changes rapidly or the sun varies in intensity on partly cloudy days. The demand for heat must be anticipated far enough in advance so that the boiler is prepared to furnish the quantity of heat that is needed at the right time.

Temperature control in the greenhouse during the heating season is provided by good coordination and regulation of heating lines and ventilation. Whether the operation of the heating lines and ventilators is manual or automated, it must be carefully supervised to produce the proper temperature range and even heating. No matter what controls are used, they must operate equally effectively during the night, day, holidays, weekends, and workdays.

Special Heat Requirements

Higher temperatures are used for the propagation of plants. Propagation benches for rooting cuttings and grafting benches or cases are maintained about 6°C warmer than the temperature used for growing the crop. Seed flats also are kept in warmer temperatures for the best germination of seed. In spite of the relatively small area concerned with propagation, there is a large number of plants involved; and the temperature requirements are critical.

The propagation areas may be in shaded locations so that they do not receive direct light or heat from the sun. Flower production areas are always in full sun, and if the heating system is operated solely for them, some provision must be made for furnishing heat solely to the propagation area on sunny days.

Some plants are propagated at the time of year when the heating system is not normally used for the production areas. The heating system must then be put in operation just for the propagation area or an alternate heating system must be used. Thermostatically controlled electric soil-heating cable is an excellent means of furnishing the uniform, warm temperatures needed in propagation areas.

With some crops, temperatures need to be varied at certain stages of growth to produce the desired kind or amount of growth. The size of structure and the control of the heating system that will provide the conditions needed for the specific crop are required. There is an advantage in having "crop-size" houses so that the temperature can be controlled as needed for the crop without affecting a crop at another stage of growth. In the early stages the quality and rate of growth of snapdragons are better at 16°C than at 10°C, but it is not possible to provide these different temperatures if young plants and flowering plants are grown in the same structure. In many instances there is an advantage in growing chrysanthemums at a warmer temperature during the early stages of growth than at the time of flowering, and the timing of holiday production of cut flowers and pot plants is adjusted by the regulation of temperature. This is possible only if the supply of heat can be controlled as needed for the crop.

The problem of proper temperature is not just a matter of producing more or less growth, but also of producing the kind of growth desired. With many cultivars of chrysanthemum, flower buds form and develop properly only within a limited temperature range, and the azalea forms flower buds in warm temperatures but develops or matures them in cooler temperatures. There are many other examples of the effect of temperature on flowering.

Because several disease organisms may grow and thrive in the same temperature and moisture conditions that are furnished for the greenhouse crop plants, it is essential that they be eliminated from the surroundings. Steaming soil, tools, benches, and surroundings is the best method of eliminating disease organisms, and it also controls soil pests and the growth of weeds in the soil. A source of steam is needed the year-round for this purpose; if the steam boiler cannot be used, a steam generator should be provided just for this purpose.

Providing Steam for Treatment of Soil and Equipment

Steaming soil is the best method of controlling disease organisms, pests, and weeds. In addition it gives many soils a better structure which promotes better soil drainage and improved root growth. For proper steaming of soil all portions of it must be heated to 118°C and maintained at that temperature for a minimum time of 30 minutes. This will require about 124,000 Btu of

Comparison of Customary and Metric Units of Volume

Customary	Metric (approximate)
1 cubic foot	0.03 cubic meter
1 cubic yard	0.77 cubic meter

heat per hour (about 56 kilograms of steam) per cubic meter of soil, or, in a bench, per 6.5 square meters of soil. Since there is approximately a 50 percent loss of heat between the boiler and the soil to be steamed, twice the amount of heat must be generated at the boiler as will be used efficiently in heating the soil: 248,000 Btu or about 112 kilograms of steam per hour. A boiler rated at 200 horsepower would produce about 6,695,000 Btu or 3,100 kilograms of steam per hour, which would be capable of steaming approximately 27.5 cubic meters of soil or 186 square meters of 15-centimeter-deep bench soil (three benches 105 centimeters by 61 meters).

If steam is not available from the heating system, a steam boiler or generator should be obtained just for the purpose of providing steam for treating soil. Such a boiler would be smaller than those used for heating systems, but a 40-horsepower unit would furnish enough steam for steaming a single bench 105 centimeters by 30.5 meters. Portable steam generators, or oil-fired units on wheels, are available also. There may be an advantage in being able to move them to the vicinity in which they are needed, but because of their small size they can steam only about a 15-meter bench at a time.

Either low-pressure or high-pressure steam can be used for soil steaming because, regardless of the pressure at which the steam is piped to the bench, the pressure drops immediately when the steam is released into the soil. The only advantage in using high-pressure steam is that smaller pipe for the same quantity of heat can be used in transporting the steam from the boiler to the bench. High-pressure steam generators for industrial cleaning are usually not satisfactory as a source of steam because they produce only a low volume of steam despite the high pressure.

Reducing Temperatures in the Greenhouse

As noted earlier, plants produce the best growth within a fairly narrow temperature range. Heating systems are used to increase the temperature during cool weather, and cooling systems may be used during the time of the year when the temperatures are too high. Since heat is removed from the surroundings as water changes from the liquid to the vapor state (evaporates), it is possible to cool greenhouse air and plants by introducing some water into the greenhouse atmosphere. The amount of heat removal (cooling) that is possible depends on the temperature of the air indoors and outdoors and the relative humidity of the air. Maximum cooling is possible when the relative humidity of the air is low and the temperatures are not extremely high. In most areas it is found that greenhouse air temperatures can be reduced about 6 to 12°C, which is sufficient to allow a definite improvement in plant growth. Greenhouse air temperatures often are 73°C and may reach a maximum of around 80°C during the heat of the summer.

Figure 2-23 Exhaust fans for a fan and pad cooling system. Note that the ridge ventilators are closed during the operation of this system. *(Acme Engineering and Manufacturing Corp. photograph.)*

Since the growth of many types of plants is adversely affected at temperatures above 68°C, the temperature reduction that is possible with cooling systems is sufficient to bring the greenhouse temperatures within a suitable range.

With the moist pad system (fan and pad), exhaust fans are placed in one wall of the greenhouse, and the moist pad in the opposite wall. All other air entries are closed during the operation of the fan and pad system, and as the exhaust fans evacuate some of the air from the greenhouse, air from the outdoors enters through the moistened pad. As the air passes through the moistened pad, some of the water changes from the liquid state to the vapor state, removing heat from the air. Then as the cooled air passes across the greenhouse, heat is transferred to it from the warm plants and the surrounding air.

Design of the Fan and Pad Cooling System

When possible, it is best to locate the exhaust fans in one wall with the moist pad in the opposite wall, and the pad should be on the windward side. With separate houses the airflow is established lengthwise if possible, as this can be done more efficiently than across the rather short width of the house. With ridge and furrow ranges the airflow may be either lengthwise or across the houses depending on how they are situated, but there is an advantage in moving the air across the houses, as the gutters between the houses then function as baffles to keep the airflow at the plant level. In making the decision on the direction of airflow through the greenhouse, it is also necessary to consider whether the necessary size and number of fans can be located in the wall and whether the opposite wall will accommodate the required size of pad. It is not possible to plan to move air farther than about 70 meters, as the pad required for such a distance would be too large for the opposite wall. A distance of 46 meters is considered the maximum for greatest efficiency in cooling. Because of the many different greenhouse designs, the installation of the fan and pad systems has to be adjusted for the particular situation, and in some instances fans are mounted in the roof instead of in the wall.

The rate of airflow should be from 2.3 to 3.2 cubic meters per minute per square meter of ground covered by the greenhouse. The higher rate of airflow is used in situations in which the distance from pad to fan is short, and in areas of the country in which the humidity is comparatively high. For a greenhouse 12.2 by 61 meters, the air would have to move at the rate of 1,637 (744 times 2.3) to 2,381 (744 times 3.2) cubic meters per minute, depending on the circumstances. Since approximately 1 square meter of moist pad is required per 49 cubic meters of air moved per minute, from 33 to 49 square meters of pad would be needed. This need could be satisfied by a pad about 3 meters high in one end wall or by a pad about 1 meter high the length of one sidewall.

For a 12.2- by 61-meter house without other obstructions around it, a 3-meter pad would be provided in the windward end wall; in the other end wall would be four exhaust fans with a capacity of about 400 cubic meters per minute each. If it were necessary to establish air movement across this house, a pad about one meter wide could be installed the length of the windward sidewall; and eight exhaust fans with a capacity of about 280 cubic meters per minute each would be located in the opposite sidewall. A pad only 1 meter high would provide a narrow stratum or band of cool air, and the crops could grow above it. Hence the pad height should be greater than the minimum for a larger area of cooled air in the greenhouse.

Since the air enters the greenhouse through the pad, there is some resistance. Fans should therefore be selected according to their rating at 0.3-centimeter static pressure. The fans are mounted in boxes that are provided with automatic shutters that open when the fan operates but remain closed during nonoperation of the fans. In order to provide uniform air movement throughout the greenhouse, the exhaust fans should be spaced no further apart than about 8 meters. Exhaust fans are available with either 110- or 220-volt motors, and 220-volt motors are generally used if that power is available.

Pads must be uniformly porous enough so that the air will flow through them evenly, and absorbent so that they will retain some water. Shredded wood serves this purpose well. It is fashioned into pads about 5 centimeters thick and in lengths and widths for convenient installation in various situations.

Comparison of Customary and Metric Units of Capacity

Customary	Metric (approximate)
1 ounce	0.03 liter
1 quart	1.00 liter
1 gallon	3.80 liters
100 gallons	380.00 liters

The pad is moistened by water trickled through it from a trough installed above the pad. The excess water may be wasted or it may be collected in a tank and pumped up to the trough for recirculation through the pad. A sufficient amount of water must be supplied to keep the pad uniformly moist, at least 4 liters of water per minute per linear meter of pad regardless of the height of the pad. Water loss in the pad is approximately 3 percent. In a system that recirculates the water, the make-up water is added to the tank by a float-operated water valve. If the water is recirculated through the pad, it is possible to treat the water for improved operation. Some detergent should be added to the water in the tank to facilitate the wetting of the pad. Any of several household detergents can be used satisfactorily, and the amount to use depends on the hardness of the water; if too much is used, excessive foaming is produced. It is possible that insects and other small pests may be swept through the pad along with the air from outdoors, and every effort should be made to keep the area outside the pads free from pests. In addition to this control, there is an advantage in using pesticide for thrips in the pad water as they have the ability to soar from considerable distances.

The pad deteriorates with use and should be replaced often enough to ensure the best results from the cooling system. It becomes plugged with dirt, minerals, debris, and algae, causing a reduced airflow. The wood fibers rot gradually, allowing some sagging and producing holes in the pad that permit the entrance of uncooled air. Washing the pad from the inside with a forceful stream of water directed through the pad will often dislodge foreign matter and improve the efficiency of the system.

There is a big advantage in having the pads installed in the greenhouse in such a way that they can be placed in or removed from operation on very short notice, to provide for the use of the cooling system at will during the unpredictable temperature fluctuations in the spring and fall. The best solution seems to be to provide large wall ventilators with the pad located inside the wall. Then the greenhouse can be opened or closed rapidly by simply opening or closing the ventilators. If the installation of the pad necessitates the removal of the greenhouse wall, it is almost impossible to guess when the wall should be removed in the spring and when it should be replaced in the fall.

Cool Storage

Many greenhouse crops require cool temperatures at some stage of development. Cut flowers should be stored overnight in water in refrigerators maintained at about 7°C or lower. Some cut flowers can be held satisfactorily for several days in storages operated at 1°C, and some rooted and unrooted cuttings can be kept in good condition for several weeks at that temperature. Some bulbs and plants require a period of cool storage in order to flower satisfactorily in the shortest time. And some holiday pot plants can be held in cool storage when they flower before the scheduled time.

Refrigerated storage may not be an absolute necessity at each greenhouse, but there are few greenhouses that could not use it to good advantage if it were available. Reliable companies specializing in refrigerated storages

Figure 2-24 Whenever possible the wet pad should be located within the greenhouse so that the house can be opened and closed as the weather demands. This type of sidewall ventilator operating equipment allows the wet pad to be installed inside the wall.

should be consulted in order to obtain the most economical construction and operation. Cooling units that are "frostfree" and without strong drafts are most desirable.

EQUIPMENT FOR COMMERCIAL FLOWER FORCING

Some of the equipment used in flower and plant production is standard equipment used in industrial or other types of agricultural production or adaptations of this equipment. Other items have been designed for specific uses in the greenhouse.

Equipment for the Control of Light

The sun is the primary source of light in the greenhouse, and the structure is designed so that it will admit the maximum amount of sunlight. All available sunlight is needed for plants in the greenhouse from fall to spring, but some reduction in light is usually required during the summer. This reduction in the amount of light at that time of the year can be handled by the use of screening material within the greenhouse or by the application of shading material to the outer surface of the greenhouse.

When screening materials are used within the greenhouse, they may be a fixed installation for the season or they may be removable so that they may be adjusted on short notice as needed. The fixed installation usually costs less, but it is difficult to provide the light intensity needed for the plants in the variable periods in the spring and fall. The removable installations either require some labor expense in adjusting them or rather costly equipment to simplify or automate the movement of the screening material.

The density of the screening material that is needed depends on the crop or the stage of growth. Propagation areas may need considerable reduction in light intensity depending on the use of moisture in the area. An 80 percent reduction in light intensity could be used when the area does not have a misting system and a 50 percent reduction in amount of light should be sufficient when an effective mist system is used. Foliage plants in general should be provided with about 65 percent light reduction, and those that require less light should be given 80 percent reduction. For general crop growth, 50 percent light reduction frequently is used during the summer. For protection of standard chrysanthemum flowers, it is common practice to use from 30 to 50 percent reduction in light intensity during the summer. Manufacturers of shading materials list the light reduction percentage of their products.

Several different kinds of screening materials are suitable. The cotton fabrics such as tobacco cloth, cheesecloth, and lightweight muslins usually cost less, but they are less durable than synthetic fabrics such as Saran, polypropylene, and polyester. Each type of fabric may have standard widths in which it is made, and these can be sewed together for continuous coverage of larger areas.

A shading material may be sprayed on the exterior of the greenhouse covering instead of or in addition to the screening material that is used within the greenhouse during the summer. These commonly are called shading compounds, and several formulations are manufactured. The objectives are to provide uniform coverage, good adherence during the summer, and easy removal in the fall. It always is difficult to know when to make the application in the spring and the removal in the fall because of the changeable climate at those times of the year.

In addition to the compound that is sprayed, a sprayer is required. This could be the sprayer that is used for application of pesticides, or it could be a sprayer used solely for this purpose. In some large installations, the shading spray is applied by aircraft.

The crops that need short photoperiods for flowering in naturally long days must be covered with fabric that excludes light. Black fabric is used. Cotton was the fabric used initially, and it still is used. In addition several types of plastic covers are used. There is a wide range in costs and durability of these materials. Also some materials can be handled better than others. The decision of which type of photoperiod-shading material to use needs to be based on these three factors—initial cost, durability, and handling characteristics.

Shading for the control of photoperiod requires daily handling. The covers are drawn in the evening and withdrawn in the morning. If this is a bench by bench operation, much manual labor and time are required. For this method of covering, two or three wires are installed the length of the bench about 15 centimeters above the maximum height of the plants and supported about every 3 to 4 meters. The width of the cover must be sufficient to extend from the bench bottom on one side over the top of the plants to the bench bottom on the other side. The entire length of the bench must be covered and the ends enclosed to exclude light. The length of the covers usually is about 15 meters because that length can be handled easily and also, when gathered together, does not cause a large area of shade over the plants during the day. This method of handling the black fabric requires two individuals per bench working in unison on opposite sides of the bench.

If larger areas are to be shaded, it is much more efficient to suspend the black fabric over the entire area so that several benches can be handled at a time. The fabric may be suspended from rollers in tracks or from wires. The fabric then may be drawn and withdrawn manually or by motor.

Electric Light Equipment   In addition to industrial-type lighting that is used in workrooms, boiler rooms, offices, and for security purposes outdoors, there are some uses of electric lights that are specific for the greenhouse business. The main work that is done in greenhouses during the night is periodic checking of temperature and ventilation. Only minimum lighting is used for this purpose. The night worker uses a flashlight, and the only electric lights provided in the greenhouse may be by the ventilator operators and the thermometers.

In some instances electric lights are used either for the sole source of light for plants or as light that is supplementary to sunlight. It is much more expensive to use electric light than sunlight as the sole source of light for plants, but this expense is justified in some situations. For some research studies, it is possible to get a degree of control with electric lights that is not possible with sunlight. In commercial work the increase in production costs when using electric lights would have to be met by a corresponding increase in quality and quantity of product. This seems possible only with plants that grow well in lower light intensities, and then probably only when they are small in size so that a large number of plants utilize the lighted area.

Fluorescent light has been used successfully as the sole source of light in some propagation areas. The tubes are placed together as closely as possible and within 30 centimeters of the top of the plants. The length of photoperiod usually is 16 hours. More recently high-intensity-discharge (HID) lamps have been used instead of fluorescent lamps. Either type of lamp can be used depending on the space limitations and the costs involved. The HID lamps require more space, and the cost of equipment may be greater than it is for fluorescent lamps.

There has been some use of HID lamps as supplementary light to sunlight in the greenhouse from fall to spring. Most of these installations have been on roses, and the growth of the plants is increased. In some instances flower production has been doubled during the period of the year the plants were lighted. However, there are differences of opinion as to whether the cost of the equipment, the cost of the power, and the additional cost of labor and materials to handle the increased production justify the installation.

Electric Lights for Photoperiod Control   Regulation of photoperiod is used for chrysanthemum, kalanchoe, poinsettia, and some other greenhouse crops. Plants vary in their sensitivity to light quantity. Poinsettia and kalanchoe are much more sensitive to light than chrysanthemum. Also there may be a variance in sensitivity among cultivars of a genus. The initial installations were made on mums, and it was recommended at that time that incandescent lamps be used to provide a minimum of 10 foot-candles of light at the top level of the plants. For benches up to 120 centimeters wide, that light intensity could be provided by 60-watt lamps spaced 120 centimeters apart and 60 centimeters above the plant tops. Most of the light installations have been made on this basis through the years. The lights are controlled by a timer, and the length of the lighting period is varied with the season of the year so that the dark period is less than the minimum required for the long-day effect. This lighting may be an extension of the natural day length, or it may be an interruption of the night. With either method, the dark periods must be less than the minimum.

It is more economical to interrupt the night than to extend the day. This lighting may be done around midnight, and it is possible to light either before or after midnight. Half the area then can be lighted at a time. Because of the reduced power demand at one time, smaller-sized wire may be used, and the rate may be lower, too, during the night.

Subsequently it was determined that photoperiodic lighting does not have to be continuous. It can be intermittent. This became known as cyclic lighting and a typical cycle was 6 minutes of light followed by 24 minutes of darkness with the cycle repeated for 4 hours from 10 P.M. to 2 A.M. With this arrangement five areas could be lighted in the 4-hour period; thus the power load would be reduced considerably at any one time. Cyclic lighting was not universally accepted commercially for photoperiodic lighting because it seemed to be less reliable even though 20-foot-candle minimums were used and it does require more sophisticated control equipment than continuous lighting.

If photoperiodic lighting is needed for large areas, it can be done most economically with fluorescent lamps that emit pink light. Some commercial installations space 120-centimeter tubes in conduit about 75 centimeters apart and about 270 centimeters above the ground, and a single line of these tubes effectively lights an area 6 meters wide. The total wattage requirement then for an area about 6 by 30 meters would be 680 watts. By comparison, lighting the traditional way with incandescent lamps would require about 6,000 watts. If the cost of current were 3 cents per kilowatthour, the costs would be 1.8 versus 18 cents per hour, in favor of the fluorescent lights. In addition smaller copper wire could be used for the fluorescent installation which would result in further significant savings.

In smaller areas, the use of fluorescent lights could present some problems in shielding plants at some distance from the light. In using incandescent lamps over each bench, it is only the adjacent benches that would need to be shielded. With pink fluorescent lamps, the second and third benches distant from the tubes probably would need to be shaded from the light.

Equipment for Control of Moisture

The application of water to crop soils is known as irrigation. Irrigation equipment has been designed for distributing water to greenhouse soils and controlling the frequency and length of irrigation.

When water is applied to aerial portions of plants, it is in the form of mist and the procedure is called misting. The objective usually is to increase relative humidity with the result that moisture loss (transpiration) from the plant is reduced. Other means for increasing humidity may be used.

Some methods are used for reducing moisture in the greenhouse.

Irrigation Equipment Various kinds of irrigation equipment have been used in greenhouses. The oldest method that still is used to some extent is hose-in-hand. Some greenhouse operators may use only that method of irrigation. A 2-centimeter hose is used, and it must be made from materials that remain pliable regardless of temperature. The irrigator uses both hands on the hose—spaced about 1 meter apart. For a right-handed worker, the right hand is just in back of the delivery end of the hose and directs the stream of water to the soil. The left hand drags the hose as the irrigator walks while watering. The hose must drag freely and not kink.

For pot-plant irrigation, each pot is watered individually with the tip end of the hose just above the soil. The faucet is only partially opened so that the water delivery is only about 12 liters per minute. A water breaker may or may not be used. For cut-flower irrigation, the faucet is fully opened. The tip end of the hose is just above the soil, and a water breaker must be used for this kind of watering. The water delivery from the hose in cut-flower irrigation is about 60 liters per minute. In either instance the irrigator's rate of movement controls the amount of water applied.

Usually it is best when water faucets are provided at the midpoint of the bench with one faucet per walk. With that sort of arrangement, the irrigator can start at the midpoint and water half of that bench to the end. On the return trip the adjoining bench is watered for the full length, and then the remaining half of the original bench back to the midpoint. If it is a pot-plant greenhouse with only hand watering, a 2-centimeter water header could be used for up to five individuals watering at one time. However, if cut flowers are grown, only one individual could water at a time if the header is 2 centimeters. At least a 2.5-centimeter header would be needed for the operation of two hoses at a time, and a 4-centimeter header would be needed in order to use four hoses at the same time. A hook of some kind should be installed in the vicinity of the faucet so that the tip end of the hose can be hung free of contamination while not in use.

Frequently a hose is provided for each walk. If there are not that many hoses, faucets and hoses should be provided with quick couplers so that hoses may be moved quickly from one location to another.

Water-Distribution Systems for Pot Plants Nozzles installed above the plants may be used for bedding plants or for small plants. This method is not practical for larger plants because the umbrella effect of the foliage causes uneven watering and the moisture on leaves and flowers may provide conditions suitable for pathogen growth.

Different kinds of nozzles are available, and the system has to be designed for the characteristics of the particular nozzle that is used. A nozzle in common usage is a deflection type that delivers a horizontal spray full circle—360°—at the rate of about 2 liters per minute. These nozzles are spaced about 1 meter apart, and they may be installed on rods for individual placement throughout the area or in pipe that is placed above the plants. A 2-centimeter pipe would supply sufficient water for 30 of these nozzles.

Larger pots—10 centimeters and up—usually are irrigated with small-diameter (about 0.15-centimeter internal diameter) plastic tubes directed to each pot. The plastic tubes are inserted into a polyethylene pipe water main for water supply. Approximately 500 pots can be supplied from one 2-centimeter poly pipe. Because of the small size of the plastic tubes servicing each pot, the rate of water flow in the tubes decreases rapidly with increase in length of the tube. For this reason, tubes of the same length must

Figure 2-25 Irrigation of pot plants by means of small-diameter plastic tubes is efficient and economical. *(Stuppy Supply Co. photograph.)*

be used on a water main. When variable-length tubes are used the pots with shorter tubes will receive more water than the pots with longer tubes. Also if one water main is fitted with 45-centimeter tubes and another water main with 60-centimeter tubes, the irrigation time to supply the same amount of water per pot would have to be longer for the water main with the longer tubes. The delivery ends of the plastic tubes usually are supplied with water breakers in order to distribute water evenly over the soil surface.

To establish the length of time the system needs to be operated to deliver a certain amount of water—for instance 1 cup per 16-centimeter pot—one of the tubes can be placed in a measuring cup and watering discontinued when the desired quantity is indicated.

Pot-plant soils may be subirrigated by capillarity from a porous substance beneath the pots. Although capillary irrigation may be used for plants in pots of any size, it is most useful for plants in small pots—9 centimeters and smaller. The porous material on which the pots are set can be fine-textured sand or fabric that will promote capillarity. The pots usually are given the initial watering with hose-in-hand in order to establish capillarity between the soil and the porous material on which the pots are set. Subsequently water is applied only to the porous material on the bench.

The requisites for a capillary irrigation system are a level and watertight bench surface, a porous layer on the surface, and a means of distributing water evenly over the porous material. Polyethylene film usually can be used for waterproof covering on the bench. Sand or several fabrics are available for use as the porous material, and water may be distributed by various means. But whatever method is used, it must be adjustable so that the porous layer may be kept wetter or drier as needed.

Water-Distribution Systems for Cut-Flower Crops In cut-flower irrigation systems, the water is distributed either by nozzles, ooze, or by piddle. Any type of system can be used satisfactorily.

The irrigation nozzles throw a horizontal spray. Some of them deliver water 360° and others either 180 or 45°. The 360° nozzles are suitable only for installation at the center of the bench, but the 180° nozzle may be placed at the center or at the side.

A 360° nozzle frequently used delivers water at the rate of about 2 liters per minute and these nozzles are installed about 1 meter apart. A 2-centimeter pipe would supply enough water for a bench 30 meters long. Steel pipe or PVC, schedule 40, pipe can be used. For benches up to 60 meters in length, 2.5-centimeter pipe would be needed. Irrigation pipe must be level so that the pipe remains full and there is no seepage from nozzles when the valve is closed.

The 180° plastic nozzles deliver water at the rate of about 0.7 liter per

Figure 2-26 Perimeter watering of bench-grown plants moistens the soil uniformly without compaction. *(From "Flower and Plant Production in the Greenhouse," Interstate Printers & Publishers, Inc., Danville, Illinois.)*

minute. They usually are self-tapped into polyethylene pipe. When the pipe is installed at the center of the bench, the nozzles would be placed 40 centimeters apart and positioned to spray the length of the pipe—or two nozzles could be installed every 80 centimeters with the spray directed in opposite directions toward the bench sides. A 2.5-centimeter pipe would supply enough water for a 30-meter bench.

The 180° plastic nozzles more frequently are installed in poly pipe placed at the sides of the bench with the spray directed toward the center from each side. These nozzles are satisfactory for use with general cut-flower crops in benches up to 105 centimeters wide or with rose plants in benches up to 120 centimeters wide. The 180° nozzles are spaced 75 centimeters apart and the ones on the opposite side are staggered rather than being placed directly opposite. A 2.5-centimeter poly pipe will supply enough water for the nozzles on a 30-meter bench.

For wider benches, 45° nozzles are alternated with 180° nozzles. The nozzles are spaced 50 centimeters apart, and they are placed so the 45° nozzles oppose 180° nozzles on the other side. A 30-meter bench can be supplied with 2.5-centimeter poly pipe, or 2-centimeter pipe can be used with two separate sources of water.

The piddle and ooze water-distribution systems for cut-flower crops use tubing made from plastic film. There are several different designs, and the installation methods and water requirements vary with the type. This information can be obtained from the manufacturer or supplier of the equipment.

Figure 2-27 Bench crops may be irrigated with collapsible plastic tubing, in this instance the Greco system. Small streams of water are emitted from the pairs of holes spaced 10 centimeters apart the length of the tubing. Note the straw incorporated into the soil for improvement of drainage. *(From "Flower and Plant Production in the Greenhouse," Interstate Printers & Publishers, Inc., Danville, Illinois.)*

Equipment for Regulation of Irrigation When water-distribution systems are used they may be installed with hand valves and operated manually or they may have electric vavles so that they can be controlled by timers. There is a definite advantage in being able to control irrigation by means of a timer. When the grower makes the selection of the benches that are to be watered, the irrigation proceeds from one bench to the next automatically. Timers for pot-plant crops should have the capability of providing irrigating times from 1 to 5 minutes. The length of irrigation time for cut-flower crops needs to be adjustable from 5 to 20 minutes.

Controllers are made for regulating irrigation for different numbers of benches. The choice of size of unit is determined by the number of benches in the area and the quantity of water that is available. If there are 20 benches to be irrigated, a controller that could handle 20 benches would be chosen if the water quantity is limited. If there is a sufficient amount of water so that two or more benches could be watered at a time, two 10-station controllers could be used.

Irrigation controllers can be set to handle watering before the workers arrive in the morning or on weekends. This allows maximum utilization of the water supply, and labor time is saved.

Misting Equipment Most propagation areas have misting lines installed above the benches. With cuttings being rooted, the system is operated just frequently enough to maintain moisture on the surface of the leaves. This reduces the rate of transpiration, and the moisture content in the cutting is maintained.

With plants being propagated from seed, the system is operated just frequently enough to keep the soil surface moist so that there will be good germination of the seeds.

The misting nozzles usually are tapped directly into the pipe. The most common type nozzle is a deflecting type that gives a horizontal, full-circle spray of mist. The nozzles are spaced about 1 meter apart, and they deliver water at the rate of about 1.5 liters per minute.

The water flow in the misting line is controlled by an electric water valve. The misting line must be installed level, and the valve must be at that level or below. There then will be no drip from the nozzles when the valve is shut. The pipe will remain full of water and misting will be instantaneous for the entire length of the misting line when the valve opens.

The timer that operates the misting system should provide misting periods of about 5 seconds with adjustable intervals between mistings from about 1 minute to 1 hour.

Equipment for Handling Fertilizer

Greenhouse growers determine the need for fertilizer applications by having analyses made of soil or leaves for the mineral nutrient content. These are laboratory procedures that are best handled by specialists in that business. Soil analysis should be made on a regular basis, and leaf analysis usually is done only if there is evidence of trouble that cannot be identified by other means.

Every greenhouse operator, however, should have the equipment to determine the total amount of salts (soluble salts) present in the soil and the pH. The instrument for making the soluble salt determination is the Solu Bridge, and pH can be evaluated by color change with sensitive paper used for that purpose. The Solu Bridge is an electronic instrument that can measure conductivity in a soil solution. The greater the concentration of salts in the soil solution, the higher the Solu Bridge reading. Low readings indicate that a fertilizer application should be made, and high readings signify that the soil should be leached with water.

Fertilizer applications may be made either in the dry or the liquid form. Fertilizer applied in dry form may be distributed over the soil as uniformly as possible and mixed into the soil as the soil is prepared for planting, or it may be distributed evenly over the soil surface after planting. Usually these are operations by hand. Special equipment for the distribution of fertilizer in the dry form for greenhouse crops is not commonly available.

Application of fertilizer in liquid form has been done for years, but methods have changed as materials and equipment have been introduced. The earliest procedures were the application of manure water. Manure was added to large tanks containing water, and the manure water was pumped through pipes to the various greenhouses where it was applied to the soil. When fertilizers became available as soluble, chemical salts, they eventually replaced manure as the fertilizer source. In some instances, this method of fertilizer application still is used. The equipment required is a tank large enough for the area to be treated, a water pump large enough to supply the water volume needed, and pipe lines from tank to greenhouse areas. Usually the tank method of fertilizer application is designed for periodic use rather than for use with each irrigation.

Subsequently devices were designed or adapted to add liquid fertilizer concentrate to water as it is dispensed in irrigation. Some of the advantages in equipment of this type are that large tanks are not required and a more uniform supply of fertilizer in the soil is provided. These devices usually are known as proportioners. There are basically two types of proportioners, and because of the way they function they may be called positive displacement and pressure difference. The positive-displacement type of fertilizer proportioner generally is more reliable than the pressure-difference type.

The positive-displacement type of fertilizer proportioner frequently is called an injector because it injects a uniform volume of fertilizer concentrate into a unit volume of irrigation water. Manufacturers of this equipment use various means of sensing irrigation water volume and injection of fertilizer concentrate.

The pressure-difference type of fertilizer proportioner commonly develops the pressure difference by means of a Venturi in which the irrigation water is routed through a reduced-size pipe or orifice. An elementary kind

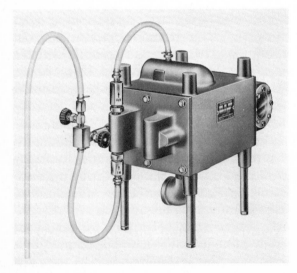

Figure 2-28 The Smith Measuremix fertilizer injectors are operated solely by the water passing through them, which gives positive, accurate injection of fertilizer concentrate into the irrigation water. Units in common usage vary in capacity from 12 to 60 liters per minute for the portable model, R-3, to 80 to 380 liters per minute for the 5-centimeter model, R-8. Larger models are available. *(Smith Precision Products, Inc. photograph.)*

of proportioner of this type commonly is referred to as a siphon. A variable amount of fertilizer concentrate may be proportioned into the irrigation water with this type of device depending on the rate of water flow and the water pressure.

In selecting a fertilizer proportioner, the important considerations are suitability for the maximum and minimum water-flow rates, proportioning reliability, durability, and serviceability.

Some fertilizer proportioners are portable, and they are moved from area to area as needed.

The fertilizer proportioners that are permanently installed must be piped with a bypass so that either water or injected water can be used for irrigation as desired. The piping in the greenhouse must be arranged so that the injected water has access only to irrigation systems. The water-supply system for boiler, toilets, pads, fountains, and other uses must be separate from the irrigation water supply.

Fertilizer injectors must be checked periodically for accuracy. The manufacturers have recommended checking procedures for their units, and it is important that the check be made at least quarterly.

Pest and Pathogen Control Equipment

In addition to equipment for applying pest and pathogen control materials there must be a secure storage area, accurate means for measuring the materials, protective gear for personnel, and an adequate place for personnel to cleanse themselves.

The most common means of applying pesticides is by hydraulic spraying because the control materials usually are in the form that can be used in that way. It is possible that some control materials are available that may be applied as a dust, granule, fog, fumigant, or aerosol. Those methods may be used as alternate means of application, but a good means of hydraulic spraying will be needed for the standard method of application.

When applying pesticides and pathocides the plant surfaces must be covered completely and uniformly without excessive run-off to the soil. This requires the dispersion of the spray liquid into very small particles, and this results when the spray liquid is forced at high pressure through the tiny orifices of the sprayer nozzles. Sprayer pumps that develop 17.6 kilograms per square centimeter pressure are satisfactory. The sprayer pumps may be powered by either electric motors or gas engines.

The sprayer may be stationary with the spray piped to outlets within the greenhouses, or it may be portable so that it can be wheeled to the greenhouse where it will be used. Portable power sprayers for use in the greenhouse have tanks from about 38 to 114 liters in volume. The pumps on the smaller sprayers may develop only about 7 kilograms per square centimeter pressure which makes them less efficient than the larger units.

When portable sprayers are used, usually they are equipped with long enough hoses so that all areas of the benches on either side can be reached when the sprayer is positioned in the center walk of the greenhouse.

Pesticides are not available often in dust form. If the material that is needed can be obtained as a dust, that method of application should be used because very little preparation is required and only a short time is needed for making the application. Dusting is a particularly efficient way to handle isolated infestations. It can be done promptly and should control the infestation in the initial stages. Small manual dusters may be used for this purpose.

Not many pesticides are marketed in the granular form, and there are few if any applicators that are made specifically for applying this form of pesticide. The granules need to be applied uniformly to the soil surface without contaminating the surroundings. Growers have adapted various other kinds of equipment for the job of making the granular application.

Foggers use oil-base pesticides that were formulated for use with specific equipment. There are only a limited number of pesticides that can be used with this kind of equipment. Also the oil that is dispersed along with chemical is toxic to some kinds of plants. Before investing in fogging equipment, growers should determine how suitable it is for their crops.

No special equipment is required for use with fumigators, but there are very few pesticides that can be dispersed in this way.

The most complete protective equipment is needed for the individual who makes the aerosol application, but the only applicating equipment needed is the hose, tube, and nozzle assembly that attaches to the aerosol. There are very few pesticides that can be prepared for aerosol dispersion.

Equipment for Application of Other Agricultural Chemicals

Most of the other agricultural chemicals either are sprayed over the plants or are drenched on the soil. In either instance it is a hydraulic application.

Growth-regulant materials are used on several greenhouse crops. When they are applied as a spray, 4 liters of the spray liquid will give coverage to plants occupying 20 square meters of space. Much of the growth-regulant spraying can be handled with small compression sprayers with tank volumes from about 4 to 12 liters. However, these sprayers are more effective if they are the type that is pressurized from compressed air tanks rather than pumped by hand. The sprayers used for application of growth-regulant materials should be used for that purpose only.

In the greenhouse, weed control in crop soils is one of the results of steaming the soils before planting. Noncrop areas such as under benches and walks do need some weed-control measures. Most of the herbicides have the potential of damaging crop plants as well as weeds, and these materials must be used in such a way that there is no contact with the crop plants. Herbicides that volatilize cannot be used because they could affect crop plants at some distance from where they are used. Some of the herbicides that do not volatilize have been used in the greenhouse, but they must be handled very carefully. Coarse sprays are used and directed only at the weeds so there is no possibility of the spray reaching the crop plants. Small, hand-pumped sprayers usually are suitable for weed-control work. These sprayers, however, must be used only for weed control.

Equipment for Preparation of Soil for Planting

Greenhouse soils may be anything from field soils that are naturally derived to gravel. But most often they are mixtures of two or more materials. The mixing is done by hand or machine, and the prime objectives are to provide a soil that drains readily in greenhouse conditions and has a suitable mineral nutrient content. Various ingredients have been used for greenhouse soil mixtures through the years. The initial mixing procedures involved adding organic matter and possibly some aggregate to field soils to improve the water-drainage characteristics of the soil. Manure was a popular ingredient in soil mixtures for years. This product varied in straw and fertilizer content, and the resulting mixtures were quite different in spite of having the same quantities of soil and manure in them each time.

Manure seldom is used in greenhouse soil mixtures anymore, but chopped straw often is used—particularly with cut-flower crops.

Peat has been used in soil mixtures for years and continues to be widely used. There are several different kinds and grades of peat. Some are powdery and others are fibrous, and pH varies considerably. It is the fibrous peats that are of most value in greenhouse soil mixtures, and the pH will need to be evaluated and adjusted as needed.

Eventually some greenhouse soil mixtures were made that contained no field soils. A single material was used in some instances. Gravel was used for some cut-flower crops, and peat was used for some container crops. They still are used for some crops. Peat has been used as one ingredient in several different soil mixtures, and the other ingredients have been various materials such as sand, perlite, vermiculite, or other materials.

More recently ground bark has been a principle ingredient in some soil mixtures.

The soil mixtures that contain no field soils usually are used only for crops grown in containers. The longer-term cut-flower crops can be grown in soil mixtures that do not contain field soils, but ingredients need to be used that provide stable drainage characteristics for the entire period of use.

Some firms have developed soil mixtures that they sell on the open market, and some greenhouse pot-plant growers have discontinued mixing their own soils in favor of the purchased product.

Greenhouse operators who do mix soil will need a soil shredder, a soil mixer, and soil-steaming equipment. The equipment required for the preparation of potting soils is different from that needed for cut-flower soils. If field soil is used in the soil mixture, a shredder will be needed. The shredder is used to break the clods into smaller pieces so that a uniform soil mixture can be made, but the shredder must not pulverize the soil.

Various sizes of soil shredders are available, from the small ones that are manually loaded by shovel to the ones that are large enough to require loading by tractor. Also the larger shredders may have conveyors or elevators to handle the soil into or out of the shredder.

Shredders are used commonly in the preparation of potting soils but rarely with cut-flower soils.

Mixers of some sort are needed for potting soils. Small batches of soil can be mixed satisfactorily with shovel-in-hand. Larger soil batches are blended in mixers in which the various ingredients are placed in the ratio desired. In many instances concrete mixers have been adapted for this purpose. Some growers have found that mixers designed for blending feed mixtures are more satisfactory than concrete mixers for the ingredients that they use. Whatever mixer is used, it must provide a uniform blend of materials in the mixture. The difference in density of the ingredients may cause a mixing problem, and the moisture content of all materials needs to be correct.

With cut-flower soils, the mixing is done with tillers. Excellent tilling can be done with the use of spade forks by hand, but this requires more labor and time than is available sometimes. Most commonly rotary tillers powered with gasoline engines are used. The ingredients that are to be mixed with the field soil are layered on top of the soil before tilling. Some common problems with the rotary tillers are that they pulverize the soil, do not get to the bottom or corners and edges of the bench or bed, and are difficult to operate in the confined space in the greenhouse. The best answer in many situations is a combination of rotary tilling and hand spading.

Greenhouse soils need to be steamed before planting because this is the best method for elimination of pests, pathogens, and weeds in the soil. The soil should be steamed in place where it will be used. Cut-flower soils are prepared for planting, steamed, and planted with only a minimum of handling before planting. The best arrangement for steaming potting soils is

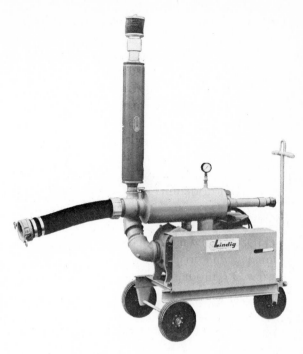

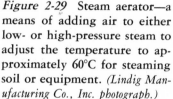

Figure 2-29 Steam aerator—a means of adding air to either low- or high-pressure steam to adjust the temperature to approximately 60°C for steaming soil or equipment. *(Lindig Manufacturing Co., Inc. photograph.)*

the cart designed for steaming as well as potting. This eliminates soil moving and handling that may introduce some contamination. Thorough discussions of soil steaming are in *California Experiment Station Manual 23* and *Pennsylvania Flower Growers Manual—Geraniums.* These manuals are excellent references for soil-treatment procedures to be used before planting.

Growers of crops in containers in quantity find that time can be saved if they use mechanical equipment to fill the containers with soil and also possibly to mark or drill the soil for planting. Some of this equipment is available on the market, but frequently the soil-handling system must be custom-made for the specific situation.

Materials-Handling Equipment

The pot-plant grower has much more material to handle than the cut-flower grower, and the greenhouse and benching arrangements determine the type of handling equipment to be used. Many older greenhouse ranges were arranged so that everything had to be moved by hand, but more recently provisions have been made for mechanical handling of some materials. Pot-plant greenhouses are constructed so that wheeled vehicles can be operated in them. At least one walk in the greenhouse is wide enough for the vehicles and it is smoothly surfaced.

In many instances movement of pot plants into and out of greenhouses has been facilitated considerably by arrangement of benches across the houses instead of lengthwise. This makes a shorter trip down narrow walks to the wide walk on which the benches abut.

Trolley-type conveyors that operate from an overhead rail are rather easily installed in greenhouses and can be very efficient movers of pot plants. There has not been enough consideration given to the use of this type of system in the greenhouse.

Before building greenhouses, the pot-plant grower should spend some time viewing movement of materials in some warehouses. Some of the procedures that they use could suggest methods that are adaptable to the greenhouse.

Repair and Construction Equipment

Any greenhouse operator needs to be a bit of an engineer. It is almost impossible to rely solely on specialist professionals to handle the maintenance of the physical facilities. Owners of smaller greenhouse businesses must be able to handle most of these jobs themselves—boiler repair and operation, painting, glazing, pipe fitting, carpentry, concrete work, gas engine maintenance and motor repair, and routine maintenance of electrical and refrigeration equipment.

The larger greenhouse operation will need to have one or more individuals who handle the engineering problems on the place.

The larger or more complicated engineering jobs in the greenhouse business will need to be handled by specialists in the particular field. It is the routine and day-by-day miscellany of engineering tasks that must be handled right on the place, and tools and equipment will be needed for this part of the business.

Plant Growth and Development

3

Plants have life, and they are capable of growth, development, and reproduction. These are characteristics not only of the plant as a whole but of the individual cells of which the plant is composed. The cell is the unit of structure of plants, and increase in size of plants occurs because some of the cells of the plant divide and then subsequently enlarge. Cell division is a form of reproduction, and the portions of the plant in which it occurs are known as meristems.

METABOLISM IN PLANTS

Cells in living things contain protoplasm. The properties associated with life reside in the protoplasm. If plants are going to be able to grow and develop, they will need additional amounts of protoplasm and building materials. This requires sources of food and energy, and there must be a means within the plant of converting some substances to other kinds of material. The name for these activities is metabolism, and it can occur within the individual cells of plants.

Photosynthesis

Plants (green plants) are uniquely equipped to provide food. When they are in a suitable environment they can manufacture food from some materials received from their surroundings. The basic food manufacturing takes place in the chloroplasts, located in the protoplasm of the cells, and the product is sugar. This food manufacturing process is called photosynthesis, and it can take place when the environment of the plants supplies radiant energy [visible light—irradiation of about 420 to 670 nm (nanometers)], carbon dioxide, and water.

Chloroplasts contain green pigments called chlorophylls, and because of this color relationship it is easy to identify the portions of the plant which are capable of manufacturing sugar. In many kinds of plants, the leaves are the largest green areas. For this reason, the leaf is generally named as the site of sugar manufacturing in plants. The more leaf area there is per plant—larger leaves or greater number of leaves—the more sugar that can be manufactured by the plant. And consequently, because of the greater food supply, plant growth can be increased.

The main route of entry of light radiation and carbon dioxide gas into the plant is in the leaves. The light radiation is absorbed directly by the chloroplasts. The rate of photosynthesis is affected by light quantity as well as light quality. The blue and red portions of the spectrum are more effective than the green portion. Within limits, the greater the light quantity that is available to the plant the more food that can be manufactured by it. The effective light quantity is the result of the combination of light intensity and the length of time the light occurs.

Carbon dioxide gas enters the plant primarily through the leaf stomates; however, some entry occurs through the epidermal tissues. The carbon dioxide diffuses into the plant. The direction of diffusion is from an area of higher concentration of carbon dioxide to an area of lesser concentration.

Water enters the plant primarily through the newly developed tissues of root tips. For this reason, if water is to enter plants there must not only be a water supply in the soil, but root growth must be continuous so that there are suitable places of entry for the water. The passage of water from the soil to the interior of the plant is mainly by means of osmosis. The direction of water movement will be from the place of greater concentration of water to the area of lesser concentration of water. After water enters the plant, it may diffuse into the xylem which is a tubular system in which water can move to various portions of the plant.

Considerable quantities of water are needed for the good growth and development of plants. In addition to its use as one of the ingredients in the manufacture of sugar in the plant, water is about 80 percent of the fresh weight of plants, and there is continual loss of water from plants. Water loss from plants is primarily by diffusion of water vapor from the plant tissues to the surrounding atmosphere. This is known as transpiration. The main avenues of exit of water from plants are through the stomates. Because the water that is transpired is in the vapor form, its exit from the plant cannot be observed. However, if the water loss by means of transpiration exceeds the rate of water entry into the plant, the effect is wilting of the plant, which is very obvious.

Translocation

The sugar that is manufactured in plant cells is soluble. It may diffuse through cell walls and it may translocate to various parts of the plant in the phloem tissue. This transportation of sugar throughout the plant makes growth possible in all portions of the plant. The most obvious beneficiary of the mobility of sugar is the root, but the growth of other parts of the plant also is made possible by movement of sugar from the cells where it is made to other cells in which it cannot be manufactured.

Assimilation and Synthesis

The sugar within the plant may be converted to other foods or building materials, or it may be oxidized (respiration), which results in an energy change and the formation of some by-products.

The food or building materials that are formed may consist only of the carbon, hydrogen, and oxygen which are the basic constituents of sugar, or proteins may be formed that contain minerals in addition to the carbon, hydrogen, and oxygen. The soil is the source of mineral nutrients required for combination with sugar or sugar derivatives in the synthesis of some of the material in plants. Plant proteins contain nitrogen and sulfur and in some instances other minerals in addition to carbon, hydrogen, and oxygen.

The synthesis of other materials from sugar within the plant occurs within the cells. The resulting products may be classed as other forms of food, building materials, or substances that enter into or control processes within plants.

Some of the products formed are transitional. They are somewhat momentary but essential steps en route to the formation of an end product.

The synthesis of protoplasm and cell wall materials from food is called assimilation.

Several types of carbohydrates may be present in plants. There may be one or many kinds of sugar, starch, and alcohols.

Cellulose and pectic compounds are found in cell walls. Lignin is a component of some cell walls, but it is derived from amino acids or proteins.

Many plants contain fats, waxes, lipids, oils, cutin, and suberin. Fats and oils may be important reserves of food in some seeds, and fats and lipids are components of some cell membranes. The fragrance or aroma characteristic of some plants is due to essential oils that are present in some portion of the plant. Waxes and cutin may be on the outer wall of some epidermal cells, and suberin is a component of some cell walls.

Protoplasm consists primarily of protein materials. This includes the enzymes, auxins, and the green pigments, chlorophylls.

The other plant pigments are carbohydrate materials. There are several carotenoids with color ranges from yellow to red to brown. The anthocyanins are red to blue to purple, and the anthoxanthins are yellow to orange.

Respiration

Oxidation of foods takes place in living things. This is known as respiration, and in plants it may be either aerobic or anaerobic. Aerobic respiration is most common in plants, and the discussion here deals solely with that kind of respiration. During the process there is a change in energy, and heat, carbon dioxide, and water are by-products.

The term respiration, when used in reference to animals, includes some procedures that do not take place in plants. In animals the respiratory act that is most obvious is breathing. Those individuals who have associated breathing with respiration will have to realize that there is a difference in plants. Plants do not breathe. But they do need a continuous supply of oxygen, and it diffuses into the plant from the surrounding atmosphere. In the aerial portions of the plant, oxygen enters mainly through the stomates, and in the roots entry of oxygen is in the new tissues close to the root tip.

Respiration occurs in all living cells of plants. The food that is oxidized is soluble, and usually is sugars. The oxidation of foods is a series of involved reactions in which the energy transfer is to adenosine triphosphate molecules and the heat, water, and carbon dioxide evolved are dissipated throughout the cells and into the surrounding atmosphere.

The rate of respiration is greatest in meristematic tissues. While respiration is occurring—and this is continuously—there must be an adequate supply of food. The plant must be in an environment that promotes photosynthesis. And oxygen must be available to all portions of the plant—roots as well as shoots. It is easy to ignore the oxygen requirements of roots, and it is more difficult, or at least it requires more understanding and planning, to provide adequate air for roots. For root growth, respiration must occur in the cells of the roots, and this can proceed at a satisfactory rate only if there is enough oxygen in the soil to diffuse into the roots continuously.

Enzymes

These are substances in the cells that promote metabolic processes. Enzymes are protein materials which are catalysts for some chemical reactions that occur in the cells. Their presence and need must be understood. Specific enzymes are required for various metabolic processes. They do not enter into the reaction, but without them the process would not occur.

With some enzyme systems specific minerals either activate or inhibit the catalytic reaction without becoming chemically combined with the enzyme.

Hormones

Hormones are substances synthesized in one portion of the plant that can cause pronounced physiological effects when they are translocated to another portion of the plant in very small quantities. The sites of hormone synthesis are meristematic or very young tissues.

Some of the hormones are auxins that may affect cell elongation, root formation, initiation of flowers, or abscission of leaves, or may cause phototropism and geotropism. Other hormones that can regulate plant growth are giberellins, cytokinins, vitamins, and ethylene.

ROOTS AND SHOOTS

Roots and shoots have many similar characteristics, but there are some distinct differences. With few exceptions root growth is downward into the ground, and shoot growth is upright above ground. This orientation of growth probably is caused by the unequal distribution of an auxin in root and shoot cells because of the influence of gravity. It is called geotropism—positive geotropism in roots and negative geotropism in shoots.

Some plants show the effects of geotropism more than others. Gladiolus and snapdragon cut-flower stems when placed horizontally will develop upright growth of the stem tips. Because of this they need to be shipped and stored in an upright position. When snapdragon or gladiolus cut flowers are placed on the horizontal in flower arrangements, the stem tips will reorient upright.

In bulbs planted upside down, the roots still grow downward and the shoots upward. They emerge from the bulb as though the root growth will be up and the shoot growth down, but then the direction of growth makes a 180° change in direction and roots and shoots pass each other en route.

Some tissues are continuous from roots to shoots. The water- and

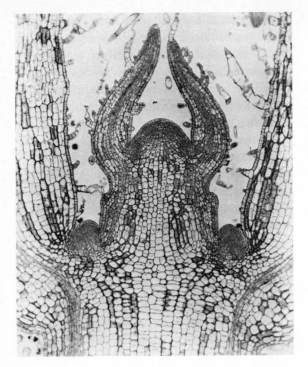

Figure 3-1 Longitudinal section of the apical stem tip of coleus. The apical meristem is between the first two, only partly developed leaves. Just below, appearing as shoulders on the sides of the stem, are bases of the second pair of leaves, which are borne opposite to the first pair. Farther below is the third pair of leaves, which have a young lateral bud in each of their axils. The distance from the top of the apical meristem to the base of the section is 0.86 millimeter. *(Photomicrograph by Tillman Johnson. From "Introduction to Plant Physiology," D. Van Nostrand Company, Inc., New York.)*

food-conducting vessels are continuous tissues from root tips to stem tips.

Growth in Length

Growth in length of both roots and shoots results from cell division in the apical meristems and the subsequent enlargement of the cells.

Root growth continues endlessly in most kinds of plants with little or no change in kinds of cells and tissues that are formed, and the outward appearance of the root remains virtually the same. Branching may occur at irregular intervals with the branches having the same kind of growth and appearance as the root from which they arose.

There is considerable differentiation in growth in shoots resulting in the development of various tissues and structures. Shoot growth may develop stems, leaves, new shoots, flowers, fruit, seed, and possibly other structures.

Growth in Diameter

Growth in diameter of roots and shoots originates in lateral meristems called cambiums. Most of this growth occurs in the vascular cambiums. The cells that divide here differentiate to form xylem tissues to the inside of the cambium and phloem tissues to the outside of the cambium.

Stem Nodes and Internodes

Plant stems vary tremendously in appearance, but they all have the typical node and internode construction with the potential that leaves, shoots, and flowers may develop at the nodes.

Stems usually are above-ground structures; however, some stems do locate in the ground. This can cause some confusion in deciding whether the structure is stem or root. Whether they are above or below ground, stems will have the typical node and internode construction with the possibility of the development of other structures at the nodes.

Some plants have stems that grow horizontally at or just below the ground surface. These are called rhizomes. Ferns may have rhizomes, and the plants that form at the nodes can be separated from the parent plant for reproduction.

The underground structures with some kinds of plants are comparatively large and are called bulbs or tubers. The structures properly called bulbs are stems, and they have leaves (scales) at the nodes that enclose the small stem tip. Some of the greenhouse plants that have bulbs are narcissus, hyacinth, iris, lily, and tulip.

Corms look something like bulbs and often are mistakenly called bulbs. They are stems, but they do not have scales that enclose the stem tip. Crocus and gladiolus have corms.

Some plants have structures that are called tubers. Some of these are stem tubers and others are root tubers. The stem tubers have nodes and internodes and roots develop from the underside of the tuber. Caladium, calla, canna, and gloxinia have stem tubers. With root tubers the stems develop only from the top end of the tuber. Dahlia and some begonias have root tubers.

Indeterminate and Determinate Stem Growth

Stem growth may be indeterminate or determinate. In indeterminate stem growth, the stem continues to increase in length as stem tissues and leaves, known as vegetative growth, continue to develop. Some of the greenhouse plants that have indeterminate stem growth are saintpaulia, begonia, calla, cyclamen, cymbidium, fuchsia, geranium, gloxinia, impatiens, lantana, pansy, and petunia. Flowering in plants that have indeterminate growth develops at the nodes below the terminal tip of the stem.

In determinate growth, stem-tip growth terminates with the development of a flower or flowers. Usually stem and leaves develop from the stem tip for a period of time, and then there is differentiation to the development of a flower or flowers. This is called reproductive growth because the flowers have the potential of forming fruit and seed from which the plant may be reproduced. Some of the greenhouse crop plants that have determinate growth are ageratum, aster, azalea, calceolaria, canna, carnation, cattleya, chrysanthemum, cineraria, narcissus, dahlia, gladiolus, hyacinth, hydrangea, iris, kalanchoe, Easter lily, marigold, poinsettia, rose, snapdragon, tulip, and zinnia.

In most plants when stem growth terminates with the formation of a flower, new shoot growth develops at a node or nodes below the stem tip, and subsequently growth in these shoots may terminate with the formation of a flower or flowers.

Branching in Plants

It was noted previously that shoots may develop at nodes in plants. When vegetative shoots develop at nodes below the terminal apex of the stem, they are referred to as branches. Branching in plants is controlled by a hormone (auxin) produced in the apical meristem and translocated to the lateral meristems.

The apical meristems of plant species or cultivars apparently vary considerably in the length of time they continue to produce this hormone. This hormone prevents the formation of lateral shoots. Some plant species or cultivars form lateral shoots at an early stage of growth and develop a branched or bush-type of plant growth, and other kinds of plants do not develop lateral shoots until terminal flowers form or the terminal apex of the plant is removed. In either instance the source of the hormone is removed.

The kinds of plants that form lateral shoots at an early stage commonly are called self-branching plants. The pot-plant cultivars that branch at an early stage usually form a compact plant that is more acceptable on the market. This characteristic has been the basis for the selection of some commercial cultivars of kalanchoe, geranium, cineraria, calceolaria, and begonia. The kinds of plants that do not form branches readily may be used for pot plants if branching is induced by removing the terminal tip (pinching) of the plant at an early stage of growth. This practice is used with such greenhouse plants as azalea, chrysanthemum, hydrangea, and poinsettia.

With some plants that are used for cut-flower crops, it may be desired to produce a plant with more than one stem before flowers are produced. This can be done by pinching at an early stage of growth, a common practice with such crops as carnation and rose and an occasional practice with chrysanthemum and snapdragon. With carnation and rose plants pinching may be continued on the new shoots that develop so that a multibranched plant is formed before the start of flower production.

Metabolism in Roots and Shoots

It is possible that all of the metabolic processes may occur in cells of both roots and shoots. It is not likely, however, that photosynthesis will take place in greenhouse crop plant roots. Cells of the roots are dependent primarily on the cells of the leaves for their continuous supply of sugar, and they need this supply of food so that they can synthesize the material needed for continuous root growth.

Respiration occurs in the root cells in the same fashion as it does in the cells of the shoot, but the source of food is the cells of the leaves and the source of oxygen is the soil. Most of the oxygen used in respiration in the shoot cells diffuses into the plant tissues via the stomates.

The shoot cells are dependent on the root cells for their supply of water and minerals.

Metabolism in Flowers

Most of the metabolic processes that occur in other shoot cells can occur in the cells of flowers. In most flowers it is apparent that the cells have been more active in synthesizing pigments of some kind.

Many flowers have characteristic fragrances because of the essential oils that are synthesized in their cells.

Dormancy and Quiescence

The term dormant is used commonly with greenhouse crop plants to describe plants or plant structures that are not in active growth. The rose cut-flower plants are started from "dormant" started-eye plants, "dormant" hydrangea plants are used to start this crop for the Easter market, bulbs and seeds usually are considered to be "dormant," and the azalea plants brought into the greenhouse for forcing are called "dormant" plants. It is true that active growth may be lacking in these plants or plant structures, but the reasons for the lack of growth are different and should be distinguished.

It is most helpful to make the distinction on the basis of active growth—or the desired type of growth—resulting when the plants are in surroundings that generally produce active growth in plants. In spite of being in good growing conditions, some kinds of plants will not produce the desired growth because of some conditions within the plants. Azalea and hydrangea flowers will not develop and open in the fall if the warm temperatures suitable for the earlier good growth of the plant are maintained. Bulbs, because of conditions within them, will not produce flowers, or flowering will be much delayed when they are planted directly after being dug from the field and placed in growing conditions suitable for most kinds of plants. These are examples of dormancy in plants. It is caused by some internal conditions in these plants or plant structures.

The conditions within the azaleas and hydrangeas that caused dormancy of the flower buds can be terminated if the plants are placed in temperatures of 10°C or lower for several weeks. This is known as vernalization. Following this cool temperature treatment, the flowers of these kinds of plants will develop in environments that are generally good for plant growth.

Some kinds of bulbs require warm-temperature treatments before cool, vernalization temperatures for several weeks, and then they will produce flowers when they are placed in generally good growing conditions.

In most plants, growth will not be active when the environment generally is not suitable for growth. Frequently the lack of active growth is because of cool temperatures. Started-eye rose plants are not in active growth because they have been placed in temperatures of 7°C or lower. Active growth in many kinds of seed is prevented by keeping the seed in dry surroundings. In either instance the lack of active growth is caused by an unfavorable factor in the environment. When the environment is made generally favorable, active growth occurs. These are examples of quiesence in plants.

Dormancy in seed is possible, but it does not occur in seed of the greenhouse crop plants.

Either actively growing plants or quiescent plants are forced in the greenhouse. Some of these plants may have been dormant sometime previously, but if procedures have been adequate, these plants will be quiescent at the time forcing starts.

LEAVES AND BRACTS

These are distinctive structures that are formed in stems. The term bract may be used for structures that are leaflike but have some characteristics that distinguish them from the leaves of the plant. They may be smaller than the leaves or of different shape. Bracts sometimes are located immediately below the flower, and in some instances they have pigments in addition to or other than the green pigment of the leaves on the same plant.

In some plants the structure commonly referred to as the flower petal is the colorful bract that actually is just below the flower. Two greenhouse crop plants that have showy bracts that are often mistaken for flower petals are poinsettia and calla.

Leaf Characteristics

Leaves develop at the stem nodes. Some kinds of plants have one leaf per node, and others have two leaves or more per node. The arrangement, form, size, and color of the leaves are characteristic of each plant cultivar and are a means of distinguishing one cultivar from another.

The leaf blade may be attached directly to the stem (sessile), as in carnation and zinnia, or it may be stalked (have petioles), as in rose and geranium.

Saintpaulia and azalea have leaves with single blades and are known as simple leaves. When the leaf has more than one blade (leaflet) as in rose and brassaia, it is called a compound leaf.

Some leaf blade margins are lobed (chrysanthemum), some are serrate (rose), and some are entire or smooth (lily).

Many leaves have green pigmentation, some have various pigments (croton), and others have green and cream-colored variegation (dieffenbachia).

FLOWERS

Flowers contain the sexual structures of plants—either male or female or both. Most greenhouse crop plants have bisexual flowers. Each flower contains both male and female structures. The male structure is called the stamen, and the female structure is called the pistil.

Some kinds of plants have female flowers in addition to bisexual flowers. These plants are aster, chrysanthemum, cineraria, dahlia, marigold, and zinnia.

Some greenhouse plants are monoecious: They have unisexual flowers of each sex—some male flowers (staminate) and some female flowers (pistillate)—on the same plant. The monoecious plants are begonia, calla, and poinsettia.

In addition to sexual structures, flowers may have a stalk (a peduncle or pedicels), a receptacle, sepals, and petals.

Terminal Flowers

In some plants the flowers are terminal. These are plants with determinate growth in which the differentiation of cells in the apical meristem changes from the formation of stem and leaf structures to flower structures. Some of the greenhouse crop plants with terminal flowers are ageratum, aster, azalea, calceolaria, canna, carnation, cattleya, chrysanthemum, cineraria, daffodil, dahlia, gladiolus, hyacinth, hydrangea, iris, kalanchoe, Easter lily, marigold, poinsettia, rose, snapdragon, tulip, and zinnia.

Lateral Flowers

The plants that have indeterminate growth have lateral flowers. The flowers develop at nodes below the terminal tip, and the apical meristem continues to differentiate leaf and stem tissues. Greenhouse crop plants that have lateral flowers are African violet, begonia, calla, cyclamen, cymbidium, fuchsia, geranium, gloxinia, impatiens, lantana, pansy, and petunia.

The Showy Portion of Flowers

All flowers have sexual structures, either male or female or both, but sepals and petals may or may not be present in some kinds of flowers. The greenhouse crop plants that have petals are African violet, ageratum, azalea, calceolaria, carnation, cyclamen, geranium, gladiolus, gloxinia, hyacinth, impatiens, kalanchoe, lantana, Easter lily, pansy, petunia, rose, and snapdragon.

In the hydrangea inflorescence it is the sepals that are the showy portion of the flowers.

The plants in which the showy part of the flower is a combination of petals and sepals are begonia, cattleya, cymbidium, narcissus, fuchsia, and iris.

In calla and poinsettia the bracts below the flowers are the showy portions.

Inflorescence

Some plants have a solitary flower per stem, and others have a cluster of flowers on each stem. The flower clusters are called inflorescences. The greenhouse plants that have solitary flowers are cyclamen, daffodil, gloxinia, impatiens, iris, pansy, petunia, and tulip.

There are two general types of inflorescences based on the direction of floret development in the inflorescence. In racemose development the lower or outermost florets develop first and the central or topmost floret develops last. In cymose development the central or topmost floret develops first and the lowest or outermost floret develops last.

There are several types of cluster arrangements of florets in inflorescences that have racemose development. In a raceme inflorescence stalked florets are arranged on an elongated stem. Greenhouse flowers that are racemes are begonia, canna, cattleya, cymbidium, fuchsia, hyacinth, and Easter lily.

Azalea has umbel inflorescence, in which florets with stalks of equal length arise from the terminal tip of the stem.

Gladiolus and snapdragon have spike inflorescence, in which the florets are sessile to an elongated stem. Snapdragon florets may have short stalks, and for this reason the snapdragon sometimes is classed as a raceme. Greenhouse operators, however, continue to call it a spike.

In a head inflorescence the florets are closely clustered and sessile to the stem tip. The greenhouse plants that have head inflorescences are ageratum, aster, chrysanthemum, cineraria, dahlia, lantana, marigold, and zinnia.

There is only one type of cymose floret development. It is called cyme. The greenhouse plants that have cyme inflorescence are saintpaulia, calceolaria, carnation, geranium, hydrangea, kalanchoe, poinsettia, and rose.

PLANT REPRODUCTION

With a few exceptions, plants can be reproduced by either sexual or vegetative (asexual) means. Usually, however, one method of reproduction for a given kind of plant is more suitable and is the common method used commercially.

Sexual plant reproduction only occurs by means of seed. Vegetative reproduction may be from any vegetative portion of the plant, although with greenhouse plants the parts used most commonly are stem tip, stem segment, leaf, and offsets.

Sexual Reproduction

Plants that develop flowers have the potential of sexual reproduction. When pollen from the male structure of the flower is transferred to the stigma of the female structure, seed may subsequently form that contains an embryo plant. When the seed is removed from the parent plant and placed in suitable surroundings, the embryo plant may develop into a mature plant. This is plant reproduction by sexual means.

Some of the greenhouse plants that commonly are reproduced by means of seed are ageratum, araucaria, ardisia, aster, begonia, cacti, calceolaria, cineraria, cyclamen, dahlia, geranium, gloxinia, impatiens, kalanchoe, marigold, palms, pansy, petunia, brassaia, snapdragon, and zinnia. Other greenhouse plants are reproduced from seed in some instances.

Seed may be produced by self-pollination and fertilization in which the pollen transfer is between structures in one flower or between flowers on the same plant. When self-pollination occurs in a homozygous (pure line) plant, the resulting seed has the potential of producing a plant with the same characteristics as the parent plant.

If the plant that is self-pollinated is heterozygous (not pure line), the characteristics of the seedlings from the seed produced on this plant may vary considerably from those of the parent, and the results may be hard to predict.

Cultivars with characteristics differing from those of the parent or parents may result from self-pollination of a heterozygous individual or from cross-pollination of either heterozygous individuals or two different homozygous individuals. If the cultivars that result from seed from heterozygous parents have characteristics of commercial value, those cultivars then must be reproduced by vegetative means in order to maintain the same characteristics in the progeny. The crosses that are made between two different homozygous individuals will result in seed that reproduces cultivars of the same characteristics each time those same parents are used in the same way. The propagator then has a means of reproducing these cultivars by seed—if the required pure-line parents are maintained.

Following pollination and subsequent fertilization, seeds develop from ovules within the pistil as the pistil and sometimes adjoining structures mature into a fruit. The production and preparation of seed for use in the greenhouse usually is handled by specialists, and the seed is ready for sowing when it is received by the grower. Seeds have an embryo plant, a food supply, and coats. If seed is kept in suitable conditions, it usually can be kept in good condition for an extended period of time before sowing. Some seed must be handled promptly, and this information should be obtained from the seed specialist.

The seed is quiescent when it is received and changes to active growth when it is placed in a moist and warm environment. The metabolic processes within the cells of the embryo plant are at a low ebb during quiescence, but with the addition of water and warm temperature growth and development can start. The seed coats fracture and eventually the roots and shoots of the new plant emerge. If the seed is tiny, the first evidence of growth may be the appearance of green coloration at the soil surface as chlorophyll forms in the cells of the new plant. With the formation of chlorophyll, food will be manufactured in the cells followed by the synthesis of other materials. Then the rate of respiration will increase, providing energy, and the seedling will grow rapidly.

Large seed usually has sufficient stored food to supply the young plant in the early stages of growth. For this reason larger seed can be planted below the surface of the soil, but small seed must be sown on the surface so that food manufacturing can start as soon as the seedling emerges.

Vegetative Reproduction

It generally is considered that a single cell of a plant has the capability of reproducing the entire plant. This is the ultimate in vegetative reproduction. It has been referred to as the totipotency of plant cells. It may not be commercially practical to reproduce plants from single, excised cells, but knowing that this is a possibility adds to the understanding of plant growth and development.

There are various ways in which plants can be reproduced vegetatively. Most of these methods involve rather large masses of plant material when compared to a single cell, but more recently procedures have been devised for vegetative reproduction of plants from tiny amounts of plant tissue. In some instances this procedure is used directly for the propagation of plants, and in other instances it is used to produce stock plants that are free of pathogens, including virus. This is referred to as tissue culture. To produce virus-free stock, the apical meristem is cultured. When tissue culture is used to propagate plants, tissue from various portions of the plant may be used. This rapid multiplication of plants may be more successful with one kind of tissue than another, and this may vary with plant species and cultivar.

Tissue culture is an involved laboratory procedure that requires aseptic conditions and highly trained personnel. This is a microtechnique in which the cuttings are so tiny they must be made while being viewed by microscope. It is not a propagation method that will be used at most greenhouses, but it may become common for greenhouse operators to obtain young plants of some species or cultivars from specialists who propagate plants by means of tissue culture.

One of the first commercial uses of tissue culture was with orchids, and this changed production procedures with these crops completely because it then was possible to get large numbers of identical individuals at one time. As tissue-culture procedures are developed more fully, there will no doubt be some major changes in production schedules for other crops. The rapid multiplication of plants by means of tissue culture apparently will be more practical with some kinds of plants than with others.

The specialists who operate tissue-culture laboratories must also include in their procedures the means for detection and isolation or elimination of mutants. Mutation is a potential problem, and the unplanned rapid multiplication of mutants needs to be prevented.

Various vegetative structures are used for the usual (macrotechnique) commercial reproduction of plants. Stem tips are used for the greatest number of greenhouse plants, but other plants are reproduced from leaves, stem segments, bulbs (including corms, stem tubers, and root tubers), spores, and bark buds. The greenhouse plants that may be reproduced from stem-tip cuttings are ageratum, aglaonema, azalea, begonia, carnation, chrysanthemum, dracaena, fittonia, fuchsia, geranium, hedera, hydrangea, impatiens, kalanchoe, lantana, maranta, peperomia, philodendron, pilea, pittosporum, and poinsettia.

Stem-segment cuttings may be used for dieffenbachia, dracaena, philodendron, epipremnum, and syngonium.

Reproduction by means of bulbs is used with narcissus, hyacinth, iris, lily, and tulip. With crocus and gladiolus the propagative structure is corm. Stem tubers are used for caladium, calla, canna, and gloxinia, and root tubers are used for dahlia and some begonia.

Leaf cuttings may be used for some begonia, saintpaulia, and sansevieria.

Ficus and croton may be reproduced by means of air layering stem tips.

Rose is most commonly reproduced by a specialized grafting procedure called budding in which a bark bud of the greenhouse cultivar is inserted in the bark of a rootstock plant.

Some ferns are reproduced by spores and others by offset of plants that develop at the nodes of rhizomes.

In vegetative reproduction, growth must originate from mature cells (with the exception of some tissue culture), and with the stem and leaf cuttings, bulbs, corms, and stem tubers the first order of growth must be the differentiation of root cells. There may be some food supply available in the plant portion being used for propagation, but since there are no roots the water and mineral supply to the cells is extremely limited. Until roots are formed and are functioning, food manufacturing and synthesis will be limited. Every effort must be made to provide the best conditions for the growth and development of roots.

The bulbs, corms, and tubers usually have the most favorable supply of food. Stem segment and leaf cuttings have the smallest food supply for use during propagation, and after roots are formed food manufacturing cannot start until shoots are developed.

With propagation by budding, the bark bud is separated from the greenhouse cultivar at the vascular cambium and is then inserted in the bark of the rootstock plant so that it is in contact with that vascular cambium. The union between these two meristematic surfaces should be prompt. Sometime after the union is complete, the portion of the rootstock plant just above the bud is removed, and growth then develops in the bud with subsequent formation of stem and leaves.

HEREDITY IN PLANTS

Living things are able to pass various properties on to their progeny. In sexual reproduction some of the properties of each parent are transmitted to the offspring, resulting in individuals with characteristics that may or may not resemble some of the characteristics of either parent. With plants that are reproduced vegetatively, it is most probable that the progeny will have the same properties as the parent plant. This is a method of producing individuals that are exactly alike. They have the same properties and characteristics.

In plants reproduced sexually, the progeny will have the same inherited properties as the parent plant only when the plant is pure line and self-pollinated.

The heritable factors or units of inheritance are the genes on the chromosomes. Plants that have identical inherited properties may be said to have the same genetic makeup or to be of the same genotype.

It has been discussed previously that each cell of a single plant has identical genetic properties. Individual cells excised from any portion of the plant have the potential of reproducing an individual with the same characteristics as the parent plant. This is the general mode of operation, but there are instances in which there is a genetic deviation in a cell and this deviate heredity is transmitted to the progeny of this cell. This is called mutation (sporting), and the change in characteristics may be observed only in the tissues or structures that developed from the mutant cell.

Mutation is change. Some mutations improve some characteristics of the plant, and others result in unfavorable qualities in plants. When the mutant portion of the plant has desirable characteristics, it is possible to reproduce the plant vegetatively from the mutated portion in order to develop plants with this changed heredity. Many excellent greenhouse cultivars were developed through mutation. In other instances, some good cultivars have had to be discontinued because unfavorable mutations had gone unnoticed until after widespread reproduction of the mutant.

PLANT NAMES

All greenhouse plants have proper names, and many also have common names. With some of these plants the proper name or a portion of it is also the common name.

Proper names of plants are in Latin form and usually are referred to as botanical names. The naming of plants is governed by the internationally accepted rules in the *International Code of Botanical Nomenclature.* Much of the naming of greenhouse plants is further governed by the *International Code of Nomenclature of Cultivated Plants.* The plant names that are used in botanical or horticultural reference books are based on either one or both of these international regulations. These botanical or horticultural names are meaningful because they place plants in groupings with other plants of similar characteristics.

Unfortunately, rules and concepts of plant nomenclature change, and as a result there is a lack of uniformity in plant names in the literature. In this book, primarily three references have been used for plant names. *Hortus Third,* Macmillan Publishing Company, Inc., has been used as the standard guide, and further reference was made to *Exotic Plant Manual,* Roehrs Company, and *Manual of Cultivated Plants,* Macmillan Publishing Company, Inc.

For some of the greenhouse plants, botanical and common names often are used interchangeably. With other greenhouse plants, either the botanical or the common name is used. The three references above index the plant names by genus. When the botanical name is known the plant description can be located easily.

Hortus Third and *Exotic Plant Manual* have separate indexes of plant common names, and *Manual of Cultivated Plants* includes some common names in the general index so that plant descriptions can also be located by common name.

Exotic Plant Manual groups the plant photographs by some readily identifiable charactertistics—vining plants in one section and those with colorful foliage in another, for instance. This is an aid in locating the botanical name for plants known only by sight.

Environmental Effects on Plants

4

The greenhouse provides an adjustable environment for plants. Within limits, the greenhouse operator is able to regulate the various elements of the environment for the best growth and development of the crop plants. The portion of the plant that grows in the soil is affected directly by soil conditions, and changes in the above-ground environment may first affect the upper portions of the plant.

The total environment must be considered in evaluating effects on plants, but an orderly approach is to appraise the ground and the above-ground environments separately.

THE ABOVE-GROUND ENVIRONMENT

This generally is considered to be a gaseous environment, but an important factor above ground is radiant energy—either light or heat. There are other forms of substances above ground that affect plants, too. Occasionally there may be liquids, and there are effects from solids such as structures, equipment, noncrop plants, pests, pathogens, and animals, including human beings. These all are parts of the surroundings that affect the growth and development of the plants.

Figure 4-1 The effect of environmental conditions on leaf size. The rose leaf on the left is from a plant in optimum conditions. The leaf on the right shows the effects of unsuitable environmental conditions, which could be water deficiency from various causes; too high light intensity; deficiencies in some minerals, particularly nitrogen; or temperatures which are too high.

Light and the Electromagnetic Spectrum

Plants are greatly affected by some portions of the electromagnetic spectrum, and it is possible that there are some effects from other portions of the spectrum that have not been identified. The component rays of the electromagnetic spectrum can be identified by their wavelengths. The unit of measure to express size of wavelengths is the nanometer (nm). A nanometer is one-millionth of a millimeter. Cosmic rays have the shortest wavelength (less than 0.0001 nm) in the spectrum, and they have no known effect on plants. The next ray classification, gamma rays (0.0001 to 0.01 nm), can have effects on the genetic properties of plants, and plant breeders may irradiate certain portions of plants in order to produce mutations and develop plants with different or more desirable characteristics. There are no established effects of electromagnetic radiation of long wavelengths (100,000 nm and up—electric rays) on plants, although some effects have been suggested.

Irradiance from the Sun The electromagnetic radiation that reaches the earth from the sun is the portion of the spectrum from 310 nm (ultraviolet rays) to 2,300 nm (infrared rays). The human eye perceives the radiation of wavelengths 390 (violet rays) to 760 nm (red rays), and this usually is referred to as visible light. This light is a blend of all of the rays of the visible spectrum and produces white light unless it is refracted by passing through clear substances of differing densities. The light refraction caused when light rays pass from air to water particles to air produces the rainbow which displays all of the colors of the visible spectrum—violet, indigo blue, green, yellow, orange, and red.

Plants do not "see" light, but various components of plant cells are affected specifically by radiation of different wavelengths. This causes changes in metabolism that produce growth and development that have come to be known as characteristic for that kind of environment. When the sun is the light source, the full spectrum of radiation is available to the plants, and it is not practical to make adjustments that would limit rays of certain wavelengths and increase others. There are, however, variations in atmospheric conditions that cause changes in light qualities that reach the plant. Some of the most common atmospheric conditions which could affect the transmission of rays of various wavelengths are cloud cover, variations in gaseous components of the air, and other pollutants in the air.

If the source of light is other than from the sun, it is possible to provide light of various qualities. Electric lamps can be designed so that their radiation will be primarily in the red area of the spectrum—or in the blue portion—and each type could be used for some specific growth effect in plants.

Electric Sources of Light and Light Quality Two methods are used to produce light by means of electricity. With incandescent lamps the light evolves when the filament becomes hot and glows as electricity is passed through the tungsten filament. The radiation that is emitted from the incandescent lamp is at the red end of the spectrum. The color of this light is yellow-orange. Considerable heat also is produced from the red rays emitted beyond the visible spectrum. The other method of producing electric light is by electric or arc discharge. With these types of lamps the electric current flows through metallic vapor, and the emitted radiation is characteristic of the metal that is used. Mercury vapor commonly is used and produces radiation from the blue end of the spectrum—a portion of it ultraviolet. When mercury vapor is used the lamp may be coated on the inside with fluorescent powders that have the property of absorbing the ultraviolet radiation and reemitting it in the visible portion of the spectrum. Depending on the kind of powder that is used, these lamps will emit light of varying degrees of whiteness. When sodium is used as the metal vapor in electric-discharge lamps, the radiation that is given off is in the orange portion of the spectrum. Other metal vapors may be used that will produce light of different qualities. However, there is no single electric lamp that is able to simulate daylight.

Light Quantity Plants are affected by the quantity of light that they receive. This is the cumulative total of light—the intensity for the time that it was in effect.

The unit of measurement of light intensity that is used commonly by commercial flower and plant producers is the foot-candle. By use of a foot-candle meter (not a photographic light meter), the light intensity in terms of foot-candles at any given moment can be determined. Some other means of measurement have to be used, however, to determine the quantity of light energy available to a plant for a period of time. One means of determining radiant energy received per unit area per unit of time is in terms of gram calories per square centimeter per minute, and one unit is called a langley. There is no exact mathematical relationship between foot-candles and langleys, but a 10,000 foot-candle light intensity for 1 minute is approximately 1.5 langleys.

The intensity of light energy received from the sun on a clear summer day in Ohio builds gradually from 0 in the morning to a maximum of around 10,000 foot-candles at midday and then decreases gradually to 0 in the evening, and for that typical summer day in Ohio, the total light energy quantity for the day would be about 500 langleys. In contrast the maximum intensity of light energy received from the sun for the same location on a January day might be about 300 foot-candles with the total light energy quantity for the day of less than 100 langleys. In many geographical areas, the intensity of the sunlight during the summer exceeds the amount required for good plant growth and development, and some means may be used for the reduction in light intensity at that time. In all areas of the United States during the winter there is a deficiency of light for good plant growth, and means must be taken to increase the amount of light available to the crop plants.

The potential light energy quantity available from electric lamps understandably is very small as compared with the sun. In laboratory situations, it is possible to provide plants with irradiance to about 4,000 foot-candles, but for commercial production it is not economically feasible to plan for more than 1,000 foot-candles—and even this amount only for special situations in which the financial returns justify the expenditure. Even though the light intensity from an electric lamp is relatively small at any given moment, the full amount of that intensity is available for the entire period of lighting. The total quantity of light energy that a plant receives from electric lamps that provide an intensity of 500 foot-candles for 16 hours daily might be just as great as the total light energy quantity that a plant would receive in a greenhouse in which the sunlight is adjusted to a maximum of 1,000 foot-candles at midday with a natural day length of 15½ hours.

The changes in plant characteristics that are caused by variations in the light that is available to them may be direct effects of the light on physiological processes within the plant, or they may be indirect effects. Increased growth would generally be expected with increase in light quantity because of the greater amount of sugar manufactured, but with further increase in light quantity the rate of growth may decrease because the temperature increase with the additional light causes an excessive increase in respiration depleting the food supply. In other instances, the characteristic response does not result because other environmental factors are not suitable. Flowers may not develop in a photoperiodic plant in the proper day length because the temperature is not right, or pigment synthesis may not increase characteristically with increased light quantity if the mineral nutrition for the plant is not correct.

Although it has been established that plant growth and development may be affected by light quantity, light quality, and light duration, it is primarily the regulation of light quantity and light duration that is involved in the commercial production of greenhouse plants. Light quality can be adjusted when the source is electric lamps, and this is taken into consideration when that source of light is used. The sun still is the basic source of light for greenhouse plants, and it is not practical to attempt to regulate this light quality in spite of growth effects that might result.

Usually for greenhouse crop plants the natural light intensity is some-what excessive in the summer and deficient in the winter. This varies with the geographical area, the crops that are grown, and the stage of growth of the plants. The greenhouse plants may be considered in three light-intensity groups: those whose growth and development are best in relatively high light intensity, medium light intensity, and low light intensity. In Ohio, during the summer, the high-light-intensity group may have best growth and development if provided with 30 to 50 percent shade, the medium-light-intensity group 50 to 65 percent, and the low-light-intensity group 65 to 80 percent. A large share of the greenhouse plants are in the high-light-intensity group—azalea, chrysanthemum, bedding plants, hydrangea, and rose. Some of the plants in the medium-light-intensity group are saintpaulia, many of the foliage plants, gloxinia, and cattleya. The aglaonemas and aphelandras are in the low-light-intensity group.

In addition, the growth and development of most plants will be best if they are given some additional shading during propagation and in the early stages of growth. Flower development and color will be better with some plants when they are given additional shading at the time of flowering.

The light conditions during the winter may be satisfactory for the plants in the low-light-intensity group, but for the other plants their growth will be characteristic of plants grown in deficient light intensity. In some instances it may be possible to supplement the light quantity for the plants at this time with electric lamps. Increased flower production or reduced length of crop time has been demonstrated with mums, roses, and some other crops when high-intensity-discharge (HID) lamps are used to supplement natural light in the winter, but it has not been generally accepted commercially because of costs involved.

In general, some of the growth and development characteristics that could be expected of plants with favorable light-intensity conditions are increased height, heavier stems, greater leaf area, shorter internodes, more roots, earlier flowering, more flowers, larger flowers, and increased pigment formation.

When the light intensity is too great, it might be expected that there would be a reduction in the amount of pigmentation, smaller leaves, smaller flowers, and dessication or burning of areas in flowers or leaves.

Light Duration or Photoperiod There are two types of effects of the duration of light on plants. The longer the daily duration of light, the greater the quantity of light available for the plant. This type of effect has been summarized in the preceding paragraphs. This effect is directly related to light intensity during the daily light period. If the light intensity is 50 foot-candles or more during the period, some effect may be observed. The other type of effect can occur with light of low intensity—in some instances 1 foot-candle or less—or of high intensity, but is caused by the relationship of the lengths of the daily light and dark periods, regardless of light intensity. This is known as photoperiodism.

Because the photoperiodic effect can be regulated by light of very low intensity, long photoperiods can be supplied during naturally short days by extending the day length with electric lamps or shortening the daily dark period by interruption with a period of low-intensity light. And in naturally long days, the daily light period can be limited by placing something over the plants that will exclude the light for a portion of each day. Photoperiodism affects flowering in some plants. This is an easily observed effect and certainly one of considerable interest in the flower and plant production business. There are, however, several other effects of photoperiodism.

The receptor of light in the plant for the photoperiodic effects is blue-green pigments called phytochromes, and apparently it is red to far-red light that is absorbed by the phytochromes. It is considered that the photoperiodic effects are caused by hormones synthesized in some cells and translocated to other areas of the plant. It is generally believed that newly matured leaves in many kinds of plants are the sites of the greatest amount of synthesis of these hormones. The hormone that controls flowering has been called florigen. Photoperiod controls the germination of some seed, and this indicates the presence of phytochrome in seeds also.

There has been much confusion, and there probably will continue to be, about some of the effects of photoperiod. In some instances the effects may be clear and unquestioned, while in other situations it is difficult to evaluate effects from other environmental factors that are varible, or different observers may use limited evaluations. Some plant scientists in reporting on effects of photoperiod on flower formation refer to flower induction or the first stages of flower formation with the assumption that development of the flower will continue to maturity. This leads to some misconceptions because some kinds of plants may have flower induction with one set of environmental conditions but the development of the flower will not continue unless some factor or factors of the environment change.

What are short days and what are long days? In either instance, the period that is involved is 24 hours in which a portion of the period is day (or lighted) and the other portion is night (or shaded). The term photoperiod refers to the day or lighted portion of the period. The short photoperiod is supplied during naturally long days by extending the night by placing a "lightproof" cover over the plants in the evening and withdrawing it in the morning. The length of the effective short day is not necessarily the same for each kind of plant. With kalanchoe the short day is considered to be 10 hours and with chrysanthemum a 12-hour day may be used to promote flowering.

During naturally short days, long photoperiods are provided either by extending the day length at sundown or by interrupting the night by light from electric lamps. When the day length is extended, it must be done for a sufficient length of time, so that for kalanchoe the long photoperiod is more than 10 hours and the night is less than 14 hours and with chrysanthemum there is more than a 12-hour day and less than a 12-hour night. When the long photoperiod is provided by interrupting the night, the interruption must be placed so that neither segment of the night is more than 13 hours for kalanchoe or more than 11 hours for mums. This can be done by making the light interruption on either side of midnight and changing the length of lighting time with the season.

Natural day length varies with latitude. In Ohio, for kalanchoe, the days are considered naturally short from October 15 to February 15 and for chrysanthemum from the first week in September to the first week in March. For kalanchoe production in Ohio the recommendations for providing long days during naturally short days are: September and March, light 1 hour; October and February, light 2 hours; November and January, light 3 hours; and December, light 4 hours. With chrysanthemums grown in Ohio when long days are needed, the common recommendation is to interrupt the night the year-round using 2 hours of light in June and July, 3 hours of light in August to September and April to May, and 4 hours of light from October to March. Incandescent lamps commonly are used because they are economical to install and provide the quality of light (red) that is most effective in photoperiodism. However, photoperiodic lighting with pink fluorescent lamps is more economical when large areas are involved.

Photoperiod control is used for a few greenhouse crop plants regularly, and on other plants on occasion. Year-round flowering of chrysanthemum and kalanchoe is possible by providing long photoperiods in which the plants grow vegetatively, producing stems and leaves, followed by short photoperiods in which the plants grow reproductively, producing flowers. The same procedure can be used for poinsettia but is not in regular usage because this crop is produced mainly for the Christmas market, and with slight regulation the poinsettia cultivars flower naturally at that time. If flowering is to be delayed, poinsettias can be given long photoperiods starting about mid-September and continuing until the first week in October. In some instances poinsettias are given short photoperiods in order to produce a crop in flower for an early marketing promotion, or to produce a Christmas crop if the area where they will be grown is close to a lighted area. Poinsettias are more sensitive to lights than chrysanthemums are, and lights from street lighting, sales areas, or parking lots adjacent to the greenhouse may keep the plants growing vegetatively unless they are given shade.

Cattleya orchid crops used to be produced at various times of the year by using cultivars that flowered naturally at about those times or could be adjusted in time of flowering somewhat by regulation of temperature. Fewer cultivars now are used, and the time of flower crop production is regulated by control of the photoperiod as well as of temperature.

Azaleas generally are not classed as short-day plants, but for year-round production they are given long photoperiods and higher temperatures to promote vegetative growth. Thus they have similarities with other plants classed as short-day plants.

Flowering in several additional greenhouse crop plants is affected by photoperiodism to some degree. These are promotional effects of long photoperiods, but the relationship does not seem to be as clear-cut as it is with some of the short-day greenhouse crop plants. The plants for which there is some benefit from long photoperiods are aster, begonia, carnation, lily, petunia, and calceolaria, and possibly snapdragon and geranium could also be listed. In general, there is early flowering and increased stem length with long photoperiods.

Effects of Other Factors on the Photoperiodic Response   There are some interesting relationships between photoperiod and temperature and effects on plants. Flower induction and/or development in some mum cultivars will proceed only if both the temperature and the photoperiod are correct. Flowering occurs in calceolaria during short days if the temperature is 10°C or below, but when long days are supplied flowering takes place at 16°C and warmer and the time required for flowering is shorter.

If petunias are grown at temperatures below 16°C, they will be short and well-branched, and will flower relatively slowly regardless of length of photoperiod. If petunias are grown in short days at temperatures of 16°C and above, they will be short and well-branched, and will flower earlier, but day-length control is not in common usage with bedding plant growers. Petunias grown at 16°C and above in long photoperiods do not branch and they flower early.

When Easter lily bulbs are placed in temperatures of 10°C or cooler (precooled) in the fall, they can be forced into flower for the Easter market. If the bulbs were not given sufficient precooling before start of forcing, the plants may be given long photoperiods as soon as they emerge from the soil and for the same number of days as were missed in precooling. The long photoperiods produce the same flower-promotion effect as the bulb pre-cooling.

It can be expected that photoperiodic induction of flowering will proceed most satisfactorily if all other environmental factors are suitable. Some temperature effects have been discussed. In addition, the environment should be favorable for food manufacture, and water and mineral supplies should be somewhat limited.

It is possible that plants will have unusual growth and development when they are in fluctuating photoperiod conditions that variably cause vegetative growth, reproductive growth, and then vegetative growth again. In some instances the growth will be deformed and disease might be suspected. This is quite a common problem with chrysanthemum. Because of electrical malfunctions enough days of short photoperiod might be interspersed to cause the start of flower formation followed by reversion to vegetative growth when the electrical error is corrected. Depending on the length of time involved and the stage of growth, the best action might be to continue the short photoperiod, causing flower development on shorter stems, rather than risking flower malformation by returning to the long-day regime.

Figure 4-2 Chrysanthemum crown buds can be caused by light leakage, day-length fluctuations, or high temperatures. Left: normal flower buds. Right: crown buds. *(Yoder Bros., Inc. photograph.)*

Malformed chrysanthemum flowers also can occur when there are light leaks during short photoperiods. Kalanchoe and poinsettia are very sensitive to light, and small quantities of light during short photoperiods will cause vegetative growth of these plants.

Light Effects in Seed Germination Seeds of some plants respond to light. After water is inbibed, the germination of some seeds is affected by the light environment, and with others it is a combination of temperature and light that controls germination. There appear to be many possible involvements. With greenhouse crop plants it has been established that light is necessary for the germination of some seed, the seed of a few kinds of plants will germinate only in the dark, and the seed of many kinds of plants will germinate either in dark or light environments. Fortunately, the light-requiring seed is small and should be sown on the soil surface for other reasons, too, and the dark-requiring seed is large enough so that it may be sown below the surface of the soil. Some of the plants that have seed that germinates in the light are ageratum, begonia, browallia, calceolaria, cineraria, coleus, exacum, feverfew, gloxinia, impatiens, kalanchoe, nicotiana, petunia, primula, saintpaulia, salvia, and snapdragon. The plants known to have seed that germinates in the dark are calendula, centaurea, cyclamen, gomphrena, larkspur, nasturtium, pansy, and phlox.

Effects of Post-Harvest Light Consideration needs to be given to environmental effects on flowers and plants after harvest—during preparation for marketing, shipping, and in the hands of the consumer. Whether the product is cut flowers or potted plants, it is living material with metabolism, growth, and development affected by the environment. Frequently, flowers and plants are stored and shipped in the dark, followed by marketing and then consumer use at low light intensities. Usually the most noticeable effects are loss of pigmentation—leaves become yellow and flower colors fade. With some plants the leaves will separate (abscise) from the stems and drop.

Above-Ground Temperature

The primary source of heat in the greenhouse is the sun. A large portion of the light energy that enters the greenhouse from the sun converts to heat energy when the light is absorbed by the plants, soil, equipment, and structure. The heat then may be transferred to other objects and to the air by means of radiation, convection, or conduction.

Temperature is the evaluation of heat intensity, and the sensing device is a thermometer. Until recently, thermometers with the Fahrenheit scale were used in the United States. With this temperature scale, the freezing point of water is 32°F, the boiling point of water is 212°F, normal body temperature for human beings is 98.6°F, and common air temperatures at night for commercial greenhouses are 50 to 70°F, depending on the crop being grown. With the conversion of various measurements in the United States to metric scales, temperature will be measured with thermometers of the Celsius (or centigrade) scale. With this scale the freezing point of water is 0°C, the boiling point of water is 100°C, normal body temperature for human beings is 37°C, and common air temperatures at night for commercial greenhouses are 10 to 21°C, depending on the crops being grown. Generally in this book references to temperature use the Celsius scale.

In referring to temperatures for greenhouse crops, the night temperature is used, and it is understood that the day temperature will be about 3°C higher on cloudy days and about 6°C higher on clear days. For a 10°C crop such as carnation or snapdragon, the daytime temperature would be from 13 to 16°C, depending on cloud cover.

Greenhouses are constructed so that they will admit the maximum amount of light, and this incidentally sometimes provides more heat than is desired during the day. When outdoor temperatures are cool, the excess heat may be vented to the exterior, but when outdoor temperatures are warm some means of air cooling must be used if greenhouse temperatures are to be reduced. Many greenhouse operators install fan and pad systems in which the incoming air is routed through wet pads and the air temperature is reduced as the water is evaporated from the pads.

During cool weather at night and on cloudy days, alternate sources of heat are needed for the greenhouse. Through the years various kinds of fuel have been used for the generation of heat—coal, oil, and gas. There also has been interest in entrapment and storage of solar heat for distribution in the greenhouse when needed.

Regardless of the source and distribution of heat, the greenhouse operator has to be committed to such exact regulation of temperature that it does not vary more than 1°C from the temperature considered best for plant growth and development. General practice has been to measure air temperatures with thermometers, and if enough of them are used and are placed at plant levels they will give a reasonable approximation of the plant temperature.

Temperature Effects on Other Factors   Temperature affects other environmental factors which may result in some indirect effects on plant growth and development. With increase in temperature, more water is evaporated from the surroundings—soil, structure, equipment, plants—and the warmer air has the capacity to hold more water vapor.

With increase in temperature, air circulation increases because of the convection currents established. This provides greater distribution and mixture of the various gases in the air, including water vapor.

The growth and reproduction of plant pathogens is affected by temperature; some develop more rapidly at higher temperatures than others.

In general, pests reproduce more rapidly with increase in temperature, and the increase in this portion of the environment of the plant can be expected to have noticeable effects on growth and development.

Typical Greenhouse Temperatures Depending on the crop, the night temperature used for greenhouse plants generally is from 10 to about 21°C, and the plants sometimes are categorized by the temperature that is considered best for their growth and development. Some of the 10°C plants are calceolaria (or 16°C when given long days), calla, carnation, cineraria, cyclamen (or sometimes 18 to 20°C), bedding plants (also 16°C), and snapdragon (also 16°C).

The plants usually grown at 16°C night temperatures are chrysanthemum, most bulbs, rose, begonia, hydrangea, Easter lily, and poinsettia.

The 18°C plants are azalea, gloxinia, saintpaulia, and kalanchoe.

Most foliage plants are supplied 21°C night temperatures.

These are rather broad and general temperature classifications. There are many variations and exceptions to the rule, but these are planned on the basis of the specific effect they will have on plant growth and development. Greenhouse temperatures below 10°C are seldom used unless plants are being precooled (vernalized) or fully mature plants are being held for marketing. Day temperatures frequently exceed 21°C during the summer, and this may not be of concern until they get above 30°C. The rates of metabolic processes within plants increase with increase in temperature, but the rate of increase is greater for respiration than it is for photosynthesis and other syntheses, resulting in a net loss of food in plants at high temperatures.

Some Effects with Increase in Temperature Some of the most common effects on plants of high temperatures during the summer are smaller leaves and flowers, reduced amount of pigmentation resulting in bleached appearance of leaves and flowers, and shorter stems. In some plants flower development is more rapid and there will be a greater number of flowers, but they will be small and will have short stems. This is typical in rose and carnation. In some chrysanthemum cultivars, flower development is delayed in high temperatures, and this causes later flowering on long stems.

When temperatures are too high during low light intensity in the winter, stems will be small in diameter, leaves and flowers will be small, and pigmentation will be decreased.

With increase in temperature, it can be expected that the rate of transpiration will increase. The rate of water absorption in the roots will increase also if there are sufficient roots, if water is available in the soil, and if the temperature increase in the soil is comparable to the temperature increase in the leaves. Wilting results when the amount of water lost by transpiration exceeds the amount of water absorbed by the roots.

Plant growth usually is better when warmer temperatures are used in propagation. There are some exceptions, but 21°C commonly is used for propagation by seed because this promotes best germination of seed and growth of seedling.

With plants being propagated vegetatively, root development is best at temperatures about 6°C warmer than the temperatures that will be used later in the production of the crop. Root and shoot growth of newly planted cuttings and seedlings usually is best if temperatures are about 3°C warmer than those used later for the more mature plant.

Temperature adjustment may be used to hasten or delay the development of flowers to meet specific market times. This adjustment in temperature may be from 1 to 3°C, and such temperature manipulation is used with several holiday crops—an increase in temperature will promote flower development and a decrease will delay it.

Flower initiation occurs in some plants more satisfactorily at temperatures 1 to 3°C above the temperature used later for the development of the flower. For this reason, plants such as chrysanthemum, begonia, and poinsettia may be grown on the warm side of 16°C at flower-formation time.

Some Effects with Lower Temperatures Some plants will flower much more rapidly if they are placed in cool temperatures at an earlier stage of growth. This is known as vernalization. The temperature to produce this effect must be 10°C or below, and this cool treatment must be given for several weeks—6 weeks for many of the greenhouse plants. Flowering of bulbs forced in the greenhouse is promoted by the temperature treatments that they receive in the fall, and this includes cool temperature, which with bulbs is called precooling. Some bulbs may be given the cool treatment before or after they are planted, but if it is after planting it must be preceded by a warm period (above 10°C) for a few weeks to promote root growth. The other greenhouse plants involved in vernalization are azalea and hydrangea. After the flower buds are well-developed in the stem tips, the plants are supplied cool temperatures for several weeks before they are returned to the greenhouse for forcing into flower.

At least with some plants, vernalization can be accomplished to some extent by means other than cool temperatures. As mentioned previously with Easter lily, long photoperiods for the newly emerging shoot can complete the vernalization if it was not completed by cool temperature. With azalea, it is possible to provide vernalization at some times or to some extent by applying gibberellins to the plants, but this may be of very limited commercial use.

Cool temperatures cause increased pigmentation in some plants. With some chrysanthemum cultivars white florets become pink, yellow florets bronze, and bronze florets deeper bronze. The increased pigmentation may be uniformly distributed or streaked. Geranium lower leaves may have red pigmentation in cool temperatures.

Cold water on saintpaulia leaves can cause chlorotic areas. This is a temperature effect on the chlorophyll pigments in this plant, and for this reason saintpaulias are irrigated so that cold water does not contact the leaves.

Unless there is a serious malfunction, freezing temperature should not be a problem in the greenhouse. But some plants are grown outdoors in the summer, and in northern climates they must be moved indoors or given temperature protection in the fall. Probably the most vulnerable crop is azalea. At this stage of growth in the fall, the flower buds can be killed by brief exposure to temperatures around the freezing point. There will be no outward evidence of damage immediately, but eventually the flower buds turn brown and abscise. Hydrangea is another crop plant subject to damage by freezing in the fall.

Greenhouse operators need cool storage facilities. The extent and type of facility depend on the crops and the methods of operation. In northern climates, vernalization treatments can be given outdoors, or for more precise control and ease in handling, storages with mechanical cooling may be provided. The maximum temperature in such a storage is 10°C, and some storages may be equipped for a minimum temperature around 1°C.

Other than use in providing vernalization for some crops, cool storages are the means for holding flowers or plants during marketing or before planting. General-purpose cool storages are operated at about 7°C, but for longer-term storage minimum termperatures are used. The purpose is to establish as nearly as possible a state of quiescence in the plant or portion of the plant being held. Because of the cool temperatures the rate of metabolic processes is so low that there is little or no growth and development. Seed may be stored more successfully in cool storage. Unrooted cuttings may be held in cool storage for several days before propagation, and carnation unrooted cuttings may be stored in good condition for several months. Rooted cuttings may be held in cool storage for several days before planting. It is common practice to hold cut flowers in cool storage at least overnight.

This is called hardening, and the object is to provide maximum absorption of water as well as cooling. The flower stems should be placed in warm (approximately 43°C) water before they are placed in cool storage. When cut flowers are to be held for the maximum length of time, the stems are not placed in water before storage and the temperature used is about 1°C. Some flowers can be held successfully for several days to a few weeks in these conditions.

Some flowering pot plants are held in cool storage before marketing. This usually is short-term storage.

Cool storage is not used for foliage plants.

Temperature control during shipping of flowers and plants is very important. This may require a source of refrigeration in the vehicle in warm weather and a source of heat in cold weather. Foliage plants and cut flowers cannot be successfully transported in the same vehicle because of the different holding temperatures that are needed. Plant products cannot be transported in some types of common carriers because they do not have temperature protection in their vehicles or at the terminals.

Gases Above Ground

Oxygen, carbon dioxide, and water vapor are gaseous components of the air that are essential for some of the metabolic processes occurring in plants. Much of the time the quantity of oxygen and carbon dioxide in the air is in the same proportion outdoors and inside the greenhouse, and these quantities are satisfactory for good plant growth and development. The quantity of water vapor in the air outdoors and in the greenhouse is variable. The amount of water vapor in the greenhouse environment should be adjusted at some times.

Effects of Oxygen Oxygen is used in the plant in the process of respiration, and this process must go on continuously if life is to be maintained. Usually the supply of oxygen is sufficient.

There is the possibility of a limited oxygen supply in some greenhouses if they are tightly closed for extended periods of time during extremely cold weather. Possibly, a more likely cause of oxygen deficiency in the greenhouse atmosphere is combustion in heaters or carbon dioxide generators used in some greenhouses. If they do not have an adequate intake air vent from the exterior, the oxygen in the air indoors may be depleted. If normal venting procedures are discontinued in very cold weather, there may be very little infiltration of air from the outside even in glass houses because the laps between glass segments may be sealed with frost. Greenhouses covered with film plastic have virtually no infiltration of air at any time.

If the products of combustion are not adequately vented to the exterior, heaters and generators may add some noxious gases to the greenhouse air. If the fuel contains some sulfur as a contaminant, the sulfur dioxide that is emitted can cause leaf and flower spots and burns. As the oxygen supply is depleted in the greenhouse, products of incomplete combustion can be formed, such as carbon monoxide, ethylene, and others, causing epinastic curvature, leaf and flower burns, and in some instances failure to flower or various types of flower malformation.

Effects of Carbon Dioxide   The normal amount of carbon dioxide in the air (approximately 300 ppm) supports the photosynthetic activity in the plant cells adequately so that there is enough food made for good plant growth and development. However, with some of the greenhouse plants, if the quantity of carbon dioxide in the atmosphere is increased, growth is increased and length of time to flowering is decreased. Because photosynthesis is a daytime activity, the additional carbon dioxide is provided only at that time, and it can be done effectively only when the weather is cool enough so that the greenhouse can be closed so that the gas will be retained. Commercial use of supplemental carbon dioxide is based on the costs involved versus the results obtained, and for this reason the procedure is not used universally.

Water Vapor Above Ground   Water vapor in the greenhouse atmosphere has some important direct and indirect effects on plants. The quantity of water vapor in the air can be determined with an instrument known as a sling psychrometer, and the results are given in terms of relative humidity. This is a percentage figure in which a relative humidity value of 50 percent indicates that the air at that moment contains one-half the amount of water that it would at saturation. But, because warm air has a higher saturation value than cool air, if there is a rise in temperature of this same air the relative humidity value decreases correspondingly, or if there is a decrease in temperature there is a corresponding increase in relative humidity. Visible evidence in the greenhouse of this relationship is the formation of liquid water or solid ice on the inside surface of the glass roof with a difference in temperature between inside and outside. The greater the difference in temperature, the more water or ice that is formed on the glass. The temperature of the air at the glass surface is low enough so that the saturation point is reached—100% relative humidity—and the water vapor at that location in the greenhouse changes to liquid water or to ice. This procedure causes drier air in the greenhouse, less light transmitted in to the plants, and, with some types of greenhouses, water dripping on plants.

During cold weather, because of this constant removal of water vapor from the greenhouse air, the above-ground environment will be drier than it is in more moderate weather. The effects of the dry air may be more noticeable on plants in propagation or with young plants just being started in growth.

Effects of Water Vapor on Other Factors Moisture formation on the inner surface of the greenhouse will measurably reduce the light intensity in the greenhouse and this in turn affects the growth of the plants. The light situation in the greenhouses further north becomes critical when there are extended periods in which the temperature is in the vicinity of $-26°C$. At that great temperature differential between inside and out, frost continues to be added to the inside of the glass even on clear days.

Most greenhouses covered with glass are constructed in such a way that the moisture on the inside of the glass flows down drip grooves and eventually to the base of the house. In greenhouses covered with film plastic, the moisture on the inner surface of the film will shower periodically on personnel and plants. This may promote some disease problems. When rigid plastic is used for covering greenhouses, if it is attached directly to the purlins the water will drip from each purlin.

When the sun is the source of heat in the greenhouse, the plant temperature usually will be higher than the air temperature. When the sun disappears, the plant temperature usually will be below the air temperature unless an alternate source of heat is supplied before the sun sets. With plant temperatures lower than that of the air, it is possible that some moisture will deposit on the plant surfaces, providing suitable conditions for growth of pathogens. This can be prevented by starting the heating system before the heating effectiveness of the sun diminishes and continuing to vent. The cool air from outdoors that replaces the vented air also will be of lower relative humidity as it becomes heated in the greenhouse. The air circulation associated with this venting helps, too, because it mixes air of higher relative humidity in the immediate vicinity of the plants with the entire air mass, lowering the water vapor quantity around the plants.

Effects of Water Vapor on Plant Growth Plants that are grown in a dry atmosphere (low relative humidity) are shorter, leaves and flowers are smaller, stems are upright and stiff, and there is less new shoot development.

The most practical method for increasing relative humidity is by evaporation of water. Some of this water will evaporate from the soil in which the plants are located, but the moisture in that soil needs to be regulated for the benefit of the plant roots rather than for any direct effect on air moisture. Water may be used liberally in walks and under benches; this contributes to raising the relative humidity. Also if the plants are of the right type or at the right stage of growth, they may be misted briefly but frequently, wetting the leaves without adding water to the soil. This reduces water loss from the plants (transpiration) as well as raises the relative humidity of the atmosphere. This is common practice in propagation houses, and also is used with newly planted stock.

Noxious Gases Of the noxious gases in the greenhouse atmosphere, some originate from manufacturing plants or other sources outside of the greenhouse. These gases could be sulfur dioxide, fluorides, or smog (PAN, ozone, and others), and in some instances chlorine, borates, or ammonia. If the source of the noxious gas cannot be controlled, it might be necessary to move the greenhouse operation to another location.

Other noxious gases are generated within the greenhouse, and when the problem is identified the correction can be made. As mentioned earlier, both sulfur dioxide and ethylene may be produced by malfunctioning heating units at the greenhouse.

There are numerous reports of greenhouse crop damage from the vapors of herbicides used or stored adjacent to the greenhouse. These may cause anything from distorted growth to death of the plant.

Mercury vapors cause flower bud damage in rose; the source of the mercury has been found in thermometers or in fungicides included in paint used in the greenhouse.

Many of the most common substances used for treating wood emit vapors which are toxic to plants. Copper naphthenate is a wood treatment that is safe to use around plants.

Most soil sterilants, even though they may be applied as a liquid, produce vapors that are toxic to greenhouse plants. Usually they are safely used only when there are no crop plants in the greenhouse.

Several pesticides are dispersed in the gaseous form. These methods of

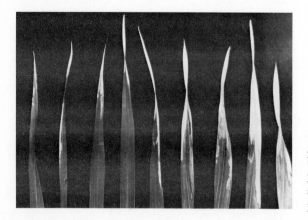

Figure 4-3 Fluorine damage to gladiolus leaves. This gas is a by-product of some industrial processes. Other air pollutants are also responsible for some plant damages.

Figure 4-4 Mercury damage on roses.

treatment are by means of fumigator, aerosol, fogger, or heating line or heating element. With all of these pesticide application methods, heat is the energy causing the dispersal, and the uniformity of distribution is affected by the temperature that is maintained in the applicator and in the greenhouse atmosphere. The greenhouse air temperature should be 25°C. Lower temperatures may cause deposition of toxic amounts of pesticide on some portions of the plants. Higher temperatures, too, may be a problem because the increased activity of the gas may cause the absorption of toxic amounts of the material in some tissues.

Uneven distribution of pesticide in the gaseous form results with air movement in the greenhouse, and this may cause some plant damage as well as variable control of pests. Greenhouses must be closed tightly during treatment, and treatment should be made only when there is not much wind outdoors.

Sometimes plants are damaged when the gaseous pesticide is too concentrated in an area because fumigators are not adequately spaced or foggers or aerosols are not transported at the right rate of speed or by appropriate routes.

Individuals making applications of pesticides in the gaseous form must be fully protected from contact with the gas—sufficient protection to prevent inhalation, ingestion, or dermal contact with the gas. The greenhouse must be closed for a minimum of 2 hours after treatment and then must be adequately aerated before personnel are admitted.

If plant surfaces are wet at the time of the gaseous application of some pesticides, there may be absorption of toxic amounts of the pesticide in some of those areas on the plant.

In foggers, the pesticide is dispersed in oil, and the oil particles that are dispersed with the fog are toxic to some kinds of plants.

Some pesticides may be dispersed as a dust over the plants. It is possible

Figure 4-5 Leaf spot on African violet leaves caused by cold water.

that the material may be finely pulverized and applied directly over the plants, but more frequently mixtures are prepared that contain 10 percent or less of the chemical mixed with an inert dust. The dust is ejected above the plants on forceful air streams and then it settles on plants and ground. Most dust applications leave a noticeable residue on the plant surfaces that may reduce the attractiveness of the product, but actual damage to plant growth is not usual.

Liquids Above Ground

The most common liquid used above ground in the greenhouse is water; however, the water may have various materials dissolved or dispersed in it and sometimes it contains oils or surfactants that aid in the dispersion of other materials in the water.

Mention has been made of drips of water from overhead caused by condensation of water on the inner surface of the greenhouse covering. Also, if the greenhouse covering is not completely sealed there will be some dripping when it rains. Either of these sources of water may cause poor growth of plants in the areas where the soil is kept too wet. The incidence of disease may be higher because of the wet conditions.

Irrigation and Mist Water In irrigation the objective is to apply water to the soil, but frequently, because of the methods that are used, the entire plant or portions of it may become wet. Because the growth of plant pathogens is promoted in moist surroundings, irrigation is scheduled for the morning so that plant surfaces dry and excessive air moisture decreases in the shortest possible time. Flowers are very susceptible to disease in moist surroundings, and when plants are in flower water from any source should be kept off the flowers.

In propagation, brief periods of misting are used at intervals so the leaves remain wet without adding more moisture to the soil. This procedure maintains adequate moisture within the plant until roots are formed.

Newly planted plants may be misted periodically for several days until new roots are formed. The air around small plants usually is drier because the contribution to air moisture by means of transpiration is negligible because of the small total area of leaves involved.

Hydraulic Spraying The most common means of application of pesticides and fungicides to plants is by hydraulic spray, and usually some surfactant (spreader) is present or is added to the pesticide so that the spray flows evenly over the plant surfaces. Surfactants must be chosen carefully and used properly because some of them can be toxic to plants.

Pesticides and fungicides for hydraulic application may be wettable powders, emulsions, or flowables. Some chemicals can be obtained in only one form and others may be availabe in more than one form. Generally the wettable powder and the flowable forms are safer to use on greenhouse plants than the emulsions. Emulsions contain oils which have the potential of damaging plant tissues. Damage to plants from the use of emulsions is more likely when temperatures are higher or lower than usual. At the higher temperatures the oils are more volatile and penetrate the tissues more readily, destroying some of the tissues. At cool temperatures and low light intensity the oil volatilizes so slowly into the atmosphere that it is absorbed into the tissues, thus destroying them. Emulsions can be used more safely on outdoor crops because in those conditions the oil usually volatilizes into the atmosphere faster than it does in the greenhouse. Emulsions and flowables have the feature of leaving no noticeable residue on the plant after application. Wettable powders leave a visible residue on the plant surfaces and this may affect their market price.

Flowers are more easily damaged from pesticide and fungicide applications than other plant structures. It is important to schedule spray applications so that pests and pathogens are under control before flowering time.

There are few, if any, all-purpose pesticides. The grower must identify the pest and then use the pesticide that is known to control that specific pest. If there are two or more pests that need to be controlled, two or more pesticides may need to be used. Before using pesticides together in the same spray application, it must be determined if the materials are compatible. A more common problem concerns the use of two or more pesticides in the emulsion form because with each added pesticide another portion of oil also is added, and it is the greater quantity of oil that might be most damaging to the plant.

Plants are damaged when excess amounts of pesticides or fungicides are used through carelessness or faulty mathematics. Also, a control material may not be phytotoxic to one cultivar but may injure another closely related cultivar. A record needs to be kept of each application so that if a problem with plant development occurs the record can be checked for a relationship between the damage observed and the substance used.

Growth Regulators Several preparations are marketed for use in controlling growth and development in plants. These generally are referred to as growth regulators. Some of these materials promote growth, and others may delay, limit, or inhibit it. There are many ways in which growth regulators can be used for limiting or controlling the amount or type of growth in greenhouse plants.

Some of the earliest uses of growth regulants involved synthetic auxins

Figure 4-6 Spraying with B-Nine at the time of disbudding of some chrysanthemum cultivars will reduce the length of the stem or "neck" and also may cause the flower to be more incurved. *(Yoder Bros., Inc. photograph.)*

used to promote rooting in cuttings during propagation. The use of these materials is standard practice. The preparation may be sprayed or dusted on the base of the cutting, or in some instances the entire cutting may be sprayed or immersed in the substance.

Many growth regulators have been developed through the years, and it appears that this will be an active field of endeavor in succeeding years. Only a portion of the products has practical use with greenhouse crop plants. Those that can be used on greenhouse crops must have label registration for this specific purpose, and they must be used in that manner. Because of frequent introduction of new products and revisions in uses of existing products, specific information on growth regulators and their use must be obtained from sources that are constantly updated. The various state extension services usually are the best sources of this information.

Growth regulators are used commercially for limitation of growth in chrysanthemum, poinsettia, Easter lily, hydrangea, petunia, some of the other bedding plants, and some of the foliage plants. Most of these uses are for producing plants that are more compact in growth—stems shorter and larger in diameter. Associated with this, usually, is improved quality of leaf development in which they have better substance and are darker green. With most plants the effect of the growth substance on flower development is not of consequence—there might be some delay in time of flowering or a slight effect on pigmentation—but with azalea there is a promotion of flowering following the application of some growth retardants.

One of the growth regulators that produces ethylene is used on bromeliads for the promotion of flowering, but its use delays flowering in geranium and promotes branching.

Various gibberellins are used to promote growth in other agricultural crop plants, but they seem to have only limited use with greenhouse crop plants.

Figure 4-7 B-Nine sprays at the time of disbudding some chrysanthemum cultivars may adversely affect their flower form. *(Yoder Bros., Inc. photograph.)*

Some products have been developed that destroy the meristematic tissues of the stem tips without unfavorable effects on the other portions of the plant. Such a growth regulator can be used as a means for pinching stems and producing branching. These materials sometimes are called chemical pinchers. They are used to some extent with azaleas. There is considerable interest in obtaining materials that would perform this task in chrysanthemum, but this commercial application lies in the future.

Pests Above Ground

Pests are animals that can be bothersome or damaging to plants. Sometimes human beings are the most bothersome animal around plants, but the discussion of their association with plants will conclude this chapter. Of all plant pests, the largest group involved is the insects. Some of the noninsect animal pests are mites (arachnids), nematodes (roundworms), slugs (mollusks), mice and rats, and cats and dogs.

Before greenhouse operators can attempt to control pests, they must know which pests are involved so that the right pesticide material can be used. There are few if any pesticides that can control a great number of different pests. The following descriptions may be sufficient to make positive identification of the pest. If there is any question, advice should be obtained from a specialist.

Some of the pests transmit virus pathogens to plants as they feed on them. Aphids, leafhoppers, and mites seem to be more frequently involved in spreading virus diseases in this way.

Insect Pests Some of the insect pests are born alive, and the young look like a small version of the adults. The majority of the insects, however, hatch from eggs and then go through various stages of development (metamorphosis) in which their form, appearance, and activity may be quite different from those of the adult. The damage to plants is a result of the insect's feeding activity on the plant. Some insects feed by biting and chewing, and others only eat liquid and can suck or siphon plant juices.

Aphids are about 0.3 centimeter long and usually occur in large colonies in the new growth at the tips of the stems. They are commonly called plant lice or green lice. Sex seems to be inconsequential to aphids. Virgin females are capable of giving birth to 100 young a day for about 1 month. Typically aphids are not winged; however, when housing or food supply becomes a problem, winged females make their appearance and fly off to establish new colonies. Other than observing the pest itself, the results of its habitation are characteristic and usually evident. Aphids excrete a honeydew which promotes a noticeable, sooty fungal growth, and bits of cast skin are scattered over the area. Aphids may infest most greenhouse crop plants, but they are most persistent on chrysanthemum. The species sometimes found in the greenhouse are melon aphid *(Aphis gossypi),* green with black mottling; chrysanthemum aphid *(Macrosiphoniella sanborni),* dark brown to black; and green peach aphid *(Myzus persicae),* yellow-green in summer and pink to red from fall to spring. Aphids are suckers, and their feeding activity damages areas of the meristem with the result that when these tissues develop those damaged areas cannot enlarge along with the normal areas. This causes twists, puckers, and general malformation in the new growth.

Figure 4-8 Aphids on a rose stem. These pests usually infest the stem-tip portions of plants.

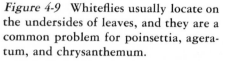

Figure 4-9 Whiteflies usually locate on the undersides of leaves, and they are a common problem for poinsettia, ageratum, and chrysanthemum.

The appearance of the malformed growth follows the aphid infestation by several days to a few weeks, and frequently it is long enough after the pest was eradicated so that the damage is not associated with the infestation unless a notation of it was made at the time it occurred.

Adult whiteflies *(Trialeurodes vaporariorum)* are four-winged, about 0.15 centimeter long, and, appropriately enough, white. They feed on the undersurface of newly matured leaves, and when they are disturbed their departure to other plants a short distance away is with a characteristic flurry. The total life cycle of the whitefly in the greenhouse is about 1 month and in that period the female whitefly lays about 100 eggs. These are deposited in circles of about 20 eggs on the undersurface of young leaves, and they hatch in about 1 week. There are stages of larval development that feed by sucking on the undersurface of the leaf. The feeding causes a speckling or mottling of the upper surface of the leaf. There is a pupal stage of about 10 days, and the adult that emerges must lay eggs in less than 1 week. Some of the most popular whitefly hosts are poinsettia, chrysanthemum, tomato, ageratum, and some other bedding plants. Whiteflies excrete a glistening honeydew that eventually is covered with a black mold. Leaves that have been severely damaged by the feeding of whiteflies may turn yellow and drop from the plant.

Fully grown thrips are only 0.1 centimeter in length and normally are not observed in the air. Their presence on plants may not be suspected until damage caused by their feeding on plant tissues suggests a close inspection for them. Thrips feed by rasping the surface of the plant tissues and then sucking the juices. They inhabit mainly the young, terminal portions of the plant. The adult may or may not have wings. When wings do develop they are feathery and give this pest the capability of soaring great distances on air currents. The life cycle from egg through larval and pupal stages to adult is about 3 weeks. The most common thrips in the greenhouse are onion thrips *(Thrips tabaci)* and greenhouse thrips *(Heliothrips haemorrhoidalis)*. When thrips feed on more mature leaves and flowers, the damage is observed as irregular streaks on the surfaces, first white and then turning brown. When thrips infest very young tissues, the results can be various degrees of malformed growth which sometimes is so extensive that the entire tip is destroyed. Because thrips infestations often come from adjacent field crops, the time of their arrival is determined by outdoor weather conditions and the stage of development of the outdoor field crop. Two methods of inspecting for thrips are tapping the plant part over a white paper and observing the thrips as they drop to the paper, or observing the base of petals or florets by quickly pushing them apart and seeing thrips scurrying for cover.

The adult leaf miner is a black fly about 0.2 centimeter long. In their 3-week lifetime they lay approximately 100 eggs in newly matured leaves. The maggot hatches in about 5 days and then eats the inner tissues of the leaf for about 2 weeks, leaving light-colored blotches or paths in the leaf where it has mined the inner tissues. The pupal stage usually is in the ground until the adult emerges in about 2 weeks. The most common leaf miners in the greenhouse are serpentine leaf miner *(Liriomyza* species) in which the adult is black with yellow markings and a yellow head, and chrysanthemum leaf miner *(Phytomyza atriconis)* in which the adult is an entirely black fly and a little larger. Leaf miners usually are not continuous inhabitants of the greenhouse. When they do appear, chrysanthemums are a likely host.

The adult mealybug is about 0.5 centimeter long and has a reddish body covered with whitish, powdery, waxlike material. The adult and the earlier development stages are crawlers, but move slowly. It is possible but not probable that adult, winged male flies might develop. The females have the capability of either laying eggs or giving birth to young. Mealybugs excrete honeydew that eventually becomes covered with black, sooty mold. They may have about a 3-week life cycle, but in some instances it will be considerably longer if the nymphs are quiescent during some unfavorable conditions. Many foliage plants are hosts of mealybugs and other greenhouse plants can be hosts. The aerial mealybugs in the greenhouse are *Pseudococcus* species. Mealybugs may locate on various portions of the plant, but frequently on the stem at the base of leaves or shoots. They are suckers and heavy infestations may destroy leaves or shoots. There are some subterranean species of mealybugs.

Scale insects are even less motile than mealybugs. Some nymph stages are crawlers, but the adult female is legless. The adult male is winged but does not feed. There are several different kinds of scale insects. The primary hosts in the greenhouse are foliage plants. Scales are suckers.

There are several pests of greenhouse plants in which the adult stage is moth and the larval stage is caterpillar. These larvae are commonly but improperly called worms. Caterpillars bite and chew. They ingest solids (leaves, stems, or flowers), some of them one or the other and some of them all three. Both the adult and larval stages operate at night. It takes some nocturnal visits to discover them. Some of the damage that they cause may resemble damage caused by slugs, but when slugs are involved dried slime trails will also be in evidence, and caterpillars leave telltale droppings. Frequently it is difficult to determine which caterpillar pest is involved in the damage. It may be necessary to view type of damage, characteristics of the caterpillar, or characteristics of the adult moth before making a decision. Some of the caterpillar pests inhabiting the greenhouse are beet armyworm, corn earworm, cutworms, European corn borer, leaf rollers, leaf tiers, loopers, and plume moths.

The beet armyworm *(Spodoptera exiqa)* is a serious pest on chrysanthemum and some other greenhouse crops. The moth has a wingspread of about 3 centimeters, the front wings are mottled gray, and the eggs are laid in groups and covered with body hair. The caterpillar is about 2 centimeters long and olive to dark green in color with a dark stripe on its back and yellow stripes with pink dots on each side. It matches leaf color well and movement is sluggish; for those reasons it may not be noticed until plant damage is apparent. It may eat quarter-size areas in the leaf leaving either upper or lower transparent, outer tissue intact. It also feeds on flower buds and flowers.

Figure 4-10 **Beet armyworm larva.** *(Ohio Agricultural Research and Development Center photograph.)*

Figure 4-11 **Variegated cut-worm larva on geranium.** *(Ohio Agricultural Research and Development Center photograph.)*

Corn earworm *(Heliothis zea)* moth wingspread is about 4.5 centimeters, the forewings are straw-colored with black variegation, the hindwings are cream-colored with dark band at margin, and the eggs are pinhead size and placed individually. The caterpillar is about 5 centimeters long and is variously colored and striped with a yellowish-brown head. They feed on the upper portions of the plant, frequently eating buds and flowers.

The cutworm *(Peridroma saucia)* moth has a wingspread of about 3.5 centimeters, the forewings are dark brown streaked with various lighter colors, and the hindwings are lighter in color and unmarked. The eggs are laid in masses or in rows. The caterpillar is about 3.5 centimeters long and has smooth skin, gray or brown with dark markings and a series of yellow dots down the middle of the back. They may chew the plants off at the base or higher or they may feed on buds or shoots.

The European corn borer *(Ostrinia nubilalis)* moth has a wingspread of about 2.5 centimeters, the forewings of the female are tan with dark wavy lines, the male forewings are dark brown with dark and pale wavy lines, and the eggs are laid shinglelike in masses. The caterpillar is about 2.5 centimeters long and gray-pink in color with a black head. They are primarily stem borers.

The omnivorous leaf roller *(Platinota stultana)* moth has a wingspread of

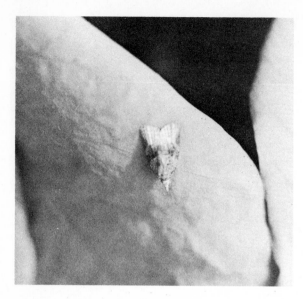

Figure 4-12 **Omnivorous leaf roller adult.** *(Ohio Agricultural Research and Development Center photograph.)*

about 2.5 centimeters, the forewings are dark brown, and the eggs are laid in overlapping masses. The caterpillars are about 1 centimeter long; the newly hatched ones are yellowish with brown heads and the mature ones are yellow-brown-green with a transparent stripe down the back. They tie terminal leaves together in a roll and feed in the roll or they may bore into buds and flowers. They have been a serious pest on greenhouse roses and some other crops.

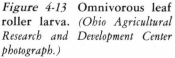

Figure 4-13 **Omnivorous leaf roller larva.** *(Ohio Agricultural Research and Development Center photograph.)*

Figure 4-14 **Cabbage looper adult.** *(Ohio Agricultural Research and Development Center photograph.)*

The leaf tier *(Oeobia rubicalis)* moth has a wingspread of about 2.5 centimeters, the forewings are light brown with dark wavy lines, and the eggs are laid in overlapping masses. The caterpillar is about 2 centimeters long and is light green and has a dark green stripe down the middle of the back bordered by white stripes with two black dots behind the head. They tie portions of the leaf together with webbing and eat from inside. Various greenhouse crops are hosts.

The looper *(Trichoplusia ni)* moth is about 2.5 centimeters long, the forewings are dark brown with lighter mottlings and a silver spot at the center, and the eggs are laid singly. The caterpillar is about 2.5 centimeters long and is pale green with two stripes. It moves by looping its body. They eat any portion toward the top of the plant.

The plume moth *(Platyptilia* species) adult has a wingspread of about 2.5 centimeters and the wings are tan with scattered gray and brown spots. The wings are split into featherlike divisions or plumes. The eggs are laid singly. The caterpillar is about 2.5 centimeters long and yellow, green, or purple with a black head. They infest geraniums and some other greenhouse crops. They may bore into flower buds and stems, and they do some leaf rolling.

Other Animal Pests Slugs *(Limax maximus)* are mollusks that are mainly nocturnal and eat leaves and flowers. During the daytime they remain in moist surroundings around the ground, and when they make their nightly visits they leave a slime trail from hiding place to dining area. Slugs have

Figure 4-15 Damage to chrysanthemum leaves by slugs. These pests attack many kinds of plants and feed on flowers as well as leaves. They prefer a humid environment. Usually during the day they are in moist areas beneath pots, flats, or trash, and they feed at night. *(Yoder Bros., Inc. photograph.)*

both male and female structures in the same body, may function as either sex, and are capable of self-fertilization. They lay eggs and the young that hatch appear to be small editions of the adult. They may infest any greenhouse crop, but they are particularly bothersome with bedding plants.

Mites are arachnids (spiders) and are never winged. Sex is determined by egg fertilization—males develop from unfertilized eggs and females from fertilized eggs. They have larval and nymph stages of development that in general appearance are much the same as the adults. The two most common mites in the greenhouse are cyclamen mite and two-spotted mite (red spider). Cyclamen mites *(Steneotarsonemus pallidus)* are very tiny, less than

Figure 4-16 Cyclamen mite infestation on cyclamen. These pests sometimes are found on snapdragon, chrysanthemum, and English ivy. They are difficult to observe because they are so small, but the cupping and crippling of the terminal leaves are characteristic of their presence.

Figure 4-17 Symptoms on the top surface of a rose leaf of two-spotted mite (red spider) infestation on the under surface of the leaf. The leaf on the right is infested. These pests usually feed on the bottom surfaces of leaves. They are small and difficult to observe, but the results of their feeding produce the characteristic speckling of the top surface of the leaves. Two-spotted mites are pests that are common to most greenhouse plants.

0.03 centimeter in length. They cannot be observed without the use of a magnifying lens. Other than cyclamen, the favorite hosts of cyclamen mites are saintpaulia, hedera, and some other foliage plants. The mites infest the meristematic tissues at the tip of the plant. They are suckers, and their feeding on these undeveloped tissues causes much malformation as growth proceeds. Leaves may be curled, twisted, and much reduced in size. Growth may cease and buds may be destroyed. With plants that have hairy leaves, such as saintpaulia, there seems to be pronounced development of hairs on the dwarfed and malformed leaves. The female may live for about 1 month and lay about 100 eggs. The entire life cycle is completed in a little over 1 month.

The two-spotted mite *(Tetranychus urticae)* is about 0.05 centimeter long, visible but just barely so. Most greenhouse plants can be hosts for two-spotted mites (red spider), and frequently they are the most widespread and destructive pest in the greenhouse. The female has a life span of less than 1 month, and in that period lays about 100 eggs. The life cycle from egg to larva to nymph and adult is completed in about 10 days. The eggs are laid on the underside of leaves, and usually young and adults feed there. They are suckers, and their feeding on the underside of the leaf causes a speckled appearance on the upper surface of the leaf. This speckling is noticeable and characteristic of a two-spotted mite infestation. They locate most often on older leaves toward the base of the plant; however, when the infestation is extensive, they may cover all portions of the plant and they then produce webbing over the infested parts. In spite of their small size, their food consumption from the plant can be so great that growth of the infested portion may be terminated. When flowers are infested, some of the florets or petals may become desiccated and turn brown. Before effective chemical controls were developed for two-spotted mites, growers flushed them from the plants with forceful streams of water (syringing). This was common practice with rose plants. Two-spotted mites reproduce very rapidly in the high temperatures during the summer, and control measures at that time of the year are very critical.

Although nematodes are animals (roundworms), because of their very tiny size they most often are included in studies and work in plant pathology. Some of the nematodes that infest aerial portions of plants are *Aphelenchoides fragariae, Aphelenchoides ritzima,* and *Ditylenchus dipsaci.* Begonia, peperomia, saintpaulia, ferns, and chrysanthemum can be hosts for foliar nematodes, and the damage to the leaves can look similar to that from pathogen activity that causes some of the leaf diseases. Nematodes also are called eelworms.

Figure 4-18 Foliar nematode infestations often cause a characteristic pie-shaped section of dead leaf tissue.

Rats and mice sometimes seek refuge in greenhouses. Although plants are not their primary source of food, they do snack on them on occasion. Mice may select carnation buds as their favorite food in the greenhouse.

Cats and dogs get involved either as companions to greenhouse personnel or as protectors of plants or property. In spite of the beneficial reasons for their presence, they can also get into some activities that interfere with plant growth and development, such as tipping pots or breaking leaves, stems, or flowers.

Pathogens Above Ground

With pests, there is some chance of using a see-and-treat method of control successfully. Many of the pests are large enough to be seen before damage is inflicted on the plant, or if there is some damage further harm may be terminated completely by proper treatment of pest. The situation is quite different with pathogens. The propagules of many pathogens are present in the environment but cannot be seen. Spores are the most common propagules in fungi. When they start to grow in or on a crop plant, their presence is not known until growth on the surface of the plant is observed or there is sufficient damage to plant growth and development that the presence of a pathogen is indicated. At this point it may or may not be possible, depending on the pathogen involved, to control further growth of the pathogen. The disease caused by the pathogen may not only continue to exist but may worsen regardless of attempts to contain continued development of the pathogen, because when the pathogen is inside the plant most fungicides are not effective. If there are materials that could be used to inactivate the pathogen, they may damage the crop plant also.

The sensible approach in disease control is to take definitive action ahead of time. As far as possible cultivars should be used that are resistant to specific diseases, procedures should be used to exclude pathogens from the greenhouse, steps should be taken to eliminate pathogens that may be present, and the environment should be regulated so that it is not suitable for pathogen growth.

Through selection and hybridization some cultivars have been developed that are less susceptible to some diseases. It is possible to use some chrysanthemum cultivars that are not subject to botrytis blight *(Botrytis cinerea),* snapdragon cultivars that are less susceptible to rust *(Puccinia antirrhini),* and some dieffenbachia species that seldom are afflicted with bacterial leaf spot *(Xanthomonas dieffenbachiae),* but it may not be possible to get rose cultivars of the desired flowering characteristics that are not susceptible to powdery mildew *(Sphaerotheca pannosa* var. *rosae)* or poinsettias that are not subject to soft rot *(Erwinia carotovora* var. *chrysanthemi).* If the cultivars being used are known to be subject to certain diseases, all efforts will need to be made to exclude or eliminate pathogens and provide an environment not suitable for their growth.

It does not seem to be feasible commercially to somehow filter all incoming air into the greenhouse so that it will be known to be pathogen-free. It is possible, however, to establish procedures that will limit the entrance into the greenhouse of infected plants and contaminated equipment. Many pathogens could be eliminated by use of chemicals. With the crops that are disease-susceptible, it should be assumed that there will be chance infiltration of the pathogen, and chemical controls should be used on a preventive basis. Other environmental factors should also be regulated on the same basis so that growth of pathogens is not favored.

Many disease symptoms are similar even though they are caused by different pathogens. With each disease problem, it must definitely be established which pathogen is attacking the plant so that correct control methods will be used. Greenhouse operators should confer frequently with specialists about diseases, the pathogens that are responsible for the problem, and methods of control.

Probably the most common disease of aerial portions of greenhouse crop plants is botrytis blight caused by *Botrytis cinerea.* The infection often gets started in old or damaged tissues of leaves or flowers, producing brown, rotted areas. Infection may start in some stems and result in stem rot. In moist conditions the pathogen flourishes and produces large masses of mycelium and spores. Botrytis blight commonly is located on the following plant structures: standard mums, outer or lower florets; geranium, center florets, leaf spots, and stem rot; bedding plants, older florets and lower

Figure 4-19 A botrytis blight infection on a standard mum flower. *(Department of Plant Pathology, Pennsylvania State University, University Park, Pennsylvania photograph.)*

Figure 4-20 Powdery mildew is the most prevalent disease of greenhouse roses. The leaf on the right exhibits the characteristic white, powdery, crinkled areas.

leaves; snapdragon, lowest florets and stem in that area; saintpaulia, older florets and leaf petioles; begonia, leaves, flowers, or stem; hydrangea, flower buds; and poinsettia, bracts. The incidence of botrytis blight can be limited if water, heat, and air movement are regulated so that plant surfaces remain dry.

Powdery mildew is a major disease problem of greenhouse rose plants. The pathogen causing rose powdery mildew is *Sphaerotheca pannosa* var. *rosae.* Mainly the leaves are infected, but at times stems and petals may have the disease. Several kinds of plants have powdery mildew disease. As the name suggests, a white, powdery surface develops on the infected part, but different pathogens may be involved on each kind of plant. Other host plants and pathogens are: mum *(Erysiphe cichoracearum),* saintpaulia *(Oidium* spe-

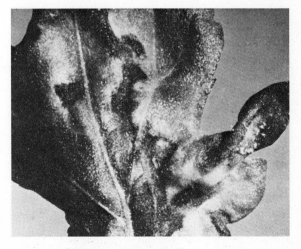

Figure 4-21 Powdery mildew infection in chrysanthemum. The best means of prevention is regulation of temperature, moisture, and air circulation so that moisture is not present on the leaf surface. *(From a Koda-chrome by C. W. Ellett.)*

Figure 4-22 Leaf-spot symptoms of bacterial stem rot in
geranium. *(Department of Plant
Pathology, The Pennsylvania State
University, University Park, Pennsylvania photograph.)*

cies), begonia *(Oidium* species), snapdragon *(Oidium* species), hydrangea
(Erysiphe polygoni), and kalanchoe *(Sphaerotheca humuli* var. *fuliginea).* Regulation of relative humidity, temperature, and air movement is critical in the
control of this disease.

Bacterial leaf spot disease usually starts with small, blisterlike spots on
the leaves that eventually coalesce to form larger, water-soaked areas. The
pathogens are *Xanthomonas* species, and some of the plants that become
infected are begonia, dieffenbachia, geranium, hedera, and philodendron.
The spread of bacterial pathogens usually can be controlled when the plant
surfaces are kept dry.

There are several serious virus diseases of greenhouse plants, and
probably the best known ones are those of chrysanthemums, carnation,
Easter lily, and geraniums. The viruses can have many different effects on
the host plants, including chlorosis, mottling, crinkling, mosaic, yellows,
stunting, and flower distortion. The virus must be eliminated from propagative stock by some means of culturing. The viruses may be transmitted from
diseased plants to virus-free plants by people or some insects.

Aerial Portions of Other Plants, Structures, and Equipment

The other plants may be either inside or outside the greenhouse. First
consideration needs to be given to neighboring crop plants. When plants of a
crop are planted or placed closely together, they cast more shade on one
another than when planted or placed farther apart. This reduction in light
intensity may not be of consequence with the summer crop, but it could be a
critical factor in plant growth during the winter.

If taller plants are placed to the sunward side or if plants are placed
overhead in baskets or on shelves, the reduction in light quantity will have
an effect on the shaded plants. This change in light environment can be
beneficial or harmful depending on the plants involved.

Figure 4-23 Dodder, a parasitic plant, is observed occasionally on outdoor plants but seldom on those in the greenhouse.

Tall plants, such as trees, immediately outside the greenhouse affect the available light intensity for the greenhouse plants if they are on the sunward side of the greenhouse.

Plants other than crop plants either inside or outside the greenhouse (weeds or ornamentals) usually do not get as good attention as the crop plants and invariably they harbor pests or pathogens that later may infest the crop plants. Such factors of the environment can produce some serious effects with the crop plants.

Plant debris or residues allowed to gather in or around the greenhouse also will produce a constant source of pathogen spores.

The location relationship of plants with structures and equipment affects the environment for those plants. The shade cast by overhead objects such as gutters, withdrawn shade cloth, or other impedimenta may cause the type of growth associated with reduced light intensity. Or the relationship in distance with pads or fans may give temperature or air-movement effects that cause growth differences in some plants.

THE BELOW-GROUND ENVIRONMENT

The below-ground environment is the soil, and at least for greenhouse crop plants it is helpful to consider that the portion of the environment of the plant in which the roots develop is soil. Soils can have extreme variability, but in spite of many apparent differences there are some factors that must exist in all soils that are suitable for plant growth. These basic factors are physical stability or anchorage for the plant, suitable temperatures, adequate water, freedom from toxins and other harmful materials, sufficient aeration, and a supply of available mineral nutrients.

Outdoors, the plants grow in naturally derived soils. They may be cultivated and modified to some extent by human beings, but basically they form and develop under natural conditions. In some instances greenhouse operators place structures over the ground and plant crops in the soil in the same manner that they would outdoors. More frequently, however, greenhouse crop plants are grown in soil in benches or in containers; the soil is especially mixed or prepared for the way in which it will be used. The base material for the greenhouse mixed soil may be naturally derived soils (field soils), or it may be a mixture of other materials not originally classed as soils.

For some experimental work, water may be the best soil to use. Sand or sand with some additives is used as soil in some instances for either experimental or commercial plant production. Regardless of the appearance, name, or former use of the material, if it supplies the basic factors needed by the plant for growth and development, it is a good soil.

Naturally Derived Soils

There are many stages in development of soil, and there are many different kinds of naturally derived soils, depending primarily on the parent material (rocks) available, the climate, the kind and amount of plant growth, and the topography of the area. The soils of concern here are those that are considered mature soils. This is a stage of soil development in which the soil profile has horizons above the parent material that have characteristics suitable for plant growth. This is soil that can be used for cultivation and the production of agricultural crops. The portion of the soil above the parent material is referred to as solum, and it develops from weathering of the parent material, organic residues from plants or animals, and possibly some material transported to the area by water, ice, or wind.

Soil Solids The solid portion of many naturally derived soils is mainly inorganic residues from the parent material and frequently has the same mineral identity as the parent material. The size of these residue particles can vary greatly. Large particles are called sand, somewhat smaller ones silt, and the smallest particles are known as clay; these names are used to describe the texture of the soil depending on which particle size is predominant. These soils are called mineral or inorganic soils.

When conditions favorable for excellent plant growth are followed by conditions that cause slow decomposition of this organic matter, the

Table 4-1 *Some Properties of Individual Soil Particles*

Textural name	Diameter, millimeters*	No. of particles per gram	Square centimeters/gram surface area
Clay	Less than 0.002	90,260,853,860	11,342.5
Silt	0.002–0.05	5,776,674	453.7
Sand	0.05 –2.0	5,777	45.4

*As established by the U.S. Department of Agriculture.

resulting soil has a high organic content. These are called organic soils, and examples of these are peats and mucks.

Soil Pores The solid portion of the soil accounts for about 50 percent of the total soil volume, and the balance of this total volume consists of spaces between the solid particles. These spaces are called pores.

The size of pores (diameter) is determined largely by the size of the solid particles—small particles fit more closely together, leaving a greater number of pores, but these are of small diameter. Thus sandy soils have relatively few pores but they are of large diameter, and nongranulated clay soils have the maximum number of pores and they are of small diameter. The volume relationship in these soils is very similar. The volume of the pores in either clay or sandy soils is about 50 percent of the total soil volume regardless of differences in number and size of pores in these two different soils.

Effects of Pore Size on Aeration In normal situations soil pores contain either water or air. This probably should be stated another way. If soil pores do not contain water, they contain air. The air of the above-ground atmosphere is available and will diffuse into the soil pores when that space is not occupied by water. Whether or not the soil pores contain water is dependent on the availability of water, the diameter and length of the pores, and the water-drainage conditions below the soil. The availability of water does not need further comment at this time, but water drainage away from the soil definitely affects the contents of soil pores and the drainage properties must be established.

Water moves downward in the soil because of the effect of gravity, and the rate of movement of water in soil pores is dependent on the size and length of the pores. The larger diameter pores and the longer pores drain most rapidly. Because of the difference in pore diameter, sandy soils drain more rapidly than clay soils, and in soils that have pores of the same diameter water drainage will be fastest in the deeper soils. Even those naturally derived soils that have small pore diameters may drain well outdoors because of the long length of the pores, but when the same soil is placed in shallow containers, such as the typical greenhouse bench or pot, the pores may remain filled with water because of the reduced water head in the short pores. For this reason, field soils brought into the greenhouse usually need to be amended so that they will have larger pores that drain more completely.

Greenhouse growers commonly refer to sandy soils as light and clay soils as heavy. It is true that there usually is a weight differential in these two soils, but this difference in weight is caused by the quantity of water retained rather than any difference in weight of the solid components of these soils. Field-crop farmers use the terms light and heavy soils in reference to tillage characteristics.

Soil particles do not always remain as single entities. They may group together forming aggregates, and this aggregation of particles is referred to as soil structure. The forming of soil aggregates is promoted in the presence of some colloids. Organic matter produces colloidal material, and usually soils containing organic matter have more aggregation. Because of the increase in particle size with aggregation, the soil pores have increased diameter, and this aggregated soil drains more freely and is classed as having better structure.

Soil Minerals The mineral composition of the parent material from which the soils developed is the source of minerals in the soil. Some additional minerals may be added from the organic matter components of the soil. With a few exceptions, the naturally derived soils have the mineral nutrients needed for plant growth and development. Those that are in short supply can be added to the soil by means of fertilizer applications.

The minerals in the soil may be dissolved in the water in the soil pores or they may be adsorbed to the surface of the soil particles. The smaller the soil particle, the greater the exposed surface area for adsorption of either minerals or water.

Mixed Soils for the Greenhouse

Various methods are used for mixing soils for the greenhouse. Field (naturally derived) soils may be used with necessary amendments, or soils may be manufactured using miscellaneous ingredients. When field soils are used as the basic ingredient of the soil mix, it first must be determined that herbicides have not been used on the soil because some that are used safely on field crops are toxic to greenhouse crops. Then soils are selected that appear to have good water-drainage characteristics. Organic matter and/or various inorganic aggregates are mixed with the soil to improve drainage, pH adjustment is made if needed, fertilizers containing calcium, phosphorus, and possibly other mineral nutrients are added, and the mixture is steamed or otherwise treated to eliminate pests and pathogens.

For years peat moss has been used as soil for some greenhouse plants, primarily azaleas and some of the foliage plants. When suitable peat can be obtained it probably will continue to be used for some of these crops. It also has been used as soil in the propagation of many kinds of plants. Fine-textured peat moss is suitable for propagation by seed, but for other uses coarse, fibrous peat provides the air-moisture relationship more favorable for plant growth. Some adjustment in pH may be needed depending on the crop and the source of the peat.

Peat is used for the basic ingredient in several soil mixes that have perlite or vermiculite as inorganic components. These peat mixes usually include fertilizers containing phosphorus, calcium, and possibly other mineral nutrients, depending on how the mix will be used.

The preparation and use of sand or peat or mixtures of sand and peat for container-grown crops are described in University of California Manual 23, *The U.C. System for Producing Healthy Container-Grown Plants.* Various fertilizer combinations are suggested for incorporation in these sand and peat mixtures.

Some soil mixes using ground bark combined with sand, vermiculite, or other inorganic materials and some added mineral nutrients have been formulated.

It is possible that the manufactured soils can provide the environmental factors needed by plants as well as or maybe better than naturally derived soils. There may be less margin for error with the manufactured soils than there is with amended field soils. The manufacturer, whether a grower or in the mix business, needs to consistently develop the product that provides the appropriate air-moisture relationship, supplies the necessary mineral nutrients, and is free of pests, pathogens, and any material detrimental to plant growth and development.

Soil Temperature

Root growth and development is very slow at soil temperatures below 7°C. Generally it is considered that soil temperatures adjust promptly to air temperatures, and because forcing temperatures usually are 10°C or higher, soil temperatures are satisfactory for root growth.

Standard practice has been to measure air temperatures only for general growing procedures and assume that the soil temperature is approximately the same and does not need adjustment. When the sun is the source of heat, the soil temperatures may be higher than the air temperatures. When the heating system is the source of heat, it is possible that there will be a temperature differential between soil and air temperatues depending on the method of heat distribution that is used.

Earlier concepts of heat distribution in the greenhouse favored the placement of heating lines below or beside benches. With such placement, soil temperatures could exceed air temperatures. Many greenhouse installations have been made with the primary distribution of heat overhead. With such methods of heat distribution, soil temperatures probably are cooler than air temperatures at some time during the heating period, but this may not be a significant problem in general growing procedures. Now, because of interest in conservation of fuel by the maximum retention of heat in the greenhouse, there is renewed use of distribution of heat at the soil level rather than at higher levels. This may limit the use of some heating systems and may complicate installation, but it marks a return to better control of soil temperatures.

Effects of Increase in Soil Temperature It can be expected that with increase in soil temperatures up to about 25°C, there will be an increase in the rate of metabolic processes within the root with increased growth and development. Because warmer temperatures promote root growth, propagation areas are designed with facilities to supply soil temperatures from 20 to 25°C. In many greenhouses this soil temperature control is provided most accurately with electricity as the source of heat.

Root growth in newly planted plants is promoted at soil temperatures from 18 to 21°C. Because of the larger areas involved, this additional heat should be provided by the general heating system.

Soil temperature has effects on the air-moisture relationship in the soil. With increase in temperature, evaporation of water is increased. This reduces the amount of water in the soil and increases the amount of air, and within limits this promotes root growth.

With an increase in soil temperature, additional water is lost from the soil by drainage. It might be more meaningful stated another way—warm soils drain more completely than cool soils. For this reason, warm soils are better aerated, placing more emphasis on using higher temperatures in propagation soils and in newly planted soils in which root development is the first objective.

Effects of Cool Soil Temperature When plants are placed in cool storage either for vernalization or for holding for marketing, the temperatures are below 10°C and the rate of root growth is very slow. The rate of water loss from the soil also is very slow, and soil aeration may become critical if the plants are irrigated too frequently. When plants are removed from cool storage, there is a period of a few days at warm temperature before there is sufficient root growth to handle the absorption of water that will be needed by the plant. During this period the plants should be placed in reduced light intensity and humid conditions in order to reduce moisture loss from them by transpiration.

Bulbs that are to be given vernalization temperatures after planting must be placed in warm temperatures (10 to 18°C) for a period of about 3 weeks after planting or until roots are well developed before the vernalizing temperatures are supplied.

Irrigation water used in greenhouses frequently is 10°C or cooler because of existing temperatures at the water source. This has a depressing effect on plant growth, and it probably is more of a factor in propagation than in growing areas. Unfortunately, there is no economical way to heat irrigation water to growing temperatures.

Irrigation

The process of supplying water to soils in which crop plants are growing is known as irrigation, and several different methods of irrigation are used with greenhouse plants. With plants growing in outdoor soils, rain is the primary method of irrigation, and there is little or no control over the quantity of water or the frequency of this irrigation. In the greenhouse both quantity of water and the frequency of application can be controlled as well as the direction in which it is supplied.

Most frequently, in the greenhouse water is applied to the upper surface of the soil; however, in some situations water is applied at the bottom level of the soil (subirrigation). This may be in large enough quantity so that the entire soil mass is supersaturated or in limited quantity so that only the bottom soil surface is wetted with movement of water to the rest of the soil mass by means of capillarity. Water may move in the soil because of gravitation, capillarity, or diffusion.

Gravitational Water   When water is applied to the top surface of the soil the effect of gravity on the water may be apparent immediately. If the soil surface is not level, the water flows to the low areas en route to moving downward through the soil. The uneven soil surface, because of its effect on water movement, has effects on plant growth. The low areas remain wetter than the higher areas. If the frequency of irrigation is based on the moisture content of the low areas, the soil in the higher areas will be too dry for good root growth. If the frequency of irrigation is based on the moisture content of the higher areas, the soil in the low areas will remain too wet for good root growth. The obvious answer is to make sure that the top surface of greenhouse soils is level. In the soil the direction of water movement is downward, because of gravity, and this movement continues unless a greater force than gravity comes into effect. The water that does make the entire trip from the top through the bottom of the soil is called gravitational water or drainage. The amount of water that is retained in the soil is called either field capacity or capillary capacity. The latter term is probably more appropriate for greenhouse soils. The assessment of the amount of drainage water must be in relation to the amount of time required for the drainage to occur.

The route that the drainage water takes through the soil is through the larger pores. These are called aeration pores, and that is a fitting term because after the passage of the drainage water they do contain air, the primary source of oxygen needed for respiration in the cells of the root. It is only with a continuously adequate supply of air in the soil that root growth and development will be good. The avowed purpose of irrigation is to supply water to the soil environment, but it is equally important that irrigation be handled in such a way that soil aeration is not impaired.

Capillary Water and Water Movement The water that is retained in the soil after the exit of the drainage water either is adsorbed to the soil particles bordering the aeration pores or it fills the small (capillary) pores among the soil particles. There is an attractive force called adhesion between water and some other substances, and in the capillary pores of the soil the adhesive force between water and the soil particles bordering these pores is greater than the force of gravity with the result that the water is retained in the pores. The adsorbed water and the water in the capillary pores are available for absorption into the roots.

Good greenhouse soil mixtures have the right combination of aeration pores and capillary pores so that air and water are available continuously in the soil for good root growth.

Although water does not move in capillary pores as a result of gravity, there is movement in these small pores due to the adhesive force between water and soil particles and the cohesive force between water particles. This water movement may be in any direction, and is called capillary movement or capillarity. It is by this means that water can move laterally and upward as well as downward. The rate of movement and the distance of movement are determined by characteristics of the soil particles and the diameter of the capillary pores. In relatively large pores the rate of capillary movement is fast but the distance covered is short. In the small pores the rate of movement is slower and the distance traveled can be greater.

In addition to movement of water in the liquid form by means of gravitation or capillarity, there is movement of water in the gaseous form in the soil by means of diffusion. Normally the relative humidity of the atmosphere in the aeration pores is very high and that water vapor diffuses in any direction from places of greater concentration of water vapor to areas where the water vapor is not as concentrated.

Subirrigation When subirrigation is used, water is introduced from below the soil, is supplied until the water level reaches the surface of the soil, and then is allowed to drain. This method of irrigation has been used commercially, but it is less adaptable than other means and for that reason has not been widely adopted.

Subirrigation was used successfully with gravel culture and was a good means of applying water to this well-aerated soil, but it has been discontinued because of the difficulty in establishing workable methods for disinfestation of bench, tank, and plumbing. In some areas gravel culture is used to an extent but with frequent irrigations applied to the top surface and water wasted rather than retained.

Capillary Irrigation Irrigation by capillarity is practiced with some of the container or potted crops. The biggest advantage with this method of irrigation is with the crops in smaller pots. With this method it is necessary to establish contact between the soil in the pot and the fibers or elements of the porous base on which the pots are set. The water that is applied to the porous base can move by capillarity to the soil and then by capillarity within the soil. There probably are, however, very few installations in which the movement of water is entirely by capillarity. Many of the irrigation systems that are referred to as capillary irrigation are in fact a type of subirrigation. The soil in the pot is in contact with the water table; thus, the capillary movement of water is only within the pot, from the water-saturated soil at the base upward. It seems apparent that an entirely capillary system of irrigation would require a relatively deep, porous layer so that the water table could be maintained some distance below the bottom of the pot.

Effects of Air-Moisture Relationships It is possible that soils of widely divergent air-moisture characteristics can be used successfully, but the greenhouse operator would need to determine the quantity of water to apply each time and the frequency with which the application should be made. However, it is considerably easier to manage irrigation correctly with soils that are coarse and porous and drain promptly. Such soils can be irrigated frequently without seriously affecting aeration. Irrigation practices must be much more precise with fine-textured soils that drain slowly. Clay soils have the reputation for poor drainage, but other soil types can have very poor drainage also because of the fine texture of the particles. These could be fine-textured sands, silts, mucks, and finely ground peats.

Figure 4-24 The effects of too frequent irrigation, too heavy soil, or too much fertilizer on pot mums. Plants on the left with good root growth develop normally, but the plants on the right were in unfavorable conditions for root growth, causing shorter stems, smaller leaves, fewer stems, and slower flower-bud development. *(Yoder Bros., Inc. photograph.)*

The air-moisture relationship in propagation soils is critical. These soils need to drain rapidly and thoroughly. The propagation soil needs to be watered well after the cuttings are stuck, but further irrigation may not be required. In addition, the intermittent mist should be regulated so that the leaves are moistened continuously without run-off to the soil.

Roots that develop in a too wet (insufficient air) environment typically are small in diameter, long, and not branched. With some kinds of plants in soils that are continuously wet, root growth may cease. When this occurs the top growth of the plant will have symptoms that indicate lack of water and deficiency of some of the required mineral nutrients in the plant. The stem growth is short and small in diameter, leaves and flowers are small, and pigments are lacking. Frequently the terminal leaves will be chlorotic and there might be symptoms of other mineral deficiencies. These shortages within the plant cannot be corrected until root growth is established again, and this can be done only by correcting the air-water relationship in the soil.

The root systems of plants grown in soils that are too dry may be extensive and well-branched and the roots may be of large diameter. Typically the stems are short and of small diameter and leaves and flowers are small and lacking in pigments. In this situation the remedy is a reevaluation of the irrigation program so that there will be sufficient water available in the soil for the plant needs. Results from the correction in water application should be evident in the new top growth in a short time because there is an established root system for handling the new supply of water and minerals.

Soil Mineral Nutrients

Naturally derived soils are variable and very complex materials. Because of this, much of the information about the mineral nutrition of plants was developed in work with other than naturally derived soils—either water or sand soils. This allowed the researchers to provide all of the basic soil environmental factors but to be able to control the variables and evaluate their effects on plant growth and development. One of the points established was that, with a possible minor exception, the mineral nutrients are in solution at the time that they enter the plant roots.

Mineral Nutrient Characteristics There are some variations in the mineral nutrients needed by plants, but it generally is understood that the following minerals can be involved in metabolic processes that occur in plants: nitrogen, phosphorus, potassium, calcium, magnesium, sulfur, boron, iron, manganese, copper, zinc, molybdenum, chlorine, and aluminum. Some of these minerals are present in all plants and their roles are well established. Other minerals may appear to be essential for some specific plants, and for this reason the lists of essential mineral nutrients vary. The relative quantities of mineral nutrients absorbed by plants are quite different, and on this basis some classifications are made of macrometabolic elements or major elements and micrometabolic elements or minor elements, but such groupings serve little purpose.

Although reference is made here only to mineral nutrients, the minerals absorbed by plants that become involved in metabolism, it does need to be acknowledged that other minerals and solutes may be absorbed into plants with no apparent involvement in plant growth and development and for that reason little or no mention is made of them. Also, although the mineral nutrients are referred to by the name of the element, they are present in the soil as a chemical compound and in the soil solution the compound dissociates to the ionic state—positively charged cations and negatively charged anions.

One of the common chemical compounds referred to as a nitrogen nutrient is ammonium nitrate (NH_4NO_3). In solution it dissociates to the positively charged cation NH_4^+ and the negatively charged anion NO_3^-, and it is the cations and anions individually that are absorbed into the root rather than the compound as such. Cations, because of their positive charge, are attracted to negatively charged particles, and anions, because of their negative charge, are attracted to positively charged particles.

Some absorption of ions into root cells occurs on a passive, diffusion basis in which the direction of movement is based on the concentration of those ions in the cell compared to their concentration in the soil solution. There is, however, an effect of temperature here (the rate of diffusion is faster in warmer temperatures); thus in warmer temperatures there is a greater uptake of mineral nutrients by plants. There also is an active form of mineral nutrient absorption that can take place, and the energy for this process derives from respiration. The rate of active absorption then depends quite largely on soil aeration because of the need for a supply of oxygen to support respiration in the root cells.

Some minerals may be insoluble in some soil solutions, or even in solutions inside the plant, but are soluble in a chelated form. There are some naturally occurring chelating agents that can solve the solubility problem of these minerals when they are present, but in situations in which some minerals frequently are insoluble they may be supplied to the soil in the chelated form. Iron is the most common example of a mineral nutrient that becomes unavailable because of insolubility.

Based on their properties, chemical compounds may be classified as acids, bases, or salts. Reference was just made to a chemical compound which is classified as a salt, ammonium nitrate (NH_4NO_3). Ammonium nitrate can be formed from the base, ammonium hydroxide (NH_4OH), and the acid, nitric acid (HNO_3). The by-product of this chemical reaction is water (H_2O). In this instance the salt is used commonly as a fertilizer in supplying nitrogen nutrients either as a cation (NH_4^+) or as the anion (NO_3^-). Theoretically the acid and base parents of ammonium nitrate could be used as fertilizers but neither of them is used in the greenhouse because of difficulty in handling and dispensing them safely. The gaseous form of ammonia (NH_3) is used as a nitrogen fertilizer for some field crops.

pH The distinguishing features of acids and bases are that when they are dissolved in water the acids form hydrogen ions (H^+) and the bases form hydroxyl ions (OH^-), and the relative concentration of these ions in the soil solution can have effects on chemical, physical, and physiological reactions. The hydrogen ion concentration (acidity) of a solution can be identified in terms of pH. The hydroxyl ion concentration (basicity) of a solution could be identified in terms of pOH, but is not, because if one is determined the other is known.

A pH value of zero (pH 0) represents the highest concentration of hydrogen ions (greatest acidity); if the report were in terms of pOH it would be pOH 14, which is the lowest concentration of hydroxyl ions (lowest basicity). When the concentrations of hydrogen and hydroxyl ions are equal, the solution is considered neutral and pH and pOH are both reported as 7. At the other end of the scale, pH 14 represents a solution of lowest concentration of hydrogen ions (and consequently the greatest concentration of hydroxyl ions), and it is called a highly basic or alkaline solution. Plant growth and development is affected by pH of the soil solution and the pH of the plant solution. The general suitable range for greenhouse plants is considered to be pH 6.0 to 6.8, but with some greenhouse plants, such as azalea, depending on other soil characteristics, the pH of the soil solution needs to be in the vicinity of pH 4.0 to 6.0. For each 1 unit of the pH scale there is a difference of 10 times in the concentration of hydrogen ions. The concentration of hydrogen ions then is 100 times greater at pH 4 than it is at pH 6.

The availability of hydrogen ions in soil or plant solutions also is dependent on the presence of other ions in the solution and on the physical effects of colloids. The carbonate ions (CO_3^{2-}) can effectively remove hydrogen ions (H^+) from the soil solution and thus raise the pH. The carbonate fertilizers used for this purpose usually are either calcium (limestone) or magnesium and calcium (dolomite). The sulfate ions (SO_4^{2-}) can cause an increase in hydrogen ions in the soil solution and thus lower the pH. The sulfate fertilizers used for this purpose usually are either ferrous or aluminum sulfates. For these reasons the choice of fertilizer to be used on a soil is based in part on the potential effect that it will have on the pH of the soil solution.

The presence of colloids in the soil depends on the amounts of clay and organic matter in the soil. An increase in the amounts of colloids can be expected with increases in the amounts of either clay or organic matter in the soil, and the effects that the colloidal systems have on the concentration of hydrogen and hydroxyl ions is known as buffer action. The colloidal systems are complex, but in general when they are present there is less change in pH, or the rate of change of pH is less for any given situation. Practically, this means that in the greenhouse soils that are largely mineral (sand or gravel) considerable change in pH is made rapidly with relatively little amounts of corrective material, but if the soils are clay or organic there may be little change in pH with relatively large additions of corrective material.

As stated previously, plant growth and development is the result of all the factors involved—not just the one under consideration at the moment. In spite of this, there is a need for considering factors individually with the purpose of putting them in proper perspective with possible effects of other factors. Some effects of mineral nutrient deficiencies and excesses follow.

Nitrogen When nitrogen is deficient in the soil, the entire plant may be lighter green in color, with the effect most visible in the older leaves. These leaves may eventually turn yellow, then dry and turn brown, but remain attached to the stem. With some plants, red pigmentation occurs in the older leaves.

The upper leaves may be smaller and borne rather stiffly in a somewhat upright position on the stem when nitrogen is deficient. Usually fewer shoots develop and they are shorter, stiffer, and of smaller diameter. The flowers may be smaller and have a reduced amount of pigmentation; however, flowers may develop more rapidly.

With excessive amounts of nitrogen, flowering can be delayed and the vegetative growth may be very succulent, with large, dark-green leaves and longer stems. Stems and leaves may be easily broken, and with some kinds of plants stem tissues may rupture, causing splitting of the stem. Flower stems may not support the flower erectly, and flower petals and florets may droop somewhat rather than remaining erect. Pigmentation in flowers usually is more intense.

Nitrogen fertilizers need to be added to greenhouse soils on a regular, continuing basis, and it is possible that either extreme deficiency or excess may develop depending on how carefully the program is developed and carried out. Typically, root growth is somewhat normal even when there is a serious shortage of nitrogen; however, excessive nitrogen may cause damage to roots and a complete cessation of root growth until the situation is corrected. When this occurs no minerals or water can be absorbed into the plant, and the growth of the above-ground portions of the plant is characteristic of the combined effects of shortages of those factors. A common symptom with many plants is chlorosis of the terminal leaves.

Plants need some nitrogen at all times in order to synthesize the proteins of which they are constructed. Because of the relatively large amount of growth produced during vegetative growth, more nitrogen is required at this time than during reproductive growth. A most critical time for nitrogen supply is in the early stages of vegetative growth. The problem is to supply enough nitrogen to promote active vegetative growth, but not so much that root development is impaired. Either extreme is bad, causing the development of mature tissues rather than meristems and resulting in reduced growth. Even if the nitrogen deficiency is later corrected, the effects on plant growth will affect the quality of the finished crop. Normally no nitrogen is supplied in propagation soils. This may be satisfactory for the usual short term that is required for propagation, but when this deficiency is maintained a bit longer the growth in the seedling or rooted cutting will be irretrievably impaired.

Phosphorus It is not likely that phosphorus deficiency will develop in greenhouse soils that incorporate field soils. Phosphorus leaches slowly from such soils, and the initial application of superphosphate at the time of mixing the soil probably will suffice. Some manufactured soils, however, may need regular additions of phosphorus. In some plants a symptom of phosphorus deficiency is purple pigmentation of the underside of the leaf petiole and the veins.

Phosphorus forms insoluble compounds with calcium, magnesium, iron, aluminum, and some other elements, and it is believed that an excess of phosphorus may cause the unavailability of some of the other minerals essential to plants. It may cause iron deficiency in azalea and some foliage plants and aluminum deficiency in hydrangea.

Figure 4-25 Leaf symptoms of potassium deficiency in chrysanthemum. Interveinal speckling is followed by desiccation and death of the marginal tissue.

Potassium In spite of the relatively large quantities of potassium absorbed in plants, apparently it does not become chemically combined with building materials in the plant. It seems to be involved entirely as a regulator of processes or as a catalyst. It translocates readily within plants from older to newer portions, and the typical deficiency symptom is a marginal chlorosis of lower leaves followed by interveinal chlorosis. The affected areas may die and turn brown, and the leaves may resemble to some extent leaves damaged by some pathogens or pests.

There does not seem to be a plant growth problem from excess potassium.

Calcium Calcium deficiency may cause malformation or lack of growth in the terminal meristems, producing short, blunt roots and shortened stem tips. This may be produced by a lack of calcium in the soil or because the calcium is unavailable in acidic soils.

Excess calcium may cause boron deficiency.

Alkalinity of the soil resulting from excess calcium may produce some typical iron chlorosis symptoms at the terminal tips of some plants.

Iron Iron is needed for the synthesis of chlorophylls in the cells of green plants, and the typical deficiency symptom is interveinal chlorosis of terminal leaves. The lower leaves remain green which implies that iron does not translocate from older to newer tissues. A deficiency of iron in the plant cells may be caused by an actual lack of iron, or it may be caused by the unavailability of the iron that is present in the soil or in the plant. The ferrous (Fe^{2+}) form of iron is the available form and the ferric (Fe^{3+}) form generally is not available.

Figure 4-26 Typical leaf symptoms of potassium deficiency in poinsettia.

Figure 4-27 Leaf symptom in rose of deficiency of available iron. This symptom may result from poor root growth for various reasons: unfavorable pH, excesses of other minerals, or an actual lack of iron.

There are no known problems from excess amounts of iron in the soil. It has been reported that apparent iron oxide spots appear on hydrangea leaves when there is excess iron available at pH 5.0 or lower.

Magnesium   Magnesium is a mineral constituent of chlorophylls, and its deficiency is indicated by the interveinal chlorosis of the lower leaves. Magnesium translocates readily from the older to newer portions of the plant. Deficiency is not common but can be prevented with use of dolomite or dolomitic limestone in the soil mixture or corrected by an application of Epsom salts ($MgSO_4$) later.

There have been no reports of effects on plants of excess quantities of magnesium in the soil.

Boron   A deficiency of boron is indicated by various growth malformations in the terminal tip including stunted terminal growth, chlorosis of leaves, and death of terminal buds and shoots. Greenhouse plants involved have been rose and carnation. Boron deficiency may be accompanied by excess calcium.

The effects of boron deficiency are very obvious and damaging, but the amount of boron involved is small. It is easy to add too much boron to the soil and get damaging effects from the excess. In rose, excess boron causes black leaf margins followed by a yellowing of the entire leaf and dropping.

Manganese   Manganese deficiency causes interveinal chlorosis first in leaves at the terminal tip and possibly progressing to lower leaves. This is in contrast to the display of chlorosis, resulting from magnesium deficiency, which appears in lower leaves.

Manganese toxicity may occur in very acidic soils or in soils that have been steamed too long.

Sulfur The sulfur deficiency symptoms are quite similar to those for nitrogen deficiency with the exception that the reduced amount of pigmentation is uniform over the entire plant. Although sulfur deficiency has not been considered a problem in the past, it might become more common in the future because of decreased use of sulfate fertilizers and increased use of manufactured soils.

Aluminum Aluminum is present in most soils, but it may be in unavailable form because of high pH or the presence of calcium and phosphorus compounds in the soil.

Aluminum affects pigment formation in some plants but other effects have not been reported. With aluminum available in hydrangea the flowers are blue, and with no aluminum the flowers are pink.

Copper Copper deficiency is not common but has been reported in rose plants in the greenhouse. In field crops, deficiencies have been reported mainly in crops on peat or muck soils. Deficiency symptoms appear in stem tips, possibly as chlorosis, stunting, or malformation.

Zinc Zinc deficiency has been reported in some field crops primarily on calcareous soils or on those that have an excessive amount of phosphorus. Zinc deficiency symptoms include chlorosis of young leaves and a great reduction in rate of shoot growth. Very small quantities of zinc are required and relatively small quantities are toxic to plants.

Molybdenum Molybdenum is required in very small quantities, but there are instances of deficiency with some field crops. Molybdenum deficiency has also been reported with poinsettia in the greenhouse. The symptoms may be chlorosis of tip leaves followed by marginal browning and upward curvature of the leaf.

Chlorine The role of chlorine in plant nutrition has not been determined, but the effects of deficiencies and excesses have been demonstrated in some field crops. It is possible that chlorine is an essential nutrient for greenhouse plants also.

Sometimes the mineral nutrients are classified as major elements (macronutrients) and minor elements (micronutrients) based on the relative amounts that are used in plants. Classifications vary with the individuals involved, but nitrogen, phosphorus, and potassium always are classed as major elements, and calcium, magnesium, and sulfur usually are included. It might be proper to include iron with the major elements because in comparison with the other nutrients usually classed as minor elements it can be used in considerably higher quantities. With boron, manganese, copper, zinc, aluminum, and molybdenum very small quantities spell the difference between deficiency and excess.

Fertilizers

Most of the 14 minerals named earlier as being essential nutrients for plant growth are present or have been present in naturally derived soils. The source of supply for the minerals (with the exception of nitrogen) is the parent material (rocks). As the rocks weather the various minerals become available. The source of supply of nitrogen is organic matter. As the plant and animal material in the naturally derived soil decay, nitrogen becomes available. If it is determined that any mineral is deficient in the soil, it is supplied to the soil in fertilizers that contain that ingredient. With most soils, nitrogen becomes deficient and must be replaced regularly.

pH Adjustment and Fertilizer Additions Before Planting The fertilizers that might be added to the soil at the time of mixing are those that adjust the pH and those that supply calcium, phosphorus, and possibly magnesium. If the soil is too acidic, usually finely ground limestone, dolomite, or dolomitic limestone is used. In addition to making the soil more alkaline, calcium is added to the soil, and when dolomite or dolomitic limestone is used magnesium also is supplied. If no adjustment is needed in pH, gypsum ($CaSO_4$) is used for a source of calcium and incidentally also supplies sulfur. When soils are too alkaline, ferrous sulfate may be added to the soil mixture. In addition to making the soil more acidic, iron and sulfur are added to the soil.

When soils are deficient in phosphorus, treble superphosphate is the main source of phosphorus. This is monocalcium phosphate. The mineral in addition to phosphorus supplied to the soil by superphosphate is calcium, an essential nutrient.

Fertilizer Applications After Planting If the soil is properly prepared for planting, there is a sufficient amount of mineral nutrients in the soil for the initial good growth of the plant. Some of the mineral supply in the soil, however, is depleted by absorption into the plant and by leaching during irrigation, and periodic applications of fertilizer are required to maintain the supply of mineral nutrients in the soil. These fertilizer applications are made to the soil surface, and the fertilizer may be applied in dry form or dissolved in water.

It is much easier to make the fertilizer application in liquid form, and most greenhouse operators have equipment for the injection of fertilizer concentrate into the irrigation water. In this way, fertilizer can be added each time the soil is irrigated. With many crops the routine fertilizer injection program uses only fertilizers containing nitrogen and potassium because those are the mineral nutrients that commonly are depleted.

When observation of the plant, soil analysis, or plant analysis indicate that other minerals should be supplied or that adjustment of pH should be made, those additional materials are added to the fertilizer concentrate.

The Soil Pests

Frequently the assumption is made that all of the pests in the greenhouse are insects. This is probably because of size and habit relationships. Many of the above-ground pests are insects, but of the pests that work on the below-ground portions of the plant there are only two or three that are insects and the others are various other animals. The insects are bulb or root aphids, fungus gnat, and garden springtail, and most of the other greenhouse soil pests are other types of animals.

The tulip bulb or iris root aphid *(Dysaphis tulipae)* is about 0.3 centimeter long. It is light green to dark green in color and covered by a white, powdery, waxlike material. It is particularly injurious to bulbs in storage. Feeding by sucking in the meristematic tissues of the bulb can cause distortions and crippling of the various structures as the plant develops.

Fungus gnat *(Bradysia* species and *Sciara* species) larvae are about 0.6 centimeter long with a white or colorless body and a shiny black head. They feed on fungi and decaying matter in the soil as well as burrowing into roots, bulbs, and stems. The adult gnat is about 0.3 centimeter long and brownish-black in color and usually is observed in swarms. The life of the adult is about 10 days and in that time it may lay 300 eggs in the cracks or crevices of moist soil. The larva hatches in about 1 week and then may feed for 2 weeks before changing to the pupal stage. The life cycle is about 1 month.

Partial control of the fungus gnat can be achieved by proper drainage and sanitation practices that will eliminate breeding grounds. Chemical control may be used for the adult above ground or the larva in the soil.

The garden springtail *(Bourletiella hortensis)* is about 0.5 centimeter long and frequently can be seen making its characteristic spring from the surface of the soil during irrigation. This particular species feeds on plant tissues, but many of the other species are scavengers.

Bulb mite *(Rhizoglyphus echinopus)* is an arachnid that is about 0.1 centimeter long and yellow-brown in color. Infested bulbs have reddish-brown color on the fleshy scales followed by general rotting of the bulb either before or after planting. When rotting does not occur the plant that develops from the bulb may be stunted and distorted because of the feeding by sucking of the mite in the meristematic tissues of the bulb.

The garden symphylan *(Scutigerella immaculata)*, also called symphlid, somewhat resembles a small version of a centipede or millipede but it is in a different classification. Springtails are mistakenly identified as symphylans, but the symphylans scurry rather than jump and are not observed on the soil surface. They are about 0.6 centimeter long and white, and they can be seen scurrying for cover when moist soil is separated. They eat newly formed roots, and this damage to the tissues may be followed by disease. When ground beds of soil are steamed, symphylans may retreat further into the soil and then return as the soil cools.

Pillbugs *(Armadillidium vulgare)* and sowbugs *(Porcellio laevis)* have somewhat similar appearances but can be distinguished by their different defensive action. The pillbug rolls into a ball when disturbed and the sowbug retreats. They are scavengers and may also feed on plant structures. They are crustaceans, related to crabs, scrimp, and lobster. Proper sanitation practices and elimination of moist breeding and hiding places can control these pests.

Nematodes are very tiny roundworms, and because of their small size work with and study of them is often placed in plant pathology rather than in entomology. Several kinds of nematodes may inhabit the soil, and some of these feed on plants and become very destructive. Nematodes have been more of a problem on rose plants than other crops, probably because this crop is started from plants grown outdoors and then continuously cropped in the greenhouse for 4 years or more. If there is a chance infestation in the plants when they are received, there is abundant time for an increase in nematode population in the greenhouse.

Their feeding activities on or in the roots can severely limit the absorption of water and mineral nutrients by the plant, with the result that the upper portions of the plant have symptoms typical of water and mineral deficiencies in the soil.

The root-knot nematode causes gall formations in the roots, and this characteristic makes it rather easy to identify its presence. Other types of nematodes can produce as much damage to plant growth, but the damage to the root is not as evident or as identifiable.

Usually the solution to nematode problems requires the assistance of a

Figure 4-28 The results of a root-knot nematode infestation on gardenia roots. Because of the extensive damage to the root system, the absorption of water and minerals will not be adequate for good growth of the plant. The visible effects on the roots of infestations of other types of nematodes may be less spectacular, but the damage may be as real.

specialist. Some chemicals are available for treating chance infestations that occur following planting.

The Soil Pathogens

Some soil-borne pathogens invade and remain localized in underground portions of the plant and possibly basal stem structures *(Pythium, Rhizoctonia, Thielaviopsis, Cylindrocladium,* and *Phytopthora).* Depending on the rate of growth of the pathogen and the amount of plant tissue involved, the aerial portions of the plant show increasingly pronounced symptoms of water and mineral nutrient deficiencies.

It can be expected when the below-ground invasion of the roots is from one side rather than general, the symptoms above ground will appear first on that side of the plant. If the involvement of the roots and/or stem base is general and the growth of the pathogen is rapid, the appearance of symptoms in the aerial portions of the plant will be generally distributed and sudden.

Other soil-borne pathogens will spread to various protions of the plant after they invade underground portions *(Fusarium, Pseudomonas, Verticilliam,*' and *Xanthomonas)*. When the rate of growth of the pathogen is not rapid and only a small root area is invaded, a single branch or two directly above the infected root may show disease symptoms while the remainder of the plant appears to have normal growth. If the growth of the pathogen is rapid and the invasion of roots and/or stem base is general, death of the entire top portion of the plant might be immediate.

Frequently bacterial disease pathogens progress more rapidly than fungal disease pathogens.

Rhizoctonia stem and root rot *(Rhizoctonia solani* is the pathogen) has the reputation of being the most prevalent stem and root rot disease of greenhouse crop plants. Most plants can be host to this pathogen. Invasion occurs at the soil line or at the base of cuttings or through roots.

Rhizoctonia microorganisms invade succulent tissues much more readily than more mature ones. For this reason cuttings or seedlings that are planted too deeply are much more susceptible to this disease because that places the younger tissues at the soil surface level or below. Rhizoctonia stem rot can be prevented, too, if irrigation is handled in such a way that the soil surface dries as rapidly as possible and remains dry for a while before the next irrigation. It is very common to discover that the plants that die in a new planting either were planted 1 or 2 centimeters deeper than those not infected or were in the low spots that did not dry as rapidly as the higher spots of a soil surface that is not level. Once the disease starts it usually progresses until the entire stem is encircled at the soil level and the plant dies.

Pythium root and stem rot *(Pythium* species) with most plants probably starts with invasion of the roots by the fungus and then the disease may or may not spread to the base of the stem. Several greenhouse plants are known hosts of pythium microorganisms. In geranium it is called blackleg because of the characteristic shiny, black rotted area that results at the base of the stem. Some of the other plants that may be infected with pythium microorganisms are saintpaulia, begonia, chrysanthemum, Easter lily, peperomia, other foliage plants, and poinsettia. Using well-drained soils and spacing irrigations so that the soil dries somewhat between irrigations can help keep this pathogen in check.

Figure 4-29 Characteristic black stems from pythium stem rot (black leg) in geranium. *(Department of Plant Pathology, The Pennsylvania State University, University Park, Pennsylvania photograph.)*

The botrytis organism *(Botrytis cinerea)* probably is better known for producing diseases of aerial portions of plants such as botrytis blights, but it also gets involved with producing stem rots at or about the surface of the soil. It is a common cause of cutting and seedling rots in propagation benches and seed flats. Usually it can be controlled by careful regulation of temperature, air movement, and water so that the surface of the soil does not stay constantly moist.

Phytophthora parasitica is another fungus that attacks plants in the propagation areas. It can be controlled usually by the same means as suggested for the control of *Botrytis cinerea.*

Fusarium wilt of carnation caused by *Fusarium oxysporum* f. *dianthi* was a serious disease for this crop until it was determined that it could be eliminated by the establishment of disease-free propagative stock and thorough steaming of propagation and growing soil. The normal progress of the disease is the death of first one shoot, followed by another, until the entire plant is dead. This species of *Fusarium* attacks other greenhouse plants, and there are other *Fusarium* species that occasionally cause disease in mums, asters, stocks, and Easter lily in the greenhouse.

Verticillium wilt *(Verticillium albo-atrum)* in chrysanthemum produces a general wilting of the plant just before flowering, after which the leaves turn pale green and then brown and die but remain attached to the stem. The entire plant then dies before the flowers mature. This was a very common disease problem until culture indexing of stock was devised to assure disease-free propagative stock.

There is some incidence of verticillium wilt in rose plants. The symptoms are the leaves dropping from a shoot followed by die-back from the tip.

Other greenhouse plants that are subject to verticillium wilt are geranium, snapdragon, cineraria, and stocks.

Possibly the most serious disease of geranium is one caused by *Xanthomonas pelargoni* and called bacterial blight. It produces several different symptoms in the plant. When the stem is infected, the vascular tissues are brown or black, the surface color is dull gray, and some of the leaves wilt. Eventually all of the leaves drop except those at the tip and the stem turns black and shrivels into a dry rot. The roots usually are black but not decayed.

Bacterial blight of geranium may start in the leaf, and when it does the infection may produce either round spots or large angular ones. The first symptom is small, water-soaked spots on the underside of the leaf. The leaves eventually wilt, and they may drop from the plant or remain attached for a few weeks.

Prevention of bacterial blight is possible only if the pathogen is eliminated from the propagative stock as well as from the propagation and growing areas.

In addition to tissue culture, culture indexing, soil steaming, and careful regulation of temperature, air, and moisture, some chemicals need to be used for the control of pathogens in the greenhouse. Their use should be in addition to rather than instead of the other controls. Listings of control chemicals and their methods of use cannot be kept current in a publication of this type. The best sources of information for recommended agricultural chemicals to be used in the greenhouse should be state extension services, university personnel, and state flower-grower organizations.

Weed Control with Greenhouse Crops

Weeds need to be controlled in the greenhouse, and generally they are eliminated in the crop soils by the steaming done in preparing the soil for planting. With some of the long-term crops such as rose and carnation, however, weeds do get started, and they can become a real problem. Because of the limited market for herbicides with floriculture crops, it is not likely that herbicides will be registered for use with these crops. Some materials have been used with some success on an experimental basis, but it is very hazardous to use herbicides on crop soils unless they have been tested and registered.

Lightweight, black polyethylene film is used to control weeds in some agricultural crops outdoors. It can also be used to good advantage with the greenhouse crops grown outdoors, and possibly more use of it should be made with some crops indoors.

When black polyethylene film is used for cut-flower crops outdoors, the soil is prepared for planting, the area is covered with the film, and the planting is done through the film. With pot-plant or other container crops grown on the ground, either outdoors or indoors, after the ground is leveled the area is covered with the film.

With either cut-flower or pot-plant crops, the film needs to be punctured at intervals so that water may pass through it.

Herbicide-Treated Field Soils Used in the Greenhouse The best statement here is that herbicide-treated field soils should not be used in the greenhouse. Before field soils are brought into the greenhouse it must definitely be established that they have not had herbicides used on them or, if they have, that enough time has elapsed to guarantee that they have dissipated. There are many different kinds of herbicides used on field crops. Before they are registered for use on a crop it is established that the weeds in question will be controlled but there will be no harmful effects on the crop plant. Materials that might be used successfully on soybeans or corn might kill or seriously damage greenhouse crop plants.

Herbicides are used so widely on field soils that it should be assumed that the soils have been treated unless it can be learned that no herbicide has been used.

The Use of Herbicides in Greenhouse Noncrop Areas The greenhouse grower definitely needs help in controlling weeds in the walks, under benches, and in some areas adjacent to the greenhouse. It does not seem likely that herbicides will be registered for this purpose because of the limited market. In the event that the grower finds some basis for approval of the use of herbicides in noncrop areas in the greenhouse, a review of some of the characteristics of herbicides could be helpful.

Herbicides can be classed in three categories by their effects on plant growth: those that prevent the germination or growth or plants from seed (yes, weeds are plants), those that destroy the aerial portions of plants on contact but do not translocate to below-ground portions of the plant, and those that may be absorbed by either the roots or the upper portions of the plant and then translocate to all portions of the plant and destroy it entirely.

Herbicides also may be classed by their method or rate of movement in the environment. Before using herbicides in noncrop areas in the greenhouse, information is needed on their water solubility, volatilization characteristics, and degradation characteristics. The water-soluble herbicides could be expected to contaminate crop-soil areas adjacent to the noncrop area treated, or they might contaminate the irrigation water if surface water is collected for this purpose. When ponds are the source of irrigation water, it must be determined if the watershed for the pond includes field lands treated with herbicides.

Herbicides that volatilize must not be used in or around the greenhouse because of the damage that they can do to adjacent crop plants.

Some of the herbicides degrade to inocuous materials upon contact with soil, and these may possibly be used in areas that later will be used for crop plants.

EFFECTS OF HUMAN BEINGS IN THE PLANT ENVIRONMENT

Plants in natural conditions may flourish or die depending on the suitability of the natural environment—the weather, other plants, pests and other animals, and other possible conditions. The plant itself really cannot do anything about it. It cannot change the environment to suit it nor can it move from one environment to another (with some possible exception of seeds being transported and happening into another environment). Plants have unique and marvelous manufacturing and synthesizing facilities, but they cannot seek and find the necessary raw material. They are dependent on those materials being supplied to them.

When greenhouse operators go into business they do it with the understanding that they will provide the conditions needed by the plants and they want to commit themselves to the task. They become the most important factor in the plants' environment and, depending on how they take care of their "ings," the plants may flourish or die. Some of the "ings" that growers add to the plant environment are knowing, thinking, planning, organizing, providing, and timing.

Cut-Flower Crop Production

5

In most of the plants that are used for cut-flower production, the flowers are borne terminally. With some kinds of plants, the plants are discarded after the one crop of flowers is cut. This is the usual procedure with chrysanthemum, bulb crops, and snapdragons.

With plants such as carnation, cattleya, and rose, the plants are continued in growth. The new shoots, which develop below the place where the flower stem was cut, eventually form flowers that are cut, and the procedure is repeated until it is determined that there would be economic advantage in replacing the plants. Several crops of flowers are cut from the plants. Carnation plants are replaced every year or every other year. Rose plants are replaced about every 4 years, and cattleya plants may not be replaced for several years.

The only kinds of plants used for cut-flower production that have lateral flowers are calla, stephanotis, and cymbidium. In the greenhouse the calla plant could be kept in continuous growth and continuous flowering, but usually irrigation is discontinued in midsummer. After the leaves dry and die, the rhizomes are dug, divided, replanted, and started back in growth. The cymbidium has a season of flowering each year, and the same plants are maintained in growth for a few years. When the plants are too large for the container, offsets are used for propagation of new plants.

OUTDOOR CROPS IN MILD CLIMATES

Quite a large variety of cut-flower crops is grown outdoors in the United States when the climate is favorable. This book is limited mainly to the production of crops in the greenhouse, but some of the outdoor cut-flower crop production does need to be mentioned. Some crops are produced outdoors in the north during the summer. This may be done by individuals who specialize only in single crops such as gladiolus or delphinium, or by greenhouse operators who grow some crops outdoors at that time of the year in addition to their indoor crops. Mums are grown outdoors as a summer crop quite frequently. Other crops might be delphinium, gladiolus, centaurea, celosia, and gypsophila.

Some of the crops that can be produced in California are marguerite, majestic, and killion daisies, and statice year-round; stocks April through June; strelitzia fall through spring; yarrow, agapanthus, and gypsophila during the summer; sweet william, candytuft, and sweet pea during the summer; and aster and chrysanthemum spring through fall.

Stock crops are flowered for several weeks during the winter in Arizona.

The Florida cut-flower production is primarily from fall through spring, and the main crops are gladiolus, chrysanthemum, statice, and gypsophila.

LAND FOR CUT-FLOWER PRODUCTION

There are several considerations in choosing the site for the cut-flower greenhouse. Most cut-flower crops require high light intensity for best growth, and for this reason the light potential for the winter needs to be evaluated.

The distance between production site and market will have effects on shipping methods, shipping costs, and the quality of the product. Cut flowers need temperature-protected conveyance and a shipping time as short as possible—1 day might be satisfactory and 3 days disastrous.

An essentially level piece of land is better for construction and for transportation. Time and expense are saved. Also, if outdoor crops are to be produced, the land may be worked without much preliminary leveling.

Is the soil suitable for flower-crop production? This may be of somewhat minor importance if the crops are going to be bench grown and there is a source of soil in the vicinity. The site has more adaptability, however, if the soil can be used with some adjustment for either greenhouse or outdoor crops. Although cut-flower soils in the greenhouse are steamed and reused, some replenishment of soil will be needed. It will be most useful if that soil is available right on the property.

STRUCTURES FOR CUT-FLOWER CROPS

Cut-flower crops need more head room than pot-plant crops. Two-meter sidewalls may be high enough for some crops, but roses and possibly some other crops will need about 3-meter sidewalls.

There are advantages in having crop-size houses so that the environment can be regulated for the specific crop. This may mean houses that are either the right size for different kinds of plants that will be grown or the right size for the same kind of plants that will be forced for different marketing times.

It is possible to grow cut-flower crops in ground beds, but usually benches that are isolated from the ground can be worked more effectively. They may be benches that are in or on the ground but completely sealed so that there is no contact between soil in the ground and soil in the bench or they may be benches raised above the soil level; however, they should only be raised the minimum amount so that the mature crop does not get above efficient working height.

Convenient working widths for cut-flower benches are from 105 to 120 centimeters.

The bench length should be based either on crop size or on efficiency in harvesting the cut flowers. Frequently a convenient length is about 30 meters. There are some advantages in this length, too, when installing water-distribution systems for irrigation.

Walk widths between benches need to be at least 45 centimeters, and those walks need to abut on a wider walk so that wheeled vehicles can be used in them.

Flowers need to be graded after they are cut, followed by a short period of cool storage before marketing. The grading room and cool storage must have good access from all of the greenhouses. Depending on marketing arrangements, the cut flowers may be brought to market in vases directly from the storage, or they may need to be packed for shipping. A packing area should be adjacent to the cool storage.

If daffodil is one of the cut-flower crops, either an outdoor area or cool storage space will be needed for vernalization treatment during the fall.

If chrysanthemum is grown and the rooted cuttings are not obtained from a specialist, a propagation area will be required for this crop.

Snapdragon, aster, and several of the miscellaneous crops are propagated from seed. A propagation area would be needed for them also. Some of these crops are planted directly from the seed flats to the bench where they will be grown, but others are planted in flats or pots before being planted in the bench. A soil supply and potting area would be needed for this purpose.

SOIL PREPARATION FOR CUT-FLOWER CROPS

If crops are to be planted directly in the ground, the first concern is water drainage—surface drainage and drainage through the soil. The surface of the beds needs to be level so that there is very little lateral flow of water at the surface. The area around the beds can be pitched so that excess water will flow away. This is particularly important with outdoor beds so that the water from heavy rains will flow away from the beds.

To ensure water drainage through the soil in ground beds, drainage tile must be placed in the ground below the beds. This is necessary either indoors or outdoors. The 8-centimeter drainage lines should be about 40 centimeters deep and 45 centimeters apart. There must be a fall of at least 3 centimeters per 30 meters in these drainage lines, and they must have free access to an open ditch or to a larger drain line that drains freely.

When cut-flower crops are grown in benches, the soil should be at least 15 centimeters deep. Shallower soils drain more slowly. In order to have the same rate of water drainage, bench soils need to be more coarse and porous than bed soils.

The bench bottoms must be sturdy enough so that they remain level, and they must be adequately supported so that drainage water can flow through the bench bottom uniformly and freely. Each time before planting it must be determined that the bench bottom is in good condition.

Ground beds need to be steam-treated between crops for the same reasons that any greenhouse soils are steamed. It might be even more important to steam ground beds because this soil is not isolated from adjacent soil that may be a source of contamination. It will always be more costly to steam ground beds because walks as well as beds must be treated, and a greater depth of soil must be treated also. Usually the best distribution of steam in ground beds is obtained when the steam is introduced through the drainage lines; however, this must be planned before the drainage system is installed so that materials are used that will withstand steam temperatures. With this method of steaming, the soil is not covered until the air is expelled from the soil by the steam. This time will be indicated by steam starting to emerge from the soil surface.

If the cut-flower crop bench bottom is in good condition for water drainage, it also will vent the air from the soil satisfactorily as the soil is being steamed. The soil must be completely tilled before steaming so that when steaming is completed only minimum handling of the soil is required before planting. The soil surface does need to be level so that the downward flow of irrigation water will be uniform throughout the soil area.

Methods for Maintaining Good Rates of Water Drainage in Soil

Cut-flower crop soils are used for long periods. The crop time not only is rather long—several months to a few years—but in most instances the soil is used for succeeding crops. Some adjustments may be made to the soil, it is steamed, and the new planting is made. The cut-flower grower needs to properly consider soil as a permanent facility and then base current handling procedures on the long-term effects.

This is an entirely different sort of soil situation from the one encountered with pot-plant crops. The use of pot-plant soils is finite, and the mixes that might be appropriate for them would be much too temporary for use with cut-flower crops.

The water drainage characteristics of soils can be improved by additions of various kinds of organic matter. If the organic matter is fibrous or coarse, it provides physical separation among soil particles, additional channels for water drainage through the soil, and increased aeration. As the organic matter decomposes in the soil, the products formed ultimately are salts and gases, but some of the transition products of decomposition are colloidal materials that may promote aggregation of soil particles and improved aeration. Generally the addition of organic matter periodically to cut-flower soils is good practice. However, the effects are somewhat temporary due to the rapid decomposition of some organic matter in the warm and moist conditions of the greenhouse. Organic matter can be expected to maintain good drainage in greenhouse soils for a period of 3 months, but its effectiveness after that time might be suspect. Some of the better organic

Figure 5-1 Adding straw to greenhouse soils and hand spading are good methods for maintaining coarse, porous soils. *(Yoder Bros., Inc. photograph.)*

materials for use in cut-flower soils are straw, fibrous peat, and peanut hulls.

For long-term crops such as carnation (1 or 2 years) and rose (4 years), it is better to consider the use of coarse mineral soils instead of the addition of organic matter to silt or clay soils. This assures good drainage and aeration for the long terms involved. It requires more frequent irrigation and more attention to supplying some mineral nutrients regularly.

If coarse mineral soils cannot be used for these long-term crops, the next best route to follow is the addition of a coarse aggregate such as haydite or calcined clay. The particle size of these aggregates should be from 1 to 1.5 centimeters. Some additional aggregate can be added between crops in order to maintain good drainage.

Rose growers through the years have used organic mulches on their soils, and this procedure can be used in the future. However, there are some advantages in using coarse, mineral soils without mulch for rose crops, and this procedure should be compared with the traditional method of soil handling.

Fertilizer and pH Adjustment in Cut-Flower Soil Preparation

With most greenhouse soils, change in pH is gradual and in the same direction rather than sudden or variable. Determinations for pH should be made regularly, and corrective treatment can be scheduled on the basis of the trend that is indicated. It is much more satisfactory to make pH adjustments as the soil is being mixed rather than after planting. If the soil needs to be made more alkaline, finely ground agricultural limestone or dolomite is added at the rate of 2.5 kilograms per 9.3 square meters. When they can be obtained, either dolomite or dolomitic limestone should be used rather than regular limestone because they will add magnesium as well as calcium to the soil.

Neither calcium nor magnesium is present in the fertilizers that commonly are used for liquid application of fertilizer after planting, and for that reason they should be incorporated into the soil at time of preparing the soil for planting. If no addition of limestone is required, the calcium and magnesium should be supplied by adding 2.5 kilograms of gypsum and 0.5 kilogram of Epsom salts per 9.3 square meters at the time of soil preparation.

When the soil is too alkaline, the pH may be lowered by applying ferrous sulfate at the rate of 0.5 kilogram per 9.3 square meters.

Organic and Slow-Release Fertilizers

The original fertilizers that were used to supply nitrogen to the soil were plant or animal residues. Although they were used to supply nitrogen, they necessarily supplied all of the other minerals of which they were composed, and this, in fact, added most and probably all of the essential mineral nutrients. In addition, these organic fertilizers have some physical effects on the soil and subsequently on the plants. The colloids formed with the decomposition of the organic matter can improve the aggregation of the soil and promote better water drainage, and they also may increase the buffer action of the soil. This all makes a rather strong case for the use of organic fertilizers, but in spite of this their use has been replaced to a large extent by the application of chemical compounds (salts) that contain specific mineral nutrients in the amount required. Some of the disadvantages of using organic fertilizers are the large volume required, difficulty in handling, odors involved, lack of uniformity of product, and the high price per unit of mineral nutrient.

The organic fertilizers usually are incorporated into the soil before planting, and some that have been used are manures, dried blood, bone meal, cottonseed meal, tankage, sludge, and tobacco stems. In addition to these, some organic materials are added to soils for the announced purpose of improving water drainage through the soil, but they may have some effects on the colloid quantity and quality of the soil and consequent effects on buffering, the pH of the soil solution, and the mineral content of the soil. Some of these common soil additives are peat, chopped straw, corncobs, leaf mold, peanut hulls, shredded bark, and sawdust.

In some situations it is desirable to add fertilizers containing nitrogen, phosphorus, and potassium to the soil at the time of mixing. When soluble chemical compounds are used there is a potential problem of adding too much and causing some plant damage. There are some products on the market that provide for the slow release of the nutrients, and these generally are better to use for this purpose. Osmocote and Magamp are two slow-release fertilizers that may be incorporated into the soil when it is being prepared for planting. When Osmocote is used the planting must be done shortly after this fertilizer is incorporated. When Magamp is used the soil may be stored briefly before being used. It is possible to mix enough of these slow-release fertilizers into the soil to supply the nutrients needed for the duration of the crop, or lesser amounts may be used if some fertilizer is going to be applied regularly with irrigation.

Osmocote is available in several analyses and rates of solubility. The fertilizer granules are coated with a resin, and in moist conditions the soluble fertilizer diffuses slowly through the resin coating. There are Osmocote formulations that have controlled release of fertilizer for 3, 8, and 12 months. All of the formulations provide nitrogen, phosphorus, and potassium.

Magamp is sold in two grades. The medium granule provides some release of minerals for about 3 months, and the coarse granule is effective for about 12 months. Magamp is a chemical compound that dissolves slowly. It is not coated. Magamp provides nitrogen, phosphorus, potassium, and magnesium.

Tilling Methods for Cut-Flower Crop Soils

When the soil is being prepared for planting, the various ingredients to be added—organic matter, aggregates, fertilizers—are distributed evenly over the surface of the soil before tilling. The tilling method used should involve the entire soil mass and distribute the various ingredients uniformly throughout the mixture. Mechanical tillers usually are used, but they have some serious limitations. They must operate just short of drainage lines and bench bottoms, and this leaves an untouched layer at the bottom that eventually will interfere with water drainage. The other problem with mechanical tillers is that many of them pulverize the soils rather than just mixing them, with the result that soil drainage is impaired.

Until some mechanical device is devised that will do as good a job as the spade fork, that will remain the best tool for tilling from the standpoint of results; at least part of the job will need to be done with the spade fork. The objections to using the spade fork for tilling are that it requires a lot of time and that the operator may do a poor or a variable mixing job.

The results of this job, however, are of significant importance, so that the owner's or manager's time could be well spent in supervising the job and making sure that water drainage away from the soil is good and that all of the soil is uniformly mixed.

The soil surface will need to be leveled after steaming. Make sure that the tools that are used for this job are disinfested before use.

Soil Disinfestation

Some method of disinfestation is necessary to control insects, disease organisms, weed seeds, and other pests that are found in soil, leaf mold, and similar materials. Serious damage is experienced yearly from the depredations of pests, not to mention the labor expended in weeding soils that are not disinfested.

Soil may be disinfested by heat or chemicals. The equipment at hand, the area to be treated, and other factors govern the choice of method, but in any case disinfestation should be practiced to produce quality crops.

Steam　Steam is the most effective method of combating pests of all types in soil. For greenhouses not heated with steam, it is possible to purchase portable or stationary boilers to generate steam for disinfestation.

The inorganic and organic matter should be added, and if superphosphate is desired, it can be incorporated before steaming. The organic matter should be mixed uniformly either manually or with a tiller. A moderately moist soil is best, since either a very wet or a very dry soil heats slowly, and many objectionable organisms will not be killed in a soil that is very dry. If the soil is somewhat dry, the soil surface should be moistened slightly just prior to steaming. After the soil is steamed, crops may be planted as soon as the soil is cool.

About 900 grams of coal is needed to disinfest 900 square centimeters of soil in a bench, and 1 square meter of soil 15 centimeters deep can be steamed per boiler horsepower. If the boiler is operated at an overload, a corresponding increase in area can be steamed. The temperature at the coolest part of the soil should reach 83°C and remain there for 30 minutes. Several points should be measured since the areas nearest to and farthest from the entrance of steam will most likely be the coolest. An ordinary dairy thermometer is suitable. A less accurate but satisfactory method is to place several potatoes in the bench at various locations; when they are cooked, the soil is disinfested. Soil should not be steamed for more than 4 hours because of the possibility of the formation or release of toxic substances. If the steam pressure is too low, or too great an area is being heated, the desired temperature may not be attained. With tubing or steam conductors buried in the soil, it is suggested that the maximum distance to be steamed be not more than 15 linear meters on a 120-centimeter-wide bench. However, with higher steam pressure a pipe header in the form of an H will supply steam for 30 linear meters, 15 meters on each side of the header. A U-shaped header is used on shorter lines. Steam is admitted to each type of header by means of a connection in the middle of the crossbar.

Figure 5-2 Steam treatment of soil for the control of disease organisms, pests, and weeds. In this instance, the steam will be introduced into agricultural tile buried in the soil. The bench is completely covered with the vinyl film during steaming.

Sometimes permanent tile lines are installed in ground beds, and they should be no more than 30 centimeters deep. It is necessary periodically to reset some tile or replace broken sections to permit unobstructed flow of steam.

A covering is placed over the soil to confine the steam. Some of the rubberized or plastic cloths with or without a fabric base are useful.

The cover should extend over the outside of the bench so that the inner surface of the sidewalls will be steamed as well as the soil and the bench bottom. Insects and disease organisms in the cracks and fissures of the sidewalls of both wooden and concrete benches can reinfest soil in the bench if the sidewalls are not steamed.

The conductor to carry the steam can be one of several kinds. Formerly 9-centimeter agricultural tiles were used, but they are heavy and cumbersome and break easily. Perforated, galvanized downspouting can be employed, but it rusts rapidly and its life is short. Old boiler flues are too heavy and generally corrode quickly. The most satisfactory material is about 250-centimeter sections of aluminum alloy tubing since it will not corrode, is lightweight, and resists crushing. To allow for escape of steam from the tubing, holes about 0.5 centimeter in diameter should be drilled 30 centimeters apart on opposite sides of the tubing. With a 120-centimeter-wide bench two lines of tubing should be buried in the soil approximately 60 centimeters apart, and with 150-centimeter benches three lines of tubing should be used. The soil should be pulled away from the sides of the bench because otherwise it may not become hot enough in that area.

Instead of burying the tubing, it may be laid on the surface of the soil. Canvas hose is also a satisfactory conductor of steam if laid on the soil surface. The steamtight covering is placed over the conductor and held down by laying pipe near the edge of the bench. Some cloths cling to the side of the bench when wet and do not require fastening down. The steam is introduced, and at first it billows the cloth, but when pressure builds up, the steam is forced down through the soil. Very often steam penetration of the soil is not uniform with the conductor on the surface, and some parts may not be steamed adequately. Benches with posts in them are difficult to steam in this manner because the cloth cannot be made steamtight around the posts.

Because concrete benches crack easily when heated, the steam should be introduced slowly at first and increased in volume after 30 minutes. It is not necessary to maintain such high pressure that the steam forces the cloth away from the sides of the bench. This may burn crops in adjoining benches. Just enough steam should be admitted to keep the cloth billowed if it is the kind that clings to the bench side or is held down in some manner.

Aerated steam, obtained by combining air from a blower with the steam, enables disinfestation of soil at a lower temperature. At a uniform soil temperature of 60°C the detrimental organisms are killed, yet many of the beneficial forms remain. The latter are helpful if a disease organism is accidentally introduced into the soil, because they prevent, by their competition, the rapid and widespread growth of the disease-causing organism. In the case of soils steamed at 82°C or higher, many beneficial organisms are killed and reinoculation with a detrimental organism may result in greater losses than if the soil had not been steamed in the first place.

Effects of Steaming   Steam disinfestation causes certain physical, chemical, and biological changes to occur.

Physically, granulation occurs, presumably because of the effect of heat, causing the soil colloids to shrink and to cement particles of soil together. One of the common mistakes after steaming is the failure to water heavily enough to wet all the soil. The water runs through the noncapillary pores rapidly so that many of the capillary pores may not be wetted. The first time steamed soil is watered, several applications should be made so that the soil colloids will swell, slow down the rapid exit of water, and cause wetting of all the soil particles.

Chemical changes are mostly concerned with some form of nitrogen. The nitrate nitrogen level drops for the first 3 weeks after steaming because ammonifying bacteria are changing it to ammonia. The ammonium nitrogen level reaches a peak in 3 weeks, and when the nitrifying bacteria population has built up in a matter of 5 to 6 weeks, ammonia is not present in any appreciable quantity. Heavy watering will remove excessive nitrates as well as wet all the soil, as has been discussed under physical effects. Too frequent watering on poorly drained soils can cause the formation of nitrites instead of nitrates.

Biological changes occur because of the effect of heat on the various organisms. Not all bacteria are killed with 6 hours of steaming, and it is doubtful if the mortality could ever be 100 percent in the conditions under which the soil is steamed. Nematodes, symphylids, grubs, and other similar pests are killed when the soil temperature remains at 82°C for 30 minutes. In ground beds, nematodes are killed in the steamed area, but the cooler areas below are a source for reinfestation. Symphylids usually migrate to cooler areas, and steaming ground beds for control of this pest is usually ineffective. In ground beds with a concrete bottom that is not badly cracked, control of these pests is as good as in raised benches.

Unfortunately, some florists have the idea that steam disinfestation will take care of all disease problems in the soil. Since a commercial greenhouse can never be as aseptic as a hospital, contamination is bound to occur and steaming, together with care in watering and other good cultural practices, is necessary to keep soil-borne-disease problems at a minimum.

Hot Water   Disinfestation of soil by this method is ineffective because the temperature does not remain sufficiently high long enough to do much good. Clay pots placed in vats or tanks of boiling water can be disinfested satisfactorily.

Formaldehyde Drench   Formaldehyde is a disinfestant and can be used to disinfest outdoor soil where steam is not available, but it does not control nematodes. The soil is loosened up well by spading and is then saturated with a solution made by diluting 4 liters of commercial formalin with 19 liters of water. From 2 to 4 liters of the solution should be applied to 900 square centimeters of the soil. The amount that can be applied depends on the depth, dryness, and composition of the soil. After treatment, the ground should be covered with a plastic or rubberized cloth for 24 hours and then allowed to dry and air out. It may take from 10 days to 2 weeks for all the formaldehyde to escape so that the bed can be planted. As long as any odor of formaldehyde can be detected in the soil, planting is unsafe. This method of disinfestation is objectionable because some types of soil are badly puddled.

Tear Gas   Disinfestation of the soil with tear gas can be done when steam is not available; however, it is objectionable because of its noxious vapor, and fumes in the greenhouse will kill plants. The soil is prepared in the usual way and treated with tear gas by injecting manually with a special applicator or a continuous-flow applicator pulled through the soil. The soil should be medium moist, and the soil temperature at least 16°C.

The soil is marked in 25-centimeter squares, and from 2 to 4 cubic centimeters of tear gas is injected into each hole, placing the material 12 centimeters deep in the soil. To prevent the escape of the gas, the holes are closed by stepping on them when using the manual injector. The area should be covered with plastic or rubberized cloth for 3 days or sprinkled periodically with a fine spray of water to keep the soil moist to a depth of 1 centimeter. After 3 days the cover is removed, the soil allowed to dry, and when no tear gas odor is present, it is safe to plant. This usually takes at least 14 days after removal of the cover.

Piles of soil can be treated as outlined above, by treating layers approximately 30 centimeters deep. Considerable time must be allowed for the fumes to escape from the center of piles 60 centimeters or more in height. Turning the piles with a shovel is helpful in aerating them to allow the gas to escape.

Tear gas is toxic to plants, and it is virtually impossible to treat soil in a greenhouse unless it is empty of plants. Tear gas controls soil insects, weeds, and nematodes in rotted roots. High concentrations must be used for weed seeds, many disease organisms, and nematodes in unrotted roots. When treating soil, a gas mask is desirable, but unpleasant to wear for long periods in hot weather.

Methyl Bromide This fumigant is effective against soil insects, nematodes in unrotted roots, weeds, and many disease organisms. It is injected into soil in a manner similar to the injection of tear gas, and usually 8 cubic centimeters is placed on 25-centimeter centers. Methyl bromide is odorless and toxic to humans, and the use of a gas mask is imperative. Any numbness of fingers, toes, or cheeks, or any staggering, double vision, nausea, or dizziness is an indication that fumes have been inhaled. The affected person should be kept warm and taken to a doctor at once.

Some plants are very sensitive to methyl bromide.

DD This chemical is specific for nematodes and insects in the soil. It is nonvolatile and does not require a covering over the soil. The soil should be prepared as usual and injected with 2 to 3 cubic centimeters on 25-centimeter centers. Two weeks should be allowed after treatment before planting.

Figure 5-3 Chemical treatment of Florida chrysanthemum fields for control of pests and disease organisms. *(Dorcas Flowers photograph.)*

Vapam This material is useful for control of nematodes and weeds and is fairly effective for killing various soil fungi. It is used at a rate of 1 liter to 9 square meters injected into the soil on 18-centimeter centers, or applied as a surface drench. A water seal for 10 to 14 days is maintained, and following this an aeration period of at least 2 weeks is usually allowed before planting.

PLANTING, SPACING, AND SUPPORTING CUT-FLOWER CROPS

Cut-flower crops are immobile. After they are planted they cannot be moved. The distance used between plants when they are planted is thought to be the spacing that will yield the best financial return per unit area. The young plant will have more space than needed for a few weeks, and the mature plant may be somewhat crowded. With some kinds of plants, giving each plant an increased amount of space might result in more flowers or in larger flowers, but the financial return per unit area might be less.

All of the plants with the exception of the bulb crops need support so that the flower stems grow upright and straight. Although it is true that shoots grow upward (negative geotropism), if the stem is not sturdy enough to support the weight there will be some horizontal deflection, with the tip growth again orienting upwards and causing crooked flower stems.

Several support devices have been used through the years, but now most crops are supported by horizontal networks. A common spacing of network is 15 by 20 centimeters. Some kinds of plants just require one network. It is placed on the ground at planting time and then raised as the plant grows so that the top portion of the stem is limited in its sideward movement, resulting in straight, upward growth. Single-network supports are used for mums and snaps.

Rose and carnation plants need several horizontal networks to support the stems because there are several different heights of growth and the plants are tall. The networks are installed above the young plants, and as the shoots grow they are poked into the proper squares.

The networks must be firmly supported on the bench about every 3 meters because of the weight of the stems at maturity.

Before planting, the soil surface must be leveled so that when it is irrigated following planting the water will drain uniformly through all areas of the soil rather than running first to low spots and then down. Planting always is done in straight rows across and down the bench. This can be done by planting through the support network or by marking the soil. Plants at various stages of growth may be planted, depending on the kind of plant. Several years ago seedlings or rooted cuttings were grown in small pots for a few weeks and then transplanted to the benches. This is done in some instances now, but frequently they are planted directly in the bench. Snapdragons are planted directly from the seed flat when the plants are less than 2 centimeters tall. They must be handled lightly and watered-in carefully. They seem to be much too small to plant, but growth is better and faster when they are planted that soon.

Chrysanthemums and carnations are planted as rooted cuttings. They must be planted as shallow as possible. Root growth then is much more rapid, and also there is less possibility of disease.

When planting seedlings and rooted cuttings, they must be protected from drying during planting. Usually it is best to have a moist cloth over the roots of the plants awaiting planting. As soon as possible after planting, the soil around each plant should be watered. This is a spot-watering procedure in which only the soil in the immediate vicinity of the plant is watered. Those individual spots are thoroughly watered, but the areas between plants are left dry. On the next irrigation, water is applied to the entire soil area.

During sunny and warm weather, partial shade should be placed above the benches and the humidity in the greenhouse should be increased by liberal use of water under benches and in the walks and periodic light misting over the plants.

In cold weather, the heating lines around the bench should be operated so that the soil temperature will be increased somewhat; the soil also will dry more rapidly, giving the better soil aeration that promotes root growth. New root growth should be evident within 2 or 3 days after planting.

Some of the plants should be inspected daily for root growth because that is the evidence that signals the need for continuation or change of procedures.

Rose has been propagated in a variety of ways. Most commonly now it is by budding, and dormant (quiescent) started-eye plants are received for planting. They have been in cool storage and are quiescent. When they are placed in suitable conditions, growth will start. Roots and canes were pruned before the plants were placed in cool storage, and usually on arrival at the greenhouse there is no evidence of the start of new growth.

Before planting it is a somewhat common procedure to place the cases of plants at 16°C for a day or two until there is some swelling of buds in the canes. These are huge plants by comparison, but they must be given the same good root-promoting conditions after planting as were given the seedlings and rooted cuttings: cautious watering of soil, heat around the bench, partial shade over the plants, and high humidity.

Regardless of what kind of plants are being planted, extreme care must be taken to see that no disease pathogens are introduced during planting— on the tools, plant containers, or shoes of the planter. The soil has been steamed but will remain pathogen-free only if pathogens are not introduced.

IRRIGATION OF CUT-FLOWER CROPS

Cut-flower crops can be irrigated with hose-in-hand, but this requires a patient and dedicated waterer. When this method of irrigation is used, half of the bench is watered from each side. In ordinary greenhouse conditions, a 2-centimeter hose will deliver about 60 liters of water per minute when the faucet is opened fully. This is a forceful stream of water, and a water breaker should be used at the end of the hose to reduce soil spattering and compaction. Enough water should be applied so that water drains through the soil. This means applying water at about 2 liters per 900 square centimeters of soil. The irrigator needs to keep the delivery end of the hose just above the soil surface. The right-handed individual drags the hose with the left hand while directing the water along each row of plants halfway across the bench. This slow or halting walk down the bench requires about 7 minutes to irrigate each side of a bench that is 120 centimeters by 30 meters. Because of the amount of time involved in irrigation by hose-in-hand, most greenhouse operators have installed water-distribution systems so that entire benches can be irrigated simply by opening a water valve.

For cut-flower crops, the water-distribution systems are either nozzle, ooze, or piddle types. Each type of system has its advantages and can be used satisfactorily. Several types of nozzles are available, and they may be installed at the center of the bench or along each edge. The amount of water delivery per nozzle needs to be determined so that the right size of water service can be used and the correct length of irrigation time can be scheduled. The nozzles throw a horizontal spray just above soil level. Some of them are designed to deliver water full circle (360°), while others may have delivery of 180° or less. Some potential problems with nozzle systems of water distribution are unequal distribution because of blockage by plant stems or leaves, excessive wetting of aerial portions of some kinds of plants, and undesired wetting of walks or adjacent plants and personnel. In addition to operation of the valve that activates the system, the grower must make periodic inspections to ascertain that each nozzle is functioning correctly. When the valve is closed, the grower must make sure that it does not leak.

The piddle water-distribution systems use plastic tubes that deliver water variously depending on the system from an ooze to a squirt or piddle. The piddlers have two holes about every 10 centimeters the length of the tube so that water is directed laterally in both directions from the tube. Two or more tubes spaced equidistantly are installed for the length of the bench.

The piddles are tiny, and there must be some lateral movement of water in the soil to get uniform wetting of the entire soil mass. A somewhat common practice with piddle water-distribution systems is to double-operate them by activating them for approximately half the necessary irrigation time and then completing the irrigation in a couple of hours. The first activation establishes some lateral capillarity, with the result that the water distribution is more uniform over the area. In addition to operation of the valve that activates the system, the grower must make periodic inspections to make sure that there is no blockage of piddle holes and that the valve closes completely so that there is no leakage when the system should be off.

The water-distribution systems require a greater rate of water flow than the hose-in-hand system, approximately twice the amount of water per unit of time. If the greenhouse is piped so that the maximum flow of water will just accommodate one person with a hose, some plumbing will have to be done before mechanical systems are installed. When water-distribution systems are installed, personnel then become available for operation of more than one unit at a time. When the water-supply facilities are installed for the greenhouse, the total potential water demand needs to be anticipated. This is discussed further in Chap. 2.

FERTILIZER APPLICATION FOR CUT-FLOWER CROPS

Fertilizers containing calcium and magnesium should be applied at the time of soil preparation as discussed earlier. Fertilizers containing nitrogen and potassium, and on occasion phosphorus, usually should be applied with each irrigation. The injection equipment for fertilizer application is discussed in Chap. 2.

It is possible to apply fertilizers in the dry form to cut-flower soils. The soil should be moist at the time of application, and irrigation should follow the application. Care must be taken to keep the fertilizer off the aerial portions of the plant. Usually the plants should be syringed with water to dislodge any fertilizer on the plant.

There may be occasional need for applications of fertilizers containing minor elements. In some instances they may be added at the time of soil preparation, and at other times by means of injection into the irrigation water.

Fertilizers for Dry Application to the Soil Surface

The organic fertilizers and some of the manufactured, slow-release fertilizers discussed earlier can be applied to the surface of the soil, and in addition several other fertilizers can be used in this way. To prevent root injury, the soil must be moist before application is made of a dry fertilizer, and then the soil must be irrigated afterward. The fertilizers that are used for dry application may be completely soluble or only partially soluble, and they

Table 5-1   Analysis and Use of Some Common Fertilizer Materials

| Name of fertilizer | Analysis | Rate of application | | General reaction |
		Grams per 9.3 square meters	Grams per 3.8 liters	
Ammonium nitrate	33-0-0	225	6	Acid
Ammonium sulfate	20-0-0	450	14	Acid
Calcium nitrate	15-0-0	450	14	Alkaline
Sodium nitrate	15-0-0	450	14	Alkaline
Urea	45-0-0	225	4	Neutral
Treble super phosphate	0-45-0	2,250	Insoluble	Neutral
Muriate of potash	0-0-60	450	14	Neutral
Sulfate of potash	0-0-50	450	14	Neutral
Ammonium phosphate (di)	21-53-0	225	6	Acid
Potassium nitrate	13-0-44	450	14	Neutral
Chelated iron	Iron	Not recommended	3	Acid
Iron sulfate (ferrous sulfate)	Iron	450	14	Very acid
Lime or limestone	Calcium	2,250	Insoluble	Alkaline
Gypsum (calcium sulfate)	Calcium	2,250	Insoluble	Neutral

may contain one or more minerals. If nitrogen is one of the minerals present in the fertilizer, the rate of application is based on it. A 5-10-5 fertilizer is applied at the rate of 1,300 grams per 9.3 square meters of soil, a 10-6-4 fertilizer is used at 650 grams per 9.3 square meters, and a 15-0-0 analysis fertilizer at 450 grams per 9.3 square meters.

These fertilizers may be chemical compounds that contain only one kind of material and usually only one or two minerals, or they may be mixed fertilizers than contain several materials and more than one mineral. Typically the mixed fertilizers are a combination of the minerals that commonly need to be added to the soil, and they are sometimes called complete fertilizers. The usual sources for the various minerals in mixed fertilizers are ammonium sulfate and ammonium liquors for nitrogen, superphosphate for phosphorus, and potassium chloride for potassium. The combined total declared analysis for mixed fertilizers for dry application is around 20 percent, and the undeclared remainder of the fertilizer contains some minerals that may or may not be needed, such as calcium, magnesium, sulfur, and chloride. Mixed fertilizers from different manufacturers may have various qualities that make them better for a specific use, and these qualities may be apparent from the labeling on the package or may be learned from experience and testing of the particular product.

It is possible to satisfy all the mineral requirements of plants using only dry applications of fertilizers, but in many instances it is best to use a combination of methods of application. Because of the limited solubility of some of these fertilizers, it is possible to provide a limited but continuous supply of minerals. In some situations there is an advantage in providing the allied constituents of the dry fertilizer such as calcium and magnesium. Some of the disadvantages in making dry applications of fertilizer are the lack of uniform distribution, greater labor time required for application, the unavoidable damage of plants by placement of fertilizer directly upon them, and the fluctuation of mineral content in the soil between applications.

Fertilizers for Liquid Application

Some of the same fertilizers can be used for liquid application as for dry application, and this is determined by the solubility of the fertilizer. If it is completely soluble in water at the rate at which it will be used, the fertilizer can be used for liquid applications. Some of these fertilizers may be chemical compounds that contain one or possibly two minerals, but the mixed fertilizers may be made from several materials containing nitrogen, phosphorus, and potassium as well as other minerals. The commercially prepared and packaged fertilizers for liquid application often contain a total analysis of nitrogen, phosphorus, and potassium of about 60 percent. These are commonly called high-analysis fertilizers. In order to provide complete

Table 5-2   *Various Fertilizer Analyses from Combination of Some Common fertilizers**

Ammonium nitrate (33-0-0)	Calcium nitrate (15-0-0)	Diammonium phosphate (21-53-0)	Potassium nitrate (13-0-44)	*Fertilizer analysis*
1 part	None	None	1 part	23-0-22
1 part	None	None	2 parts	20-0-30
None	1 part	None	1 part	14-0-22
None	2 parts	None	1 part	14-0-15
None	None	1 part	1 part	18-26-22

*To assure good mixing the proper amount of each chemical compound should be added to the water in the tank and thoroughly mixed. If it is desired to use 450 grams of a 23-0-22 analysis fertilizer per 3.8 liters of water in the fertilizer concentrate, 225 grams of ammonium nitrate and 225 grams of potassium nitrate should be added per 3.8 liters of water.

solubility together with high analysis, the manufacturer of these fertilizers may use urea, potassium nitrate, ammonium nitrate, or ammonium phosphate for the nitrogen sources; ammonium phosphate and potassium phosphate for the phosphorus sources; and potassium nitrate and potassium phosphate for the potassium sources. Various combinations of these materials can be used to produce fertilizers of different analyses. Depending on the manufacturer, these mixed fertilizers may also contain some chelated minerals that are used in small quantities as well as a dye that will indicate when fertilizer is present in the irrigation water.

If the proper materials are obtained and the mixing is done very carefully, it is possible for growers to prepare fertilizer mixtures themselves as they need them. The most useful materials for this purpose are potassium nitrate, calcium nitrate, ammonium nitrate, and di-ammonium phosphate.

If phosphorus and calcium fertilizers are incorporated into the soil before planting, it is usually satisfactory to use fertilizers that contain only nitrogen and potassium during the production of most crops.

Methods for Making Liquid Applications of Fertilizer

Various methods may be used satisfactorily. The tank method is an accurate means of supplying fertilizer to soils, and it may be one of the most economical systems to install. It is used mainly for applying fertilizers periodically rather than with each irrigation. With a fertilizer containing approximately 20 percent nitrogen, about 1,300 grams of fertilizer is used per 380 liters of water in the tank. This liquid fertilizer should be applied to the soil at the rate of 1 liter per 900 square centimeters.

Other methods of making liquid applications of fertilizer involve the use of some type of proportioner to add a fertilizer concentrate to the water as it is being used in irrigation. The most reliable proportioners are the injectors as they add the same volume of fertilizer per volume of water regardless of varying conditions, and this ratio or proportion does not change. There really are only two problems with good-quality units: (1) The water motors can be damaged if the water source contains sand or silt. If a clean water source is not available, a strainer should be used. (2) Undissolved particles in the fertilizer concentrate may cause malfunction of the check valves in the injector.

The common proportions for injectors are 1 to 100 and 1 to 200. An injector with 1 to 100 proportion will inject 1 unit of fertilizer concentrate into the irrigation water in every 100 units that is dispensed, and an injector with 1 to 200 proportion will inject 1 unit of fertilizer concentrate in every 200 units of water that is dispensed from the injector. If the same amount of fertilizer is desired in the irrigation water, the fertilizer concentrate for the 1

Table 5-3 Amount of Nitrogen Fertilizer to Use with Potassium Nitrate for 200 ppm Each Nitrogen and Potassium*

Fertilizer	Analysis	Grams per 3.8 liters of water
Ammonium nitrate	33-0-0	142
Calcium nitrate	15-0-0	312
Ammonium sulfate	20-0-0	241
Urea	45-0-0	114

*Use 213 grams of potassium nitrate (13-0-44) per 3.8 liters of concentrate water plus any one of these listed nitrogen fertilizers for 200 ppm each nitrogen and potassium with a 1 to 100 ratio fertilizer injector. For a 1 to 200 ratio injector use twice these amounts.

to 200 injector would be twice as great as for the 1 to 100 injector. Most of the injectors are positive displacement hydraulic pumps or water motors, which are operated solely by the water that passes through them.

Injectors provide a convenient and reliable means of adding fertilizer regularly to the irrigation water, and their main use is in supplying fertilizer with each irrigation rather than periodically. If properly handled, this can provide uniform amounts of minerals in the soil at all times. When fertilizer is applied with each irrigation, the water should contain approximately 200 ppm each of nitrogen and potassium. Tables 5-3 and 5-4 list the amounts of several different fertilizers which can be used to obtain this concentration.

When fertilizer is applied with each irrigation, heavy irrigation must normally be used—applying water at the rate of 2 liters per 900 square

Table 5-4. Amount of Nitrogen Fertilizer to Use with Potassium Chloride (Muriate of Potash) for 200 ppm Each Nitrogen and Potassium*

Fertilizer	Analysis	Grams per 4 liters of water
Ammonium nitrate	33–0–0	230
Ammonium sulfate	20–0–0	390
Urea	44–0–0	170

*Use 160 grams of potassium chloride (0–0–60) per 3.8 liters of concentrate water plus any one of these listed nitrogen fertilizers for 200 ppm each nitrogen and potassium with a 1 to 100 ratio fertilizer injector. For a 1 to 200 ratio injector use twice these amounts.

centimeters of soil. This will leach some of the fertilizer with each irrigation, but using lesser amounts of water will cause excessive amounts of minerals in the soil with resultant crop damage.

Soil and Plant Analysis

It is best to use a combination of methods to evaluate the mineral status of the soil and plant. The soil should be tested before planting to ensure proper corrective action and proper programming of fertilization. After planting, the soil should be tested often enough to assure that the proper minerals are available, and this will require testing once a month or more often until it is established that the fertilizer program is right. Careful observation of the plants during this period is essential in order to verify the soil-test reports.

Timeliness is very important. If it takes several weeks to receive the soil-test report from a complete soil analysis, it will be necessary to use, in addition, some less detailed tests that produce immediate reports.

Plant analysis is a detailed laboratory procedure that has been used to a limited extent more recently. It does furnish information on the status of minerals right in the plant, and it may be particularly helpful when some unusual mineral situations exist.

Different methods of soil testing are used throughout the country, and the values that are reported by one testing method will not necessarily be comparable to the values used in another. Methods for determining pH are standard, and the values reported from any testing service should be the same for a given soil. Most soil-testing services give reports on the quantity of available nitrogen (expressed as nitrate nitrogen), phosphorus, potassium, and calcium in parts per million. Each soil-test report should be recorded and compared with previous tests of the same soil, as observation of the status of each mineral from test to test may give more useful information than the results from a single test. Phosphorus, pH, and calcium values should be quite stable and not change rapidly. If the tests indicate a general progression either way, some corrective action can be taken before trouble is encountered; usually, however, it is possible to make adjustments in the soil for pH, phosphorus, and calcium before planting that will satisfy the requirements for the entire crop. If a single test indicates values that are radically different from those in previous tests, another test should be made as quickly as possible to determine whether a mistake was made in sampling or the soil was given some unusual treatment between tests. Nitrogen values—and to a lesser degree potassium values—can fluctuate considerably between tests, and tests should be made frequently enough to evaluate their status and take corrective action. If the pH, phosphorus, and calcium

Figure 5-4 Solu Bridge soil tester for rapid determination of total soluble mineral (soluble salts) content of soil or water. *(Beckman Instruments, Inc. photograph.)*

quantities were properly adjusted before planting, only nitrogen or potassium applications may have to be made during the production of the crop. As indicated earlier, for many crops the soil pH should be approximately 6.5.

In addition to reports on pH and the amounts of minerals, most soil-test services include an analysis of the amount of soluble salts in the soil. The soluble salts value indicates the total quantity of minerals that are available in the soil; even though it does not specify which minerals are included in the total, it is essential to keep advised of the total quantity as plants will not grow in an excess of minerals. The amount of soluble salts in soil is assessed by an instrument called "Solu Bridge," which determines the amount of salts in the soil solution by the relative amount of conductance of electric current through it. Readings can be made rapidly with the Solu Bridge, and it is operated easily. Most greenhouse operators should have their own Solu Bridge for making quick determinations of soluble salts, and more detailed reports could be obtained periodically from a soil-testing service. In making the Solu Bridge determination, some testing services use one part of soil to two parts of water, and others use one part of soil to five parts of water. Table 5-5 gives the recommendations based on values reported by either method.

High soluble salts, a common problem in greenhouse soils, are caused by the addition of large quantities of fertilizer, poor drainage conditions, or failure to apply a sufficient quantity of water at each irrigation. If a high soluble salts condition exists before planting, the situation can be corrected by the addition of soil or organic matter that is low in minerals. If the high soluble salts problem occurs after planting, the first step is to determine

*Table 5-5 Interpretation of Solu Bridge Values**

Solu Bridge readings		
1 soil to 2 water	1 soil to 5 water	Interpretation
Below 0.15	0.08–0.30	Too low. May be all right for seed germination, but too low for seedlings or plants
0.15–0.50		Satisfactory only if soil is high in organic matter
0.50–1.80	0.30–0.80	Satisfactory range for established plants, but upper level may be too high for some seedlings
1.80–2.25	0.80–1.00	Slightly higher than desirable
2.25–3.40	1.00–1.50	Plants usually stunted or at least not growing rapidly
3.40 and up	1.50 and up	Plants dwarfed severely with the crop often economic failure

*Because Solu Bridge values may be determined using either one part soil to two parts water or one part soil to five parts water, both values are listed. About 1965 the manufacturer changed the scale of the Solu Bridge. Units manufactured before that time will indicate readings 100 times greater than those listed here (the reading 0.50 on new equipment is the same as 50 on older units).

whether the drainage through soil and bench is adequate. With good drainage, heavy applications of water (leaching) can then be made in a short period of time to remove the excess minerals. In order to prevent the soil from remaining constantly wet for an extended time, successive heavy irrigations should be made immediately following each other on the same day. It is also possible that the soluble salts problem can be decreased if the source of minerals is changed. In many instances sulfates and chlorides that originate in ammonium sulfate and potassium chloride fertilizers cause most of the soluble salts, and they can be eliminated in the future by changing to such fertilizers as potassium nitrate, ammonium nitrate, and calcium nitrate as sources of nitrogen.

Extremely high salts content in water supplies is not common, but it does occur occasionally and can be determined by the Solu Bridge. Table 2-1 lists guides that can be used in evaluating the suitability of water because of salts content.

Most greenhouse operators should do some of their own soil testing to provide a rapid means of determining the status of minerals in the soil. The results may at times not be as accurate as soil testing by a regular service, but it is a helpful supplement. The Junior Simplex Soil Test Outfit made by the Edwards Laboratory, Box 318, Norwalk, Ohio, provides tests for the most

Figure 5-5 Desiccation and death of the leaf margin due to insufficient water in the plant because of inability of the roots to absorb water following damage from high concentration of soluble minerals (soluble salts) in the soil.

common minerals as well as a simplified determination for pH, and it could be used to advantage in many greenhouses. The Solu Bridge manufactured by Beckman Instruments, Inc., 89 Commerce Road, Cedar Grove, New Jersey, is another valuable tool for proper management of minerals. The procedures are not difficult, and they can be done rapidly. It is a means of making an immediate decision on whether a soil mineral problem exists, and this can be followed by a detailed soil test to determine which minerals are involved. The cause of poor plant growth in the greenhouse may not be

Figure 5-6 Snapdragon is particularly sensitive to high concentrations of soluble salts. Root growth is limited, leaves are chlorotic, and there is little growth of stem. *(Yoder Bros., Inc. photograph.)*

apparent readily, and the appearance of the plants could indicate either mineral (soluble salts) excesses or mineral deficiency. The Solu Bridge can answer such a question in a matter of minutes.

The status of minerals within plants can be determined by plant analysis (tissue tests). This is a rather lengthy laboratory procedure that is used as a research tool but has been adapted for some uses on commercial crops. It does assess the mineral situation directly in the plant, and it may be a valuable additional means of determining the kind and amount of minerals to be supplied to the plant. Procedures vary, but commonly the plant sample is made from leaves recently matured toward the top of the plant. The sample is dried and analyzed, and the mineral content is reported in percentage of dry matter or parts per million depending upon the element. The interpretation of results varies with the crop, the sampling procedures, and the experience of the individuals making the analysis; but there is some agreement that the optimum content for most plants is about the same. The more typical acceptable values are nitrogen, 3.0 to 5.0 percent; phosphorus, 0.4 to 0.6 percent; potassium, 2 to 4 percent; magnesium, above 0.3 percent; calcium, above 1 percent; and boron, above 30 ppm.

Aside from soil or plant tests and observation of deficiency symptoms, the use of fertilizers must be tempered by the general growth of the plant and the environmental conditions that are provided for the plants. Minerals cannot be used by plants until they are absorbed, and since the primary means of entry is through the roots, minerals will be absorbed into the plant only if the roots are active and growing. The grower must observe the root growth constantly and adjust soil, drainage, or irrigation so that the best root growth is obtained. Adding fertilizers to soils when root growth is poor will actually cause harm. The condition of root growth can be used as a means of assessing several conditions that have been provided for the plants. If good, active root growth (many white root tips) is observed, this is sufficient evidence that soil aeration, drainage, and irrigation practices are satisfactory and that there is not too much fertilizer in the soil. If the roots are not in active growth (few white root tips) or they appear to be damaged, it could be caused by a soil, water, pest, or fertilizer situation or a combination of them. Whatever the cause of poor root growth, it must be corrected before the fertilizer application is made.

The use of fertilizer must be coordinated with other environmental conditions. If light or temperature conditions are not satisfactory, the plant will not use as great a quantity of minerals as it would in better conditions. The addition of fertilizer should also be based on the size of plants, kind of plants, and stage of development.

Fertilizer injectors are highly recommended because elements are applied on the basis of existing light and temperature conditions. The mineral requirements of some types of plants are greater than others, and, in general, large plants use more minerals than small plants. Plants that are in vigorous vegetative growth should usually be more adequately supplied with minerals than plants during the flower-forming stage of growth.

PINCHING AND PRUNING CUT-FLOWER CROP PLANTS

Pinching may be done on cut-flower crops either to produce more stems on the plant or to control the timing of the flower crop. Some kinds of plants are never pinched. The aster cultivars that are grown in the greenhouse are self-branching plants. Each plant produces about six shoots in natural conditions, and each shoot eventually develops a terminal flower.

With bulb crops, the shoots are not pinched. One flower per bulb is the maximum for iris. Because double-nose bulbs are used with daffodil, two or more flowers usually develop per bulb planted.

Some kinds of plants may or may not be pinched depending on the situation. If the plants are pinched the plants are planted farther apart, several shoots develop at the nodes below the pinch, and flowering is delayed approximately 2 weeks. Formerly snapdragon was grown pinched, and it was not unusual to continue the plants in growth after the first flower crop was cut. The shoots that developed after the first crop would be pruned to four. The snapdragon plants to be grown pinched were planted on about 20-centimeter squares.

Now snapdragon is grown single stem—not pinched—and the plants are spaced from 10 by 10 centimeters to 10 by 15 centimeters, depending on the time of the year they will flower.

Chrysanthemum was grown more commonly as pinched plants that were pruned to two or three stems, but now frequently they are grown with single stems. The pinched plants may be spaced 15 by 20 centimeters and the single-stem plants 10 by 15 centimeters, although there are variations in this spacing according to the season of the year.

Successive pinching might be done with rose and carnation plants in order to produce multiple-branched plants. Pinching on carnation plants is discontinued in early September and flowering is from fall on.

With rose plants some pinching is done during the entire time the plants are grown. Pinching is done continuously to improve the quality of the stems, and pinching is done at some scheduled times to produce flower crops for specified market times. Pinching must become second nature with rose growers.

CUTTING AND GRADING CUT-FLOWER CROPS

Cut flowers must be harvested at the right stage of maturity and either marketed or placed in cool storage until time of marketing. The morning is the best time of the day to cut the flowers, although rose flowers necessarily must be cut both morning and afternoon because they mature so rapidly.

The flower cutter has two decisions to make with each cut: Is the flower at the right stage of maturity for cutting and at what position on the stem should the cut be made? The latter question is relatively unimportant with crops such as mum and snapdragon because the plants will be discarded after the flowers are harvested, but the correct answer to both questions is essential with rose and carnation plants. With these plants the position of the cut on the stem affects the development of the succeeding flower crops.

After the flowers are cut they are placed in water in vases and then subsequently in cool temperatures in cool storage until they are marketed.

The cut flowers may be graded and wrapped either before or after they are placed in cool storage. Various procedures are used because of differences in facilities and crops, but the objective is to get the flowers in cool temperatures as soon as possible after cutting. These cool storages are maintained at about 7°C, and they are short-term storages, usually overnight.

If the cut flowers are scheduled for relatively long periods of cool storage, the flowers are not placed in water after cutting. They are enclosed in films or containers that retain moisture and placed in storages operated at about 1°C. When they are removed from this storage, the stems are cut and the flowers are placed in vases that contain water at about 33°C. The flowers then are graded and placed in the storages maintained at 7°C until they are marketed.

Some kinds of cut flowers can be held in cool storage for several days without any adverse effects on the subsequent keeping qualities of the flower, and other kinds of cut flowers may be kept for several weeks satisfactorily. Whenever possible, however, cut flowers are marketed as soon as possible after they are cut.

Storages for orchids are maintained at 13°C, and they may be held for relatively long periods at this temperature without harmful effects.

TRANSPORTATION OF CUT FLOWERS

Within the greenhouse, it is helpful if the cut flowers can be rapidly transported from the greenhouses to the grading and storage areas in vases on carts.

When cut flowers are marketed locally, usually they are transported to the market in the vases in which they were stored. When cut flowers are shipped to market, it must be in temperature-controlled conditions. In the winter they must be protected from freezing, and in the summer they must be protected from high temperatures. Common carriers may provide some degree of temperature control, but packaging methods also give some protection from adverse temperatures. Insulated containers may be used, and in hot weather ice may be added to the cartons.

Most of the cut flowers may be shipped in the horizontal position satisfactorily, but snapdragon and gladiolus show the effects of negative geotropism readily, and they must be shipped in the vertical position. If they are shipped horizontally, the stem tips will curve upward.

Two other critical factors in transportation of cut flowers is the length of time in transit and the cost of transportation. These factors favor the local producer and become a real problem for the producer who must ship to distant markets. There was a day when cut flowers were shipped successfully long distances in the United States via Railroad Express, but that method of transportation disappeared. It seems most likely that there will not be any one method of cut-flower transportation that will be the best for all areas of the country for all times. Currently the best choices are either air freight or specialized truck carriers. Finding the quickest and most economical method of transportation probably will continue to be an interesting problem for the cut-flower producer.

PEST AND PATHOGEN CONTROL FOR CUT-FLOWER CROPS

Most cut-flower crops need routine pest control programs. In most instances pathogens can be kept in control when elimination procedures are carefully followed and the environment is regulated in the best way for good growth of plants. Pest and pathogen control is discussed in Chaps. 2 and 4.

ROTATIONS FOR CUT-FLOWER CROPS

Rotations for cut-flower crops are not nearly as involved as they are for pot-plant crops. The immobility of the cut-flower crops limits the number of rotation possibilities. To some extent it is also a different type of rotation that is practiced with cut-flower crops. The objective of any rotation is the utilization of the production area in such a way that the greatest net return is realized per unit of area. Sometimes a good rotation will schedule brief periods of unplanted areas in spite of the common remark that no money can be made from empty benches.

It is difficult to devise economically sound rotations in which an area is used alternately for cut-flower crops and pot-plant crops. The different types of crops may require more change in the facility than is justified by the gross return. At least, the costs involved need to be determined before that type of rotation is scheduled.

Producers of rose cut-flower crops usually rotate roses with roses, and this can be done to good advantage. The dormant rose plants are available for planting anytime after the first of the year, and the rose grower may schedule a portion of the replanting for mid-February after the Valentine's Day crop is cut and the balance of the replanting in mid-May after the Mother's Day crop is cut. The first crop of flowers from the February planting can be scheduled for the Mother's Day market, and the first crops from the May planting can be scheduled for flowering during the summer when other plants normally are cut back.

With that start, the rose grower then rotates rose cut-flower crops by the method of cutting back and then pinching the plants. Certain areas of plants may be pinched in such a way that there will be continuous flowering month after month. Other areas of plants may be pinched in such a way that flower crops will be produced for specific markets such as Sweetest Day, Christmas, Valentine's Day, Easter, and Mother's Day. Normally the rose grower will have little need to attempt to rotate rose flower crops from an area with other flower crops from the same area.

The mum cut-flower grower usually develops a steady demand month in and month out for that product and attempts to keep an area in continuous mum rotation. Because plant growth is slower in some seasons than in others, however, the mum grower cannot develop a rotation that will provide the same quantity of cut mums per week from a given area. Five or six weeks more growing time may be needed for the mum crops flowered in December through February than those flowered in June through September. A cut-mum grower who in fact needs as much flower production in the winter as in the summer either must have some additional benches available for planting in August through October or should use some of the benches in the area for some other crops in the period April through July. Some of the cut-chrysanthemum growers use some of the benches in the area for additional production of the spray kind of mums during the summer because there is no Florida production of them at that time. Other summer crops that possibly could be used in the rotation would be snapdragon, statice, gypsophila, zinnia, and celosia. If the market could use any of these additional crops during the summer, those benches then could be used for additional cut mums to be flowered during the winter.

Carnations usually are rotated with carnations, but possibly a rotation that could be used to good advantage is rotating carnation with snapdragon. In this rotation carnation rooted cuttings are planted in May after the Mother's Day crop for flowering from fall through the following summer. They are followed with snapdragon seedlings planted in late summer and early fall for flowering in winter and spring. The snapdragon is followed with carnation rooted cuttings planted in the spring.

Carnation cut-flower cropping is controlled by pinching and lighting. The stems pinched in late summer and early fall produce shoots that flower during the winter. Subsequent flowering comes from shoots produced from flower stems that are cut. In natural conditions carnation flower production increases greatly in late May and June. However, if the plants are lighted in January through February, most of this flower production can be advanced for the better market conditions in April and May.

CUT-FLOWER CROPS

Carnations, chrysanthemums, and roses are the cut-flower crops of the greatest economic importance; however, several other crops are produced commercially. Actually, the amount of production is affected by market demand, and the potential sales of the various crops can be affected by the general economy of the country, changes in customs and styles, and improvements in production procedures or cultivars. The advent of year-round production of chrysanthemums has made a radical change in the production of that crop, and the reduced use of corsage flowers has affected the amount of production of such crops as camellias, gardenias, and orchids.

Aster *(Callistephus chinensis—Compositae)*

High-quality asters can be produced the year-round provided the seedlings are lighted during short days from the time that they emerge until flowering. The same type of lighting as used for mums can be employed, but the light intensity required is less, so that the bulbs can either be spaced farther apart or be of lower wattage. The primary effect of supplementary illumination during short days is elongation of stems. Asters will produce flowers in short days but on very short stems. Asters at 10°C nights will be fully double with strong stems. At higher temperatures they will grow reasonably well but will be weaker stemmed and have fewer florets.

Lighted asters can be used to good advantage by producing a crop earlier than the natural-flowering asters in the summer or as a short-term crop that fits into mum, snapdragon, or other rotations. The summer crop is commonly produced in the cloth house. The seed can be sown in the middle of March, the seedlings potted as soon as they can be handled, and the plants placed outdoors after frost in May. The seedlings are lighted from the seed flat until they are set out in the cloth house. About 4 months is required for flowering from seed sown in the spring, and as long as $5\frac{1}{2}$ months is required for flowering from seed sown in November. The Royal-type asters are considered the most suitable for forcing.

Asters should not be pinched since they are self-branching and 8 to 10 flowers are produced per plant. Each shoot developing from the main stem is disbudded to a single flower. The plants can be spaced 20 by 20 centimeters in the bench.

Fusarium wilt can be a very serious disease. The organism is soil-borne, and thorough soil steaming is the best control. Fusarium trouble is almost certain if successive aster crops are grown on the same soil without steaming. Some disease-resistant strains have been developed, but apparently there are different strains of the fusarium organism, and asters resistant to the western fusarium strain may be susceptible to the eastern strain, or vice versa.

Yellows is a virus disease that is transmitted from weeds or other host plants to the aster primarily by the leafhopper. A properly constructed cloth house will exclude the leafhoppers.

Rust may attack the plants if the foliage is kept moist by rain, dew, or careless watering.

Aphids, red spider, thrips, blister beetles, and leaf miner are the common insect pests.

Baby's Breath *(Gypsophila elegans—Caryophyllaceae)*

The annual gypsophila, *Gypsophila elegans,* may be grown either outdoors or as a greenhouse crop. In northern climates the seed is sown in March through April for flowering in June through October outdoors. The seed germinates in 1½ weeks at 21°C. The plants are spaced at about 28 centimeters.

For greenhouse flowering, the annual gypsophila seed is sown in December through April for flowering in March through July. The plants usually are grown in flats at 10-centimeter spacing and 10°C temperature.

Perennial gypsophila, *Gypsophila paniculata* "Bristol Fairy," may be grown outdoors either from rooted cuttings or from grafted plants.

Florida plantings are made in September through February for flowering from December through June.

Bachelor's Button *(Centaurea cyanus—Compositae)*

For a greenhouse flower crop in April to May the seed should be sown in November through December. The seed germinates in 1½ weeks at 18°C, in the dark.

The plants should be spaced 30 by 30 centimeters, and one or two support networks are required. The night temperature should be 10°C.

Calla *(Zantedeschia aethiopica—Araceae)*

This plant is a native of Egypt which may be grown outdoors in mild climates or in greenhouses throughout the year.

It is propagated by means of division of the rhizomes. The rhizomes are potted in August, and flowering starts in the fall and continues in the winter and spring until the plants are dried off in early summer. They are started back in growth in late summer or early fall. The need for the dormant period caused by drying is questionable, as the growth and flowering would proceed in the summer if the plants were watered regularly.

Callas may be grown in beds or in pots. If they are in pots, they must be large enough to give adequate space for the large rhizomes and root system. Callas are subject to root rot, and the spread of this disease may be more easily controlled among plants in pots. With bed-grown callas, it usually is easier to provide the uniform moisture conditions necessary for good growth.

Full sunlight should be provided, but partial shade should be used for callas grown during the summer. Growth and flowering are best at 13°C night temperatures, with the day temperatures about 3 to 6°C higher. There is no apparent effect of day length or temperature on flower formation and development.

Root rot of callas is common and may be caused by phytophthora dry rot or erwinia (soft rot). The rhizomes must be carefully inspected before planting, and any rotten spots completely cut out. Soil and containers must be thoroughly steamed before use. Red spiders, thrips, and mealybugs are occasional pests on callas, but they are controlled by normal measures.

Candytuft *(Iberis odorata* and *Iberis umbellata—Cruciferae)*

Annual candytuft flower colors are white, pink, lavender, and red. It is propagated from seed that germinates in 3 weeks at 18°C.

Seed sown in October to November will produce plants in flower in April to May at 10°C. For a late May flower crop, seed can be sown in mid-January.

The plants should be spaced 15 by 15 centimeters, and they can be supported with one network.

Carnation *(Dianthus caryophyllus—Caryophyllaceae)*

The carnation is a native of southern Europe. Theophrastus wrote about carnations in his *History of Plants*, but it was not until the sixteenth century that carnations were widely used. The perpetual flowering type used for commercial purposes at the present time was originated by Dalmais in France in 1840 and introduced into the United States in 1856.

Carnations are propagated by means of rooted stem-tip cuttings, and the main propagation is scheduled for the spring so that the young plants will be planted during the good growing conditions of spring and early summer. The plants are usually pinched once or more to produce a branched plant, and the time of planting and the method and amount of pinching determine when flower production will start. The carnation stem terminates with a flower after approximately 18 sets of leaves have been formed regardless of the day length, but growth and flower development are more rapid in high-light and high-temperature conditions.

Carnation plants could be cropped indefinitely, and in some instances the plants are grown for 2 or 3 years with continuous production of flowers. Such a system of management saves replanting costs and may increase production, but the quality of the flowers is not always as good with the older plants. In a 1-year rotation, the plants are benched in the spring; flower production starts in the fall and continues until the plants are removed the following spring.

Standard carnation cultivars produce large flowers of about 7.5 centimeters in diameter, and only a lone, terminal flower is allowed to develop per stem. The lateral flower buds should be removed (disbudded) as soon as they are large enough to be handled conveniently. Carnation production is primarily in the large, standard cultivars; however, some miniature or spray

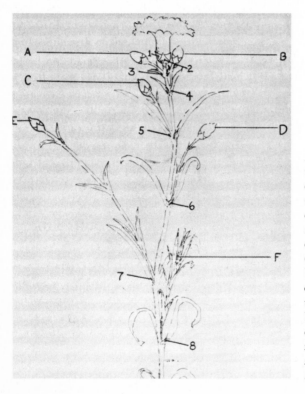

Figure 5-7 If standard carnation cultivars were not disbudded, the lateral flower buds (A–E) would be at this stage of development when the terminal flower matured. These lateral shoots should be removed (disbudded) as soon as they can be handled. The shoot (F) at the eighth node should be vegetative. Shoots should not be disbudded below this point as succeeding flower crops develop rapidly from them. *(From Research Bulletin 786, Ohio Agricultural Experiment Station.)*

cultivars are grown. These are smaller flowered cultivars, and the lateral flower buds as well as the terminal flower are allowed to develop so that a spray of flowers is produced per stem. Often the terminal flower bud is removed so that several of the laterals will be in flower simultaneously.

Propagation   Success or failure of the carnation crop starts with the selection of cuttings. The bases for selection are productivity, flower qualities, habit of growth, quality of the shoot, stage of development of the shoot, and disease or pest infestation. The first three of these characteristics will be known only if the plant from which the cuttings originate is observed carefully for several months and accurate records are maintained. This must be something more than merely taking cuttings from some plants of a given cultivar. Plants can and do change by mutation; and unless the growth and production of the plant are observed carefully, it will not be known whether good or unfavorable characteristics are being propagated.

The quality and the stage of development of the shoot are determined by the conditions that are provided for the stock plants and the management of them. The stem-tip cutting must be of good diameter and have closely spaced leaves. The stock plants should be segregated, and they should be provided with the best growing conditions and care. The cutting must be in vegetative growth at the time that it is taken from the stock plant, and evidence of this is closely spaced leaves. The stock plants must be pinched and the cuttings harvested regularly when the shoots are long enough to make cuttings. If cuttings are made from long shoots, flower buds will have started to develop in the shoot tip. Such cuttings grow slowly and produce poor-quality plants.

If the stock plants are segregated, it is much easier to provide complete control of pests. Regular treatments will have to be made for the control of two-spotted mites, aphids, and possibly other pests.

There are several diseases of carnations, and most of the pathogens can be transmitted with the propagating stock. Virus, bacterial wilt, and fusarium wilt pathogens may be present and growing within the stem tip without any external symptoms of the disease being evident. The presence of these pathogens can be determined by a detailed laboratory procedure known as culturing. Stock that is free of infestation is used for developing blocks of stock plants, and the stems that show evidence of disease during culturing are discarded. This procedure is known as culture-indexing. The presence of virus can be determined by the reaction of certain host plants to the sap or graft of the carnation being tested, but it is a long procedure. Virus in carnations can be eliminated by the use of heat therapy and meristem culture. Virus-free stock must be renewed frequently because reinfestation is possible by means of aphids or handling the plants.

Rhizoctonia solani is a soil-borne fungus that is usually not transmitted by the cutting if normal sanitary measures are used. Spores of the fusarium stem rot organism, however, can be carried very easily on the surface of the carnation cutting, but the presence of neither of these pathogens could be expected to be determined by culturing. The elimination of rhizoctonia and fusarium stem rot pathogens from carnation stem tips being propagated is accomplished by the practice of strict sanitation and the use of some chemical controls.

The selection and production of high-quality carnation cuttings requires a degree of specialization that is not possible for the grower whose primary business is the production of carnation flowers. A grower who feels a need to propagate cuttings rather than buying them all from the specialist should at least obtain all the propagation stock from a specialist who can ensure that the stock has been carefully selected for best production and quality characteristics and that it is disease-free. It is then possible for the carnation grower to produce good cuttings with proper management and good growing conditions.

It is possible to set the time of propagation quite accurately if it is known when the carnations are going to be benched. The propagation date should be determined so that just the right amount of time is allowed for growing the young plants. The length of time between propagation and benching will depend on how the young plants are handled.

Plants that are placed in 6-centimeter pots will have to be transplanted in a month for the best growth. If a 8-centimeter pot is used, the plants will need moving within 2 months. For a June 1 benching the cuttings should be stuck in the propagation bench on March 1 if the young plants are going to be placed in 8-centimeter pots or on April 1 if 6-centimeter pots will be used. If it is necessary to propagate earlier or to bench the plants later, some provision must be made for transplanting to larger containers.

When direct benching is practiced, the cuttings should be stuck 3 to 4 weeks before the benching time. Fifteen-centimeter stem tips should be removed from the stock plants by breaking them sideways by hand. There is some danger of disease transmission if a knife is used. There is no need to break them from the plant at the node or the internode as either type of cutting roots very well.

If the cuttings cannot be stuck at once, they should be placed in refrigerated storage or under a moist cloth. If it is desired to hold them for several days or weeks, the cuttings will remain in good condition for periods of 2 to 3 months and possibly longer if the temperature is maintained at 1°C and they are protected from drying.

The storage of unrooted cuttings is very useful for building a supply of cuttings from a limited number of stock plants. The cuttings can be propagated in one lot, and that will allow the young plants to be started at one time, which assures better handling of cuttings and young plants.

Carnation cuttings root in 3 to 4 weeks if they are placed in a favorable environment, and it is not necessary to use growth substances. The propagation bench must provide for excellent drainage, and supplementary heat is usually needed so that the soil can be maintained at a higher temperature than the air. If the soil temperature is 20°C and the air temperature 13°C the cuttings root readily.

Whenever possible, intermittent mist should be provided for the propagation bench, and it should be controlled so that the leaves just remain wet. During warm weather and in good light, this may require about 5 seconds of mist every minute; during cooler and darker weather, a 5-second misting every 10 minutes may be sufficient.

The cuttings should be removed from the propagation bench when the roots are about 1 centimeter long. If it is necessary to keep them in the bench for a longer period of time, they can be furnished a high-analysis complete fertilizer at the rate of 30 grams per 8 liters of water.

It is possible to store rooted cuttings for a few weeks in a refrigerator if the temperature can be carefully controlled. The procedure is essentially the same as that used for the storage of unrooted cuttings, but even in ideal conditions the rooted cuttings may not store well for more than 8 weeks. The best results are obtained with cuttings from the good growing periods of the year and under conditions of refrigeration where there is less than 1°C variation above the freezing point.

Planting, Spacing, and Supporting Carnations should be planted as shallowly as possible to develop rapid root growth and give the young plants a faster start. There is also less possibility of infestation with the rhizoctonia stem rot pathogen. The plants should be set so shallowly that quite a number of them topple at the first watering and need to be reset.

Plants should be spaced in the bench about 15 by 20 centimeters apart. In some instances two rows of plants are planted together across the bench and the double rows are spaced about 30 centimeters apart. The advantages of this method of planting are that cutting of the flowers is facilitated, irrigation and fertilizer applications can be done more easily, there is improved airflow through the plants in fan and pad cooled houses, and possibly better light for the plants at the middle of the bench is provided.

Carnations should be supported so that the stems grow upright by using several layers of wire, or wire and string, networks. The first network is placed about 15 centimeters above the soil, and the succeeding networks are gradually spaced farther apart until the top ones are about 30 centimeters apart. Welded wire fabric with 15- by 20-centimeter spacing may be used instead of wire and string networks.

Carnation plants weigh heavily on the support wires. The wires must be stretched tightly the length of the bench and well anchored, and the networks must be supported about every 3 meters down the bench with stable metal or wooden supports.

Light and Temperature   The best growth of carnations is obtained in localities of high light intensity during the winter and cool temperatures during the summer.

Excellent growth of carnations can be obtained at 10°C night temperature with 13 or 16°C daytime temperatures, depending on whether the day is cloudy or clear.

Troubles   Splitting of the calyx is the most common problem with carnation flowers. Some cultivars or selections split much more readily than others; hence the cultivars that do not split excessively should be used. Apparently splitting is related to variable rates of growth caused primarily by temperature fluctuations or by changes from conditions unfavorable for good growth to those that are favorable due to management of fertility, moisture, or temperature.

Splitting is most common during the periods of the year when temperatures fluctuate rapidly and greatly, as in the fall and spring. Splitting can be aggravated at these times if the heating system is not being operated and the night temperatures drop lower than anticipated.

Various devices are used to prevent or repair calyx splitting, including rubberbands, ties, plastic collars, or pins that are placed on the calyx to hold it together. Their use is accepted in some markets without penalty, but in others the potential price is reduced.

Sleepiness is the condition in which the carnation petals cup upward. Many customers believe this indicates that the cut flowers have been stored too long before being marketed, but it is actually a symptom produced by ethylene gas that may affect either fresh or old flowers. Some of the most common sources of ethylene are fruits, vegetables, or greens that are stored in refrigerators, and decaying plant material in the vicinity of the carnation flowers. It is possible that some other gases or products of combustion may cause sleepiness in carnations.

Weak stems are common during the winter months. This is aggravated by reduced light because of dirty glass, excessive use of nitrogen fertilizer, and constantly wet soil. Cooler temperatures and a greater amount of light are aids in producing stronger stems in the winter.

Grassy growth and excessive development of side shoots are caused by a mutation, and cuttings should not be made from such plants because this characteristic will be reproduced in the new plants.

Some soils are deficient in boron, and carnation plants readily indicate the shortage with characteristic symptoms of malformed flower buds, short stems, and excessive branching toward the tips of the stems. Boron may be applied to the soil with each irrigation by injection with borax at the rate of 14 grams per 3.8 kiloliters of water, or it may be applied once a year at the rate of 28 grams of borax per 9.3 square meters of soil. Greater amounts of borax may be toxic to the plants.

The successful carnation disease-control program is based on selection of disease-free cuttings and thorough steaming of sand, soil, benches, pots, and any equipment that is to be used around the plants. Proper ventilation and heating practices are helpful in the control of some of the diseases, and there are fungicides that can be used in some cases when the other measures of control fall short.

Rhizoctonia stem rot affects the plant at the soil line. The rotting of the tissues begins at the surface of the stem and proceeds to the inner portions. It may be just a week or two from infection until the plant is dead. Rhizoctonia stem rot develops rapidly in a constantly moist environment and at lower temperatures than bacterial wilt. The organism is soil-borne, and very often a careful steaming program will eliminate the source of trouble. Planting shallowly and allowing the soil to dry somewhat between waterings will help keep this organism in check.

Fusarium wilt *(Fusarium oxysporum* f. *dianthi)* is a fungus which grows in the water-conducting tissues of the stem. The plants may be infected for several months before definite wilt symptoms or death occur. The progress of the disease is more rapid in hot weather than during the winter. When the wilting is first noticed, the roots usually show no evidence of rot. Since the organism grows in the inner tissues, it is possible to take cuttings that are infected but may not exhibit characteristic disease symptoms. A source of disease-free cuttings is essential, as well as thorough steaming of soil, benches, and equipment. There are no effective chemical controls.

Botrytis blight is often serious on soft or white-flowered cultivars. Portions of the petals appear water-soaked, and later a gray mold develops. The fungus thrives at a wide variety of temperatures but grows best in a humid atmosphere. Keeping the ventilators open with some heat to circulate the air is effective.

Bacterial wilt is caused by a bacterial organism *(Pseudomonas caryophylli)* that thrives only at high temperatures. Very little trouble with bacterial wilt should be experienced in localities where night temperatures are below 24°C. This bacterium grows in the stem and produces symptoms that are quite similar to the fusarium wilt symptoms; however, the roots are invariably rotted, and a sticky ooze is evident in stem and roots. The means of control are the same as for fusarium wilt.

Fusarium stem rot *(Fusarium roseum* f. *ceralis)* is a fungus disease usually prevalent in the propagation bench or among the young plants. The rot starts on the surface and progresses inward. The organism may be introduced on the surface of cuttings, or it may be soil-borne. A stem rot or a root rot or both may occur. Careful steaming and close attention to watering practices are the best means of control.

Fusarium stem rot also is a serious disease of mature carnation plants. The pathogen may start in growth in the stem remaining after the flower is cut. Subsequently that stem dies, followed by adjoining branches as the pathogen continues in growth.

Rust is no longer a serious disease problem if the plants are kept constantly under glass. The primary source of infection in older methods of culture came from growing the plants in the field. Rust spores may not germinate unless there is free water on the plant.

Mosaic, streak, and yellows are virus diseases of carnations which have been so serious that some susceptible cultivars have virtually been eliminated because of them. Earlier this had been ascribed to "running out" of the cultivar. Unfortunately, very often the symptoms of the disease are not noticeable at the time cuttings are taken. Thus it is very easy to propagate the disease in the new plantings. To eliminate the virus diseases, the stock plants must be closely observed over a long period of time to assure that the cuttings are not diseased.

Meristem culture is a procedure that may be used to produce carnation plants that are free of virus. It is a detailed laboratory technique in which the excised tip of the plant (meristem) is grown in aseptic conditions on nutrient media. The stem tips are taken from plants that have been grown at high temperature; and they are virus-free because the growth of the stem tip at high temperatures is faster than the development of virus into the new tissues.

Pests Red spider is the most serious pest on carnations. In winter the cool temperatures at which the plants are grown keep the population in check, but in spring, with warmer weather, they multiply rapidly. This pest is very serious in summer and fall when the temperatures are high. Young plants can be so heavily infested that the leaves dry up and the plants will be worthless.

Aphids disfigure the young growth and may cripple it severely.

Thrips cause streaks in the flowers, and generally they are most noticeable in periods of warmer weather. Affected flowers are unmarketable. Regular spraying or dusting is essential.

Pinching Carnation plants can vary considerably in rate of growth during the early stages. They should be pinched on the basis of stage of growth. Some plants will probably be at the right stage 4 weeks after planting, and others not until later. It may take 2 or 3 weeks to complete the first pinch on a block of plants.

When possible, the plants should be allowed to grow until the side shoots have cleared the leaves. That will often mean that the stem is in bud by the time the first pinch is made. Whenever possible, three cleared shoots and about five sets of leaves should remain on the plant below the pinch. With the Sim cultivars, that makes the pinch roughly 15 centimeters above the soil level. It is particularly important to pinch high on the Sim cultivars during hot weather; harder pinching very often produces only one shoot per pinch.

Multiple pinching is the cultural method that is most commonly employed. It is sometimes referred to as double pinching or pinch and a half. The attempt is made to pinch the plants in such a manner that the resulting flower crops are produced during the periods of the year when carnations are in greatest demand. The carnation is used the year-round, but the demand is usually greatest from December through June. It takes about 5 months for a flower to develop from a stem pinched in mid-July. Stems pinched before then produce flowers in a shorter period of time, and the

Figure 5-8 Position of pinch to be made before August 1 on carnation stems. In the early stages of growth, carnation stems are compact with leaves closely spaced and very little stem visible between sets of leaves (left). The shoots should be allowed to develop until internodal stem is visible, and the pinch should be made as indicated above six or more sets of leaves (right).

stems that are pinched later take a longer time to produce flowers. If the second pinches are going to be made in July, it is necessary to make the first pinch about May 1.

Not all the shoots grow at the same rate. When the first pinch is made on the first of May, some shoots will develop sufficiently for a June pinch, and others in July and August or later. The top shoots develop most rapidly and usually receive the second pinch. The lower shoots are slower and very often are not pinched. The shoots that arise from the June pinches will start to flower in September.

A schedule that has given excellent results in the Middle West is as follows: Stick the cuttings March 1, place the rooted cuttings in 8-centimeter pots March 25, make the first pinch May 1, bench the plants on 18- or 20-centimeter squares in early June, and start pinching the most advanced shoots in June. Pinching should continue until late July. After that time the shoots that are in flower bud can be pinched periodically. If the latter type of pinching is continued until September 15, the very early fall flowers will be eliminated, but the late winter and early spring production will be increased, which provides for steady production from late November on.

This schedule was developed particularly to allow for benching the plants after the spring rush. It is especially difficult for the retail grower to bench carnation plants before June 1. Some adjustments can be made in the schedule, but later propagation and benching are usually not satisfactory

Figure 5-9 Position of pinch to be made on carnation stems after August 1. Pinching should be continued until early September, but from August 1 until that time only the stems that have formed flower buds (right) should be pinched. This will eliminate early fall flowers but will increase flower production in January, February, and March. During this period, vegetative stems (left) should not be pinched as they will form flowers which will mature from November on.

because the last pinches then are made later and the flower production does not start until later in the winter.

Excellent plant growth can be expected from March through May because of the favorable light and temperature conditions at that time. If the rotation of crops can be worked out, it is best to bench the plants as soon as possible in the spring. The time of propagation is simply placed earlier to provide the rooted cuttings for the spring benching.

Flower development in carnations occurs at a faster rate during periods of high light intensity and high temperatures. Apparently the first stages of flower formation take place at about the same rate regardless of light and temperature conditions, but from that point on, the rate of development is dependent on weather conditions. In the Middle West this difference in rate of development may mean that the shoot that develops from a pinch will flower in 90 to 250 days, depending on the time of year the shoot is pinched. Rapid flower development in periods of high light intensity accounts for the early crop in the fall when abnormally bright weather is experienced, and the slowdown in flower production during the dull days of winter is well known.

There is relatively little that can be done to modify the weather conditions sufficiently to cause a change in the rate of flower development. However, adjustment can be made in the time of pinching so that the right amount of time is planned between pinching and flowering for that specific time of the year. For the Middle West it can be expected in general that about 90 days is required for flowering from a May pinch and about 150 days from an October 1 pinch. In areas where the summer light and temperatures are not quite as intense, the rate of flower development will not be as rapid at that time of the year. Where the winter light intensity is greater, flower development will be more rapid than it is in the Middle West.

It is impossible to talk sensibly about the effect of pinching and weather conditions and their relationship to time of flower production unless there is a clear understanding of the method of pinching. Flower production will be much slower on stems that are pinched to two leaves than on stems that are pinched higher, so that five or six sets of leaves are left below the pinch. As described earlier, five or six sets of leaves should be left on the stem below the first pinch. The succeeding pinches should be made in much the same manner. This is particularly important when the pinching is done during hot weather. The plants will be built up more rapidly by this method of pinching, and flower development will be faster.

Rotations Various rotations of carnations can be used depending on the requirements for flower production. If carnations are followed by carnations in 1-year crops, the rooted cuttings or young plants are usually benched in late May or early June. Flower production then starts in the fall and continues until the plants are removed in the next spring or early summer. This rotation produces good-quality flowers during the time of the year when they are usually in greatest demand, but there is no flower production during the summer, although in most areas there is a continuing market for flowers during that period and carnations could be sold at a favorable price if they were produced.

There was a time when it was physically impossible to continue to grow carnations throughout the summer because of the excessive disease and pest infestations during the hot weather. More careful selection of stock has virtually eliminated the disease problem, and the better miticides that are available control two-spotted mite effectively. In addition, it is possible to grow good-quality flowers in the summer in the cooler temperatures of houses that are equipped with fan and pad or mist cooling systems.

A 2-year rotation can be used in which half the area is planted each year, and this provides for flower production from the entire area from fall through spring and from half the area during the summer. It is possible also to have a portion of the area on a 1-year rotation and the rest of the area on a 2-year rotation. The amount of area on a 2-year rotation would be determined by the quantity of flower production desired during the summer. Two-year crops save the cost of new plants and planting costs, but the plants may be tall and unmanageable, the quality of the flowers may not be as good, and it may not be possible to time crops as well as with 1-year crops.

Carnations can be rotated with other crops, and snapdragons can be used best for this purpose. Whatever production area is needed for flowers in the summer is left in production until fall, and then it is followed by either one or two crops of snapdragons before being planted with carnations again. The benches vacated by carnations in late August could produce snapdragon crops in December and early May and be available for planting with carnations in late May. The carnation-snapdragon rotation works well; and if some snapdragons can be sold profitably in the winter, this may be the best way to produce good-quality carnations and still have summertime production. Rotations with chrysanthemums are possible if the problem of providing 10°C temperature for carnations and 16°C temperature for the chrysanthemums can be resolved.

Any rotation that is used must provide the right distribution of colors at the various times of the year. White and pink carnations are in greatest demand, and in most areas the year-round demand for all colors is quite uniform, with the exception of red. The market for red carnations is best at Christmas, Valentine's Day, and Mother's Day.

Cutting the Flowers Carnations should be cut only when they are at the right stage of development, which can best be judged by observing the center of the flower. The center petals should be expanded so that the flower forms a hemisphere. Generally it is better to cut flowers tighter in the summer than during the winter. The flowers are usually cut from a given area two or three times a week.

It is best to use a knife in making the cut. Breaking the stem off very often injures the shoot developing at that node. The height at which the stem is cut is important and should be based on the effect that it has on the plant rather than on the length of stem on the cut flower. Cutting long stems in the fall is poor economy. The fall cut needs to be made high enough so that the plant is built up, and the return crop from a high cut will be considerably faster. Judicious cutting in September and October will increase the April and May crop.

If the plants are going to be discarded in July, the flowers may be cut with as long stems as desired after January. Stems from which flowers are cut

Figure 5-10 Position for cutting carnation flowers. For the most rapid return crop and greatest yield, the flower stem should be cut as indicated above two or more lateral shoots.

at that time of the year do not have time to develop a return crop of flowers before the plants are discarded.

The proper height of cutting can best be described as in the area where the leaves are well spaced. If the cut is made down too far, it will be where there is very little distance between leaves. It is usually advisable to cut above two side shoots whenever it can be done.

Cultivars Changes in the cultivars that are planted take place rather rapidly. If the new introductions have desirable characteristics, they receive wide acceptance readily. In spite of this, it appears that the cultivar William Sim and its host of mutants will be very popular for several years. This group of carnations has many fine characteristics, and about its only fault is willowy stems in areas of poor light.

There is some interest in producing various shades or tints of flower colors, and this is more common in some areas of the country than in others. It is possible to get various exotic or "decorator" tints in white carnations by placing the flower stems in dye solutions. The dye is absorbed by the stems and transmitted to the flower.

Storage Carnation flowers can be kept in good condition for a longer time if they are well grown. Flowers that are produced in adverse conditions do not keep as well. After cutting, the flowers should be kept in cool temperatures as this greatly increases the useful life of the cut flower. If the flowers are to be marketed promptly, they should be placed in vases of water as soon as possible after cutting and held at a uniform 4°C temperature until they are in the hands of the consumer. Preservative solutions used whenever the stems are placed in water—at the greenhouse, the wholesale store, the retail shop, or in the consumer's home—will provide longer life. It will be necessary for the flowers to be in warmer temperatures during grading, shipping, and selling, but this should be only for brief periods.

Immediately after cutting, if there is to be a delay in marketing, the flowers should be placed in a 1°C temperature in closed containers that do not absorb moisture but do allow the transfer of some air. The stems are not placed in water before or during this storage period, and the flowers may be held in good condition up to 4 weeks. When the flowers are removed from this storage, the stems should be recut and they should be placed in vases of a warm 30°C preservative solution in an air temperature of 4°C.

Ethylene gas causes carnation flowers to look sleepy and age rapidly. The common sources of ethylene in storages are fruits, vegetables, some greens, and diseased or decaying organic matter. Very small quantities of ethylene can cause a large amount of damage to carnation flowers, and care must be taken to see that the storage is clean and does not contain items that generate ethylene. Carbon dioxide generators that are not operating properly can produce ethylene or other toxic gases.

Marketing Carnations are usually packaged 25 flowers per bunch.

Carnations are sold by various methods—from retail greenhouses directly to the consumer, from wholesale greenhouses directly to flower shops, and from greenhouses through wholesale commission stores to flower shops. Regardless of the method of selling, some sales efforts are required, and there are selling costs involved. The average selling costs are 20 to 25 percent of the selling price.

Carnations are used daily the year-round, but they are in greater demand for Christmas, Valentine's Day, Easter, and Mother's Day. The price fluctuates with the market demand, and the holiday price often is about twice as high as it is at other times.

Celosia *(Celosia cristata—Amaranthaceae)*

This is a common bedding plant that sometimes is grown commercially outdoors as a cut flower. The tall cultivars suitable for cut flowers have either yellow or red flowers.

For planting outdoors in May the seed should be sown about April 1. The seed germinates in $1\frac{1}{2}$ weeks at 21°C. For later flower crops, the seed may be sown directly outdoors.

The common name of cockscomb identifies the shape of the flower, but there are plumosa types in which the flowers are feathery plumes.

Chrysanthemum *(Chrysanthemum* X *morifolium—Compositae)*

The chrysanthemum is commonly supposed to be a native of Japan and serves to the present day as the national flower of that country. However, according to Chinese history, the flower was cultivated in China more than 2,000 years ago, while the first available record of its use in Japan dates back to A.D. 1186, when the swords of the reigning Mikados were decorated with designs of the flower.

The earliest record of the introduction of the chrysanthemum into Europe relates to its cultivation in Holland by a merchant of Danzig, Jacob Breynius. In 1688 he described two types under the name of *Matricaria japonica* in red, white, purple, yellow, flesh, and crimson tints.

No reference to the cultivation of the chrysanthemum in France is found before 1789, when M. Blanchard, a merchant of Marseilles, brought home three varieties from China, one white, one violet, and one purple, of which the last survived. In 1827 M. Bernet found perfectly matured seeds, and from these new cultivars were obtained. This is the first record of successful production of seed, although many English and French gardeners made ineffectual efforts previous to that time.

John Salter gave a great impetus to the cultivation of the flower when he established a nursery at Versailles in 1838. He obtained a complete collection of the best kinds in France and Europe and began to raise seedlings, the most noted of which were Anne Salter, Marie, King of Crimson, and Queen of England.

In 1843 Robert Fortune was sent to China by the Royal Horticultural Society of London in search of rare plants. On his return in 1846 he brought back, among other curiosities, two small-flowered chrysanthemums which were known as the Chusan daisy and the Chinese *C. minimum.*

The importation of Japanese chrysanthemums to England dates back to 1862, when Fortune introduced several cultivars, some of which were spotted and striped, others of fantastic forms called Dragons, and one a beautifully marked white flower having the appearance of a pink rather than a chrysanthemum. Others among them had petals like long thick hairs, red in color but tipped with yellow. Still others resembled the camellia and vied with it in great size and brillant coloring. At the same time the Japanese work *Phonsan Zowfu* pictured a considerable variety of forms, among them a narrow-petaled kind known as *C. striatum* and a single with small pink rays which may have been the wild form of *C. morifolium.*

The development of the chrysanthemum before its introduction into England is not recorded. Hemsley stated in 1889 that "it is impossible to determine the parentage" of some of the double chrysanthemums, and it is highly probable that some of them are hybrids of *C. indicum,* the small yellow, and *C. morifolium.* The same may be said of some of the early figures of double cultivars of chrysanthemums, which authors have identified with one or the other of the two wild species. The slender Chusan Daisy, the parent of all the pompons, for example, is probably of mixed origin, though it may be pure *C. indicum.* The true *C. indicum* is found in its wild state from Hong Kong to Peking, the ray and disk flowers both being yellow. This species is not a native of India, and therefore Linnaeus' specification is inappropriate. It is a perennial shrubby plant, erect and rigid, growing to a height of 60 to 90 centimeters, with thin, flaccid, pinnately parted, and acute-toothed leaves. The flowers are yellow. The rays are shorter than the diameter of the disk.

C. morifolium is found in Luchu Archipelago and the Chinese central province of Hupeh. It is more robust than *C. indicum,* the leaves are thicker and tomentose, and the ray flowers are of a different color from the disk flowers. The gracilis variety of *C. morifolium* is known only from the mountains near Peking, from southern Manchuria, and from Japan. The plants vary in color, having lilac, rose, and deep-rose ray flowers. Japanese specimens differ from the Chinese specimens in having decidedly hairy leaves.

The early history of the cultivation of the chrysanthemum in the United States is not available. Doubtless it was introduced in America soon after its development in England in 1795, because the florists of that period were active in obtaining novelties from their Eastern correspondents. It appears that the cultivated chrysanthemum was introduced into the United States much earlier than is ordinarily supposed. By the time the Massachusetts Horticultural Society was incorporated in 1829, the interest in this flower had increased considerably. There were certainly 17 or 18 known cultivars recognized. From this time on, interest in the chrysanthemum rapidly developed.

It was not until after the middle of the last century that the chrysanthemum began to be regarded as a greenhouse plant. Previous to that time it had been grown almost exclusively as a garden flower in regions where the fall season was favorable for its development.

Beginning in 1889, chrysanthemum development in this country centered about Elmer D. Smith, who introduced his first seedlings at an exhibit in Indianapolis in the fall of 1889. The cultivars shown were medium-sized, incurved, and quite similar to those now grown as disbudded pompons. In all, Smith originated, named, and disseminated over 500 cultivars, many of which have stood the test of years and are still looked upon with favor.

Smith was followed by several hybridists who produced cultivars of commercial value, and many new cultivars are introduced each year. The business of developing new chrysanthemum cultivars, producing disease-free stock, and selling rooted cuttings is one of the largest phases of the flower industry. Yoder Brothers, Inc., and later other organizations, have been increasingly active in this field since the early 1940s.

There are many shapes, sizes, and colors of chrysanthemum flowers, and they have excellent keeping qualities. The chrysanthemum cut flower is produced in great quantities throughout the country for the daily market, but there is usually no increased demand for holidays. The production of year-round chrysanthemums is made possible by supplying artificially long or short days as needed for the growth and flowering of this plant. The development of the practical application of daylight to chrysanthemums was made by Laurie and his co-workers in 1930.

Chrysanthemums are propagated by means of stem-tip cuttings. The rooted cuttings are planted and grown in long days until the stem is of the proper length, and then short days are provided until the plant flowers. After the flower is cut, the plant is removed, the soil is reworked, and a new crop of rooted cuttings is planted for the next crop of flowers. Depending on how they are handled, approximately three crops of flowers can be produced per area per year.

Flower Types The chrysanthemum is actually an inflorescence of florets on a head. Some of the florets which have distinct petals are known as ray florets; they are pistillate or contain only female flower parts. The florets with extremely short petals are called disk florets, and they contain both male and female flower parts. The flowers are classified by the kind and arrangement of florets. Singles have one or more outer rows of ray florets with disk florets at the center, in a daisy-type arrangement.

Anemones have the same floret arrangement as singles, but the petals of the center florets are more developed, showing their tubular shape and forming a cushion.

Pompons have ray florets over the entire flower. The disk florets are hidden by the ray florets, which form a formal, globular, or ball-shaped flower.

Decoratives have a floret arrangement that is similar to pompons, but the petals of the outer ray florets are longer than the inner ones, giving the flower a flatter appearance.

Incurved types are larger flowered cultivars that have a floret arrangement somewhat similar to that of pompons. The long petals of the ray florets curve upward and inward, forming a large, globular flower.

Reflexed types also have ray florets with long petals, but the outer florets reflex downward, forming a less formal flower.

Spiders have tubular ray florets, and the outer florets are often much longer than the ones in the center. In some cultivars the tubes are hooked at the ends.

Fujis are somewhat similar in appearance to spiders, but the tubular ray florets are straight tubes and not hooked on the ends. The center ray florets are approximately the same length as the outer florets, giving the fuji a brushlike appearance.

Classification of Chrysanthemum Crops Chrysanthemums are also classed as standards, sprays, or disbuds by the type of growth or the method by which they are handled. Standards are large flowers produced with one flower to a stem (all the lateral flower buds are removed or disbudded). Incurved and reflexed flowers and to a limited extent spiders and fujis are used for standard production. Standards may be grown as either single-stem or pinched crops; if they are pinched, the plants usually are pruned to only two stems per plant, as the goal is large flowers. It is the large, incurved cultivars that are produced in greatest quantity, with flowers from 10 to 15 centimeters in diameter and stems about 75 centimeters long. Standards are

Figure 5-11 Types of chrysanthemum flowers. Left to right from the top: incurved, spider, pompon, decorative, single, anemone. *(Yoder Bros., Inc. photograph.)*

produced the year-round in many northern and western greenhouses and on a limited basis outdoors in Florida.

Sprays are smaller flowered cultivars that are produced with many flowers or a spray of flowers per stem; the lateral flower buds are not removed. Several different flower types are grown as sprays, and the pompon type is the most common. In some areas of the country the term pompon or pom is used interchangeably with or instead of the term sprays. Single, decorative, and anemone flower types are all used as sprays, and they are more commonly grown as pinched crops with either two or three stems per plant. Sprays are produced in some of the northern and western greenhouses the year-round, and they are grown outdoors from fall through spring on a large scale in Florida. In other areas of the country, sprays may be grown outdoors or under cloth during the time of the year when temperatures are favorable for good growth. Sprays are grown with about 75-centimeter stems and are of medium weight, so that four to six stems may make a 250-gram bunch.

Disbuds are grown with one flower per stem in the same manner as standards, but usually the flower is a size smaller and the stem shorter. The smaller size may be due to the cultivar of chrysanthemum that is used or to the method of growing. The large-flowered types—incurved, reflexed, spider, and fuji—may be used for disbuds as well as some of the small-flowered types. Some decoratives, anemones, pompons, and singles can be used for disbuds if they form a large enough flower when they are disbudded. Disbuds are usually spaced closer together in the bench so that there will be more production of the medium-sized disbuds than there is of the large-sized standards. Disbuds are produced in greenhouses primarily for local area sales.

Flowering in chrysanthemum is controlled by length of day—or rather length of night. During long days chrysanthemums form leaves, and the stems increase in length, and during short days flowers are formed in the stem apex, and growth in length terminates with the flower. In natural conditions the chrysanthemum grows in length and produces leaves during the long days of summer; but in the shorter days of late summer and early fall, flower buds form, and the plant flowers. Some chrysanthemums form and develop flower buds more rapidly than others, and on the basis of this response the cultivars are classed in groups according to the number of weeks required for flowering after the start of short days. The fastest response to short days is 7 weeks, and the slowest response is 15 weeks. The 7- and 8-week cultivars are often used as garden plants in the North because in natural outdoor conditions they will flower in October before the killing frosts. Farther south, the 9-, 10-, and 11-week cultivars may be used for garden plants, as freezing weather occurs after their natural flowering period

Table 5-6 *Classification of Chrysanthemum Cultivars and Date of Flower Bud Formation and Maturity*

Pinching date	Probable date of flower bud formation	Date cultivar matures	Classification of cultivar
July 4	Aug. 20	Oct. 5–Oct. 14	7-week
July 11	Aug. 23	Oct. 15–Oct. 23	8-week
July 18	Aug. 26	Oct. 25–Nov. 1	9-week
July 25	Sept. 1	Nov. 5–Nov. 14	10-week
Aug. 1	Sept. 4	Nov. 15–Nov. 23	11-week
Aug. 8	Sept. 8	Nov. 25–Dec. 1	12-week
Aug. 15	Sept. 12	Dec. 5–Dec. 14	13-week
Aug. 22	Sept. 15	Dec. 15–Dec. 23	14-week
Aug. 29	Sept. 18	Dec. 25–Jan. 1	15-week

in November. It is the 9-, 10-, and 11-week cultivars that are used to the greatest extent in year-round mum programs in greenhouses.

For years chrysanthemum flowers were produced only during the natural season, and flowering occurred from October to January by planting a selection from 8-week cultivars through 15-week cultivars. Since it was learned that vegetative growth or flowering could be produced in the chrysanthemum as desired by regulating the length of day artificially, chrysanthemum flowers have been produced at any time of the year.

Some chrysanthemums still are produced in the natural conditions of summer and fall, but the greatest proportion of the chrysanthemum production is in carefully controlled light and temperature conditions the year-round. The plants are started from rooted stem-tip cuttings under long days to produce leaves and increase in stem length. When the stem is long enough, short days are furnished to produce flower buds followed by flowers. The chrysanthemum is about a 4-month crop from the planting of the rooted cutting to the production of flowers. After the crop is harvested, the remainder of the plant is removed, the soil is cultivated and steamed, and the rooted cuttings for the next crop are planted. Depending upon how they are handled, approximately three crops of flowers can be produced per area per year.

Propagation Most chrysanthemum flower producers purchase rooted cuttings from specialist propagators because they have the facilities to produce disease-free, good-quality cuttings, and the right cultivars at the time they are needed. Chrysanthemums are subject to many diseases, some

Figure 5-12 Propagation benches for rooting chrysanthemum stem-tip cuttings. Left: mist line not operating. Right: mist line in operation. The misting system is activated by clock at regular intervals so that a film of moisture remains on the leaves.

of which can be transmitted with the cuttings. Most chrysanthemum stock was infested at one time with verticillium wilt and probably still would be if it were not for the procedure of culture-indexing designed by Dr. A. W. Dimock and developed for commercial use by Yoder Bros., Inc. Culture-indexing is a laboratory procedure designed originally to determine the presence of the verticillium pathogen in plants and later adapted to include methods for determining the presence of several different pathogens. It is essential to have a procedure such as culture-indexing to identify disease-free stock, as the plant may appear to be perfectly healthy and yet harbor the disease organisms that will later produce the characteristic disease symptoms.

The specialist propagator also has facilities for selecting the best strains or clones of cultivars. Plants sport or mutate continually. The striking mutations such as change of flower color are easily observed, but more subtle changes such as smaller flowers, fewer petals, less vigor, or greater or weaker stem strength may go unnoticed unless the stock is studied and the best characteristics are continually selected.

Most flower producers do not have the facilities for producing disease-free stock or selecting the best clones for propagation. If producers do not purchase all their cuttings from the specialist propagator, they should at least purchase their nucleus propagation stock from the specialist and replace this stock often enough to assure freedom from disease and the best selection of cultivars.

Chrysanthemum stock plants should be grown at a minimum of 16°C and provided long days so that they continue to be vegetative. Cultivars differ considerably in rate of growth, and this changes with the weather conditions of the various seasons of the year. Eight-centimeter stem-tip cuttings are taken from the stock plants when the shoots are long enough so that shoots with two or three leaves will be left on the plant. It takes about a month from the time a stem is pinched or a cutting is taken until the next crop of cuttings is ready for removal from the plant. The shoots on the stock plants should not be allowed to grow for a long time before the cuttings are taken, as such stem tips may have started to form flower buds in spite of having been in long days.

In addition to providing the normally good temperature, light, moisture, air, and mineral environment for the stock plant, the planting and pinching of the stock plants must be carefully scheduled so that the right number of cuttings of the proper cultivars is available at the right time. Scheduling may not be a big problem for a crop or two, but for a year-round program in which cuttings are planted weekly and cultivars changed seasonally, it becomes a management problem fraught with many pitfalls.

Rooting the cutting is the lesser problem with chrysanthemums since it is a rather routine procedure as compared to the many details involved in producing the supply of stem-tip cuttings. Several materials can be used satisfactorily for the rooting soil, but mixtures of horticultural-grade perlite and German peat moss are used most commonly. Chrysanthemum cuttings are stuck about 2 centimeters apart in the rows, and the rows are spaced 5 centimeters apart. The cuttings are stuck just deep enough so that they remain upright.

The air temperature should be 16°C and the propagation bench temperature 21°C for rooting the chrysanthemum. Other propagation procedures should follow the general practices outlined in Chap. 4. Chrysanthemums require about 2 weeks for rooting, and they should be lifted from the propagation bench when the roots are 1 centimeter long.

Chrysanthemum cuttings do not store as well as carnation cuttings, but either unrooted or rooted cuttings can be held satisfactorily for a few weeks at 1°C if all conditions are right.

Planting, Spacing, and Supporting There are three primary concerns for the newly planted rooted cutting: minimizing water loss from the cutting, promoting rapid root growth, and having some nitrogen available for the plant. The best method of reducing water loss from the cutting is to mist the plants often enough so that the leaves remain moist, and in extremely hot weather a light shade may be placed above the plants. Root growth is aided by a favorable air supply in the soil. Shallow planting helps, and during the winter when soils dry slowly, the plants should be spot watered, leaving dry areas between the rows of plants. In cold weather additional heat around the newly planted area will dry the soil more rapidly and promote root growth. The young plants do not require a lot of nitrogen in the very early stages, but some is needed. If nitrogen is lacking at the time of planting, it should be supplied when the plants are watered in.

The amount of space that the plant is allowed in the bench is one factor that determines the amount of light that is available for the plant and possibly to a lesser extent the competition among plants for fertilizer and water. Within limits the farther apart the plants are spaced, the better the growth. Plants should be spaced at the distance that will produce the quality and quantity of flowers that can be sold at a profit. A spacing of about 15 to 20 centimers is used for plants that will be pinched and about 10 to 15 centimeters for plants that will be grown single-stem. Actually the spacing should be varied from one season to another, allowing more space per plant during periods of inadequate light.

If the plants are grown single-stem, they are not pinched, and therefore only one stem per plant is produced. This method of culture saves some growing time, and it is possible that better quality flowers can be produced, particularly during the winter. Single-stem culture requires about twice as many plants as pinched culture, but the saving in production time about equals the cost of the additional plants.

Various methods can be used to support chrysanthemums so that they will grow erect, but the most satisfactory system is welded wire fabric. If cultivars are used that grow to about the same height, a single layer of wire fabric can be used per bench. At planting time the fabric is placed at the soil level, and planting is done through it. As the plants grow, the wire fabric is raised so that the upper portions of the plants are supported upright. When it is installed, the wire fabric is stretched as tightly as possible and fastened to bars at each end that can be moved up and down on the end posts. About every 3 meters along the bench, upright members with crossbars are provided for support of the wire. These uprights also are the means for supporting lights and black shading fabric.

Light The chrysanthemum will grow most rapidly under conditions of high light intensity. In summer, shade on the roof makes the greenhouse a somewhat more desirable place to work, but will delay development of the plants. Plants grown under reduced light will be somewhat taller and thinner stemmed and will have larger leaves. If used, shade material on the roof should be very thin, and all of it should be off by late August.

In the winter, light is at a premium in greenhouses, and everything possible must be done to provide the greatest amount of light. The quantity of light that the plants receive at any time of the year is one of the determining factors in the amount of photosynthesis that will take place in the plants, which affects the amount and quality of growth. The best light intensity range for photosynthesis in chrysanthemums is probably from 3,000 to 10,000 foot-candles. As the light intensity in some winter days does not exceed a few hundred foot-candles, photosynthesis is limited at that time, and plant growth is reduced.

Chrysanthemums are affected also by the length of the daily light or dark period, a quality known as photoperiodism. In the initial studies, the effects were ascribed to the length of daily light, and chrysanthemums were called short-day plants because chrysanthemum flower buds form and develop in short days. Later studies established that it would have been more appropriate to use the term long night rather than short day, but at least commercially, chrysanthemums continue to be called short-day plants even though some of the procedures that are used are actually based on the effect of the dark period. More recently it has been learned that it is a blue pigment, called "phytochrome," in plants that actually changes in short or long days. It is this pigment, probably acting as an enzyme, that causes the photoperiodic effects. It has been demonstrated that the photoperiodic response is due not only to the daily length of day or night but also to the type or quality of light. The red end of the light spectrum, about 580 to 720 nm, produces the long-day response. Yet if plants are subjected to far-red light, about 720 to 800 nm, just the opposite effect is caused: The plants react as though they were in short days.

The commercial significance of the effect of light quality on chrysanthemums is that light that is rich in red rays should be used for extending the day length artificially. The incandescent lamp that is commonly used does provide that quality of light, but if fluorescent lamps are used, pink or red tubes will provide the red light needed. Theoretically it would be possible to produce short days for chrysanthemums by irradiating them with far-red light during naturally long days, and it is possible that this or some related procedure may be developed in the future. Experimentally, far-red illumination has only been partially effective in producing the short-day effect in some chrysanthemum cultivars.

Low-intensity light is effective in providing the day-length response. Some chrysanthemum cultivars respond to intensities as low as 1 or 2 foot-candles; however, a minimum of 10 foot-candles of light is usually maintained when long days are furnished artificially. This amount of light is easily provided by several different lighting arrangements, but one of the most common is the use of 60-watt lamps spaced 120 centimeters apart and 60 centimeters above the plants. With such an arrangement the lights must be raised as the plants grow in height.

In long days chrysanthemums form leaves and continue to grow in height. In order to produce this vegetative growth in naturally short days, the plants are supplied with artificial light sometime during the dark period daily. When this work was first started with chrysanthemums by Laurie and associates, the artificial light was added at the end of the day to make a long day. Later work demonstrated that the long-day effect was really the effect of short nights—a daily dark period no longer than $9\frac{1}{2}$ hours which can be provided by lighting for a rather long period of time at either end of the day or lighting for a shorter period during the middle of the night. Various methods are used commercially, but generally the lights are added each night of August and May for 2 hours; of September through October and March through April for 3 hours; and of November through February for 4 hours. In order to reduce the power load at any one time, half the area may be lighted immediately before midnight and the other half immediately after midnight.

There has been some interest in cyclic or flash lighting for chrysanthemums. Several procedures have been used in a limited way. The one that has received some commercial acceptance provides a 4-hour lighting period each night, but the area is divided into five units that are lighted for 6 minutes every 30 minutes using a light intensity of 20 foot-candles. This procedure can reduce the total power load at any one time and may lower the total quantity of power that is used, but it must be realized that cyclic lighting is based on furnishing the minimum quantity of light. Slight variations in conditions may cause some problems; hence such a system can be used only if it is properly designed and supervised.

Chrysanthemums may be given partial shade during the time of the year when light intensity is high, in order to improve flower color and prevent petal burn. This partial shade is provided best by erecting cheesecloth or lightweight muslin above the plants as they start to flower. This is good procedure to follow in most areas of the country from May through September.

Artificial short days for chrysanthemums during naturally long days are provided by placing black fabric over the plants. Black cotton cloth or in some instances black polyethylene are used for this shading, which must assure almost total darkness for the plants (2 foot-candles or less when the sunlight intensity is 4,000 foot-candles). For the short-day effect, a daily dark period of at least $9\frac{1}{2}$ hours must be provided; commercially a daily dark period of 12 to 15 hours is used so that the fabric may be applied and removed by regular work crews. This method of applying the black shade fabric may be the most economical in the use of labor, but there may be some deleterious effects on the plants. Covering the plants with black fabric for too long a period daily may limit the amount of photosynthesis and may cause temperatures that are too high for the proper growth and development of the plants. This problem is compounded in areas that observe daylight savings time. After daylight savings time begins in the spring, if black fabric is applied at the same clock time as before, it will actually go on an hour earlier by sun time; this will reduce the effective light on the plants and increase the temperature under the cover. For best response of the plants, the black fabric should be applied daily at about 8 P.M. and removed at 8 A.M. This may be a problem if manual labor is used, but an automated operation can be performed under control of a time clock.

Black fabrics are used over the plants beginning in early March and continuing to the end of September in order to have controlled short days. Some black fabric may need to be used during naturally short days to prevent chance lighting of areas that should be in short days; this is done best by using drop cloths between the areas lighted and the short-day areas.

Black fabric shading should be done daily during the period when artificially short days are being provided; however, it is possible to skip shading once a week without serious consequences other than delaying the

Figure 5-13 The effect of continuity of short photoperiods on the flowering of spray chrysanthemum. Left to right: shaded 7, 6, 5, and 4 days per week. *(Yoder Bros., Inc. photograph.)*

flowering date by about the same number of days that are skipped. The only reason for skipping shading once a week is to give the shade pullers a weekly break. The black fabric treatment does not need to be continued until the flowers are cut, but with most cultivars of standard mums it should be continued until the flower buds are as large as a nickel, and with sprays it should be continued until the flower buds show color.

When the length of day is manipulated mechanically, the environment is changed abruptly from long days to short days, but in natural conditions there is a gradual shift from one critical day length to the other—and in fact there is probably some shifting back and forth for a few days between long days and short days. The effect of abrupt versus gradual day-length transition has been a subject of speculation and some research, but it is believed that abrupt change may be as good as gradual. In some instances, however, a few short days are interspersed into the end of the long-day period, a custom known commercially as interrupted lighting. This procedure can increase the number of ray florets in standards during winter flowering, but the effect varies with cultivars and some other environmental conditions. It is a procedure that has apparently been used to good advantage by some growers, but it has not been adopted as a general practice. There are some variations in the number of days of interruption that is used, but a common recommendation is 9 days of short days toward the end of the long-day period, followed by 12 days of long days and then short days to flowering.

Temperature Although the chrysanthemum has for years been called a "cool crop" because it flowers in the fall, many cultivars will not form flower buds at cool temperatures. Depending upon the maturity date of the cultivar, flower buds form between mid-August and late September, at

Figure 5-14 For most rapid flowering, chrysanthemum should be given short photoperiods each day after the treatment is started. (*Yoder Bros., Inc. photograph.*)

which time the night temperature should be maintained at 16°C to ensure proper bud formation. In the Middle West, the night temperature is generally at least 16°C, but occasionally the late cultivars will be blind if no heat is used in cool September weather.

After the flower buds have developed to a size that is visible, the temperature may be lowered a degree every two nights to 13°C to enhance the quality of the cultivar. This reduction of temperature is of prime importance, particularly with many of the cultivars which are in the 12- to 15-week groups. Maintenance of a high temperature (16°C or higher) will actually delay development. Thus with late cultivars (12- to 15-week) the night temperature should be warm to form flower buds and then gradually cooled after buds are visible so that they will develop. When grown too cool in September, flower buds will not form, the stems will be blind, and the growth will often be rosetted. Heat delay has been commonly associated with hot summer temperatures, but it may be encountered in December with some cultivars growing too close to the heating pipes or in a 16°C greenhouse.

In periods of warm fall weather the pink, bronze, and red cultivars may fade. If the air is kept too cool, many white cultivars will become pink-tinged and yellow flowers will turn bronze, but this may also be true of flowers that are too old.

Cooling greenhouses in summer with fan and pad improves the quality of the growth. The maintenance of a warm temperature at the time of flower bud formation is one of the key factors in successful culture of mums out of season. Although there are a few cultivars that form flower buds in cool temperatures, almost all the cultivars must have a minimum of 16°C at night when short-day treatment is started. In fact, in very dark weather a night temperature of 18°C is recommended to ensure uniform flower bud formation. As soon as the buds are barely visible, the night temperature can be lowered from 18 to 16°C. With many of the 12- to 15-week cultivars, night temperatures of 13 to 15°C will actually promote development of the buds, whereas a temperature of 16°C or higher will cause delay. Quality of the flowers of many cultivars is improved if the air temperature can be lowered to 13°C, but this may be impossible if there are plants in all stages of development in the same house.

In summer, delay caused by excessive heat is quite common on some cultivars. Night temperatures above 30°C are known to delay development (not formation) of flower buds. This may be partially alleviated by uncovering the plants during the darkness and promoting the circulation and admittance of cooler outside air by fans. Cooling by fan and pad is effective in overcoming heat delay, but care must be exercised, or botrytis blight may ruin the flowers as a result of the high humidity.

The pink, bronze, and red colors fade in hot weather, though there are some cultivars which are more satisfactory than others. It is believed that the pigment is prevented from forming by the high temperature. Older flowers fade rapidly, particularly in hot weather. In winter certain white cultivars may show a pink tinge even at 16°C, which indicates it is too cool.

Troubles Poor growth in the early stages is often caused by too much fertilizer, poor drainage conditions, or lack of fertilizer. If roots are not growing, excess fertilizer or poor drainage or both should be suspected. In such a situation the top leaves may be yellow. If the root system is good, but there are little top growth and small greenish leaves, it is quite likely that there is a deficiency of fertilizer. The plants need some nitrogen continuously in the early stage of growth, and without it the top growth will be permanently stunted.

Various flower bud formation and development problems can be caused by unfavorable light or temperature conditions. If the plants are in short days but too low temperatures, flower buds may not be formed and the growth is compact or rosetted. If the plants are in short days but in too high temperatures, flower buds (crown buds) may be formed and the growth usually is elongated. Crown buds form more readily in some cultivars than in others, but they will form in most cultivars even in long days when the stem is allowed to grow long enough before short days are started. Formation of crown buds in plants within a few weeks after planting is an indication that the stock plants were not lighted properly or that the cuttings were taken from shoots that were too long.

Malformed flowers can be caused by diseases or pests, but they also can be caused by giving the plants various combinations of short and long days.

Figure 5-15 Variable photoperiod causes delay in chrysanthemum flower bud development and produces malformed or crown buds. The plant on the right received short photoperiods continuously. The plant on the left had some long photoperiods interspersed with the short photoperiods. *(Yoder Bros., Inc. photograph.)*

Figure 5-16 Sunburn on chrysanthemum flowers. Some cultivars are more susceptible than others. It can be prevented by placing a partial shade above the plants before the flowers start to open. The burn appears as an arc or circle on the flower because florets at the same stage of development are affected. Botrytis blight usually affects the oldest, outer florets, and sunburn occurs on the more recently formed florets toward the center of the flower. *(Yoder Bros., Inc. photograph.)*

Such situations arise from failures of electrical equipment, poor shading fabric, or failures of personnel to handle either lighting or shading properly.

Petal burn or sun scald is often confused with botrytis blight, but they can be distinguished because *Botrytis cinerea* infests the tips of the oldest petals and burn occurs on the younger petals at the center of the flower. The burn usually appears as an arc or circle at the center of the flower because the petals at the same stage of development are affected. Burn is a problem with standard chrysanthemums during hot weather, and it can be prevented by supplying light shade over the plants as the flower buds start to show color.

Diseases Bacterial stem rot is most destructive in hot weather. Infected cuttings appear normal but soon begin to wilt, and the inner stem is hollow and blackened. A check in growth such as pinching appears to accentuate the trouble.

Botrytis blight, or gray mold, is a disease in which the petals turn brown and appear water-soaked. It is troublesome when the air is moist and so is best alleviated by using heat and ventilation plus circulating fans to keep the air moving.

Dodder is a parasitic plant found mostly on outside plantings. It uses food from the mum plant and causes cessation of growth.

Powdery mildew is prevalent under conditions of high humidity, particularly in dark weather. The white powdery fungus on the leaves is unsightly, and in severe cases the stems may be affected.

Root-knot nematodes cause gall-like knots on the roots and in general severely stunt the plants.

Rust appears as small blisters which erupt, exposing the brownish spores.

Septoria leaf spot, or black spot, is a fungus that causes irregular black blotches on the foliage. Infected leaves usually turn yellow and drop.

Stem rot caused by *Rhizoctonia solani* is common if the cuttings are planted too deeply, are overwatered, or are placed in very heavy soil. Rotted areas are noted at the soil line or below.

Stunt is a slow-moving virus disease that severely dwarfs the plants and causes fading of flowers of pink, red, and bronze cultivars.

Verticillium wilt, or Siedewitz disease, is caused by a vascular fungus that affects most cultivars. Leaves on one side of the stem or the entire stem usually turn gray-green and wilt perceptibly. By the time the plant is in flower, the foliage is usually dead, and the flowers are small. Verticillium wilt never kills the plant, and cuttings taken from infected stock will generally have the fungus within them.

Yellows is a virus that affects the flowers. A portion or all of the flower is yellow-green rather than the normal color, and the flowers are generally smaller. Aphids and leafhoppers that feed on infected plants spread the trouble, as does handling the plants.

Pythium stem and root rot affects some cultivars of chrysanthemum much more readily than others. The use of the pythium-susceptible cultivars must be avoided in outdoor areas where the means of environmental control are not adequate. Soil and handling equipment must be thoroughly steamed.

Ascochyta or ray blight is best known for the characteristic malformed flowers following an invasion of this pathogen, but other portions of the plant may be involved and the leaf symptom may resemble septoria leaf spot. This organism germinates only if there is water on the plant and is therefore much more common on outdoor crops than in the greenhouse.

Pests Aphids disfigure the young growth and are unsightly. There are various kinds and colors of aphids, and they are especially difficult to kill when they attack the stem tip and are protected by the enfolded leaves.

Chrysanthemum midge makes galls on the foliage and stems. Inside the galls of an affected plant are larvae which have hatched from orange-colored eggs laid by the female flies. The larvae feed about 28 days, and emerge to mate and repeat the cycle.

Cutworms eat the foliage or flowers. Of special interest is the corn earworm, which in a short period of time can devastate a crop of standards in flower.

Cyclamen mite is found at the very tip of the stem, but it is too small to be seen without the aid of a magnifying glass. These pests cause malformation of the new growth, and in severe cases growth practically ceases.

Foliar nematode is an eelworm which moves from leaf to leaf through films of moisture. It enters the leaf through the stomates and causes development of brown wedge- or pie-shaped areas in the foliage between the veins. The damage usually is noticed in the basal foliage, and infested foliage usually dies. Keeping foliage dry prevents the worm's spread, but this is not always practical.

Grasshoppers chew the leaves and flowers and in severe cases will devour the young stems.

Leaf miner larvae tunnel through the foliage between the upper and lower epidermis and make irregular light-colored patterns in the leaf. The injured leaf may be split apart and separated into upper and lower surfaces.

Leaf rollers are whitish-green caterpillars that chew the underside of the foliage, leaving the upper epidermis, which dries until it looks like parchment. They roll the leaves together by means of a web and emerge as brown moths to mate and repeat the cycle.

Mealybugs occasionally infest mums and are easily distinguished by the white cottony masses covering the gray pests in the axils of the leaves.

Red spider is a serious pest because it sucks the juices from the leaves and causes a light mottling. It also infests flowers and, if not controlled, can build up large populations in a short time.

Slugs and snails chew ragged holes in the foliage and occasionally attack the flowers.

Sowbugs chew the young stems and may attack the roots.

Spittlebugs are rarely troublesome but may sting the young growth and cause minor disfigurations. A frothy white mass identifies this pest.

Symphylans stunt the growth through their injury to the root system.

Tarnished plant bugs sting the stem, causing excessive branching or even blindness.

Termites may become troublesome in wooden benches with wooden legs. They bore into the stems of the plants and cause wilting.

Thrips are a very serious pest at certain seasons. They rasp the foliage and flowers and cause light-colored streaks on the foliage and deep-colored petals and brownish steaks on yellow and white petals.

Whitefly is unsightly. The nymphs suck the juices of the leaves but seldom noticeably injure the plants.

Pinching, Pruning, and Disbudding Chrysanthemums may be grown as either pinched or single-stem plants, and no matter which method is used, approximately the same amount of space is allowed per flowering stem. Plants can be planted 15 by 20 centimeters apart, pinched, and pruned to two stems; in comparison, single-stem plants would be planted 10 by 15 centimeters. To maintain the same spacing per flowering stem in a pinched plant pruned to three stems, the plants would be spaced 20 by 23 centimeters.

Figure 5-17 The length of time between pinching and start of short photoperiod for chrysanthemum must be scheduled carefully for the best flower arrangement or formation. In spray mums it affects the height at which the terminal flower develops and the length of the lateral flower stems.

All the activities associated with producing chrysanthemums are carefully scheduled so that the right-quality flowers are produced at the desired time. One of these activities is pinching. Time is allowed in the schedule for the plant to make enough terminal growth after planting so that the pinch can be made in the new growth. A soft pinch should be used; remove as short a stem tip as possible. Shoot growth from the leaf axils below the pinch will then be rapid and of good quality. The length of time that long days are used after the pinch also is scheduled carefully so that the stem attains the proper length and is in vegetative growth at the time short days are started. If the plants are given long days for too long a time after the pinch, flower buds (crown buds) start to form but do not develop completely. Crown bud formation is eliminated when the times of planting, pinching, long days, and short days are scheduled properly; and the terminal flower bud that forms during short days continues to develop during the short days to a mature flower.

Following pinching, several shoots develop, and these must be limited, depending on the amount of space that is allowed per plant. The top two or three shoots are usually of the best quality. For this reason, the cuttings are spaced widely enough apart at planting that there will be sufficient room for two stems per plant, and when shoots develop after the pinch, all but the two top shoots are pruned. In some instances three shoots are retained on the outside rows of plants if the good light conditions in this position justify it. Pruning should be done as soon as the shoots are big enough to be handled.

Disbudding is the process of removing flower buds that are not desired on the chrysanthemum stem. A lone, large flower per stem is wanted in standards and disbuds; and in order to produce this, the lateral flower buds must be removed (disbudded). Disbudding must be done as soon as the flower buds can be handled because if they are left on too long, the size of the terminal flower is reduced, and it matures more slowly.

Some disbudding of spray mums may be done, but this is a selective type of flower bud removal to improve the arrangement of flowers in the spray. The most common disbudding on sprays is the removal of the terminal flower bud to make the lateral flowers more effective and to create a looser arrangement of the flower spray.

Rotations and Cropping   Chrysanthemums may be grown during the natural season, making weekly plantings from late June until the middle of August and cutting flowers from late October to late December. Natural-

Figure 5-18 With standard mums, the lateral flower buds should be removed (disbudded) as soon as they can be handled. *Left:* before disbudding. *Right:* after disbudding.

season crops require no artificial light or shade, which effects savings in production costs, but this may attract more growers into producing fall chrysanthemums and thereby produce an oversupply and reduced prices. Natural-season mums can be rotated with bedding plants, spring pot plants, or a spring crop of tomatoes. Natural-season crops have their early growth in the warm temperatures of summer and early fall, and they are finished in the fall at about 10°C. The cool finish saves fuel and does improve the flower quality, but it delays flowering.

When it was realized that there were commercial possibilities in the use of artificial light or shade to control mum flowering, the first attempts were to lengthen the natural season by lighting some plants for flowering after the natural season and shading others for flowering before the start of natural-season flowering. Gradually procedures were developed for flowering chrysanthemums at any time of the year. For flowering from late August until early October no artificial light needs to be used as the natural days are long enough, but black fabric must be used during this period when short days are needed. For flowering from mid-November until early April no

Figure 5-19 A planting machine used for chrysanthemum cuttings (unrooted cuttings in this instance) in Florida. *(Dorcas Flowers photograph.)*

Figure 5-20 Newly planted chrysanthemum fields in Florida. Note the electric lights for providing long photoperiods. *(Dorcas Flowers photograph.)*

black fabric shade needs to be used as the natural day length is short enough, but the plants have to be lighted during the early stages of growth. For flowering at other times of the year both artificial light and shade have to be supplied.

When large-scale production of mums was started outdoors in Florida, flowers were produced from late November until May; and the plants had to be provided with artificial light but not black fabric. Each year the flowering season has been extended, and so black fabric shading does have to be used for the spring and early summer crops.

In northern states crops cannot be planted outdoors until the first part of May because of frosts, and they may be safe from frost until early October. This allows for some outdoor production in the North from late August to October; however, the flowering season can be extended by starting a few crops indoors in pots and planting them outside in May, or by providing some protection from the frost in October and early November.

Outdoor production in any part of the country is better under tobacco cloth or plastic screen than it is in the open fields, and it is limited primarily to sprays, as standards are more susceptible to damage from rain, wind, and diseases.

Chrysanthemums are produced the year-round in many greenhouses throughout the country, and the objective often is to produce approximately the same quantity of flowers each week. This becomes an interesting problem in management as varying lengths of time are required to produce chrysanthemums, depending on the seasonal weather conditions. It is not unusual to have to make some compromise between having the bench space occupied continuously and producing the crops at the time of greatest need. In order to do the best job of utilizing the available space and producing flowers at the right times, it is necessary to develop a schedule for the mum production area about 2 years in advance. This is an elementary but indispensable schedule that lists each planting unit, date of flowering, date of replanting, date of second flowering, and so forth. It usually is satisfactory to allow 1 week between the scheduled flowering date and the date of replanting because the flowers should all be cut by the scheduled date, which provides 1 week for reworking and steaming the soil in preparation for the replanting.

Year-round scheduling of chrysanthemums could be a simple operation if the same length of time could be used for each crop regardless of the time of the year. If, for instance, each crop required 18 weeks from planting to cutting, a 19-unit area could be planted weekly the year-round; and with a week between flowering and planting, a crop of flowers would be cut each week of the year. The growth of chrysanthemums varies with weather conditions, and pinched crops require from 17 weeks for flowering in late summer to 21 weeks in midwinter. Single-stem crops require 15 to 18 weeks. In order to produce a flower crop approximately weekly the year-round, about 20 units are needed for pinched crops and 17 units for single-stem crops. A unit can be a bench, several benches, or a house depending on the size of the operation.

Adequate lighting and shading must be provided for the entire area, and a minimum night temperature of 16°C is used.

Various rotations of mums with other crops may be used, but it is not practical to interplant chrysanthemums in either carnation or snapdragon areas as the temperature requirements are different. Because chrysanthemums are a short-term crop, it often is possible to produce a crop in an area vacated by roses or carnations between the time of removing the plants and the time for replanting.

Cutting Flowers Most growers allow the flowers to open too far before cutting. Cutting the stems while the flowers are slightly on the "green" side is preferred because it offers a better quality product for the customer. In general, spray types should be cut when the central flower is open and the surrounding flowers are well developed, and cultivars which shed pollen badly will have to be cut before they become unsightly. Standards should be cut before the center florets are fully expanded.

Stems should be reasonably soft where the cut is made since very hard, woody tissue may not absorb water. Entry of water into hard stems is facilitated if the stems are slightly crushed with light blows from a hammer or mallet. The lower one-third of the foliage on the stem is stripped off to prevent leaves from fouling the water, and the stems are placed in water to "soak up." Warm water is absorbed faster, but the air temperature should be cool to harden the flowers. The flowers can be graded, bunched, and packed after several hours in water. Flowers to be stored dry at 1°C need not be placed in water unless they are wilted.

There are no universally accepted grading or bunching standards, and individual growers use their own judgment and ethics. The 250-gram bunch has been used widely for the spray types, but bunches weighing 450 grams are common, particularly in glut periods. Less than five stems per bunch is not acceptable to most retailers. Because of the wide variety of spray chrysanthemums, it is difficult to establish a set of standards. The appearance of the bunch may govern the sale more than the weight or number of stems. Where stems are reasonably alike, no fewer than five should be placed in a bunch, and the bunch should weigh at least 250 grams. The length of stem need not be over 75 centimeters for most purposes.

Storage   Although chrysanthemums keep well at a cool temperature in water, their life can be extended by storing them dry at 1°C. The flowers or bunches are laid in waxed boxes or boxes lined with sheets of polyehylene and are placed at the prescribed temperature, where they may remain for as long as 3 weeks. The dry condition of the tissue plus the cool temperature reduces the rate of respiration and maturity. When the flowers are removed from storage, the stems should be cut and they should be placed in 33°C water for several hours until soaked up, at an air temperature of 10°C, and then packed for shipment. Stock infected with disease should not be stored since the trouble may spread to the entire contents of the box. Only the best-quality stock should be stored because the plant material does not improve in cold storage.

Marketing   For long-distance shipment, standards must be packed properly to prevent damage. A cushion of rolled newspaper is placed on the bottom of the box, and the flowers are laid with the "necks" resting on the newspaper. The next row of flowers is laid so the heads rest on the neck of those below, and strips of waxed paper are placed under all layers of flowers to prevent drying and injury. When the stems touch the end of the box, the same system is started at the other end of the box, and the stems are inserted underneath the heads of the flowers at the opposite end of the box. The center of the box is left open for cleats to securely fasten the stems and for ice, if needed.

The bunches of the spray types are laid in the box side by side, with one layer on top of the other from both ends until the box is filled. If the bunches have been wrapped with cellophane or waxed tissue paper, there will be a minimum of entanglement of stems and flowers and resultant breakage.

In severely cold weather 20 or 30 layers of newspaper serve as insulation; there are also patented box liners which are bettern insulators than newspaper. Heavy cardboard boxes are better insulators than wooden boxes.

Daffodil *(Narcissus pseudonarcissus—Amaryllidaceae)*

The daffodils that are forced most commonly in the greenhouse are the trumpet daffodils. The botanical name is given above. In these flowers the corona is as long or longer than the segments. King Alfred has been the most popular cultivar for years.

Daffodils with coronas that are shorter than the segments are classed as large-cupped narcissi when the corona is one-third to nearly as long as the segments, and as small-cupped narcissi when the corona is less than one-third as long as the segments. The large-cupped and small-cupped narcissi are cultivars of *Narcissus* X *incomparabilis.* Several of these cultivars are grown in the greenhouse.

Cultivars of several other species of narcissus are forced in the greenhouse. These species are *N. triandrus, N. cyclamineus, N. jonquilla, N. tazetta,* and *N. poeticus.*

A large portion of the daffodils forced in the United States are started from bulbs produced in the northwestern part of the country. Depending on the temperature treatment they are given after digging, the daffodil bulbs are supplied either as regular bulbs or precooled bulbs. The regular bulbs are shipped in late September, and they are kept at 18°C from digging to shipping time. The precooled bulbs are shipped about the middle of October, and they are kept at 9°C from digging to shipping time.

Precooled daffodil bulbs are used for flowering from late December to mid-January. For flowering from late January on, regular daffodil bulbs may be used.

The daffodil bulbs should be planted as soon as they are received. They are used most commonly for cut-flower crops, and these bulbs usually are planted in flats or boxes so small quantities can be brought into the greenhouse at intervals for forcing. From planting time to start of forcing, the planted bulbs are placed container-to-container either outdoors or in cool storage. For the first 2 or 3 weeks the temperature should be about 16°C to promote root development. The temperature then is reduced to 10°C or less.

In the northern United States the natural outdoor temperatures are satisfactory for the storage of the planted daffodil bulbs outdoors if they are covered sufficiently to prevent freezing later in the fall. Refrigerated storage space is more costly, but it is much easier to manage.

Daffodil bulbs are graded after digging, and the largest grade is called double-nose number one (DN#1). It is the grade that usually is grown in the greenhouse.

There will be growth of shoot and leaves while the daffodil bulbs are in storage. When the leaves start to emerge from the nose of the bulb, it will be only the leaves that can be felt within the sheath that encloses them. Subsequently the stem tip can be felt also, and at this stage of growth the plants can be taken in for forcing. Forcing temperature usually is 16°C.

Delphinium *(Delphinium elatum—Ranunculaceae)*

Delphinium is a perennial that is grown most commonly as an outdoor cut-flower crop. The seed may be sown about September 1 in cold frames and then transplanted outdoors in the spring at 30 by 30 centimeters.

They may be started by sowing the seed in the greenhouse in January. The seed germinates in about 18 days at 21°C night temperature and 30°C day temperature. The seedlings usually are planted in flats at 8-centimeter spacing and grown at 10°C until they are planted outdoors.

For delphinium cut-flower crops in late spring and early summer in the greenhouse, the seed is sown by August 1 and then given some protection in frames until transplanted in the greenhouse in November. The spacing should be 15 by 20 centimeters, and the temperature 10°C.

Forget-Me-Not *(Myosotis sylvatica—Boraginaceae)*

This cut-flower crop is usually grown in retail rather than in wholesale greenhouses. The small, blue flowers and short stems make it effective for foreground placement in larger arrangements or by itself in small vases.

The seed is sown during the summer. It germinates in $1\frac{1}{2}$ weeks at 13°C, in the dark. The plants are spaced 28 by 28 centimeters, and the temperature is 10°C.

Freesia *(Freesia* X *hybrida—Iridaceae)*

Usually freesia are started from corms shipped in August through November for cut-flower production from February through April. The corms are planted about 5 centimeters deep and about 8 centimeters apart. They are grown at 10°C.

The larger corms will produce two to four flower stems. The entire flower stem may be cut when the terminal flowers mature, or the first cut may be made just above the first lateral shoot when the terminal flowers are mature. This flower stem would be about 30 centimeters long. The lateral flower stems then can be cut as the flowers mature, and they will have about 20-centimeter stems.

Freesia may be started from seed sown outdoors in May. Watering is discontinued in September and the tops die. The corms then are dug and transplanted indoors in October and November.

Gladiolus *(Gladiolus* X *hortulanus—Iridaceae)*

This native of South Africa is now seldom grown in the greenhouse. Winter crops are produced in Florida, and summer crops in the northern states, with a gradual progression of crops between those periods in the intervening states. This is all outdoor production. The greatest acreage in gladiolus production is in Florida.

The gladiolus forms a thickened underground stem that is commonly called a bulb but is technically a corm. Propagation is by means of the bulblets (cormlets) which grow in clusters at the bases of the maturing bulbs. From 40 to 120 bulblets are planted per 30 centimeters of row. About 8 months later they are dug, cured for 2 months, given a hot-water treatment for the control of some diseases and pests, dried and given cool temperature (about 4°C) for 2 to 4 months, and given warm storage (24°C) for a few weeks before being planted for the second season's growing period. When the bulbs are dug after the second year's growth, they are cleaned and graded, dipped in a fungicide-pesticide, and placed in 4°C storage to terminate the rest period. Before they are planted in the production fields it must be determined that they have had a sufficient time in cool temperatures to end the rest period. The bulbs are then placed in 24°C temperatures for 1 to 3 weeks or until there is evidence of some root development. Gladiolus corms were formerly produced in the north and northwest states. More recently many of the corms have been propagated in Florida.

For flower production, No. 2 corms (3 to 4 centimeters) and larger are used. In Florida, planting is usually done from September to February at the rate of about three corms per 30 centimeters of row or an average of about 45,000 corms per acre. Land must be chosen in a frost-free area, well drained but with irrigation water available, and free of diseases, pests, and weeds. If the land has not been under cultivation previously, it may be reasonably free of disease and weeds. Land used previously for crops of any kind should be treated chemically, if at all possible, for control of pests, diseases, and weeds. If the land cannot be treated, replanting to gladiolus must be delayed as long as possible—at least 5 years.

Irrigation facilities must be available to supplement natural rainfall. Fertilizer must be applied regularly, and the kind and amount are dependent on the soil and the amount of moisture. Cultivation of gladiolus fields is usually required to control weeds and improve the aeration of the soil. If weeds are not handled by cultivation or treatment of the soil before planting, herbicides such as dacthal or diuron may be used after planting. These herbicides are effective only against germinating seeds. Periodic applications for the control of pests and diseases usually are necessary during the growth of the crop.

The flowers should be cut when the floret buds swell and the petals begin to show. The stage of development for cutting the flowers is varied with the prevailing temperature. In warm weather, flowers are cut when three to four florets show color, and in cool weather not until five or six florets are at that stage. The flowers are shipped in tight bud, and all the floret buds develop and open satisfactorily when the stems are placed in water after they are shipped to the retailer. After cutting, gladiolus are graded according to the number of florets, the overall length, and the weight and length of the flower head. The largest grade is labeled fancy, and the next grades by size are special, A, B, and C. The flowers are bunched in dozens, and they are shipped upright in hampers which hold from 10 to 24 dozen depending on the grade. If gladiolus were shipped in the horizontal position, the tips might curve upward. This is a growth response known as geotropism which also occurs in snapdragons. This effect often can be observed in flower arrangements in which either gladiolus or snapdragons are placed in the horizontal rather than upright position.

After flower harvest the corms are allowed to remain in the ground until they mature. This may be from 4 to 10 weeks after the flowers are cut. In hot, dry weather, irrigation must be continued during this period. About 2 to 3 weeks after digging, the corms are cleaned to remove the mother corm, roots, and cormlets. The corms are graded, given disease or pest treatments, and placed in 4°C storage for 2 to 4 months followed by about 24°C storage for a few weeks before replanting.

Several diseases are troublesome with gladiolus. *Curvularia trifolii* f. *gladioli* may cause rather large rotted areas on leaves, stems, or corms, and infected florets may not open. The land should be treated chemically before planting or at least 3 years should elapse between plantings of gladiolus on the same land. Irrigation should be done at the time of the day when the plants dry most rapidly.

The gladiolus botrytis blight fungus may attack leaves, flowers, or corms. It may be particularly damaging on flowers as there may be no evidence of it when they are packed, but they may be completely ruined by the time they reach their destination. The leaf infection may produce small, circular, red-brown spots as well as larger light brown areas with the typical gray mold growth on some of them. Early infections on floret petals are clear, water-soaked, pinpoint-sized spots, and they are followed by larger rotted areas covered with gray mold. Corms infected with *Botrytis cinerea* have brown or black rotted spots with some gray mold in evidence, and the corms are soft and spongy. Because *Botrytis cinerea* thrives on old flowers and trash, a good sanitation program is essential.

Stemphylium leaf blight is a disease of the leaves that produces small, round, yellow, translucent spots which show on both sides of the leaves. No other round spot on gladiolus leaves appears as bright when held against the light. Flower and corm size may be limited by this disease.

The most destructive disease of gladiolus is the brown rot of corms caused by *Fusarium oxysporum* f. *gladioli*. It may cause stunting of the plant, yellow lower leaves, curvature of leaf growth, and small flowers with weak stems and conspicuous veins in the petals. If the land cannot be treated chemically, it should not be replanted to gladiolus for at least 10 years. Wounding or bruising the corms should be avoided, and dipping or dusting the corms with some fungicides may be helpful.

Wireworms, cutworms, armyworms, thrips, red spider mites, nematodes, and leafhoppers are common pests of gladiolus. They are controlled only by persistent methods of treating the soil and thorough dusting or spraying.

Iris *(Iris* spp., bulbous–*Iridaceae)*

Although the origin of iris for forcing is uncertain, it is likely that the species *I. xiphium, I. tingitana,* and *I. filifolia* form the basis of the present-day cultivars. Although iris is a very profitable crop when grown well, blindness, or failure to flower, may occur.

West Coast iris bulbs are dug in July and then kept at various carefully controlled temperatures, depending on how they will be used later, until shipment to the greenhouse operators. Those bulbs which are to be forced late in the season (for planting November 20 and later) are shipped after digging to distribution points around the country, where they are held at 30°C until 6 weeks before time for shipment to the greenhouse and then held at 10°C for the remaining period. These are known as retarded iris.

Bulbs that will be planted in greenhouses in October and early November are placed in 32°C temperatures within 5 days after digging, and held for 10 days to accelerate the formation and subsequent development of the flowers, since at harvest time flowers are not yet formed. The bulbs then are shipped in controlled-temperature carriers to various storages where they are kept at 20°C followed by 6 weeks of 10°C temperature immediately before shipment to the greenhouse. Bulbs shipped the first two weeks in October are called "special precooled" because they are the earliest dug and most mature; those shipped from mid-October to the third week in November are called "precooled."

Some growers still receive their iris shipment in September and provide the cool storage treatments or plant the iris in boxes which are buried outdoors for the cool treatment. It is now more common, however, for all the storage treatments to be handled by the bulb growers or distributors, and for the bulbs to be shipped to the forcer at the right time for planting. Continuous flower production from mid-December to May results from weekly plantings of iris bulbs from the first week in October until March. Special precooled iris are shipped the first 2 weeks of October. For the next 6 weeks precooled iris are shipped, and for the remainder of the season bulbs which have been retarded and precooled are supplied. The Wedgwood cultivar may be forced most reliably during the entire period, and at a 16°C night temperature they flower from 10 to 11 weeks after planting. This is a short-term crop, and one which works in very well in small bench areas which may be available. This does not imply that iris may be grown in any conditions. The best available light is required, and iris must be kept well watered at all times.

Bulbs may be planted in boxes or flats, which must be at least 10 centimeters deep in order to provide the uniform moisture conditions required. Moving of flats at time of bud development may break roots and cause blasting of buds. Whether they are planted in benches or boxes, the bulbs must be given adequate space. Either 5 by 10 centimeters or 8 by 8 centimeters is satisfactory. In some instances interplanting is used. The first crop is spaced 5 by 15 centimeters, and if weekly planting is used, six equal-sized areas are planted at this spacing in 6 successive weeks. In the seventh week, bulbs are planted midway between the rows of the first planting. In the thirteenth week, bulbs are planted beside the bulbs in the area that was planted the first week, for by this time the flowers from the first planting have been cut.

Iris open well when they are placed in water if they are cut when the flower bud has opened just enough to show color. This is a definite advantage if the flowers are to be shipped, as partially opened flowers pack much better than those in full bloom. For local sales the flowers may be allowed to open more fully before they are cut. Iris are usually bunched by the dozen.

Larkspur *(Consolida orientalis—Ranunculaceae)*

For outdoor crops, the seed may be sown either in late fall or early spring at about 20-centimeter spacing in the row. The fall sowing will produce the earliest flower crop in the summer.

For a spring crop in the greenhouse, the seed is sown in September and the seedlings are transplanted to 8-centimeter pots. The seed germinates in about 3 weeks at 13°C, in the dark. The plants should be benched in November and December, spaced 30 by 30 centimeters, and grown at 10°C.

Orchid *(Orchidaceae)*

The orchid family is one of the largest, with over 20,000 recorded species; however, most of these species are the exotics of the tropics and jungles, as only a few genera are used in commercial production. Cattleya, phalaenopsis, and cymbidium orchids are the only ones that are commercially produced in quantity in greenhouses, and in addition cymbidiums and vandas are produced commercially in outdoor semitropical areas.

Orchids are special-occasion flowers used mainly for weddings, formal or "dress-up" dances, Easter, and Mother's Day. Because the cultivars flower at different times of the year and only once or twice a year, it has been necessary to use many different kinds for the production of flowers throughout the year. Flowering in cattleya can be regulated by temperature, and the time of flower production can be adjusted by providing the proper temperature. Flower bud formation in cymbidium takes place in cool temperatures, and these plants are grown in cool greenhouses or outdoors during the summer to promote flower bud formation.

Orchids have either sympodial- or monopodial-type growth. Cattleya is the best example of sympodial growth, but cymbidium also is of this type. The sympodial orchids have a prostrate rhizome whose growth terminates periodically with an upright pseudobulb, leaf, and flowers. The flowers of cattleya are terminal, and after the flowering a vegetative bud starts to grow at the base of the pseudobulb, forming a prostrate rhizome that terminates in a pseudobulb, leaf, and flowers. As this succession of growth—prostrate rhizome to upright flowering pseudobulb to prostrate rhizome—occurs, the plant eventually grows or extends over the edge of the pot and must be repotted.

Phalaenopsis has monopodial-type growth, in which the upright stem continues in uninterrupted terminal growth, producing closely spaced leaves as growth progresses, and periodically a flower stalk develops from a leaf axil. The monopodial orchids also form aerial roots from the stem as they proceed in their upward growth.

Propagation Propagation of orchids by seed is a technical procedure that is handled best by the specialist. It is a means of developing new cultivars, and some of the features sought in the new plants are heavier textured, larger, and longer lasting flowers; improved color; better flowering period; and faster and more vigorous growth and development. By knowing the characteristics of the parents, it is possible to predict the type of offspring with some degree of accuracy.

Propagation by seed is a time-consuming process: 4 to 8 years passes from the time of pollination until the flowering of the mature plant. The seed is sown on nutrient agar in aseptic surroundings, and the seedlings are transplanted to pots or small flats as soon as roots have developed.

The successful production of orchid seedlings requires detailed information, much experience, special equipment, and a devotion to the subject. It is a fascinating occupation that attracts many individuals, but most orchid growers would benefit from obtaining their seedlings from a reliable specialist. For those who want to try propagation of orchids by seed, a good reference is *The Orchids*, by Carl L. Withner, published by the Ronald Press Company.

If the seedlings are obtained from the propagator in the seed flasks, a small wire hook may be used for their removal from the flask. They are planted in either fir bark or a mixture of one-fourth fir bark, one-half German peat, and one-fourth perlite in small flats. After planting, the seedlings should be drenched with a fungicide for disease control. Uniformly moist conditions must be provided, and the seedlings should be misted frequently or covered with polyethylene film until the plants are established.

Orchid seedlings are grown at 21°C and in partially shaded locations that provide from 1,000 to 2,000 foot-candles of light. Faster growth and good-quality plants can be obtained by extending the day length to 18 hours with electric lights that furnish 2 to 5 foot-candles of light.

The plants should be fertilized regularly when they are established in the flats, using 20-20-20 or lower analysis at the rate of 56 grams per 380 liters of water with each irrigation.

When the plants are large enough they are transplanted to small clay pots, and they are then transplanted to larger pots as growth requires.

Cattleya and other orchids that form pseudobulbs can be propagated by division. The division is made so that there are at least four good pseudobulbs with each section, and they are then potted. If virus is present, it is possible to transmit it with the knife or shears that is used to make the division. To avoid contamination, the tools should be sterilized between each cut by steam or by dipping them in a solution of calcium hypochlorite.

The growth of the divisions may be slow depending on the condition of the pseudobulbs.

With cymbidium, divisions of one or more of the pseudobulbs are started in a mixture of sand and peat at 18°C and in moist surroundings. When the leaves are 15 centimeters long, the young plants are potted.

Phalaenopsis can be propagated vegetatively from growths formed on the flowering stem and known as offsets. The flowering stem may be cut into sections of at least one node, its surface may be sterilized in a calcium hypochlorite solution, and it may be planted in a fine potting mixture. Offsets form at the nodes, and when the roots of the offset are about 2 centimeters long, it is removed from the flowering stem and potted.

Tissue culture is a detailed laboratory procedure that can be used for the vegetative propagation of orchids, and now it is the primary means of cattleya reproduction. The advantages of tissue culture are that a large number of individuals can be propagated from a single clone selection in a short period of time and that the propagation of virus-free stock may be coupled with the procedure. The tissue sections are handled in aseptic conditions, and they are started in growth in a nutrient culture. Tissue culture is one of the most important developments in the commercial production of orchids.

Potting Mixtures   The same potting mixture may be used for cattleya and phalaenopsis except that for phalaenopsis the pH of the mixture must be adjusted to 6.0 with limestone, and the plants are potted more loosely than cattleya plants and watered more frequently. The roots of the monopodial-type phalaenopsis are structurally different from the roots of the sympodial-type cattleya, and root growth is best with slightly different treatment.

Osmunda fiber was used for years as a potting medium for orchids, but more recently various mixtures of bark and peat have been used. When osmunda was used, it was necessary to pot the plants very firmly; and the potting procedure occupied much of the total labor time. The osmunda was firmed with stick in hand, or in some instances potting machines were fabricated that did the firming faster. Much less firming and consequently much less potting time are required when fir bark mixtures are used.

The requirements of the potting mixtures for orchids are good aeration, uniform moisture conditions, and a source of supply of minerals. When osmunda fiber was used, it was considered that orchids should not be supplied fertilizer, as the osmunda did contain a small amount of nitrogen. However, subsequent experimental and commercial trials of growing orchids in gravel or haydite that were fertilized regularly demonstrated the basic requirements of the potting medium, which led to the use of various potting materials and regular additions of fertilizer.

A good potting mixture is made from poultry-litter-grade German peat moss, fir bark, shredded redwood bark, and horticultural-grade perlite. The proportions for a common mixture are 0.5 cubic meter fir bark, 1 bale peat moss, $\frac{1}{4}$ bale shredded redwood bark, and 0.1 cubic meter perlite. These materials must be moist but not wet before mixing, and they are mixed with a shovel before being passed through a shredder. Because of the difference in weight of the various ingredients, the mixture must be discharged downward from the shredder in order to remain well mixed.

For a coarser mixture a greater proportion of fir bark may be used. Such a mixture has better aeration but has to be watered more frequently. A coarse mixture should be firmed more when potting to produce suitably uniform moisture conditions for the roots. Apparently a pest problem is related to the coarseness of the fir bark mixture, too, as small bush snails that feed on orchid roots can be harbored in a coarse mixture. Control of this pest is easier in finer potting mixtures.

Because the rhizome of cattleya is prostrate and grows horizontally, this orchid is potted toward one edge of the pot; eventually the leading growth of the rhizome reaches the other edge of the pot. It is necessary then to repot the plant. The rhizome is cut into sections each containing four or six pseudobulbs, and each section may be repotted.

Because the growth of phalaenopsis is continuously upward, the plant eventually becomes too large and must be replaced with younger plants that have been started from offsets or seed.

Orchids are classed often by their position of growth in their natural habitats. Some orchids grow on tree trunks or branches above ground level and are classed as epiphytes. Other orchids grow in or on the ground in natural conditions and are classed as terrestrial. Cattleya and phalaenopsis are epiphytes, and cypripedium is terrestrial. Some orchids may be found as either epiphytes or terrestrials, and cymbidium is one of these. Commercially cymbidium may be grown in ground beds or in large pots or tubs, and the medium is more of a terrestrial mixture. Cymbidium potting mixtures must be well drained but retain moisture, and they are commonly made from mixtures of German peat moss, leaf mold, and sharp, coarse sand. The pH should be maintained at 5.5 to 6.0.

Although cymbidium has sympodial-type growth, the horizontal extension of the rhizome is slight, and the plant can remain in the same tub for a long time without division and repotting.

Moisture and Fertilizer Orchids are grown in coarse, well-drained mixtures, and they must be maintained moist. Irrigation must be frequent enough to keep the mixture moist and heavy enough to provide some leaching with each watering, and with cattleya and phalaenopsis the irrigation method must be such that thorough watering is accomplished without getting water on the upper portions of the plants. If watertight benches are available, subirrigation of the pots may be used. If proper breakers are used, irrigation systems using small-diameter, black polyethylene tubing can probably be installed.

The air moisture content should be maintained at approximately 70 percent relative humidity for young plants and plants in leaf; however, for plants that are in bud and flower, too much air moisture may promote some flower diseases. Continuous air movement with air-circulation fans and the proper regulation of heating lines and ventilators can provide suitable humidity.

Orchids do not grow rapidly, and large quantities of minerals are not required. Various fertilizers and rates of application are used at different greenhouses; but if the irrigation is thorough with some leaching, a 20-20-20 fertilizer may be used with alternate irrigations at the rate of 150 grams per 380 liters of water.

Light   Orchids grow best in light intensities from 3,000 to 6,000 foot-candles. At higher light intensity the leaves become yellow and may develop burned areas, and at lower light intensity the leaves are dark green and the development of the plant delayed. In many localities partial shade needs to be provided to reduce the amount of light for orchids. Light intensity can be regulated by lath shades on the roof, shading compounds sprayed or painted on the roof, or plastic screen suspended over the plants in the greenhouse. Generally some shade must be provided between February and November.

Flowering in cattleya can be controlled with day length: delayed by long days and promoted by short days. This is seldom used now, however, because the clones reproduced by tissue culture can be flowered the year-round by regulation of temperature.

Temperature   Cattleya should be grown at a 16°C night temperature and about 6°C warmer during the day; however, in some instances temperatures about 3°C lower are used during the flower-forming stage as this promotes flower initiation in some cultivars.

When possible, phalaenopsis is grown in temperatures about 3°C warmer than those used for cattleya.

Summertime temperatures should be kept below 35°C as leaves may be burned in higher temperatures. Orchid houses are commonly shaded to reduce the temperature in periods of high light intensity, and fan and pad or mist cooling is desirable.

Cymbidiums are grown in cooler temperatures—generally 3 to 6°C cooler than those used for cattleya—whenever possible. Fan and pad systems are helpful for the warm period of the year. Flowering of cymbidium is promoted by cool temperature, and as soon as possible in the fall the temperature is maintained at 7 to 13°C.

Air Continuous air movement should be provided as this helps to maintain the uniform temperature and the needed moisture conditions. High humidity when cattleyas are in bud and flower provides conditions that are suitable for development of some flower diseases.

Flowers are injured by smog, ethylene, or other air impurities that are found in industrial areas, and the best solution in such a situation may be to move to an area where the air is not contaminated.

Some trials have been made with orchids in atmospheres with increased carbon dioxide, but the results have been inconclusive.

Troubles Black areas on the leaf are caused by the sun's heating the leaf area to a point where the tissues are killed. Shade on the roof or cloth shades under the glass will prevent this.

In periods of high humidity, particularly in spring and fall when heat is not used at night, the yellow pigmented areas in the throats of cattleya orchids often turn black several days after cutting. This may be due to a fungus. Control is accomplished by use of additional heat plus ventilation. It is advisable not to refrigerate the flowers for a period of 12 hours after cutting if this difficulty is experienced.

In periods of hot, humid weather an exudate may appear on the lips of dark orchids which causes a discoloration and collapse of the tissue and ruins the flower. Heat and ventilation at night will prevent the trouble. It is often necessary to keep the night temperature higher than normal to provide the circulation of the air.

"Dry sepal" of cattleya is a problem when humidity is high, particularly in industrial areas where smog is prevalent. Certain cultivars of cattleya orchids are highly susceptible, while others are quite resistant to dry sepal damage.

Cold injury on cattleya orchids is characterized by the throat turning brown, the end of the column turning black, and the petals and sepals becoming water-soaked in appearance. Flowers of the cattleya, cymbidium, cypripedium, and vanda orchids should be stored at a temperature range of 10 to 13°C with the optimum at 13°C.

Deformed flowers of many cattleya hybrids are caused by continued temperatures of 13°C or lower during bud development, which may occur during attempts to delay the development of the flowers. This condition should not be confused with deformities which are hereditary.

Wilting of the flower, if not due to old age, is generally caused by pollination, usually by bumblebees.

Pests Scale, snails, and thrips are the worst orchid pests. Aphids, mealybugs, slugs, and millipedes may be troublesome also.

Diseases There are several virus diseases, and what is known as the cattleya virus is one of the more serious. The flower color is streaked or broken, usually rendering it unsalable, and the plant eventually dies. The virus can be transmitted by a knife when cutting rhizomes or roots, and infected plants should be discarded. The cymbidium mosaic virus causes loss of vigor on cattleya plants, and symptoms appear on the leaves as lighter colored green streaks or areas which later turn brown or black and often are sunken. The flowers are not affected.

The botrytis pathogen causes a red-brown area to develop and occurs when there is drip on the plants in cool or cold weather.

Root rot is a serious fungus disease on cattleya and is prevalent when the medium is kept too wet and cold (below 16°C).

Brown rot attacks the crown of cypripedium and phalaenopsis and is evidenced by a soft rot at the base of the leaves. Standing water in the crown should be avoided by watering early in the day and maintaining a lower humidity at night.

Cutting The cattleya flower should be cut from 3 to 5 days after the bud dehisces or splits depending on whether the weather conditions are favorable for rapid development. Cutting is facilitated if the plants are tagged each day as the buds split, and the flower on the tagged plant then is cut 3 to 5 days later. After cutting, the flower stems are placed in water at an air temperature of 13 to 16°C. Orchid flowers should never be placed in temperatures lower than 10°C because transparent "water spots" may appear on the petals or the flowers may wilt.

Phalaenopsis flowers are cut when they are fully open, either individually or as an entire spray. If the spray is cut above the bracts on the lower stem, a new flowering shoot will develop.

Cymbidium flowers can be cut individually, but more often the entire spike is removed and the individual flowers are cut at the time of grading and packing. The flower stems should be placed in water after cutting; and if they are kept in an air temperature of 13°C, they will keep for several weeks. Of all the cut flowers, the cymbidium has the best keeping qualities.

Shipping For shipping, the flower stems are inserted through gum rubber caps into small tubes filled with water. The opening of the rubber cap must be sufficiently large so that it does not restrict water movement in the stem. The tubes are taped or sewn to the bottom of the boxes, with the flowers on crumpled or shredded wax paper. Enough shredded wax paper is used around the flowers so that they do not rub on each other or on rough surfaces in transit.

Rose *(Rosa hybrida—Rosaceae)*

The present-day cultivars are all hybrids which have been derived from crosses between *R. gallica* and *R. chinensis*, from which came the Hybrid Chinese. *R. chinensis* was also crossed with *R. centifolia* to produce *R. edward*. This in turn crossed with *R. gallica*, which resulted in *R. bourbon*. A triple cross of the Hybrid Chinese, *R. bourbon*, and *R. damascena* in two successive generations developed the present-day hybrid perpetuals. To secure continuity of bloom, a further cross of the hybrid perpetuals with *R. chinensis odorata* resulted in the hybrid tea, which is the type largely used for forcing purposes, as it combines the necessary qualities of productiveness, fragrance, attractiveness of bud, and multiplicity of colors.

The hybrid tea rose forms a large terminal flower per stem, and if any lateral flower buds form, they are disbudded. The demand for red roses is greatest, and some yellow, pink, and white hybrid tea roses are grown also. Roses are in particular demand for holidays, and the plants are handled in such a way that greater production is realized at those times.

Some floribunda roses are grown. They are smaller flowered cultivars that may produce a lone terminal flower per stem, or lateral flower buds may form and be retained so that there is a spray of flowers per stem. Several of the floribunda cultivars have better keeping qualities than the hybrid teas, and because of this the demand for them has increased. Light pink is the most popular color, followed by red, orange, yellow, bicolor, and white. Typically only about 10 percent of the rose range may be used for floribunda production, but that would account for more than 10 percent of the total flower production, as floribunda plants may produce up to twice as many flowers as hybrid teas.

Roses usually are planted in the spring, and flower production may start 2 to 3 months after planting. Rose stems form leaves and increase in length in the early stages of growth. Eventually flower parts start to form in the stem tip, and growth terminates with a flower. When the flower is cut, new shoot growth starts in the axils of the leaves below the cut, and the growth and flowering cycle is repeated. Growth and flowering are faster in good light and warm weather, but flowers are formed in the rose at any time regardless of the day length or season. Rose plants may be pruned or cut back during the second and third summers in order to keep them within height limits, but other than that the plants are cropped continuously for approximately 4 years before they are discarded and replaced with new plants.

Propagation Roses are reproduced vegetatively by means of cuttings, grafts, and buds to produce the plants for the production of flowers. Each method has good features, and equally good results can be obtained with any method, depending on how it is handled. However, budded plants are used more commonly than rooted cuttings or grafted plants because they can be handled better in typical situations that exist. Budded plants are dormant (quiescent) when they are received from the propagator, and they remain quiescent and in good condition when properly refrigerated. They may be kept quiescent in refrigerated storage from December until June or planted at any time during that period with good results, and this provides a flexible planting program that is needed in many instances. Rooted cuttings and grafted plants are actively growing plants—or at least they should be—and the only way that good plants can be produced is by providing the best growing conditions at all times. This is particularly important in the early stages of growth. The time of propagation must be coordinated carefully with the time of planting so that the plants can be kept growing actively all the time. It is not possible to delay planting and still achieve good results with either rooted cuttings or grafted plants, but when they are handled properly, they can be just as good as budded plants.

Sexual propagation is used only for the production of new cultivars. Rose breeding requires special techniques and equipment, and it can be handled only by the specialist.

Budded plants are produced in a year's time on the West Coast or in Arizona, and they may be either started-eye or dormant-eye plants. *R. manetti* is used for the understock; hardwood cuttings of this plant are lined out in the fields in December, the budding is done from late April to mid-June, and the mature, budded plants are dug in December.

Budding may start as early as the latter part of April, that is, as soon as the bark starts "slipping" and the cuttings have attained fair size. If budding is done too early, the process will be difficult and the cuttings dislodged or the roots injured. If done too late, the bark is too thick and will cover the bud.

The bud wood of the desired cultivar is obtained from either outdoors or the greenhouse, making sure it is ripe and free of mosaic. It is cut into lengths of 30 centimeters and stripped of all thorns, and the leaves are cut off, allowing a short petiole to remain, while being careful not to injure the bark near a bud. A knife is used if difficulty is encountered in removing the thorns. The scions are then wrapped in moist burlap or plastic bags to prevent desiccation.

Stocks to be budded are furrowed 8 centimeters deep on each side by a single plow, a previous irrigation being required if the ground is too hard. Too deep furrowing will cause the wind to blow the stocks over and injure the roots. The budding process is done in groups of three—by a hoer, a budder, and a tier. The hoer scrapes the soil away from the plant and cleans the clinging soil from the bark by a burlap strip tied to the end of a stick. The budder, carrying bud stocks in a small box protected from the sun, makes the cut and inserts the bud. The tier follows and ties the bud with small rubber strips which decay and fall off in about 3 weeks. The first application of water is given 10 days after the budding and is continued periodically throughout the growing season.

The tops of the plants for started-eye plants are cut off about 2 centimeters above the inserted bud. This is done 3 weeks after budding in order to force the bud into growth. The stock tops may be partially cut through and then bent over, which allows food from the top to nourish the root. The stock top is later completely severed. The shoot that develops is pinched to three eyes to force out bottom breaks. This plant becomes the started-eye type of plant, so named because the eye or bud that was inserted was forced to start or grow during the summer. The tops of other plants are not removed until the plants are dug, and because the eye or bud did not grow during the summer, the plant is known as a dormant-eye.

All plants are dug in December, graded, and packed for shipment to greenhouse operators. With started-eye plants the XXX grade is preferred, as there should be several heavy shoots per plant. The tops of the dormant-bud plants are used as hardwood cuttings for the next year's plants. Mosaic is spread rapidly as a result of this random used of hardwood cuttings. Even though a manetti cutting is free of mosaic when stuck in the field, if the bud that is inserted is infected with mosaic, the disease spreads through the manetti plant, and when it is used as stock the following year, all plants budded on it will be infected. Because certain types of mosaic lower the vitality of the plant, the use of selected stool blocks free of mosaic and the use of mosaic-free buds are practices which would meet the approval of the forcers of greenhouse roses. Producers of plants estimate that from the time the cuttings are stuck until the plants are shipped, losses may run about 50 percent. This is due to failure of cuttings to root, failure of buds to unite and grow, breakage, pests, and other factors.

Occasionally some budding is done in the flower-production greenhouses, and this is called "top budding" as buds of new cultivars are inserted in the top portions of producing plants so that the flower qualities of the new cultivars can be observed, or in order to increase bud wood of the new cultivar. The bud is inserted in a T cut and tied with a rubber strip, and 3 weeks after budding the shoot above the inserted bud is cut off to start growth in the new bud.

Grafting of rose plants is a greenhouse operation that formerly was used by some operators to produce a portion or all of the plants that they needed for replanting their greenhouses. In some instances they also grafted additional plants for resale to other rose growers. *R. manetti* usually was used for understock, and it was obtained from West Coast or European growers. The grafts were made from February through April. The plants were set in closed cases or under mist until the graft knitted, and then they were placed in regular greenhouse conditions to produce some top growth before planting. Grafting can be a very successful method of propagation if it is carefully timed so that the plants are benched as rapidly as possible, good growing conditions are provided at all times, and plant growth is continuous and unchecked.

Rooted cuttings of roses are commonly called "own-roots." This term arose and is in general usage because it acknowledges that the rooted cutting has the roots of its own cultivar, but the roots of grafts or buds are *R. manetti*. There are controversies on whether roses grow better on their own or manetti roots. This may be an academic question as rose soils are heavily mulched, and roots form above the graft or bud so that even grafted or budded plants grow on their own roots, too.

Some rose growers use rooted cuttings for a portion or all of their rose plant requirements. Two eye cuttings are used, and they root in about 5 weeks with a bench temperature of 21°C and an air temperature of 16°C. Several rooting materials are satisfactory, and mixtures of perlite and peat moss are commonly used. The cuttings are spaced 2.5 centimeters apart in the row with 8 centimeters between rows. Rose cuttings should be furnished as much light as possible without drying the cuttings. Intermittent mist systems should be used whenever possible because they provide the needed uniform moisture without excessive shading of the propagation area.

Either unrooted or rooted rose cuttings can be held in 1°C storage up to a few weeks with satisfactory results, and this can be an aid because the cuttings can then be collected for a period of time before being stuck or planted. If the cuttings are placed in plastic bags which are not sealed, they will have a good air-moisture environment during storage.

The rooted cutting may be potted or planted directly in the bench. If the cuttings are potted, they must be planted within 3 weeks after potting to avoid hardening because of limited area for root growth. When the cuttings are planted directly in the bench, they are usually provided with better growing conditions, and the end results are better.

Roses are propagated sexually only by the hybridizer in an attempt to develop new cultivars. As the color develops in the petals, the mother-plant flower is emasculated (the anthers are removed) to prevent self-pollination; and when the stigma is sticky, pollen from the staminate parent is transferred to it. The pollinated flower is then covered with a plastic bag until the seed begins to form.

In natural conditions, rose seed does not germinate until the second year after sowing, but the hybridizer shortens this time by a cold-storage period. The seed is removed from the hips (rose fruits) by crushing and fermentation, and the clean seed is then disinfected and stratified in moist peat moss at 4°C for 4 to 6 months.

Planting, Spacing, and Supporting The time of planting is based on the availability of bench space and on the development of good plant growth in sufficient time for flower crop production. Bench space becomes available primarily when old, producing rose plants are removed, and in many instances the most economical time to remove them is in May after the Mother's Day crop has been harvested. The removal of the old plants is very often timed to follow one of the holiday crops, which may be Christmas, Valentine's Day, Easter, or Mother's Day. Rose plants are kept in production for about 4 years, and about one-fourth of the rose range is replanted each year. Cropping and work are better spaced if the replanting is done over a period of a few months in the spring.

An Easter crop of flowers can be produced from plantings made in late December and January, and a Mother's Day cut can be made from plants benched in January and February. This first crop, however, must not be taken if the general growth and development of the plants are not satisfactory. Flower production starts during the summer in plants benched later in the spring.

In most areas growing conditions in the spring are the best for starting rose plants; however, if a fan and pad cooling system is provided, roses can be planted during the summer and produce good growth. The primary objective is to develop rose plants with good, heavy canes and large leaves, as such plants produce the best growth during the poor light conditions of the winter.

Rose plants are spaced about 30 by 30 centimeters, and there is no advantage in deep planting. Plants that are shallow-planted form roots more readily than ones that are planted deeper; and since mulches are applied later to rose soils, shallow planting prevents the plant from being buried too deeply in the mulch.

Some budded rose plants have such a large root system that some pruning of roots may need to be done before planting, but as large a root system as can be handled in planting should be retained. The roots should be spread in the soil rather than knotted or bunched together.

After planting, the plants must be watered in well, but during the dark and cold weather in December and January they should be spot-watered, leaving dry areas between plants. The entire soil area is then watered thoroughly at the second irrigation. When planting takes place later in the season during good light and temperature conditions, the entire soil area should be thoroughly watered with the first irrigation.

The air around the plants must be maintained as moist as possible. This provides a more suitable atmosphere for shoot development in the quiescent, budded plant, and it maintains the leaf and stem growth in grafted plants or rooted cuttings until new root growth supplies water to the plants.

Budded plants may be planted in the quiescent stage directly from refrigerated storage, or they may be "sweated out" for a few days by being kept moist at 16°C until the eyes start to swell. There are some advantages to both methods of handling, but with either one it is important to keep the tops of the plants moist. After planting, the air can be kept moist around the plants by misting periodically or by covering the plants. More uniform air moisture is usually maintained by covering unless a mechanically operated mist system is used, as it is virtually impossible to mist regularly enough with hose-in-hand. Various covers may be used successfully. The plants may be covered directly with either sphagnum moss or straw, or clear plastic or light cloth may be supported just above the plants. This is a critical period in which much better results follow with uniform humidity. The plants must be observed very carefully, and as shoot development takes place, the cover is removed gradually. Not all the plants may develop at the same rate, and it is necessary to cover the slower plants individually when the cover is removed from the entire area.

Grafted plants and rooted cuttings are actively growing plants at the time they are planted. They need to be in moist air for several days after planting, but they cannot be covered directly. It is best to mist regularly, cover with a light cloth above the plants, or use a combination of the two methods.

Rose plants need some nitrogen in the early stages of growth. If the nitrogen in the soil is low at the time of planting, a fertilizer containing nitrogen should be applied with the first irrigation.

A method of support is needed to keep rose stems erect, and either individual plant stakes or a series of networks are used. When stakes are used, a galvanized No. 9 wire stake is inserted in the soil beside each plant and attached at the top to a wire that is stretched the length of the bench. As the stems develop on the rose plant, they are tied individually to the stake. When networks are used, they may be either welded wire fabric or wire run the length of the bench between the rows of plants with string laced across the bench between the plants. The first network is installed about 45 centimeters above the soil, and succeeding grids are placed at about 35-centimeter intervals above the first. As the rose stems develop, they are guided into the upright columns formed by the networks.

Light   Light is generally considered the most important limiting factor in the growth of plants in the greenhouse. The intensity of light is highest in summer, and it is at this time that the greatest number of roses is produced by the plants unless they are cut back during this period. Under the low light conditions of winter, fewer flowers are produced.

Rose flower production can be increased by supplementary electric lighting in the period of the year when light intensity is low. This lighting can be done with high-intensity-discharge (HID) lamps. It is possible that other more effective or more reasonable means of lighting may be developed in the future. It has been established commercially that there can be a significant increase in rose flower production with HID lighting, but the costs of installation and operation of the lighting are considerable. Some growers have found that the returns justify the costs, and others believe that it is not an economical procedure.

Day length has no apparent effect on the growth and flowering of roses.

As the sunlight increases or decreases, depending upon the season, growers modify the practices of watering, fertilizing, cutting, and pinching. Cultural practices vary from season to season, depending upon light and its effect on temperature. Fertilization with nitrogen is frequent in spring, summer, and fall because of favorable light conditions for growth.

Because of the high light intensity and the resultant rise in temperature in summer, many growers in the Middle West apply a shading compound to the roof. A reduction of light intensity to about 6,000 to 8,000 foot-candles from about 10,000 to 12,000 foot-candles is apparently satisfactory. The temperature is reduced, relative humidity is increased, and generally the stems will be longer with somewhat darker green leaves. Too much shade seriously reduces growth, and mildew infections can become serious. Shade is often applied lightly in early May, is increased in June and July, and should be removed by late August. When the greenhouses are cooled by means of fan and pad little or no shade is needed on the roof. Such a condition is favorable for growth because of the high light intensity together with the cool temperatures.

Cutting and pinching practices depend upon light intensity because of their effect on food manufacture. In spring, summer, and early fall it is not always necessary to allow two 5-leaflet leaves to remain on the plant. Cuts can be made leaving knuckles, or stubs, on heavy wood from March to October, but in winter such a practice usually would result in blind shoots. As the light intensity decreases in the fall, it is important with most cultivars that two 5-leaflet leaves remain on the shoot to make food for additional flowers. Very often shoots are pinched in the fall to add foliage to the plant.

The light intensity within the greenhouse also affects the plants. In an east to west house, rose plants in the south row of a bench produce more flowers than plants in any other row. The plants in the north row are next in production, followed by the inner rows. The production per unit area from plants in wide benches with five or more rows of plants across will not be great because of the increased number of inner rows.

Temperature   Most rose cultivars are grown at a night temperature of 16°C because at that temperature the quality and quantity of roses produced are considered satisfactory. At lower temperatures growth is slower and production is reduced, but the quality of the flowers is higher. At higher temperatures growth is increased and production is greater, but the quality is not as good. Temperature affects the rate of all physiological processes, such as photosynthesis, respiration, and amino acid and protein formation in the plant, and their effect on growth is governed by the temperature maintained in the greenhouse.

The temperature on sunny days is generally maintained 5 to 8°C warmer, if possible, than the night temperature. The purpose of this is to allow for greater food manufacture in the leaves. It is believed that at temperatures above 30°C the rate of photosynthesis levels off; therefore such high temperatures are undesirable. With a reduction of light intensity on cloudy days, the temperature is raised no more than 3°C because of the reduced rate of photosynthesis.

Respiration occurs both day and night and proceeds at a faster rate as the temperature increases. Therefore loss of food can result in poorer quality roses if night and day temperatures are not regulated properly.

The synthesis of proteins and amino acids, which are vital constituents of cells, takes place in the presence of a favorable supply of carbohydrates and some form of nitrogen, so that regulation of temperature affects the materials from which new growth is made.

The rate at which temperatures should be changed from night to day, and vice versa, is not known. As the sun rises, the greenhouse is heated, and there is no difficulty in reaching the desired temperature. In fact, on bright sunny days it is usually impossible to keep the temperature from going beyond the desired point unless the greenhouse is cooled by fan and pad. Bringing down the air temperature in the evening may require quite some time in warm weather because the structure, benches, soil, and plants are warm and it may be difficult to dissipate this heat by nightfall. In cold weather lowering the temperature to the desired point is no problem.

The temperature of the water applied to the soil appears to have little measurable effect on the plants. Warm water is not effective in increasing production, and cold water drops the soil temperature several degrees for only a matter of a few hours.

Soil   Since roses remain in the bench for a period of several years, thorough preparation of soil is imperative.

Rose soils must remain coarse and porous, and with some soils it will be helpful to incorporate 1-centimeter-grade haydite or calcined clay. The amount to add varies with the soil. Heavy, clay soils will benefit from larger additions.

Mulches are used for a number of purposes in rose houses. Primarily, they reduce soil moisture loss by evaporation, but they also improve soil structure and water drainage. Mulches also keep the soil somewhat cooler in summer. Roots will permeate a mulch, and the mulch therefore adds to the area where roots can develop. As mulches decompose, carbon dioxide is released into the greenhouse atmosphere, and this may keep the carbon dioxide concentration in rose houses at a favorable level.

The chemical changes induced by a mulch are dependent upon the type of material used. Peat may lower the pH somewhat, but it usually does not affect the fertilizer levels. Corncobs generally bring about a rapid depletion of soil nitrogen, and the rose plants may become starved and hardened unless some form of nitrogen is added periodically.

When the mulch material stimulates growth of microorganisms, soil structure is improved.

Practically any organic material can serve as a mulch provided it is properly managed with respect to needed fertilizer for the plants and frequency of watering. Mulches may be applied soon after the newly benched plants are established and growing satisfactorily.

Troubles The normal flowering shoot of a greenhouse rose possesses fully expanded sepals, petals, and reproductive parts. The failure to develop a flower on the apical end of the stem is a common occurrence; such shoots are termed "blind." The sepals and petals are present, but the reproductive parts are absent or aborted. Blind wood is generally short and thin, but it may attain considerable length and thickness when it develops at the top of the plant.

The cause of blind shoots is not known. Investigations have shown that, under normal conditions of growth, the amount of blind wood varies from 35 to 40 percent at any time of year and on any plant, whether planted in an outer or inner row of the bench. Various nitrogen and potassium fertilizer levels have neither induced nor retarded blind-wood production. Severe defoliation will often temporarily increase the percentage of blind wood, and it is possible that some hormonal mechanism is responsible for blindness rather than the direct results of such environmental factors as light intensity, temperature, and nutrition.

Chlorosis of the upper foliage can be caused by lack of one or more fertilizers as well as excesses, but injury to the roots from overwatering may induce similar symptoms. Nematodes on the roots may induce a light chlorosis, but more often stunt the growth. Some insecticides and fungicides may injure the leaves of the younger growth and cause yellow blotched areas or spots to appear.

Bullheads are malformed flowers in which the center petals of the bud remain only partly developed and the bud appears flat. They are common on very vigorous shoots, particularly bottom breaks, and it is possible that there is a lack of carbohydrate to develop the petals. Thrips infestation will also cause malformed flowers.

Leaf drop is experienced frequently and can usually be traced to some check in growth. Extreme dryness followed by resumption of normal watering will cause the rapid yellowing and drop of older foliage. Fumes are also responsible, and undetermined factors in the use of aerosols for insect control have caused undue foliage drop. Sulfur fumes from the material applied to heating lines for mildew control and the products of combustion from the smokestack are also responsible. Cultivars differ in their "shedding," too. Black spot results in leaf drop, and when mildew is extremely

Figure 5-21 Left to right: malformed flower commonly called "bullhead"; loss of terminal growth or blindness; a well-developed rose flower.

severe, the leaves will fall in due course of time. Loss of roots due to any cause can result in foliage loss.

Mercury toxicity is rare, but mercury is without question the most dangerous material which can be brought into the rose house. There is one case on record in which the rose benches were painted with a bichloride of mercury solution for sterilization, and roses were then planted. The growth was so poor that the range was eventually dismantled. Zimmerman and Crocker have conducted experiments to show typical symptoms. They showed that the sterilization of bench boards with bichloride of mercury may cause damage to all plants in the house. Mercury thermometers should have no place in a rose house, as there are accurate types that do not contain mercury. When mercury is spilled, it spreads in very numerous small droplets which add up to a very large surface area. Since mercury is a liquid, it evaporates, but at a very slow rate. Therefore the mercury vapors would be present in a rose house for many years. Paints containing mercury as a fungicide should not be used.

The symptoms of mercury damage are quite specific and are easily recognized. The stem below the flower, or peduncle, on young shoots turns brown, and the fall of petals is common. Growth is stunted, and the drop of all foliage except leaves on the youngest shoots is common. The production of bluish-red flowers is the outstanding characteristic of mercury damage.

The only control known is to remove as much as possible of the soil in and under the bench in which the mercury is found or suspected. This should be discarded, but not in the vicinity of the rose range. Iron filings—the finer the better—neutralize the mercury by formation of an amalgam which does not vaporize. Mixed metal filings may be used, but iron is preferred. These should be scattered to a depth of at least 2 centimeters over all areas where the presence of mercury is suspected. Since mercury is a heavy liquid, it spreads over a wide area when dropped, so that thorough inspection of the soil for a considerable distance is warranted.

Rose plants commonly have the characteristic mineral nutrient deficiency symptoms unless some fertilizers are applied periodically in addition to the regular fertilization program. Iron fertilizers should be applied to rose soils about once a year, in the form of either ferrous sulfate at the rate of 450 grams per 9.3 square meters of soil or chelated iron at the rate of 50 grams per 9.3 square meters of soil.

In some instances boron needs to be applied to rose soils. It is provided by making a single application of borax at the rate of 25 grams per 9.3 square meters of soil.

Magnesium may be deficient in some soils, and the application once or twice a year of magnesium sulfate (Epsom salts) at the rate of 450 grams per 9.3 square meters should correct the problem.

A symptom of boron toxicity in rose plants is black leaf–blade margin followed by yellowing of the entire leaflets and abscission.

Limp necks on roses are most noticeable in the retail store or with the ultimate customer. The area of the stem just below the flower "wilts" and will not support the head. Sometimes this is due to insufficient water absorption; cutting off the lower 3 centimeters of stem and placing the cut stem in water at 38°C with a preservative will revive the flower. Lack of sufficient carbohydrates undoubtedly has some relation to this difficulty.

Diseases Powdery mildew is very common and is recognized by the whitish powder on the leaves, stems, and petals. Air currents spread the spores readily.

Downy mildew is rare but causes drop of green leaves near the base of the shoot bearing the flower. Exacting regulation of temperature and relative humidity is important in its control.

Black spot causes loss of foliage, but if the leaves are kept dry, the spores can neither spread nor germinate.

Canker organisms of various kinds cause death of stubs from cuts, and the entire plant can be killed if the infected wood is not removed. Galls may appear on the lower stems or roots.

Black mold is a disease of the grafting case, and a blackened condition of the graft union is evidence of the disease. Infected plants die.

Verticillium wilt causes yellowing of the stems, and infected stems should be removed well below the visible area of trouble and destroyed, as should stems infected with canker.

Viruses cause mottling or distortion of leaves but in general are not thought to be exceptionally damaging.

Pests Red spider is the most serious pest in that resistant strains develop and new insecticides are constantly being sought to control them.

Aphids are unsightly but generally cause little damage.

Thrips can be responsible for bullheads or otherwise malformed flowers.

Leaf rollers of various sorts chew the leaves and petals.

Root-knot and other nematodes will seriously reduce the vigor of the plants.

Pinching Rose plants are pinched in various ways to produce branched plants, larger diameter canes, cropping of flower production, and longer stemmed flowers. The type and method of pinching are determined by need.

The objective with the newly benched plants is to develop several good-diameter canes from the base of the plants, and this can be controlled

Figure 5-22 Early pinch (roll-out) on rose. The pinch should be made above 2 or 3 five-leaflet leaves which are just unfolding. When pinched at this stage, the leaves below the pinch attain maximum size, and the shoot that develops will be larger in diameter than the one pinched. This pinch should be used at any stage in the plant's development if heavier canes and larger leaves are desired.

considerably by the way the pinching is handled. Typically the rose plant starts to develop one or two heavy shoots from the base of the plant and several shoots of small diameter. The diameter of the shoots can be increased if they are pinched at an early stage. The decision on the quality of the shoot needs to be and can be made at an early stage—when the shoots are approximately 3 centimeters long. If the tip of the shoot is removed just above the second or third five-leaflet leaf as it is unfolding, the leaves on the shoot will develop to the largest possible size; and the shoots that grow after the early pinch will be of greater diameter than the original shoot. With small-diameter stems, it may be necessary to make two or more successive early pinches to produce the size of cane that is desired. This early pinch is often called a "roll-out" since only the very tip of the shoot is removed. Some shoots that are pinched early will not form new shoots, but this is not of consequence as the large leaves that form following the early pinch improve the photosynthetic capacity of the plant. Since the early pinch on newly benched plants must be made at the right stage, all the plants must be inspected and pinched daily after growth starts in the plants.

The heavy shoots that develop naturally should be allowed to grow until the flower bud is just visible, and then they should be pinched above the top five-leaflet leaf. This type of pinch is commonly called a "soft pinch." Hard pinches are made lower on the stem, leaving 2 five-leaflet leaves below the pinch, which is at about the same place where flowers are cut.

The decision on when to stop pinching and start flower production should be based on the quality of growth that exists in the plant and on the

Figure 5-23 Soft pinch on rose is made to the first five-leaflet leaf on stems just starting to form flower buds. This pinch is used in timing crops for holidays or to increase the flower stem length.

future growing conditions. Growing conditions are much better from spring through early fall than they are in the winter, and it is to be expected that the quality of the shoots that develop in the winter will not be as good as those that grow earlier. Flower production can be started sooner with plants that are started in early spring than with those that are started later, as there will still be a period of good growing conditions after flower production starts. When flowers are cut from the plant, leaves are removed also, which means that the plant must be of sufficient size by fall to have enough leaves remain on the plant after the flowers are cut. The size and number of leaves on the rose plant during the time of the year when light conditions are poor will materially affect the amount of food manufactured in the plant.

Pinching to improve the growth of the plant must be continued during the time of flower production, and this pinching is limited to shoots that are not heavy enough or long enough. Small-diameter stems should be given the early pinch—just the tip is removed when the shoot is about 3 centimeters long. When this type of pinching is practiced religiously, there should be no small-diameter canes on the plant. Stems of medium diameter that were not given the early pinch should be soft-pinched to avoid production of short-stemmed roses, for which there is generally limited sale. It is necessary to do selective, early, and soft pinching on producing rose plants to maintain good-quality growth.

Pinching is used to time crops for holidays or to shift flower production from one period to another. Rose growers in each locality know from past experience the length of time required for a rose to develop following a pinch. In order to increase flower production for holidays, they pinch the proper number of weeks before the holiday. Usually a record is kept of the number of flowers cut and the number of pinches made during this period so that it will be possible to estimate the number of flowers that will be cut for the holiday. Either a soft or a hard pinch is used. Actually the length of time required from pinch to cut varies with the weather conditions, and the pinch dates are based on averages. If the weather is better than usual, the holiday crop is produced too early, and if the weather is not as good as the average, the flower crop will be delayed and may be too late for the holiday. The rate of development of the flower buds must be watched closely during this period, and the temperature must be adjusted to speed or delay the development as needed.

If rose plants are pinched so that they will crop for a holiday, they will recrop following the holiday. If the crop will not be needed at that time, some selective pinching must be done to distribute the flower production more evenly.

Flower Production Timing In late spring or summer, $5\frac{1}{2}$ to 6 weeks is required for the production of a flower from a cut or pinch. In winter it takes approximately 8 weeks, and proportional lengths of time are necessary for spring and fall production. It is important to remember that a soft pinch requires from 3 to 7 days longer to develop a flower than does a hard pinch or cut.

The variations in temperature in a greenhouse must also be considered. If one end of the house is several degrees cooler than the other, pinching must be started 3 to 7 days in advance at the cool end.

The development of the shoots themselves is quite variable. Roses with stem lengths between 40 and 60 centimeters mature faster than do the shorter or longer grades. Usually the shorter-stemmed roses are produced on the thinner and weaker wood, which probably accounts for the slower growth, and it is presumed that the flowers on the longest-stemmed roses are not formed as soon as those of medium length, and hence require additional time to mature.

For a Christmas crop, the plants should be soft-pinched from October 17 to 21 and hard-pinched from October 21 to 25 in the latitude of central Ohio. Cultivars differ, but these dates will apply for this locality.

A portion of the crop that is cut for Christmas often comes back for Valentine's Day on February 14, although this is not to be taken as a certainty. Easter occurs at a different date each year, but approximately $7\frac{1}{2}$ weeks should be allowed when it is early and 7 weeks when it is late. A considerable number of Easter cuts will come in for Memorial Day if Easter is neither very early nor very late. By counting back from a specific day, growers can pinch and bring their crops in at the desired time. The crop can be delayed or hastened by gradually lowering or raising the temperature as much as 6°C at night. The night temperature should not be raised or lowered more than 1°C in any one night. Extremely warm, sunny weather in the late fall may cause the Christmas crop to develop too rapidly, while long periods of cloudy weather may delay it. During the last 15 to 20 days considerable attention must be given to night temperatures.

Pruning   One or more times during the period the rose plants are in the bench, they must be pruned back rather severely to prevent them from growing so tall that cutting, tying, and other operations become inefficient. Two methods are used: (1) direct pruning and (2) gradual cutback. Both have their advantages and disadvantages; it is quite likely that both methods should be used in the rose range, not necessarily for comparison but for their adaptability to the general management of the range.

Direct Pruning, or Cutback   Usually sometime after Mother's Day, when roses are not needed in such large numbers, the plants can be pruned. Formerly, severe drying was allowed, until the foliage wilted, but this is no longer practiced. Instead, the plants are simply cut back to the desired height, and the frequency of watering thereafter is reduced because of the limited use by the pruned plant. The height to which the plants are cut back the first time should not be less than 60 centimeters for most varieties because the wood is generally quite hard below this point. If after cutting back, forks, or branches, remain in preference to single canes, so much the better. Each time the plants are pruned, the cuts should be made about 15 centimeters above the previous cutback to keep in somewhat softer wood, which "breaks" more readily. Relative humidity should be kept high by syringing frequently, closing side vents, using mist, and providing a roof shade, to encourage development of new shoots.

Gradual Cutback   Gradual cutback is often called "knife pruning" since the stems are cut with a knife when the flowers are taken from the plant. The gradual pruning, or cutback, is a modification of the direct cutback since not all stems are cut off at once. The gradual cutback can be started with the Easter crop, followed again by further removal for the Mother's Day crop. By Mother's Day it is possible to have completely cut back the plants so that few flowers are present. No matter how rapidly the gradual cutback is practiced, it is important that not all cuts be made at the same time. Some shoots are in flower at the time others are breaking out following the cutback. The plants should not be cut lower than 60 centimeters in height.

This method of pruning requires more skill and time than the direct cutback, but it has the advantage of not completely eliminating production for a period of several months, as occurs with the direct system.

A combination of the two methods may be followed: The first year after planting, the roses are cut back gradually. The second year after planting they are direct-pruned. The third year after planting they are again cut back gradually. They are often removed when they are 4 years old.

Cutting Flowers Close examination of a typical flowering stem of most greenhouse roses will reveal that approximately in the center section of the stem there are two to five leaves bearing five leaflets and immediately above and below them are several three-leaflet leaves. With reference to the buds at the axil, or base, of these leaves, it will be noted that the buds on the lower one-half or two-thirds of the flowering stem of vigorous shoots are either blunt or rounded, while the buds on the upper section of the flowering stem are pointed. The shape of the bud in the axil of the leaf serves as a guide when cutting flowers. Stems with flowers should rarely be cut to a leaf that has a pointed bud at its base. Such buds usually develop into flowering stems without the normal distribution of foliage or a series of

Figure 5-24 Cutting rose flowers. With rose plants, it is generally good practice to cut "up" (leaving 2 five-leaflet leaves below the place of cutting; top arrow) in the fall and winter because this leaves a sufficient number of leaves on the plants for adequate food manufacturing in the low-light-intensity period of the year. In the spring and summer, due to good growing conditions, the flower stems may be cut "down" (below the hook; bottom arrow).

scalelike leaves. The stems with flowers should be cut to a leaf that has a rounded or blunt bud at its base. The general rule observed by most rose growers in cutting the stem is to allow 2 five-leaflet leaves to remain below the cut. This is practiced except where soft pinches have been made. In that case the cut can be made below the soft pinch, again allowing 2 five-leaflet leaves to remain on the stem. Some cultivars are often cut to a stub or "knuckle" on the more vigorous shoots because they break faster and production is increased.

If the flowering stems were cut "up" each time, allowing 2 five-leaflet leaves to remain, some of the more vigorous shoots would be much too high after several months' time. On such shoots, it is common to cut as described; then the next time cut to the leaf immediately below the hook. When the bud in the axil of this leaf develops into a mature flower, the stem is cut in the usual way. This is sometimes called "going up two and down one" and serves to prevent the more vigorous shoots from becoming too tall. The less vigorous shoots are generally handled in the usual way.

The stage at which the flowers are cut differs with the cultivar. The yellow cultivars can be cut somewhat tighter than most pink or red types, and the buds will open and unfold normally. Flowers cut too tight fail to open for the customer. Most red and pink cultivars should be allowed to develop to a stage where one or two of the outer petals begin to unfurl. In most cases the sepals will be at right angles to the stem axis, or pointing downward.

Beginning in early August it is desirable to allow as much foliage as possible to remain on the plant after cutting flowers, to build up the plants for winter. This means cutting up, except in the case of very vigorous shoots. In the spring, from mid-February on, as light intensity increases, the "up-and-down" cutting system is useful on many shoots. At all times it is desirable to try to maintain a zone, or area, where the majority of flowers are cut. If some flowering stems are very high and others quite low, cutting is more difficult.

Knuckle cuts usually are made in the spring and fall. They are flowering stems cut to a hook, or crotch, allowing approximately 1 centimeter of stub to remain. There are usually numerous latent buds present which can be seen with the naked eye, and these develop into strong shoots when the wood is heavy. If weak, thin wood is knuckle-cut, the breaks will be short and blind. In case numerous shoots develop from a knuckle cut, the weak, thin growths should be removed.

Storage If the flowers are to be shipped without delay, the stems should be placed in lukewarm water containing a preservative as soon as they are cut and in 4°C air temperature for about 12 hours before shipment. At the wholesale store and at the retail shop the flowers should be kept in preservative solution and in a 4°C temperature.

If it is necessary to delay marketing the roses, they may be held satisfactorily from a few days to as long as 2 weeks at 1°C when proper procedures are used. They are not placed in water after cutting, but instead are put in a nearly airtight container that does not absorb moisture. The temperature and moisture conditions must be carefully regulated. Upon removal from storage the stems should be recut and placed in warm (30°C) preservative solution in an air temperature of 4°C. From that time until they are sold, they should be in preservative solution and 4°C temperature. Fewer problems with limp necks and keeping quality occur when these practices are observed.

The consumer should be instructed in the use of preservative solutions for roses in the home, and should be encouraged to use them.

Marketing Standard grades for roses have not been adopted, but the methods that are in general usage base the grade on length of stem. There is little uniformity among the various regions of rose production. Some methods base grades on 5-centimeter increments starting at 25 centimeters, others use 8-centimeter increments starting at 23 centimeters, and others, in order to reduce the number of grades, use 10-centimeter increments starting at 35 centimeters.

Stem length is measured from the cut end of the stem up to and including the tip of the flower petals. In all grades the flowers should be uniformly developed, the stems should be straight and of sufficient strength to support the flower without undue bending, the flowers should be uniform in color, the foliage should be clean and unblemished, there should be no bullheads, and the flower buds should be of the size characteristic of the cultivar. All roses that do not meet these standards may be bunched together as "utility" or "work" grade. The stem length on these grades should be reduced only to the extent that the flower is adequately supported.

There are two common methods of packing roses for shipment. The one used in the eastern states, called "sheeting," consists of laying roses in rows on sheets of parchment or waxed paper, one row on top of the next, the buds of each row below those of the previous row, with ice covering the stems. This method reduced bruising, but it is inconvenient because of the necessity of lifting these layers of flowers out for display on commission house counters before sale.

The second method of bunching roses in bundles of 10, 12, or 25 is much more universally used throughout the rest of the country. The roses are either bunched in round bundles and then wrapped in parchment paper, or else they are spiral-wrapped by placing the heads together on the proper size paper and then rolling the paper with the roses to make a round pack. The spiral pack reduces bruising to the minimum. To prevent breakage of stems and looseness of pack, at least two ties are made: one around the wrap below the flower heads, and the other close to the base of the stems. Some growers use a lightweight grade of asphalt paper around the base of the stems. Handling is facilitated if the paper is heavy enough to prevent thorns from penetrating.

In place of waxed or parchment paper, the use of cellophane is suggested for greater sales appeal. The MSAD 86 type of cellophane will not discolor roses and may be cut in sheets of the desired size. The cellophane may be tied with string, held together with Scotch tape, or heat-sealed by lightly rubbing the cellophane with a sealing iron. No matter what type of wrapping is used, it should extend 5 centimeters beyond the tips of the buds.

Roses, Inc., started in 1937 by Joseph Hill and Alex Laurie, is an organization of commercial rose growers that functions primarily in the areas of promotion and public relations, and in addition sponsors some experimental work with roses. Through Roses, Inc., rose producers have a means of presenting a united front in marketing and legislative matters. For many years much of the research work on rose culture was sponsored by grants from this organization.

Schizanthus *(Schizanthus pinnatus—Solanaceae)*

The common names of butterfly flower or poorman's orchid are an indication of the delicacy of the flower. Also, the colors are brilliant, but the florets shatter. Because of this its use is limited to local sales.

For flowering from January to April, sowings are made from August to January. The seed germinates in 2 weeks at 15°C. Spacing should be about 16 by 20 centimeters and the forcing temperature 8 to 10°C.

Snapdragon *(Antirrhinum majus—Scrophulariaceae)*

The snapdragon is a perennial plant, native to the Mediterranean region. The flower is a spike inflorescence in which the lower florets open first, and, at the time of cutting, the florets are at all stages of development from fully expanded at the base of the spike to tight buds at the graceful tip of the spike. Not many spike-type flowers are grown commercially, and since they add interest and appeal to the flower arrangement, there is a constant demand for snapdragons.

Snapdragons are propagated from seed, and approximately 1 month after sowing, the seedlings are the right size for transplanting. The rate of growth and flowering of snapdragon is affected by light intensity and temperature, and plants growing during the summer will flower in as short a time as 7 weeks after they are benched. Snapdragon plants grown single-stemmed during the winter require about 22 weeks from the time they are benched until they flower.

Most snapdragons are grown as single crops; after the flowers are cut, the plants are discarded. However, in some instances two or possibly three crops of flowers are cut from the same plants before they are discarded. The main period of flowering snapdragons is during the winter and spring; but because of the good F_1 hybrid cultivars which are available for all seasons of the year, year-round flowering of snapdragons is quite common.

Flowering in the snapdragon apparently is controlled by a combination of light quantity, temperature, and day length. Some cultivars have a high light requirement and will flower satisfactorily only in the summer, while others have a low requirement and can be used for winter flowering. Snapdragons are classified into four groups according to their flowering properties at various times of the year.

Group 1 cultivars flower satisfactorily in the low-light, low-temperature, and short-day conditions of winter, and they are grown at 10°C night temperatures for flowering from mid-December through April. The group 1 cultivars flower in as short a time as 15 weeks after benching at the start of the season or in as long a time as 22 weeks at the end of the season.

Group 2 cultivars flower best in the late fall conditions from mid-November to mid-December and in the late winter conditions from mid-April through mid-May, but they may be used also for flowering during the entire period from mid-November to mid-May. The group 1 cultivars apparently are insensitive to day length, but the group 2 cultivars, like mums, will flower in a shorter period of time during the winter if they are given long days for about 2 months in the early stages of growth. Group 2 cultivars should be grown at 10 to 13°C night temperatures, and the length of time for flowering after benching will be 12 to 15 weeks in late fall and 22 to 17 weeks in late winter.

The group 3 cultivars, known as the fall or spring types, are flowered from May through mid-June and from mid-September to mid-November. These cultivars are grown at 16°C night temperatures, and they are quite sensitive to long days. Their length of time for flowering after benching is from 17 to 12 weeks in the spring and from 9 to 13 weeks in the fall.

The snapdragon cultivars in group 4 are used for flowering in the summer as they require high light, high temperature, and long days. The length of time for flowering after benching varies from 12 to 7 weeks in the period from mid-June to late August, and they may be flowered satisfactorily until mid-October.

This group classification for snapdragons is based on average conditions in Ohio. If the weather conditions are different from these, the use of the groups should be adapted to the weather conditions that can be expected.

Propagation Propagation from seed is practiced, except on rare occasions when double cultivars are propagated by cuttings. The seed is very small and must be sown on the surface of a finely screened soil.

The soil should be a light mixture with peat and sand, and the fertilizer content must be low. Shredded sphagnum, neutral peat, and vermiculite can also be used. Regardless of which material is used, it should be screened so that the seed can be sown on a smooth surface that maintains a uniform moisture supply. Since the soil has little fertilizer in it at the time the seed is sown, some fertilizer will have to be supplied after the seed germinates and true leaves are formed. Peatlite mixtures of peat and vermiculite may be used successfully for seed germination.

Subirrigation of the seed flat usually is best. The medium is thoroughly wetted without danger of washing the seeds on the surface. The flats should be placed at 21°C under intermittent mist or a plastic or glass cover until the seed germinates, at which time they are moved to an 18°C temperature.

Damping-off in the seed flat can best be handled by doing a thorough job of steaming before sowing, then sowing the seed thinly. One trade packet will generally be sufficient for two flats, and it is usually best to sow in rows. After germination strict attention must be given to moisture and ventilation. If the surface soil is kept constantly moist after germination, some damping-off can be expected.

Transplanting should take place as soon as true leaves form. Excellent results can be obtained from direct planting to the growing bench. This method is used most often with single-stem culture.

Snapdragon seed is packed 2,000 seeds per trade packet. The number of good seedlings that can be obtained per seed packet depends on the quality of the seed and the conditions that are provided during germination, but it is safe to plan on producing 800 good-quality seedlings per packet of seed. Production of fewer than this is usually due to some mishandling of propagation procedures.

Snapdragon seedlings should be transplanted as soon as they can be handled; however, if this cannot be done, the next best plan is to hold them at temperatures of 1°C until they can be planted. They can be held at this temperature several weeks and will be in better condition than if they remained in the seed flat in "growing temperatures."

Planting, Spacing, and Supporting The snapdragon seedlings should be planted as soon as they can be handled, when the plant is less than 3 centimeters high and the leaves are just unfolding. The plants grow and develop much more rapidly when they are transplanted at this early stage than they do when the seedlings are larger. The tiny plants should be handled by the leaves during planting to avoid damaging the stem. The plants should be watered well after planting; however, if the planting is done during the winter, the plants or the rows of plants should be spot-watered, leaving dry areas between the rows.

Both pinched and single-stem crops have advantages. If the plants are grown single-stem, 2 to 3 weeks can be gained, the quality is very often more uniform, and the crop cuts off in a shorter period of time. The principal disadvantage in single-stem culture is the number of seedlings required. About four times as many seedlings are necessary for a single-stem crop as for pinched plants. The initial investment in seed is greater, and more labor is required for planting. In most instances, however, the advantages of single-stem culture are much greater than the disadvantages.

For pinched-plant culture the plants should be soft-pinched to three or four sets of leaves. Either two or four shoots will develop following the pinch, depending on the stage of development of the lateral shoots at the time the pinch was made. The correct time of pinching is determined by the cultivar and by the weather conditions that can be expected. Snapdragons flower much more rapidly in the high-light-intensity–high-temperature periods of the year. The best-conceived pinching schedules can be sadly lacking in results if the anticipated weather conditions do not materialize. For instance, abnormally bright, hot autumn weather can cause the "Christmas crop" to be produced for Thanksgiving Day.

Spacing of about 20 by 20 centimeters is used for snapdragons that are pinched; however, snapdragons that are grown as a single-stem crop are

Figure 5-25 Snapdragon plants should be planted as soon as the seedlings can be handled (approximately 1 month after sowing the seed). Left: a flat of snapdragon seedlings at the right stage for planting. Right: recently planted snapdragon seedlings. The penny in the foreground is for size comparison.

spaced from 10 by 10 centimeters for flowering in the summer to 10 by 15 centimeters for the winter crop.

If cultivars are used that reach about the same height, a single network can be used to support the tops of the plants and keep them erect. The network can be made from string laced across wires that are stretched between the rows of plants the length of the bench, or it can be welded wire fabric. The network may be placed at ground level for planting and raised as the plants grow.

Soil and Fertilizer Snapdragon soils should be porous, well drained, and thoroughly steam-disinfested. The addition of poultry-litter-grade peat moss, straw, or manure will make soils more porous, and particularly fine- or heavy-textured soils can be improved by the addition of materials such as haydite, coarse perlite, or calcined clay.

The pH of the soil should be about 6.5, and if any adjustments are needed, they should be made before planting. The total fertilizer content of the soil should be low at the time of planting, but the young plant needs some nitrogen in the early stages of growth. If there is little nitrogen in the soil at the time of planting, some should be provided when the plants are watered in or at the first irrigation after that.

Light Snapdragons need to be partially shaded from the sunlight only in the early stages of growth in the seed flat, and after that growth is best in full light. In most areas of the country, the winter light conditions are not good enough at best, and every effort should be made to provide the best light possible for the plants. Growth and development of snapdragons are more rapid in high-light and high-temperature conditions, and flowering of snapdragons may be ahead of schedule in unusually bright seasons and delayed if the weather conditions are darker and cooler than usual.

The effect of day length on snapdragons varies with the cultivar, and flowering in some cultivars can be advanced in long days and delayed in short days. Some advantages may be gained by the artificial adjustment of day length for flowering snapdragons at some times of the year, but it has been more satisfactory to flower them only during the "natural season" according to the group classifications.

Temperature Snapdragons are usually considered to be a 10°C night temperature crop. This is because they are more commonly grown during the winter, and the cultivars that are used at that time of the year grow and flower best at that temperature. Snapdragons that are flowered in the spring or fall should be grown at 16°C night temperatures, while for summer flowering 18°C night temperatures can be used. The day temperature should be maintained about 6°C higher than the night temperature.

Growth of the young plants for the first 4 to 6 weeks is best at 16°C night temperatures at any time of the year; and when it is possible, that temperature should be used for the young plants of the winter crop as well.

In many areas of the country summer temperatures are higher than desired for the best growth of snapdragons. A 9°C reduction in daytime temperatures is possible with fan and pad cooling systems, and this is sufficient to produce better quality snapdragons during the summer.

Moisture   Root growth is poor in soils that are constantly wet, and root and stem diseases are more prevalent. If coarse and porous soils are used for snapdragons, the soil will drain readily so that overwatering problems will be minimized. The soil should be allowed to dry somewhat between irrigations, and this is particularly important in the dark and cool weather in the winter. Root rot organisms thrive in constantly moist soil even if it is well aerated, and the continued use of peat moss as a soil conditioner can lead to trouble.

Some leaf and stem diseases are more common in snapdragons if the relative humidity is high. Adequate ventilation and heating while ventilating should be done to keep the air moisture level at a satisfactory level.

Troubles   Chlorosis of the tip foliage indicates a root problem. The most common cause is poor drainage resulting in poor root growth; however, too much fertilizer in the soil or root pests can be the cause.

A wilt that occurs in snapdragons at about the time the flower buds are well developed has not been associated definitely with a particular pathogen, and it may be caused by either pathogens or physiological situations or a combination of them. It occurs primarily during the poor growing conditions of winter, and it is believed that poor root growth at that time is due to low temperatures, low light intensity, and too wet a soil. There is a possibility that pythium root rot may be involved in some instances.

Floret drop or shatter is not as much of a problem as it once was because resistance to shattering is one of the characteristics that hybridists have bred into the new cultivars. Other than the genetic factor, the primary causes of floret drop are pollination by bees or other insects and the effect of gases such as ethylene.

Hollow stems may occur in the winter, as a result of the low light intensity at that time. The condition can be remedied if the temperature is reduced, irrigations are spaced farther apart, and less nitrogen fertilizer is applied.

Floret skip is a problem that arises only if the snapdragons are subjected to unusually cool temperatures during formation of the spike.

Foliar die-back has no known pathogen, but it may be caused by soil or root conditions during the winter. Some of the leaves about midway in the stem die gradually from the tip, and when the condition progresses as far as the stem, the portion of the stem above the position of the affected leaves wilts.

Diseases   Rhizoctonia stem rot and damping-off are very common diseases of snapdragons, and they occur primarily in the early stages of growth. Soils and handling equipment must be carefully steam-disinfested, plants set as shallow as possible, irrigations spaced well, and continuous air movement provided.

Botrytis cinerea or gray mold can attack snapdragons at any stage of growth, and typically it produces a stem rot some place above the soil line—often midway on the stem. The spores of *B. cinerea* are very common in the greenhouse, but their presence can be reduced if good sanitary measures are used, as this pathogen thrives on trash. The area should be carefully steamed before planting, and good air movement and low relative humidity should be provided while the crop is being grown. This disease is easily controlled if heating and ventilating practices are good.

Powdery mildew should not be a problem if heating and ventilating are properly handled, and rust is even less of a problem as rust resistance has been bred into many of the varieties. Rust will germinate only if there is water on the plants, and this usually does not occur unless the greenhouses are in very poor condition or the watering practices are improper.

Pests   Aphids are the most common pests, and they often cause twisted or misshapen leaves at the tip of the plant.

Cyclamen mites are occasional pests on snapdragons. They are so tiny that they are often overlooked, but their effects can be seen on the plants, as they cause small cup-shaped leaves and severely reduced growth.

Two-spotted mites or red spider can be a problem at any time, and thrips do infest snapdragons in season. These pests, however, are rather easily controlled with several different pesticides.

Rotations and Cropping   Because of the different seasonal light and temperature conditions, snapdragon cultivars that grow and flower well in each season must be used. Table 5-7 gives the planting and flowering dates for single-stem crops throughout the year. Approximately 1 month is needed to produce a seedling of the right size for planting, and therefore seed should be sown about 1 month before each planting date. The timing listed here is based on average weather conditions in Ohio. If there are more light and higher temperatures where the snapdragons are to be grown, flowering will be faster, and the cultivars in groups 2, 3, and 4 can be used earlier in the spring and later in the fall.

The rate of flower development and the time of flowering in snapdragons are affected greatly by temperature and light. If the weather conditions vary from the average, the time of flowering will be advanced or delayed accordingly.

Table 5-7 can be used for scheduling year-round flowering with snapdragons, and a minimum of nine units is needed to provide uniform flowering throughout the year.

Table 5-7   *Snapdragon Cultivar Classification and Dates for Planting and Flowering*

Date of planting	Weeks in bench	Date of flowering	Cultivar classification
July 10	10	Sept. 15	Group 3
July 25	10	Oct. 1	Group 3
Aug. 1	11	Oct. 15	Group 3
Aug. 10	12	Nov. 1	Group 2
Aug. 15	13	Nov. 15	Group 2
Aug. 25	14	Dec. 1	Group 2
Sept. 1	15	Dec. 15	Group 1
Sept. 4	17	Jan. 1	Group 1
Sept. 7	19	Jan. 15	Group 1
Sept. 15	20	Feb. 1	Group 1
Sept. 20	21	Feb. 15	Group 1
Oct. 3	21	Mar. 1	Group 1
Oct. 15	22	Mar. 15	Group 1
Nov. 1	22	Apr. 1	Group 2
Nov. 20	21	Apr. 15	Group 2
Dec. 15	20	May 1	Group 2
Jan. 15	17	May 15	Group 3
Feb. 10	16	June 1	Group 3
Feb. 25	15	June 8	Group 3
Mar. 10	14	June 15	Group 3
Apr. 1	12	June 22	Group 3
Apr. 10	12	July 1	Group 4
Apr. 20	11	July 8	Group 4
May 1	11	July 15	Group 4
May 25	10	Aug. 1	Group 4
June 5	10	Aug. 15	Group 4
July 1	9	Sept. 1	Group 4

Snapdragons may be rotated with other crops. A winter crop of snapdragons can be followed by spring bedding plants, or carnations that are removed in the fall can be followed by a crop of snapdragons before the area is replanted to carnations. Many other rotations are possible.

Snapdragons are often grown outdoors in the North during the summer. If the first planting is in late April or May, two crops can be produced before frost in the fall. The quality of the flowers is much better if the plants are grown under cotton cloth or plastic screen.

Cutting The flowers are cut when the bottom florets are completely expanded and the tip florets are in tight bud. For single cropping, the stem may be cut at any suitable length, as the plants are discarded after the flowers are cut; however, if a second crop of flowers is to be produced from the same plants, the cut should be made above four sets of leaves. The flower stems should be placed in water immediately after cutting, in a 4°C air temperature.

Snapdragons can be stored dry at 1°C for up to 3 weeks, but this is seldom done as floret drop may result from ethylene generated by the flowers in storage.

Snapdragons are graded by spike and stem length and bunched by the dozen. If snapdragons are to be shipped for any length of time, they must be positioned upright, or the flower tips will crook. This is a geotropic effect: When the stems are laid horizontally, the tips soon turn upward. If snapdragons are shipped, they are placed upright in hamper-type containers. Because of this shipping problem, snapdragons usually are sold locally and are not shipped for long distances.

White and light pink snapdragons are used in the greatest quantities, while yellow and dark pink varieties are grown in lesser amounts. Red, bronze, and lavender colors are used seasonally according to the demand.

Statice (Annual *Limonium sinuatum* and *Psylliostachys suworowii*—Plumbaginaceae; Perennial *Limonium latifolia* and *Goniolimon tataricum*—Plumbaginaceae)

The annual species may be grown either outdoors or in the greenhouse. The perennial species are grown outdoors only.

For outdoor crops in the North, annual statice is sown as soon as possible in the spring for flowering during the summer. In Florida the annual statice is sown about August 1 for flowering in January and February.

Statice is flowered the year-round in California.

For greenhouse forcing *Limonium sinuatum* is sown in January for flowering in May. *Psylliostachys suworowii* is sown in October for flowering from March through May. Statice seed germinates in 3 weeks at 21°C. The plants are spaced 20 by 20 centimeters, and the forcing temperature is 7°C.

Stephanotis *(Stephanotis floribunda—Asclepiadaceae)*

Stephanotis is a vine with indeterminate-type growth. Vegetative growth continues in the terminal tip of the plant as flowers form in cyme inflorescences laterally. The florets are white and small and frequently are used individually in bridal bouquets.

Growers usually do not have large areas involved in stephanotis cut-flower production. Frequently rose growers grow some stephanotis in one end of a greenhouse. Because it is a vine, they may use the end wall for this production, or they may provide horizontal wires for it to grow on.

Stephanotis is usually reproduced by stem-segment cuttings. The plants may be continued in growth for a few years until they have become too large for the allotted area, and they are replaced.

Vegetative growth and flowering are promoted in high light intensity. Flowering is promoted in long photoperiods, and plants are lighted for increased flower production during the winter.

Stephanotis is grown at 16°C.

Stock *(Matthiola incana—Cruciferae)*

For greenhouse forcing, stock usually is spaced 8 by 15 centimeters, and the seed is sown directly with three seeds in each position and then thinned to the best seedling. The forcing temperature is 7 to 10°C.

For northern greenhouses sow in July for January flowering, September for March flowering, and November for April flowering.

Transvaal Daisy *(Gerbera jamesonii—Compositae)*

The gerbera has startling flower colors, and usually there is good market demand. The problems with this crop have been in production. It has not been possible to predict time of flower production, and control of plant pathogens has been difficult.

Production schedules have been based on sowing the seed in January for planting in late spring. The seed germinates in $1\frac{1}{2}$ weeks at 21°C. In northern greenhouses, cut-flower production occurs during the summer and fall. Very few flowers are produced during the winter, and flowering then starts again in the spring. The plants may be continued in production, but flower production usually is less with these plants. It is possible that gerberas could be used more successfully as a spring to fall crop on a rotation with snapdragons or other cut-flower crops. On that basis the seed could be sown in November.

The plants are spaced 30 by 30 centimeters, and the night temperature is 16°C.

Zinnia *(Zinnia elegans—Compositae)*

Zinnias can be forced in the greenhouse as cut flowers in the spring, or they can be grown outdoors for cut-flower crops during the summer. Usually the market will be local, and it will be the best in areas in which home gardening is not common.

For greenhouse forcing, the seed is sown in mid-February for April to May flowering. The seed is sown directly at 10- by 10-centimeter spacing, and the forcing temperature is 16°C. Cactus- and dahlia-flowered types are used, and they are disbudded as soon as the buds can be handled so that the solitary flower per stem is maximum size.

For outdoor cut-flower crops, it is best to sow the seed directly as soon as possible in the spring for flowering from July on. The spacing should be about 30 by 30 centimeters. Cactus- and dahlia-flowered types are used, and they should be disbudded.

Pot-Plant Crop Production

6

These are crops that are grown and marketed in containers of some kind. They have mobility, which has some good features. When the crop is started, the plants may be in small pots with each unit taking a small amount of space. As the plants grow they may be transplanted to larger pots and the pots placed far enough apart to allow enough space for the development of the mature plant. This is economical use of greenhouse space, but it requires more planning and labor than the procedure in which young plants are placed at the final spacing from the start. Regardless of which method is used, planning and organizing is required, and this involves making rotations and schedules. Examples of some rotations and schedules will follow.

THE POT-PLANT CROPS

A general classification of pot-plant crops is flowering pot plants, foliage plants, and bedding plants.

Some of the crops are grown the year-round, others are only seasonal, and some are grown in increased amounts for holiday marketing. Most pot-plant growers find that their greatest marketing period is in the spring; however, some growers expand their market by producing plants for growing-on as well as producing mature plants. They may produce rooted cuttings, seedlings, or plants in small pots to be sold to other growers for growing-on to mature plants.

For most growers, foliage plants are a year-round crop. There will be some seasonal variations, such as producing more *Araucaria heterophylla* for the Christmas market or more palms for the Easter trade, but generally they have a complete offering of foliage the year-round. Some of the flowering pot plants may be produced the year-round, such as saintpaulia, chrysanthemum, azalea, gloxinia, begonia, and kalanchoe.

Bedding plants are a seasonal item. The customer plants them outdoors, and they must be produced so that they will be ready for planting in the garden. The planting date depends on the latitude of the location. It may be as early as December and as late as June, depending on area of the country, and some bedding-plant growers expand their market by shipping south first and then gradually farther north as spring arrives in those areas.

Some plants are used as seasonal pot plants because of the effects of the natural environment. Bulbs mature in the fall, and depending on how they are handled, flower crops from them may be produced sometime between December and May.

Gloxinia tubers also mature in the fall, and when gloxinias are grown from tubers they may be planted from November through early spring for flowering from early spring to early summer. The gloxinias that are grown the year-round are started from seed.

Azaleas grown in natural season produce mature flower buds in the fall, and then they may be forced into flower sometime between December and May. The azaleas that are produced the year-round are provided with the temperature and light environment needed regardless of natural seasonal weather.

Because of temperature and light in natural conditions, calceolaria and cineraria have been grown in northern greenhouses for flowering in early spring. They have been known as cool-weather crops.

The holiday markets in the United States are Sweetest Day (the third Saturday in October), Thanksgiving (the fourth Thursday in November), Christmas (December 25), Valentine's Day (February 14), Easter (variable from late March to mid-April), Mother's Day (the second Sunday in May), and Memorial Day (the last Monday in May). Some areas of the country do not observe all of these holidays, and some areas have additional, important holidays that they observe.

In Canada, the holiday observations in addition to Sweetest Day, Christmas, Valentine's Day, Mother's Day, and Easter are Thanksgiving (the second Monday in October), Victoria Day (the Monday closest to May 24), and Jean Baptiste Day (June 24).

Any of the plants that are grown the year-round and those that are produced seasonally at that particular time of the year may be used for the various holiday markets, and in addition some plants are used mainly for specific holidays—poinsettia for Christmas, Easter lily for Easter, and hydrangea for Easter and Mother's Day.

LAND FOR POT-PLANT PRODUCTION

Two of the considerations are a source of soil and transportation. With pot-plant production a continuing supply of soil is required because the soil that the plant grows in is marketed along with the plant. If naturally derived soil is going to be used as an ingredient in the soil mixture, there are some advantages in having that soil available right on the property. As that soil supply becomes depleted, that portion of the property can be used as a storage area for soil hauled in from other areas.

If naturally derived soil is not going to be used in the soil mixture for the pot plants, a storage area will be needed for the materials that will be brought in for making the soil mixture or for storing ready-made mixes.

Pot-plant crops are mobile, but their transportation presents more problems than many other items that are moved. They are bulky to pack and heavy. If the pot plants start out in small pots (6 centimeters) set pot to pot, there would be about 25 pots per 900 square centimeters to move into and out of the greenhouse space. This requires much handling of individual pots, so small pots usually are placed in trays approximately 34 by 43 centimeters so that 48 pots can be moved at one time. If the small plants are transplanted to 16-centimeter pots, six of these pots could be placed in a flat 26 by 52 centimeters. Trays and flats of this size are convenient for a worker to handle. If a wheeled vehicle or conveyer is available, several trays or flats could be moved at one time by an individual. On any basis of movement, however, the job can be accomplished more easily if the land is level. When the pot-plant crop is mature, the pots must be moved to the packing area so that they can be packed and loaded onto trucks. In many instances when an order is assembled, the pots are selected from several different greenhouses, which requires an involved trip for each order. In this summary of pot-plant transportation, no mention is made of other moves that may be made to give the plants more space as they grow or to place them in different temperatures according to their stage of development.

All of the pot-plant moves are made more easily on level ground. There is a considerable advantage in starting with level land for pot-plant greenhouses because of the transportation problems.

In marketing pot plants, the customers may use their own vehicles and make the pickup or the grower may deliver. If the vehicles are shelved, the pot plants may be loaded on the shelves pot to pot. If the vehicles are not shelved, the pot plants must be boxed so that the cartons can be stacked in the truck. If shipment is to be made via common carrier, the pot plants must be boxed well enough so that the cartons can be thrown and upended without damage to the plants. Regardless of method of shipment, the site needs to be readily accessible to any of these individuals and the vehicles that they might use.

Transportation of the finished product must be considered before the site for the greenhouse is acquired. If pickup by customers will be the primary method of transportation, it must be determined if there are enough potential customers in the area who will pick up. If delivery to the customers will be used, it must be determined if there are enough potential customers within an area that can be serviced economically. This may be an area restricted to the neighboring city, or it may be decided to include an area about 80 to 160 kilometers (about 50 to 100 miles) in radius from the greenhouse.

If common carrier is to be used, which ones will be able to give good service to the site? The common carriers that are used must provide temperature protection for the product, and this places restrictive limitations on the carriers that are available. Shipping charges must be evaluated for the various possible site locations. The shipping charge becomes a part of the cost of the product to the customer. This may limit the marketing area.

The amount of shipping time may be critical for some of the pot plants. If some of the products need to get to the customer within 1 day or less, will sufficiently rapid transportation be available to the site?

The effect of site location on inbound shipments must be evaluated as well as the effects on outbound shipments. The inbound shipments may be plant material of some kind that would require similar service as the outbound shipments, or they may be shipments of pots, fuel, building materials, or other nonliving items. Is the site serviced readily by all types of common carriers? Generally sites in or adjacent to larger cities have faster and/or more economical service than sites that are several miles away. The site must provide ready access for trucks with trailers of 12 meters or more in length because even small shipments may be handled by vehicles of that size.

In addition to site requirements for soil source and transportation suitability, there should be space available for growing some crops outdoors. Azalea and hydrangea are grown outdoors during the summer, and land will be needed for this purpose. Also, if sufficient refrigerated space is not available for vernalization treatment of bulb crops, outdoor land will be needed for this purpose.

For areas of the same size, the utility requirements are about the same for pot-plant and cut-flower crops. The discussions on the availability, quality, and cost of water, fuel, electricity, and trash removal for greenhouses are in Chap. 2.

STRUCTURES FOR POT-PLANT CROPS

The discussions in Chap. 2 on greenhouse structures and other equipment apply in general to pot-plant crops. Some of the specific applications to pot-plant crops are covered here.

The pot-plant grower should have enough separate greenhouses so that the different light and temperature environments needed for the control of cropping can be provided. The plants then can be moved to the house that has the desired environment. This usually will result in the pot-plant grower having several smaller houses rather than fewer larger ones.

Because of the transportation problem with pot plants, the houses need to be joined in such a way that the plants can be moved easily among the houses. Within the houses the benches should be arranged so that it is a short trip from any part of the benches to a main walk where wheeled vehicles can be operated.

With the exception of the height requirement for houses for large foliage plants, pot-plant greenhouses can be minimum-height structures. There are no special requirements for framework or type of covering.

Most pot-plant growers have need for some seasonal greenhouses. These usually are houses that are used for the increased quantity of plants grown for the spring market. This may be bedding plants, or it may be additional pot plants grown for the Easter, Mother's Day, and Memorial Day markets. These houses may be used solely for these purposes, or they may be used as cool houses for azalea, hydrangea, or some of the bulb crops.

With the exception of large foliage plants and bedding plants, pot plants

Figure 6-1 Pot plants should be placed on benches which drain readily. Well-spaced, wooden bench bottoms are satisfactory. *(Yoder Bros., Inc. photograph.)*

Figure 6-2 It is best to sow seed in rows because that prevents overcrowding and improves air circulation and light availability for the seedlings. Upper left: The rows were lightly covered with sand after sowing and the label was inserted in the flat to identify the kind of plant. Upper right: The sowing of seed was completed, the label was placed on its side in the flat, the soil was thoroughly watered by subirrigation of the flat, and the flat was covered with a pane of glass to assure uniform moisture at the soil surface. Lower left: If the seed flat is placed in sunlight after sowing, it must be covered with an opaque material, such as paper, in addition to the glass, to prevent excessively high temperatures within the flat. Lower right: After the seed germinated, the glass was removed from the flat, and the label was placed upright for easy identification.

usually are grown on benches that are about 75 centimeters high and 180 centimeters wide. These are convenient working dimensions for the pot-plant crops. Raised sides on the benches are not required, and unless the bench is to be used for capillary irrigation, the bench bottom should provide maximum water drainage.

Walks in pot-plant greenhouses should be smooth and well-surfaced to facilitate rapid movement of workers. The main walks need to be hard-surfaced and wide enough to allow the use of wheeled vehicles.

Pot-plant greenhouses need one or more buildings connected to them for use in potting, assembling orders for shipment, shipping, storage, and cool storage. It is best if this area is centrally located and with easy access from any of the greenhouses. Indoor loading or unloading for one or more trucks should be provided in this area.

If some of the crops are going to be propagated on-site, a propagation area with adequate facilities must be provided. Calceolaria, cineraria, cyclamen, exacum, primula, and most bedding plants are propagated from seed. Saintpaulia is propagated from leaf cuttings, and geranium, poinsettia, hydrangea, and fuchsia are propagated from stem-tip cuttings. It is possible to make a propagation area in either a greenhouse or a structure that has opaque covering, but in either instance special provisions have to be made so that the light, temperature, moisture, and air movement are suitable for the type of propagation that will be done. The propagation area must be carefully developed. A large number of plants are handled in a small area, and the environment must be just right. Suggestions for the establishment of propagation areas are given in Chap. 2.

POTS

Pots are made from several different materials, and the suitability of the pot depends on the use to which it will be put. Clay pots are available in all sizes, and through the years they have been used successfully for all purposes. Clay pots are porous, providing some exchange of moisture and air through the pot, and this is considered to be beneficial for the moisture-air relationship in the soil. Two objectionable aspects of clay pots are that they are heavy and that algae grow on the sides, necessitating cleaning them before sale. When clay pot manufacturers treat the outside of the pots with silicone, the algae growth is markedly reduced.

Plastic pots are made from several different materials and may be either rigid or flexible. Because they are lighter than clay pots, they are commonly used for pot plants that will be shipped. Plastic pots are impervious to moisture and air, which may be a problem with soils that drain slowly or if irrigation is too frequent. Algal growth on the sides of the pots in not a problem, and therefore the plastic pots do not have to be cleaned before the pot plants are sold. Plastic pots become deformed in high temperatures and cannot be steamed. If the pots are to be reused, they must be sterilized by some other means.

Pots made from peat and wood fiber are useful in smaller sizes for seedlings or rooted cuttings. The pot is planted together with the plant. This saves the operations of knocking the plants out of small pots and sterilizing and storing the pots, and it reduces the disturbance of the roots. Peat pots are somewhat fragile to handle, and usually trays are required so that several pots can be moved at once.

The so-called "standard" pot is most universally used. Such a pot is as wide at the top as it is high (for example, 6 centimeters high and 6 centimeters across at the top, or 15 centimeters high and 15 centimeters across at the top). They are available in all sizes from 2.5 up to 40 centimeters. Pans begin usually with the 13-centimeter size and are half as high as they are wide (for example, 15 centimeters across at top and 8 centimeters high). Pans are useful with poinsettias and also for germination of seeds. Three-quarter pots and azalea pots are generally similar in that they are three-quarters as high as they are across (15 centimeters across and 11 centimeters high). The three-quarter, or azalea, pot is not as widely used as it should be. For example, many pot plants, such as azaleas, primroses, calceolarias, and chrysanthemums, look more balanced in an azalea pot than in a standard pot. In addition, less soil is used, which makes a lighter plant to move and carry. Azalea pots have a wider base than a standard pot and are not as likely to fall over. Rose pots are useful when potting *R. manetti* stock and for growing small plants or cuttings. Since they are taller than they are wide, they provide more soil for development of a larger root system and require less frequent watering. They are rarely over 8 centimeters across the top.

Containers

For years annual bedding plants were grown approximately 100 per flat, and plants were dug from them at the time of sale. Injury to the plants and

Figure 6-3 For years pots were made of clay and had one drainage hole at the bottom. Most flower pots now have several drainage holes at the bottom, and pots made of plastic often also have holes on the side at the bottom, as shown in the pot at the right. These are 15-centimeter azalea pots. The inside diameter at the top is 15 centimeters, and the height is about three-quarters that amount. Standard flower pots have the same height as width.

*Comparison of customary and metric units of pot sizes**

Customary	Metric (approximate)	Customary	Metric (approximate)
2 inches	5 centimeters	6½ inches	17 centimeters
2¼ inches	6 centimeters	7 inches	18 centimeters
2½ inches	6 centimeters	7½ inches	19 centimeters
3 inches	8 centimeters	8 inches	20 centimeters
3½ inches	9 centimeters	8½ inches	22 centimeters
4 inches	10 centimeters	9 inches	23 centimeters
4½ inches	11 centimeters	9½ inches	24 centimeters
5 inches	13 centimeters	10 inches	25 centimeters
5½ inches	14 centimeters	11 inches	28 centimeters
6 inches	15 centimeters	12 inches	30 centimeters

*Although the 16-centimeter pot is not listed here, it is expected to be very commonly used.

inconvenience have brought about sweeping changes in containers used for bedding plants.

Small containers made of thin plastic, aluminum, paper, or a paper-composition product that will hold 6 to 12 plants at maturity are preferred. Several of these containers can be placed in a conventional flat with no wasted space. At the time of sale, the individual container is taken from the flat; the plants are removed by the customer when required at the time of planting.

Pots made of peat and paper are also used. While somewhat fragile, they offer the advantage that no knocking out of pots is necessary since the entire unit of pot and plant is set out in the planting. Pots made of aluminum or plastic may also be used.

Containers should be placed on boards, fine gravel, sawdust, or similar material, rather than directly on soil, which becomes muddy and into which roots grow readily, encouraging rank, soft growth.

SOIL PREPARATION FOR POT-PLANT CROPS

The general discussion of soils is in Chap. 4; the specific applications to pot-plant crops are given here.

Peat is used as soil for azalea and some of the foliage plants. It should be peat that is coarse and fibrous. Sphagnum peat is considered the best because it decomposes slowly, has uniformly coarse texture, and is acid in reaction. It comes from bogs where sphaghum moss grows. Peats that originated from other types of bog plants such as sedge or hypnum are not as

Figure 6-4 An integrated family of plastic containers in which the plastic flat holds four dozen 5-centimeter pots, two dozen 8-centimeter pots, or either six or eight plastic packs. *(American Plant Container Co., Inc. photograph.)*

satisfactory because they decompose too rapidly. Various names have been used for peat types or brands, with the result that products of similar names may be peats of very different qualities. It is necessary to inspect the peat before purchasing to make certain that it is coarse and fibrous rather than fine and powdery. The pH of the peat also should be determined before use so that it may be adjusted as necessary.

Soils for propagation are prepared in various ways depending on the propagative part of the plant being used. Soils for propagation by seed must be fine-textured so that there is good contact between soil particle and seed for transfer of moisture. The smaller the seed, the finer textured the soil mixture must be. These soils usually need to be screened to get the uniform, fine texture. The material used may be field soil, fine sand, peat, vermiculite, or a mixture of two or more of these materials.

Soil for propagation by cuttings needs to be coarse and porous so that water drains through it readily. Rooting is faster in well-aerated soils and the quality of the roots is better, too. Various materials can be used for these propagation soils: peat, sand, vermiculite, perlite, and mixtures of any of these materials. This peat must be coarse and have fiber. Geranium, poinsettia, and cuttings of other kinds of plants may be propagated (stuck) directly in the pot in which they will be grown. The soil for this direct-stick procedure, despite being in the growing-on pot, needs to be as well-drained as any propagation soil. Some products are manufactured specifically for use in rooting cuttings. Some of these are made from peat, and others from synthetic products made for this purpose. They can be used satisfactorily.

The supply of mineral nutrients in propagation soils should be low but some nutrients must be available when roots start to form. The status of the mineral nutrients in the propagation soil must be determined before it is used. Those low in nutrients may be used, but fertilizer application should be scheduled as soon as possible after rooting.

The uses of pot-plant soils are a bit different from some of those of cut-flower soils—the soil is shallower and there is a shorter period of use. Because of the shallow depth, the pot-plant soils must be more porous than cut-flower soils in order to have the same rate of water drainage. But because of the shorter period of use it is possible to use materials in the mix that are effective for a shorter time. Whereas coarse aggregates such as haydite or calcined clay may be indispensible with rose soils that are going to be used for 4 years or longer without further amendment, the pot-plant soils actually may be in use for several weeks to a few months. Organic matter of some kind can be used very satisfactorily in pot-plant soil mixes. Porous soil mixes can be made using field soil, peat, and perlite. The peat should be coarse and fibrous, and the amount of peat used should be varied according to the texture of the field soil. If it is a fine-textured clay soil, a greater amount of peat should be used per unit volume of soil mix than if the field soil is a coarser textured sand. Greenhouse operators frequently refer to pot-plant soil mixtures as 2-1-1 or 1-1-1 depending on the volumes of field soil, peat, and perlite that were used in the mixture. However, soil mixtures of the same ratios will not have the same water-drainage characteristics unless the characteristics of the field soils and the peat are the same in each

Figure 6-5 Potting soils must be coarse and porous. This is a good potting soil mixture of soil, poultry-litter-grade peat moss, peanut hulls, and perlite. *(From "Flower and Plant Production in the Greenhouse," The Interstate Printers & Publishers, Inc., Danville, Illinois.)*

mixture. The grower needs a method of determining the soil-water drainage before the soil is used so that further changes in the mixture can be made if they are needed.

Sometimes cut-flower bench soils in the greenhouse are available to use in pot-plant soil mixtures. These soils may not need as much organic matter added to them as field soils, but usually some will be required. Also, because these soils may have had considerable fertilizer applications for the cut-flower crops, the mineral nutrient status of this soil must be determined before use. They might have too much fertilizer in them.

Some of the prepared peat mixes that may have been perfectly satisfactory for the short-term uses in propagation or with bedding plants are not satisfactory for the longer-term uses with flowering pot plants or with foliage plants. The peat that is used in these mixtures is fine-textured and not fibrous, which will result in poor drainage situations.

There have been several shredded bark mixtures on the market. They may be more or less suitable than peat mixes. It is not possible to make a general assessment of them because there are so many variables. Each mix must be evaluated on the basis of how well it provides the basic soil requirements—initially and at crop maturity. The basics still are water drainage and its effects on soil aeration and water, the availability of the required mineral nutrients, and the absence of pests, pathogens, or toxins of any kind.

Whatever the soil mixture ingredients are they must be mixed thoroughly so that the mixture is uniform. For years pot-plant growers have mixed small batches of soil by turning the pile, and a uniform mixture can be produced in this way. The various ingredients are placed on top of each other on the potting bench, and the pile is turned with a square-bladed shovel. Starting at one side of the pile, the shovel with the leading edge on the bench top is extended through the pile; then as it is withdrawn the shovel is tipped away from the pile so that the soil in it tumbles away from the pile. This procedure is repeated until the entire pile is turned that direction. Using the same procedure the pile then is turned in the other direction, giving a uniform mixing of the ingredients. If fertilizers are to be incorporated into the mixture, they should be placed on the pile with the other ingredients and mixed in the same fashion. For larger batches of soil, mechanical mixers of some kind are needed. These may be mixers designed for handling soil, or in many instances they are mixers that were designed for other products (possibly concrete or livestock feed mixers) that are now adapted to handling soil.

Field soils or peat may need to be shredded before being mixed. It is not possible to get a uniform mixture if some of the ingredients are too chunky, but the shredder must not shred so finely that the materials are pulverized.

At the time of mixing, the various ingredients for the mix need to be moist—neither dry nor wet. If the peat is entirely dry in the bale, it may be difficult to wet it so that it is uniformly moist, but if it is not moistened before mixing, it may remain dry even after thorough watering following planting. This can be a problem. It may be necessary to add a surfactant to the water in order to moisten peat before using it in the soil mixture.

At the time of preparing soil for potting, it must be determined that the pH and mineral status of the soil are suitable, and if they are not adjustment must be made at that time. For general uses, the pH should be in the range of pH 6.0 to 7.0. If the pH should be raised, finely ground dolomite can be incorporated into the soil at the rate of 45 grams per 0.03 cubic meter (1.5 kilograms per cubic meter) of soil. If dolomite cannot be obtained, finely ground agricultural limestone may be used plus Epsom salts at the rate of 9 grams per 0.03 cubic meter (300 grams per cubic meter). In addition to making the necessary pH adjustment to the soil, calcium and magnesium should be added to the soil. These are essential nutrient minerals that are best added to the soil before planting. Most soils will be improved by additions of calcium and magnesium. If no adjustment in raising pH is required, the necessary calcium and magnesium can be supplied by adding gypsum at the rate of 45 grams per 0.03 cubic meter of soil and Epsom salts at the rate of 9 grams per 0.03 cubic meter of soil.

If the pH needs to be lowered, ferrous sulfate should be added at the rate of 9 grams per 0.03 cubic meter soil. In addition, in order to supply calcium and magnesium, gypsum and Epsom salts should be added at the rates given above.

Field soils and greenhouse soil mixtures that do not contain any naturally derived soil usually are deficient in phosphorus. It is best to add phosphorus at the time of preparing the soil mixture; this can be done by adding treble superphosphate at the rate of 45 grams per 0.03 cubic meter of soil.

Other nutrient minerals may be added to the soil at the time of preparation; however, it is very important that it is determined that the soluble salt content of the soil makes this addition necessary. A Solu Bridge test should be made. If the Solu Bridge reading is low to medium, other minerals could and probably should be added. It is particularly important that soils contain some nitrogen in the early stages of plant growth. The most common method for adding other minerals to potting soils is the addition of organic or slow-release fertilizers. The organic fertilizers should be added to the soil before the mixture is steamed. The manufactured slow-release fertilizers should be added after steaming and just before the time of potting.

After mixing, pot-plant soils need to be treated to destroy weed seed, pests, and pathogens. It may be possible to use some chemicals for this treatment, but steaming is by far the best treatment. Then, after treatment, the soil must not be contaminated before it is used or while it is being used. It is best to steam the soil at the site where the potting will be done. In this way the entire area is disinfested. Tools and handling equipment also should be included in the steaming. Probably the best arrangement is the use of carts designed just for the purpose. The soil is steamed in the cart and potting is done right from the cart.

There are advantages in using aerated steam for treating soil. By introducing air into the steam, the soil is treated at 60 to 70°C instead of the 80 to 100°C temperatures that are used with steam alone. The lower temperatures with aerated steam are sufficient to destroy the pathogens. Some side benefits are: less steam is required resulting in lower fuel consumption; soil can be cooled more rapidly after treatment, and thus used sooner; there is a reduced possibility of producing toxic substances in the soil; and some beneficial microorganisms may not be destroyed.

For detailed information on treating pot-plant soils the following manuals are very good sources: *Geraniums* (second edition), edited by John W. Mastalerz, published by Pennsylvania Flower Growers, 103 Tyson Building, University Park, Pennsylvania 16802, and *The U.C. System for Producing Healthy Container-Grown Plants*, Manual 23, edited by Kenneth F. Baker, published by Agricultural Publications, 22 Giannini Hall, University of California, Berkeley, California 94720.

Pot-plant growers need an adequate-sized soil-storage facility. This is for the ingredients that go into the soil mixture. It must provide protection from weather conditions so that the field soil, peat, or any of the other materials to be used will be available for use immediately regardless of the weather.

SOWING, STICKING, POTTING, AND TRANSPLANTING

All of these tasks involve some plant material, containers, and soil. With these jobs, usually it is most efficient to assemble the items in one place where the work can proceed systematically. This may be the propagation house, the potting room, or a production greenhouse. The larger the job, the greater the need for good organization of the details.

Some of the larger jobs that may require special equipment or detailed organization are sowing bedding plant seed, transplanting bedding plant seedlings, sticking poinsettia cuttings, transplanting poinsettias, planting chrysanthemum rooted cuttings, planting lily bulbs, and planting dish gardens. Some of these are seasonal jobs and others are continuous. Many of the bedding-plant growers have devised means of filling seed flats and transplanting flats with soil using an elevated soil hopper and moving the flats on a conveyor belt. Some of the systems also include a means for marking the soil for correct placement of seed and seedlings. Depending on the market area that the bedding-plant grower services, this equipment may be used from fall to spring.

In propagation of plants by cuttings, the cuttings may be stuck in soil in the propagation bench, or they may be stuck in soil in small pots on the propagation bench. Each system has its advantages. Poinsettia is one of the crops that frequently is stuck in small pots. The pots may be arranged pot to pot at time of sticking and then spaced after rooting, or the pots may be in trays that support the pot upright at the spaced distance. The small pots may be filled with soil in the potting room and then brought to the propagation bench where the cuttings are stuck, or they may be filled with soil at the propagation bench. If they are filled at the propagation bench it must be done in such a way that excess soil is not left on the bench.

After the poinsettias (or other crop) are rooted, they will be transplanted to the pots in which they will be finished. This may be an operation in which the plants are brought to the potting bench and the pots are filled with soil by hand and the plants transplanted. Or the pots may be filled with soil by mechanical means, and the transplanting done either in the vicinity of the soil-filling equipment or at the bench where the plants will be grown.

Equipment that mechanizes some portion of the potting or transplanting operation is referred to as a potting machine. Some of these machines have the capability of actually planting or transplanting, but many of them are used solely to fill pots with soil and possibly drill a hole of the right size in the soil for the plant. They are adapted most easily when one plant is transplanted per pot, but it is possible to use them when three or more plants are planted per pot.

Most pot-plant growers have a year-round pot-mum program in which planting is done each week. Considerable time is saved if a mechanical means for filling soil in pots is used.

Planting Easter lily bulbs is a once-a-year project, but a large number of bulbs need to be planted at once. Many growers use equipment for filling the soil in lily pots.

Planting dish gardens is one of the operations that is difficult to mechanize. There are too many variables.

IRRIGATION OF POT-PLANT CROPS

Irrigation of pot-plant crops by means of hose-in-hand has been replaced by various water-distribution systems, but there will always be a need for some watering by this manual method. Each pot must be irrigated individually with the tip end of the hose just above the soil level. The faucet is only partially opened so that the force of the water flow does not dislodge soil from the pots. This requires a water-flow rate of about 12 liters per minute. The grower directs the water flow to the soil in each pot long enough to completely fill the freeboard space between soil level and the top of the pot. For a plant in a 16-centimeter pot, that means delivering approximately 1 cup (0.25 liter) of water. At this rate, about 60 pots are irrigated per minute on the straight runs with no time allowed for anything else (for example, scratching the nose or looking at the thermometer). It is a time-consuming and tedious job, and for these reasons, most growers use water-distribution systems of some kind.

The choice of type of water-distribution system depends on the size of pot, the kind of plant, the kind of benches, and possibly other considerations. The most common systems are plastic tubes to each pot, capillary mat, and nozzles placed above the plants.

The system that uses plastic tubes to each pot is practical for most plants in large pots—13-centimeter and larger—but it is not practical for use in small pots. Sometimes it is used for pots as small as 10 centimeters, but this is not usual. Polyethylene pipe usually is used as the water main on the bench, either 2 or 2.5 centimeters in diameter depending on the number of small tubes that will connect to it. Several variations in arrangement and design of this equipment have been available. The most popular tube diameter is about 0.15 centimeter (inner diameter), and the tubes are inserted in holes punched or drilled into the polyethylene pipe at the intervals that the pots are set so that one tube can be placed in each pot. A breaker usually is placed on the end of the tube so that the water is distributed more evenly over the surface of the soil. A practical arrangement for using plastic tube irrigation on a bench 180 centimeters by 30 meters on which 16-centimeter pots are placed six across the bench and 84 along the length of the bench would be to use two 2-centimeter polyethylene pipes along the length of the bench and 0.15-centimeter plastic tubes 60 centimeters long. The tubes would be inserted into the polyethylene pipe at about 36-centimeter intervals so that three pots in a row can be serviced from each pipe location. There would be 252 tubes in each polyethylene-pipe water main. The length of tube used is determined by the distance from the water main to the farthest pot with some excess length added to allow for the arc needed to get from the bench level over the top of the pot. All of the tubes serviced from the same main must be the same length or there will be a difference in the amount of water delivered per tube because the resistance to water flow varies greatly with length in tubes of that small size. In this example, the two 2-centimeter water mains should be serviced by a water header no smaller than 2.5 centimeters.

The plastic tube method of irrigation is used very successfully for hanging pots also. With larger pots two or more tubes may be placed in each pot.

Only a minimal amount of labor is involved in operating a plastic tube irrigation system. If it is manually operated, the only time required is that needed to open and close the valves, probably a matter of less than 1 minute to irrigate 500 or more pots. If the system is electrically operated, only a few seconds are needed to set the controller.

The capillary system of pot-plant irrigation is particularly useful for small pots—10 centimeters and smaller. The basic requirements here are a level and water-tight bench bottom and a porous material that can distribute water evenly over the surface of the bench bottom. A practical means for making the bench water-tight is to place polyethylene film on the bench bottom.

Various porous materials can be used for distribution of water on the bench-bottom surface. Sand can be used, and various fabric mats have been designed or adapted for this purpose. Whatever material is used must provide contact with a porous pot or with the soil in pots that are not porous so that there can be capillary movement of water to the soil in the pot.

To establish capillarity, the pots are irrigated with hose-in-hand when they are first set in the bench. Water then is supplied to the bench at a rate that maintains the capillarity but does not cause waterlogged soil in the pot. Several different methods of supplying water to the bench can be used satisfactorily, but regardless of the method, it must be carefully regulated so that the water quantity is right. Various tube arrangements are used to get the water evenly distributed, but some growers even apply the water to the bench with hose-in-hand and find that this is satisfactory.

Other than adjusting the water supply to the bench, the problems with capillary irrigation that must be met are control of algae growth on the porous surface, disinfestation between crops, and fertilizer application. Algal growth is promoted when fertilizer is applied with the water, so partial control of the algae can be obtained when the fertilizer needs of these crops are supplied by the incorporation of slow-release fertilizers in the soil mix at time of potting. Further control of algal growth may be realized by reducing the amount or the frequency of water supplied to the bench. The capillary irrigation bench does need to be disinfested periodically, and steaming is the best method. Steam, however, cannot be used if the porous material is underlaid with polyethylene film. The best solutions here would be to use either materials that can be steamed or materials that are so reasonably priced that they can be discarded between crops without a major effect on crop cost. This is another answer to the algae problem.

The best means of irrigating bedding plants usually is with nozzles installed above the plants. The nozzles may be in pipes running the length of the area and spaced in width so that there is even distribution of water to all of the plants, or the nozzles may be installed individually on rods and the rods spaced throughout the area so that the water distribution is even. Spacing for these irrigation pipes or rods cannot be determined unless the distance of water throw from the nozzles is known for the existing water pressure. The nozzle manufacturer or distributor will be able to to supply this information.

Nozzle irrigation is used for some foliage plants, but it is seldom used on flowering pot plants. There are primarily three reasons why nozzle irrigation is not used on flowering pot plants. It is difficult to get a uniform amount of water applied to each pot because of umbrella effects of the leaves; with some plants the application of water to stems and leaves may promote some diseases; and with most plants the application of water to the flowers makes them more susceptible to disease.

The regulation of irrigation is very critical with pot plants. They may be watered too often or too seldom, and the quantity of water applied may be too little or too much. The grower must make the decisions on the frequency of irrigation and the amount of water to be applied in each instance. The decisions will be based on these factors and possibly others: size of plant, size of pot, amount of root growth, drainage characteristics of the soil, kind of plant, time of day, season of the year, and anticipated weather conditions. The decision must allow water to be provided to the soil if it in fact is needed, but it must not limit aeration in the soil so that root growth is impaired. In making these decisions, the grower must be fully aware that any application of water to the soil will reduce the amount of air in the soil. The job of irrigation is not one that can be assigned to just anyone. This job requires the judgment of a well-qualified grower.

With pot plants it is possible to determine the amount and condition of root growth by knocking the plant out of the pot. There must be continuous root growth so that water and mineral nutrients can be absorbed into the plant. Evidence of this root growth is white root tips. If there is an adequate amount of white root tips observed when the plant is knocked out of the pot, this is evidence that the soil aeration has been satisfactory, there is not too much fertilizer in the soil, and there has not been damage by pests or pathogens. If the soil appears to be dry, an application of water would be advisable. If there are no or an insufficient quantity of white root tips observed, the cause must be determined before other action is taken. If there is too much fertilizer (high soluble salts) in the soil, enough water must be applied to leach out the salts. If the cause is either pest or pathogen, a suitable control must be applied. If it is suspected that the lack of current root growth is due to constantly wet soils, the frequency of irrigation must be decreased.

The total quantity of roots must be evaluated on the basis of plant size or the length of time it has been potted. Plants that recently have been potted will not have a great quantity of roots, but the new root growth should be evident on the surface of the soil ball in less than 1 week after potting if the soil environment is right. Plants that have been potted a longer time should have a correspondingly greater quantity of roots. The quantity is an indication of conditions that have existed in the past—and this is of importance—but the only indication of present conditions and the need for irrigation is the presence of white root tips.

If tube, nozzle, or other types of water distribution are used, a large number of pots can be irrigated by merely opening a water valve that supplies the system. This may be a manually operated water valve or a mechanically operated one. If mechanically operated water valves are used, they can be controlled either by a manually, mechanically, or electronically operated switch. The mechanically and electronically operated switches may be called clocks, automators, or programmers. The clocks usually provide for the operation of one or more water valves at the same time; all valves would either be open or closed. The automators and programmers have provisions for the operation of a relatively large number of valves in some kind of sequence so that only one valve will be in operation at a time, and selection can be made of which areas will receive irrigation. Clocks, automators, and programmers need to be adjustable so that the frequency of irrigation as well as the length of irrigation time can be set as needed. The decision of what setting to use can be made by the grower only after the careful evaluation of soil and roots outlined earlier has been made.

FERTILIZER APPLICATION FOR POT-PLANT CROPS

Pot-plant crops need a continuous supply of mineral nutrients from the early stages of growth to the maturity of the crop. Generally the presence of nutrients in the early stages of vegetative growth is more beneficial to the overall growth and development of the plant than it is in the later stages of growth. There is a period of a few weeks after planting in which the nutrient status of the soil is very critical, and it must be monitored very carefully. This cannot be a guessing game. An oversupply of nutrients can prevent root growth and thus there will be no absorption of water or nutrients into the plant. An absence of nutrients will not affect root growth immediately; water will be taken in but not nutrients because they are not there to be absorbed. If the soil is deficient in nutrients, they should be incorporated into the soil mixture before planting, or a fertilizer application should be scheduled for immediately after planting.

Fertilizers and their uses are discussed in Chap. 5, and the equipment for making fertilizer applications is given in Chap. 2. It is very difficult to make surface applications of dry fertilizer to pot-plant soils. Dry fertilizer should be added when needed to the soil mixture before planting, and after planting fertilizer should be applied as a liquid whenever possible. Slow-release fertilizers such as Osmocote and Magamp can be used very satisfactorily in soil mixtures before planting, but they should be made immediately before planting.

TRANSPORTATION OF POT PLANTS

Reference has been made to the mobility of pot-plant crops. A means of transportation for them is needed within and away from the greenhouse. Transportation equipment is discussed in Chap. 2.

ASSEMBLING AND WRAPPING POT PLANTS FOR SHIPPING

The individual items in a pot-plant order have to be selected and then assembled in one place for packaging and shipping. Bedding plants usually are not wrapped or packaged. They are shipped in flats in shelved trucks. Plants in small pots may be flatted, and plants in larger pots usually are sleeved. The sleeving may be done in the greenhouse or in the packing room. Flatted or sleeved pot plants may be shipped in shelved trucks without further packaging. When shelving is not available, the plants must be boxed so that the boxes may be stacked in the truck.

PEST AND PATHOGEN CONTROLS FOR POT PLANTS

Pest and pathogen control programs are needed for pot plants. This information is covered in Chaps. 2, 4, and 5.

POT-PLANT ROTATIONS

Pot-plant crops are much more adaptable to rotations than cut flowers because they are short-term crops. They may be spaced at various distances, and they can be moved from area to area. Because of the high degree of adaptability there are many different possible rotations, but very detailed planning is required to develop good rotations because several different pot-plant crops are grown in each pot-plant range, with each crop requiring increasing space as it grows. It is a complex problem to fit all of the crops into the space available so that the plants have the space and conditions that are needed and so that maximum use of the greenhouses is still made. It is easy to develop convenient rotations which do not make maximum use of the greenhouse space, but adequate financial return from the area is not realized unless all of it is used intensively.

Pot-plant rotations must be made for each specific situation. To illustrate some of the possibilities (and some of the problems) a rotation is presented here for a greenhouse range that contains a glass house with 2,790 square meters of bench space: about 4,185 square meters of ground area covered with glass, with 1,395 square meters in walks and 2,790 square meters in benches. In addition to the glass-house area there are 1,553 square meters of bed space in plastic houses (approximately 2,325 square meters under plastic) and 1,860 square meters of bed space outdoors for growing plants during the summer.

The first consideration in making a rotation is to develop a workable schedule for the production of pot plants that can be marketed at a profit. If this can be done and at the same time the entire greenhouse space can be fully occupied, the plan for rotation is completely successful.

The year-round pot-mum program consists of five hundred 16-centimeter pots per week; they are placed about three pots per 900 square centimeters for 3 weeks in an area where light and/or mist is available, which means that 15.5 square meters per crop is required, or a total of 46.5 square meters in the entire area. They are then shifted to an area at finish spacing of 1,150 square centimeters per pot, requiring 58 square meters per crop or a total of 638 square meters for the 11 weeks that the pots may be in this area before being marketed. The total area required for the year-round mum program is 679 square meters of bench space; however, in order to make some space available during the critical period in March, April, and May, the pots are shifted gradually at that time in order to gain some space for the holiday pot mums. Five mum cuttings are used per 16-centimeter pot.

The off-season azaleas are grown in the greenhouse for the entire time except for 6 weeks in refrigerated storage. This program schedules 100 plants for flowering each week from May 1 to December 1: One hundred 13- by 15-centimeter azalea plants are planted in the greenhouse benches 15 by 15 centimeters apart each week from September 1 to April 1, requiring 2.5 square meters of bench space per crop or a total of 30 square meters for the 12 weeks they remain there. The plants are then potted and spaced at 675 square centimeters per pot or 7 square meters per crop or a total of 84 square meters for the 12 weeks that the plants remain at that spacing. The total growing area needed is 112 square meters of bench space. The plants are placed in refrigerated storage for 6 weeks, and at three pots per 900 square centimeters a total of 19 square meters of bench space in storage is required. Azaleas require about 6 weeks at forcing temperatures and they are spaced at 900 square centimeters per plant. The forcing area required would be 9 square meters per crop and 65 square meters for the entire program.

This rotation plans the production of 48,000 poinsettias in 6-centimeter pots for resale in early fall to other growers and 10,000 poinsettias in 16-centimeter pans to be forced for the Christmas market. The 6-centimeter

Table 6-1   Rotation for a Greenhouse with 2,790 Square Meters of Bench Space*

Crop		Jan.	Feb.	Mar.	Apr.	May	June	July	Aug.	Sept.	Oct.	Nov.	Dec.
		Square meters of bench space											
Mums (year-round)		679	679	651	614	651	679	679	679	679	679	679	679
Azaleas (off-season)		112	112	177	177	177	177	177	177	177	177	149	112
Poinsettias		.....	.....	.....	.....	353	837	837	1,023	1,674	1,488	1,395	1,395
Azaleas (natural-season)		744	744	.....	.....	.....	.....	.....	.....	.....	.....	93	278
Hydrangeas		93	186	558	698	279	.....	.....	.....	.....	.....	.....	.....
Lilies		93	140	140	140	.....	.....	.....	.....	.....	.....	.....	93
Mums (holiday)		465	651	1,023	1,162	1,097	.....	.....	93	233	446	474	233
Tulips		93	93	93	.....	.....	.....	.....	.....	.....	.....	.....	.....
Hyacinths		93	93	93	.....	.....	.....	.....	.....	.....	.....	.....	.....
Gloxinias		.....	.....	.....	.....	233	1,023	1,023	744	.....	.....	.....	.....
Total		2,372	2,698	2,735	2,791	2,790	2,716	2,716	2,716	2,763	2,790	2,790	2,790

*In addition to the glass house with 2,790 square meters of bench space, there is a plastic house with 1,553 square meters of bed space used for storing azaleas (1,395 square meters) from October through January, for growing azaleas (1,395 square meters) during the summer, for forcing azaleas from October through March and hydrangeas (158 square meters) from October through January, for growing azaleas (744 square meters) in March, April, and May, and for forcing mums (279 square meters) in April. There is an outdoor area of 1,860 square meters of bed space for growing azaleas and hydrangeas and an outdoor area of 558 square meters of bed space for the storage of tulips and hyacinths from October to January.

plants would be rooted directly in peat pots spaced at four per 900 square centimeters for a total of 1,116 square meters. In order to supply the cuttings that are required, 600 stock plants would be started in May. The ten thousand 16-centimeter pans require 30,000 rooted cuttings, as they are planted three per pan, and 400 stock plants would be started in May to supply these cuttings. The cuttings are stuck in the propagation bench at 60 square centimeters in late August and September, which will require 186 square meters of propagation bench area. The rooted poinsettia cuttings are potted in 6-centimeter pots, and in early October three plants are panned per 16-centimeter pan. The final spacing on the 16-centimeter poinsettia pans is 1,350 square centimeters per pan. Poinsettia stock plants are started in May at a spacing of 3,600 square centimeters each and spaced to the final spacing of 8,100 square centimeters each in June through September.

It is planned to produce 30,000 natural-season azaleas in 16-centimeter pots, of which 1,000 will be forced for Christmas, 8,000 for January, 8,000 for February, 8,000 for March and April, and 5,000 for May. These plants will be started from 13- to 15-centimeter plants received in May, and half will be grown in the plastic house and the other half outdoors at a spacing of 900 square centimeters per plant. By October the azalea plants will be placed in the plastic house for storage at a spacing of two plants per 900 square centimeters. The azaleas are forced at 900 square centimeters each; the December, January, and February plants are forced in the glass houses and the March, April, and May plants are forced in the plastic house.

A total of 5,000 hydrangeas, three canes in 16-centimeter pots, is planned, of which 3,000 would be forced for Easter and 2,000 for Mother's Day. Approximately 465 square meters of bed space would be required outdoors because the plants should be grown during the summer with spacing of 900 square centimeters each. From October to January the hydrangeas are stored in the plastic houses at three pots per 900 square centimeters. For forcing, the plants are started at three pots per 900 square centimeters and spaced to 1,350 square centimeters per pot for finishing.

The rotation plans 3,000 lilies to be forced for Easter in 16-centimeter pots, and they are started at three pots per 900 square centimeters and finished at two pots per 900 square centimeters.

A total of 18,600 pot mums in 16-centimeter pots would be produced for holidays, of which 3,200 would be forced for Thanksgiving, 2,000 for Christmas, 4,000 for Easter, and 9,400 for Mother's Day. Final spacing for the pot chrysanthemum is 1,125 square centimeters per pot, and five cuttings are used per pot. In order to accommodate a portion of the pot-mum crop in April, 279 square meters of space is used in the plastic houses in addition to the glass-house space.

The tulips should be panned seven per pan in October, set three pans per 900 square centimeters outdoors, and covered with soil, straw, or other material to prevent freezing while keeping the bulbs uniformly cool. This requires an area of 279 square meters of bed space for the 9,000 pots to be forced. The tulips would be brought in for forcing in three lots in January, February, and March, and because they are set three pots per 900 square centimeters, 93 square meters of bench space is required.

The hyacinths would be handled in the same manner as the tulips with the differences that they are panned three per pan.

Gloxinias would be grown only in the summer by buying 6-centimeter potted plants in May, potting them in 15-centimeter pots, and giving them an initial spacing of three pots per 900 square centimeters. The rotation plans for 7,000 pots, which would require 233 square meters of bench space for the initial spacing and 1,023 square meters for the final spacing.

Developing a rotation on paper is one thing, and putting it into effect in the greenhouse is another, as some unplanned problems arise. One common problem is the usability of the bench space. A bench that contains 37 square meters will hold 400 pot plants spaced one per 900 square centimeters when the plan is developed on paper, and it will actually hold 400 pot plants if its dimensions are 120 centimeters by 30.5 meters, as the plants will be placed four across the bench with 100 rows down the bench. If a 37-square-meter bench has dimensions of 105 centimeters by 34.5 meters, however, usually only 339 plants would be placed on it for a one-per-900-square centimeter spacing, as the plants would be placed three across the bench with 113 rows of plants down the bench. This by no means indicates that plans should not be made because they are not entirely reliable, but it does illustrate that after the plan is made, the usability of the space should be verified before the plan is put into effect.

The whole pot-plant production program revolves around the production of plants for the holidays, primarily Christmas, Easter, and Mother's Day. Every square centimeter of space is used at these times, and it is not unusual to find that plants are spaced too closely in order to get a larger number of plants into the available space, or that a portion of the plants are grown on temporary shelving above the benches. Although either practice is questionable, it is possible to use them with some degree of success if good judgment is exercised.

There are two periods of the year when pot-plant ranges are likely to have bench space that is not being fully used—in the summer and in January and February. At those times some short-term crops can be forced if there is a market for them. In this rotation a crop of gloxinias and 6-centimeter poinsettias are planned for the summer, and azaleas, tulips, and hyacinths are scheduled for forcing in January and February.

The scheduled rotation must be somewhat flexible so that changes can be

Table 6-2 *Gross Income from a Greenhouse with 2,790 Square Meters of Bench Space*

Crop	Number of plants		Selling price, dollars		Less selling costs, dollars†	Gross income per year, dollars
	Planned	Sold	Each	Total		
Mums (year-round)	26,000	24,700	3.00	74,100.00	18,525.00	55,575.00
Azaleas (off season)	3,000	2,850	4.75	13,537.50	3,384.38	10,153.12
Poinsettias, 6-centimeter	48,000	45,600	0.35	15,960.00	3,990.00	11,970.00
Poinsettias, 15-centimeter	10,000	9,500	3.50	33,250.00	8,312.50	24,937.50
Azaleas (natural-season)	30,000	28,500	4.25	121,125.00	30,281.25	90,843.75
Hydrangeas	5,000	4,750	4.50	21,375.00	5,343.75	16,031.25
Lilies	3,000	2,550	3.25	8,287.50	2,071.88	6,215.62
Mums (holiday)	18,600	17,670	3.00	53,010.00	13,252.50	39,757.50
Tulips	9,000	8,100	2.50	20,250.00	5,062.50	15,187.50
Hyacinths	9,000	8,100	2.50	20,250.00	5,062.50	15,187.50
Gloxinias	7,000	6,650	3.50	23,275.00	5,818.75	17,456.25
Total gross income per year						303,314.99

*The difference between plants planned and plants sold is estimated to be 5 percent, with the exceptions of 15 percent for lilies and 10 percent for tulips and hyacinths.
†Selling costs for pot plants are estimated to be 25 percent of the selling price.

Table 6-3   *Income (in Dollars) per Square Meter per Month for Several Pot-Plant Crops*

Crop	Gross income per year	Income less plant costs	Income per month	Bench space per month, square meters	Income per square meter per month*
Mums (year-round)	55,575.00	42,575.00	3,548	669	5.30
Azaleas (off season)	10,153.12	7,153.12	596	160	3.73
Poinsettias, 6- and 15-centimeter	36,970.50	31,534.50	3,942	1,125	3.51
Azaleas (natural-season)	90,843.75	60,843.75	5,070	1,399	3.61
Hydrangeas	16,031.25	15,031.25	1,253	268	4.70
Lilies	6,215.62	3,965.62	793	121	6.55
Mums (holiday)	39,575.50	30,457.50	3,046	616	4.95
Tulips	15,187.50	8,437.50	1,688	167	10.11
Hyacinths	15,187.50	8,437.50	1,688	167	10.11
Gloxinias	17,456.25	15,006.25	3,752	756	4.96

*For income per square foot per month multiply by 0.093.

made as needed, but before a change is made it should be determined what the long-range effect will be. Sometimes the change that seems desirable at the moment will prove very unsatisfactory when the results of future crops are considered.

There are various reasons why the number of plants sold does not equal the number of plants planned. This number varies from crop to crop and year to year, but through the years it is estimated that the loss is about 5 percent for most pot plants. For lilies the estimate is 15 percent and for tulips and hyacinths 10 percent. The important point in this discussion is not the amount of loss, but that there is a loss. Too many plans are made on the basis that the entire quantity planned will be sold, but this seldom occurs because of cultural problems, diseases, pests, physical injury to the plants, and poor market conditions.

In this analysis of income it is estimated that selling costs for pot plants average 25 percent of the selling price. The selling cost is subtracted from the total selling price in determining the gross income from the crop.

The total gross income per year from the pot plant range in this example is $303,314.99. The total bench and bed area involved in the range is 5,273 square meters—2,790 square meters in glass houses, 1,553 square meters in plastic houses used primarily for storage but rated the same as the glass houses in computing income, and a glass-house equivalent of 930 square meters in outdoor beds, as this area is charged at one-half the glass-house rate. The gross income per square meter of bench space per year would be $57.52. It is possible that the plastic-house area used primarily for storage should be rated less than the glass-house area, and if this were done, the gross income per square meter would increase.

In order to make a comparison of income among the various crops that were grown, the original plant costs were subtracted from the gross income, and the gross income per month was determined by dividing this amount by the number of months the crop was in production. Dividing the gross income per month by the average amount of bench space used by each crop per month gives the gross income per square meter per month. The greatest value in presenting this analysis may be in suggesting a method of comparing relative incomes from greenhouse crops rather than in the actual values that were determined in the example.

FLOWERING POT PLANTS

African Violet *(Saintpaulia ionantha—Gesneriaceae)*

The African violet is a native of tropical Africa and was given its generic name in honor of Baron Walter Von St. Paul who discovered the plant. It tolerates the low light, warm temperature, and relatively dry air in the home and makes a very satisfactory flowering house plant.

Saintpaulias are produced the year-round in 6- to 10-centimeter pots; and many of the plants are purchased for use in the home although some of the larger sizes are used for hospital or other gifts. The use of these plants is not associated with any particular holiday, but sales are generally better in the spring than at other times of the year.

African violets flower the year-round with no effect of day length on flowering. The leaves and flowers arise from a compact stem producing a crown type of growth. The plants increase very little in height as they grow, but they do expand in width as new plants form at the base.

Propagation Plants are propagated by leaf cuttings taken with a petiole about 1 centimeter long to help anchor the leaf in the propagation medium. Young plants develop slowly from long petioles stuck deeply in the rooting medium. Mature leaves may be taken any time of the year, and for a 10-centimeter plant from 8 to 10 months should be allowed from the time of propagating.

A mixture of equal parts of sand and peat or sand, vermiculite, and peat is preferable to sand alone because it does not dry as fast and retains fertilizer. Ordinary greenhouse flats are filled with the rooting medium, and leaves are stuck close but not touching each other, so that there are several hundred in a flat. The flats may be placed overhead on racks in a 18°C house. Rooting will occur in 3 to 4 weeks, but shoot formation and development to a size convenient to handle take 8 to 12 weeks. Growth substances hasten rooting but often delay shoot development.

Nematodes may infest the petioles, and generally there are swellings present. Such leaves should not be used for propagation, because there is no control except to discard the plants. All flats, pots, soil mixtures, and bench areas should be steamed to prevent nematode infection.

Seed may be used with only a few cultivars which reproduce true. The majority of seedlings from a cross will be different from the parent and constitute the major source of new cultivars. Extensive breeding by amateurs has led to the introduction of far too many cultivars because of reluctance to discard inferior sorts.

The seed is fine and should be sown on the surface of a screened, well-prepared soil that is watered from below. At a temperature of 21°C, germination will occur in several weeks time. The plants are pricked off to flats approximately 3 centimeters each way and, when crowded, are placed in 6-centimeter pots and later shifted to 10-centimeter pots, where they are flowered and evaluated.

Since African violets are so readily propagated by seed or leaf cuttings, today there are numerous cultivars which are identical, or nearly so, yet have different names. Many cultivars should be discarded because they are poor; some are satisfactory as small plants, but deteriorate after reaching the flowering stage in larger pots. The large-flowered, heavy-leaved kinds are presumed to be tetraploids.

Light   Regulation of light intensity is very important. Optimum growth and flowering will be obtained at 1,100 foot-candles of light during the brightest part of the day. More than this level of light will cause compact growth and bleaching or burning of the foliage. Too little light induces stretching of the petioles and reduction of flowering. The African violet grower should purchase a light meter so that light intensity can be maintained at the optimum range at all seasons.

Regulation of the intensity can be accomplished by several means. Applying shading compounds to the roof should begin in early March, and as the sunlight increases in intensity, additional shading material is used. By June the glass should be completely covered with shading compound. In late

September some shade can be brushed or scraped off, and by late November, in Ohio, most of it should be off because of the prevalence of dark cloudy weather. Cheesecloth, muslin, and other similar cloth suspended on wires overhead may be used alone or in conjunction with shading material on the roof to regulate light intensity.

When the only source of light is fluorescent lamps, growth of the African violet is very satisfactory. The plants have heavier, darker green leaves with attractive pigmentation underneath, flowering is much more profuse, and in general the plants are far superior to those produced under the optimum conditions in the greenhouse. Leaves allowed to root and form small plants under fluorescent light and then grown in the greenhouse produce mature plants faster than if grown in the greenhouse from propagation. Therefore fluorescent lights can be quite useful in propagation where great numbers of leaves occupying a relatively small area can be lighted. The added growth obtained makes this a feasible undertaking.

The light intensity should be 600 foot-candles, and the length of exposure per day should be 15 to 18 hours. The standard cool-white tubes have proved somewhat superior to other types.

To obtain 600 foot-candles over a 120-centimeter bench, two industrial fixtures, each holding two tubes, should be suspended side by side, 30 centimeters above the tops of the plants. The 40-watt tubes are 120 centimeters long, and the area covered will be about 1.5 square meters. Instead of fixtures, strips which have the ballast and receptacle for the tubes may be mounted on plywood painted white for maximum reflection. If these strips are spaced 15 centimeters apart, the optimum light intensity can be obtained at reduced initial cost. Limited tests have shown that African violets can be lighted for 24 hours (continuously) if given 400 foot-candles of light. This eliminates the need for a time switch to operate the lights and promotes longer life for the tubes, which wear out faster when turned on and off.

The fluorescent light itself is not solely responsible for the improved growth of the plants. It is true that optimum light intensity is obtained for 15 to 18 hours, which is quite different from greenhouse light intensities, but usually environmental conditions in a room without sunlight do not vary so greatly, and growth is accelerated from the more uniform environment.

Temperature At temperatures lower than 16°C, the African violet grows very slowly, may get mildew, and will have hardened, brittle, downward-curled foliage. Best growth is obtained between 18 and 21°C, though maintenance of a 17 to 18°C temperature is more economical and quite satisfactory. At 27°C the plants grow well and flowering is profuse, but the petals are faded and small.

Potting and Spacing When the shoots at the base of the petiole are about 3 centimeters long, the leaf with the attached plants is carefully lifted and placed in a 6-centimeter pot. Such plants will become multiple-crowned (all shoots develop). Single-crowned specimens are produced by separating the crowns at the time of initial potting or after the plants have developed to some extent in 6-centimeter pots. Single-crowned plants have leaves that spread out like spokes in a wheel and are difficult to ship because of leaf breakage. Multiple-crowned plants grow into a salable plant more rapidly and ship rather easily.

The small pots are placed pot to pot in the bench, and they are kept at that spacing until time for repotting. When the leaves of the young plants extend to the edges of the pots, the plants are removed from the bench and repotted. They are shifted to the size in which they will be finished, usually either 8- or 10-centimeter azalea pots.

After repotting, the plants may be placed pot to pot on the bench, or they may be placed at the finish spacing. The method of spacing is determined by the amount of available space, the number of plants to be grown, the quality desired, and the available labor. Labor will be conserved, and plant growth will be better if the plants are set at the finish spacing. The spacing used varies with the type of plant desired, but it is about 10 centimeters for 8-centimeter pots and 15 centimeters for 10-centimeter pots.

Troubles Overwatering the African violet generally kills the roots, and the plant will have a gray-green appearance. Very often the crown will rot if kept too wet. The soil should be allowed to dry, but not to the point that the plants wilt.

The temperature of the water is very important. If the water is somewhat cooler than the leaf temperature, irregular spots, streaks, or rings develop that are white or cream-colored. The chlorophyll in the leaves will never develop in that area again. If the plants are watered early in the morning when the leaf temperature is at its lowest point, cool (not cold) water usually is safe. Warming the water to a temperature of 27°C by means of steam or hot water is the safest procedure to eliminate danger of leaf spotting. Watering before 10 A.M. will ensure that the crowns and foliage will be dry by night, which is an effective way of reducing the danger of rot or other diseases developing.

Petiole rot occurs where the petiole contacts the edge of the pot and is due to injury from the minerals that have accumulated in the pot. This is not common in production when new pots are used, but it can be a problem after the plants have grown for several months in the home. There is no pathogen involved, and the control is to prevent the leaves from touching the pot edge by covering the edge with aluminum foil or other material.

Diseases Botrytis blight may affect leaves or flowers, and the best means of control are sanitation and adequate spacing of plants. Increasing ventilation or using air-circulation fans will help also.

Root and crown rot are caused by the pythium pathogen, and soil, pots, and handling equipment must be steamed thoroughly before use. This pathogen thrives in soils that are constantly moist. The use of well-drained soil coupled with well-spaced irrigations provides more favorable conditions.

The powdery mildew pathogen may infest the leaves of African violets, but this should be no problem if heating and ventilating are done properly, providing air movement and lower humidity.

Pests Aphids and mealybugs can be troublesome. Probably the most serious pest is the cyclamen mite, which sucks the juices of the youngest leaves and causes them to be curled upward and dwarfed. The leaves also have a dense whitish pubescence on the upper surface when mite has infested the plants. Flowers are malformed, and soon the plant ceases to produce flowers, because the mite sucks juices from the young inflorescences, which prevents their development.

Thrips cause light streaks on the flowers of the darker-colored cultivars. They pollinate the flowers, which drop quickly, and seed pods form.

Nematodes, both root-knot and foliar, attack the African violet. Knots or galls may form on the roots, while swellings of the petiole or discolored brown areas appear between the main veins of the leaves, indicating their presence. Nematode-infested plants should be destroyed, and pots, soil, and bench areas steamed. Nematodes can leach from the soil in a pot and infest the bench area, so that infested plants constitute a serious hazard.

The Pritchard mealybug may live on the roots of African violets and is a small white insect covered with waxy threads. Several hundred may infest the plant roots, and losses can be great.

Azalea *(Rhododendron* X cultivars—*Ericaceae)*

All greenhouse azalea cultivars are evergreen—they retain leaves the year-round—but most are not hardy in many areas of the United States. They are damaged by cold temperatures that occur naturally outdoors during the winter. Some of the cultivars are less susceptible to cold damage and they may be used as landscape plants as well as indoor ornamentals.

Through the years some of the azalea cultivars have been classed in groups because of general characteristics or because of known or suspected parentage. Some of the earlier groupings were Kurume, Indica, and Pericat. The Kurumes usually had a great number of small flowers, and a very popular cultivar of this group was Coral Bells. Most of the cultivars classed as Kurumes probably arose from hybridization between varieties of *Rhodo-dendron obtusum*. The group known in the trade as Indicas or Belgians have a botanical listing as Indians. Generally the Indians have fewer but larger flowers, and one of the early Indians was Lentegroet. The Indians resulted originally from hybridization among *R. indicum* and *R. simsii*, or *R. indicum* and *R. mucronatum*, or varieties of these species.

The Pericat group has flower characteristics somewhat between the Kurumes and the Indians, and Sweetheart Supreme is a cultivar from this group that remains in the trade. It has been reported that the Pericats developed from crosses between cultivars of Kurumes and Indians.

Other groups of significance in greenhouse azaleas that were developed later were Rutherford (Rutherfordiana) and Whitewater.

The placing of azalea cultivars in groupings may be pertinent to hybridizers and historians but is of much less importance to greenhouse pot-plant growers. They need to know the growth and flowering characteristics of each cultivar regardless of ancestry, and there is less reference now to azalea groups. Azaleas, however, usually are listed by time of flowering in natural season—early, mid-season, or late. With this information, the grower will know how long a cold-temperature storage period is required before forcing can be started for the cultivar.

Azalea Reproduction Reproduction of azaleas is mainly by means of stem-tip cuttings and is handled commonly by specialists who sell greenhouse operators small plants for growing-on or dormant plants ready to force. The azalea propagator needs to maintain stock plants for a source of cuttings and will attempt to keep the stock plants in vegetative growth. If flower buds do form, the cutting will be pinched either at the time it is stuck in the propagation bench or as soon as it is removed after rooting. There is some difference among cultivars in the length of time required for rooting, but at 21°C soil temperature rooting requires about 6 weeks.

Natural-Season Azaleas The landscape azaleas have vegetative growth during the summer with terminal flower buds forming in late summer. The plants are in the naturally cool outdoor temperatures from fall to spring, and sometime after the natural increase in temperature in the spring flowering occurs. The greenhouse azalea cultivars would grow and develop in the same way as the landscape cultivars if they could withstand the cold temperatures outdoors in the winter.

Greenhouse azalea growers simulate outdoor conditions for their plants inside except they moderate the "winter" conditions by making this cold period shorter and not as cold. The plants grown in this way are called natural-season azaleas.

The greenhouse grower usually starts the natural-season azaleas from small plants (growing-on plants) received from the propagation specialist in April or May. The plants that will be finished in 16-centimeter pots will be the 13- by 15-centimeter growing-on plants (the diameter of the branched portion of the plant is approximately 13 to 15 centimeters). Smaller growing-on plants will be used for smaller pots and larger growing-on plants will be used for plants to be finished in larger pots. In some instances, two smaller plants instead of one larger plant are planted in the large pots. Several years ago a type of pot was designed for azaleas that was not as tall as the standard pot (it is about three-quarters the height of standard pots), and most azaleas are grown in this type of pot. Subsequently the "azalea pot" was adopted for use with other kinds of plants, and it is in general usage in pot-plant production.

Azalea soils should be coarse and fibrous peat with pH 5 to 5.5, and the young plants may be planted either in beds or pots when they are received. In the middle to northern United States, the azalea plants are grown in the greenhouse at 18°C from the time they are received in the spring, and then, usually in June, they are moved outdoors.

Azaleas are pinched (sheared) so that a bushy, compact plant develops. If the growing-on plants were not pinched shortly before they were shipped, they may be pinched at the time of planting. The plants may be pinched again, but the last pinch must not be made later than early July. A pinch then allows enough time for sufficient stem growth before growth in stem length terminates with formation of a terminal flower or flowers in late summer.

Azalea pinching may be done with knife-in-hand or by means of shears. Shearing is the faster of the two methods but is lacking somewhat in accuracy. Azaleas also may be pinched by spraying the plants with a material that kills the shoot tips but does not injure the more mature tissues. This is referred to as chemical pinching. It can be an effective and efficient means for pinching azaleas, but it must be used very carefully. The results can be affected by the stage of growth of the shoots and the environmental conditions. Chemical pinching of azaleas is used more frequently by the producer of large quantities of plants who usually has a better opportunity to provide the uniform conditions that are required for best results.

If the plants are grown outdoors during the summer, usually they are not brought indoors or given temperature protection until there is danger of freezing in the fall. There are advantages in leaving the plants outdoors as long as possible. The flower buds develop very well in the typical fall climate, and the cool night temperatures provide some vernalization so that the plants will force more rapidly and uniformly. However, the flower buds are so susceptible to damage by freezing at that stage of growth that just a short period at about the freezing temperature is sufficient to kill the flower buds.

During the summer the plants are spaced on about 30-centimeter centers. When they are taken in for cool storage they are set pot to pot.

If the natural-season azalea plants have grown satisfactorily during the summer, the flower buds will be fully developed by late September. Azalea growers judge the stage of development by the size and shape of the flower bud. If the buds seem to be too small at that time, the plants may be moved into the greenhouse for a few weeks of growth at 16°C before they are placed in cool storage.

The plants with well-developed flower buds are placed in cool temperatures (below 10°C) for vernalization. Some of the cultivars which are classed as early that have been grown in natural season may be forced into flower after 4 weeks of cool storage. Thus the earliest cultivars grown in natural season may be forced for the Christmas market. The mid-season cultivars may be forced for Valentine's Day, and the late cultivars are held in cool storage until March and forced for the Easter market. Cold frames, greenhouses, or refrigerated storage may be used for the vernalization of azaleas.

The plants must be irrigated before they are placed in cool storage, but during storage irrigation will be infrequent because the plants are dormant and the water losses low in the cool temperatures.

When azaleas are stored in greenhouses or frames, the temperature needs to be maintained between 1 and 10°C. It usually is necessary to shade greenhouses so that the temperatures are not too high during the day. There can be excessive leaf abscission with azalea plants stored in refrigerators. Usually this can be prevented by supplying the plants with 10 foot-candles of light for 12 hours per day and opening the storage periodically to vent any ethylene that may accumulate.

When short-term (6 weeks or less) refrigerated storage is involved, it is best to use 9°C. For longer-term storage, the refrigerator should be operated at 2°C.

When the natural-season azaleas are brought into the greenhouse for forcing, the plants in 16-centimeter pots are spaced on 30-centimeter centers. The night temperature should be 16 to 18°C. It will take a few days for root growth to start after the plants are brought out of cool storage. For at least the first week the plants should be misted frequently during the day to reduce water loss from the plant.

It requires about 6 weeks to force azaleas into flower in early season. The length of forcing time decreases as the season progresses. It should require only about 2 weeks to force azaleas for a late Easter.

Year-Round Azaleas The production of azaleas at periods of the year other than the natural season has been a relatively recent commercial development. Refrigeration facilities are definitely needed for the year-round production of azaleas, and there must be a constant source of supply of small plants. In many instances the year-round azalea grower will also be a propagator and produce the small plants that are needed for the program.

Some azalea cultivars are much more satisfactory for the year-round production program than others. Some of the cultivars that can be used successfully are Red Wing, Dorothy Gish, Gloria, Kingfisher, Alaska, and White Gish.

There has been a controversy for several years about the photoperiodic characteristics of azaleas. There was some evidence that short photoperiods promoted flowering. However, it was not the definite response exhibited by chrysanthemum and some other kinds of plants, and for this reason regulation of photoperiod was seldom used in the production of natural-season azaleas. The effect of photoperiod on vegetative and reproductive growth is more easily demonstrated with azaleas grown out of natural season. For this reason, the plants are provided with long photoperiods when vegetative growth is desired and with short photoperiods when reproductive growth should occur.

Various production schedules have been suggested for year-round azaleas. There is general agreement that the minimum length of time in cool storage (7°C) must be 6 weeks for the azaleas on the year-round program. The minimum amount of time from the last pinch to placing the plants in cool storage could be 12 weeks—the first 6 weeks after the pinch with long photoperiods and the last 6 weeks with short photoperiods. The temperature during this growing period should be 18°C. On this minimum-length growing program the buds will be small, but at least in some areas of the country or at some times of the year such a short growing time is a possibility.

Most azalea growers will need to develop their own time schedule based on the rate of growth at their locale for the time of the year or the kind of growing season. In some instances more growing time will be warranted either in long photoperiods or short photoperiods or both.

The year-round azaleas should be forced at 16 to 18°C, and the forcing time should take 3 to 6 weeks depending on the season of the year.

Production of Budded Azalea Plants The term "budded azaleas" is used for azalea plants that have well-developed flower buds. This type of plant is grown by growers in several parts of the United States—mainly in coastal areas of the country. They are grown in natural-season conditions and thus the plants are ready for shipping in the fall. Gulf Coast and East Coast growers ship most of their budded plants before frost in late October. Because of natural climatic conditions on the West Coast, the growers in that area are able to ship budded plants from early fall into the winter.

Most of the budded plants that are shipped are dormant plants. They require vernalization before forcing.

Many greenhouse operators buy dormant, budded azalea plants in the fall, place them in cool storage, and bring some out at regular intervals for forcing.

Troubles Chlorosis of the tip leaves usually indicates a lack of available iron in the plant, which may be caused by a lack of available iron in the soil or by a damaged root system which is not able to transfer the iron from the soil to the upper parts of the plant. If the roots are growing actively, an application of chelated iron or iron sulfate will correct the situation. If the roots are not growing well, the cause for this poor growth must be corrected first. The most common causes of poor root growth in azaleas are inadequate drainage with constantly wet soil, too much fertilizer in the soil, nematodes of various kinds, and fungus diseases.

Bypassed flower buds—caused by vegetative shoots starting in growth immediately below the flower buds—may be a problem during the forcing period. If they are allowed to continue in growth, the flower buds on those stems will not open—they will be bypassed. If the vegetative shoots are removed when they first appear, the flower buds will open normally. Most bypass growth can be prevented if conditions for flower bud formation are good while the plant is grown. Then the flower buds form not only in the terminal position in the stem but also in the lateral position, immediately below the terminal, and the stems have clusters of flower buds with no possibility of bypass shoots forming.

Leaf drop does occur, and this is associated usually with root damage because of either extremely dry or extremely wet soil or because of the use of too much fertilizer. In addition, the lack of light or presence of ethylene in storage may cause some leaf drop.

Bronzing of the leaves can be caused by cool temperatures, and it is more pronounced when the light intensity is high and the nitrogen supply is low.

Loss of roots can be caused by poor soil drainage or keeping the soil too wet, by too much fertilizer in the soil, or by allowing the soil to dry too much. If peat moss becomes too dry, it is difficult to wet; then the soil ball should be submerged in water briefly. If coarse poultry-litter-grade peat moss is used drainage usually is not a problem. An application of fertilizer can damage the roots if the soil is dry when applied, and it is good practice to irrigate just before fertilizing.

Diseases Phytophthora root rot is caused by *Phytophthora cinnamomi* and is most prevalent in soils which are poorly drained or are irrigated too frequently. Diseased plants should be rogued and the soil moisture conditions improved. *Cylindrocladium scoparium* is a fungus attacking the lower stem or roots. It grows best at warm temperatures under moist conditions. Losses from the fungus can be great and are often ascribed to other fungi. Laboratory culturing will identify the organism.

Flower spot caused by *Ovulinia azaleae* can be a serious problem for azaleas. In the early stages the spots are pinhead size and are white to rust in color, and as the infestation progresses, the spots enlarge to irregular blotches with the collapse of the entire flower. The affected flowers dry and remain on the plant, as contrasted with the normal flower drop of old flowers. This pathogen forms sclerotia that can overwinter in the soil. Infected flowers should be completely removed from the area as soon as possible, and the area should be sterilized if it is to be used for azaleas the following year.

Leaf spots caused by *Septoria azaleae* and other fungi are most troublesome when the leaves remain wet for extended periods. The leaf spotting is usually followed by leaf drop.

Rhizoctonia stem rot occurs primarily when the soil is too heavy, the plants are set too deeply, or irrigations are too frequent.

Pests Nematodes have become increasingly serious pests, and the best control is careful steaming of soil and all handling equipment. Plants infested with nematodes cease growing because of the severe damage to the roots, leaves are off-color, and the plants may wilt permanently.

Azaleas may be infested with two-spotted mites, aphids, thrips, cyclamen mites, leaf miners, leaf rollers, or mealybugs, but normal control measures are usually effective.

Growth Regulators Some chemicals retard the growth of azaleas and, when properly used, develop buds more quickly and more uniformly. The sprays should be applied to run off from the leaves to well-watered plants with dry leaves, and water should be kept off the leaves for at least 24 hours following the application. Two applications should be made about 1 week apart.

These materials are of maximum value only when used in addition to providing the best temperature and day-length conditions for formation of flower buds. Some bad effects may be expected if they are used at too great concentrations, too often, or under wrong conditions. However, when used according to label directions, they may be helpful.

Experimentally in some situations it has been possible to use the potassium salt of gibberellic acid to mature azalea flower buds instead of using cool temperature treatments. It appears, however, that commercial use is not practical.

Elatior Begonia *(Begonia* X *hiemalis—Begoniaceae)*

By selection and hybridization, Rieger, in Germany, developed improved cultivars of elatior begonias. These new introductions became known as Rieger begonias. The first ones were marketed in the 1950s, and since that time they have become an increasingly important factor in the pot-plant market. Mikkelsen introduced them in the United States, and they are grown primarily as specimen plants in about 16-centimeter pots or as hanging plants in about 25-centimeter pots. Elatior begonias can be grown the year-round, but generally larger quantities are marketed in the spring.

The upright-growing cultivars are more commonly used in the 16-centimeter pots and those that have more prostrate-type growth are used in hanging pots. Because of these characteristics, the Schwabenland cultivars were grown as specimen plants and the Aphrodite cultivars as hanging plants. Each of these blood lines of elatior begonias, however, had other specific characteristics that affected their uses. The Schwabenlands could be propagated from leaf cuttings, they could be flowered the year-round, and they were susceptible to powdery mildew. The Aphrodites could be propagated from stem-tip cuttings, they could not be flowered during the winter, and they were not susceptible to powdery mildew. Now, however, because of selection and hybridization, the characteristics of blood lines do not segregate in the same way in the cultivars, and each new individual needs to be identified by its own properties rather than being classed in some ancestral grouping.

Propagation The elatior begonias are propagated by leaf cuttings if that method can be used and by stem-tip cuttings if leaf cuttings cannot be used. Propagation is handled by specialists and the young plants are marketed to growers in 5-centimeter pots.

Light These begonias need some reduction in light intensity from spring to fall. Growth is best at about 3,000 foot-candles if the temperature can be maintained at 16 to 18°C. In warmer weather when the temperature is higher than 27°C, the light intensity should be adjusted to about 1,000 foot-candles.

Although the elatior begonias are not classed as short-day plants, vegetative growth is promoted in long days. For this reason, long days may be provided for young plants during the naturally short days from September 1 to April 15. This can be the same type of lighting that is used for mums, but even better results can be obtained when the light intensity is 20 foot-candles or more rather than the 10 foot-candle minimum usually used with mums.

Temperature Growth is best if the young plants can be started at 22°C followed by 17°C after the plants are established. The plants may be finished at 16°C.

Pinching The size of the finished plant can be regulated by pinching. For finishing plants in small pots, the plants can be grown without pinching. In most instances, these begonias are grown in larger pots with one plant pinched to produce branching. The pinch must be made deep enough so that it is below the reproductive growth.

Pests and Pathogens Some of the elatior begonia cultivars are susceptible to powdery mildew, and this disease may be a problem at any of the stages—in the greenhouse, during marketing, or in use by the customer. Whenever possible, the cultivars that are not susceptible should be grown. Careful regulation of the environment may prevent infection in the greenhouse, but it may not be possible to control the environment as well in the marketing and consumer stage.

The elatior begonias are subject to some leaf problems that may have somewhat similar symptoms. Bacterial leaf blight or bacterial leaf spot is caused by *Xanthomonas begoniae,* and foliar nematodes may infest leaves. The spread of either of these problems is promoted with water on the surface of the leaves. The plants should be irrigated so that the leaf surfaces remain dry.

Calceolaria (*Calceolaria crenatiflora—Scrophulariaceae*)

Through the years, calceolaria has been a cool-temperature crop produced for late winter and early spring. The flower colors are bright yellow or red or mixtures of the two colors. The characteristic flower shape gives the calceolaria the common name of pocketbook plant. It is propagated from seed. Formerly, *Calceolaria integrefolia* was also used as a flowering pot plant, and it was propagated by stem-tip cuttings. It no longer is in the trade.

Calceolaria seed germinates in about 2 weeks at 21°C. It is small seed and should be sown on the soil surface without covering.

Temperature and Light When the calceolaria is grown at 10°C in naturally short photoperiods, a September sowing is used for plants to be flowered in April in 13-centimeter pots.

For early flowering the seed is sown earlier and the plants are given long photoperiods (the same as chrysanthemum lighting) about 3 months before time of flowering. For a Valentine's Day crop, the seed is sown in July to August and lighting starts in mid-November.

When calceolaria is grown at 16°C or warmer, it can be flowered in a shorter period of time (about 5 months from sowing the seed to flowering in late winter and early spring) if given 6 weeks of short photoperiods followed by 18-hour photoperiods by extension of the natural day length by mum-type lighting.

It is also possible to flower calceolaria during naturally long days if they can be given 6 weeks of short photoperiods (12 hours or less) with temperatures of 20°C or less. Because of naturally high temperatures and high light intensities during the summer, it does not seem probable that the calceolaria will be a common summer crop in most areas of the United States.

Troubles Calceolaria soil must be coarse and porous so that it drains readily. In addition calceolaria must be irrigated carefully so that the soil does not remain constantly wet. Chlorotic tip leaves are a symptom of poor root growth due to wet soils.

Stem rot can be a problem if the plants are set too deeply in the soil or if the soil is kept too wet.

Aphids and whiteflies are common pests, and a program to control them will need to be used.

Cherry (*Solanum pseudocapsicum—Solanaceae*)

Known commonly as the Jerusalem, or Cleveland, cherry, this is a reasonably priced plant for Christmas sales. Seeds are sown in January or February, and the plants are grown in a 13 to 16°C house. In late May they can be placed in 13- or 15-centimeter pots and placed in frames or plunged outdoors, or the plants can be placed in beds for later potting.

During the summer the fruit is set. Overdoses of nitrogen promote excessive vegetative growth and poor fruiting. Bed-grown plants are potted in late August and placed in a 13°C house, where the fruits will be well developed by Christmas.

Christmas Cactus *(Schlumbergera bridgesii* and *Schlumbergera truncata—Cactaceae)*

There are some identity problems here. *Schlumbergera truncata* has been known as *Zygocactus truncatus*, but apparently this plant is properly a *Schlumbergera* and will be classified as such in the future. Also, it has been commonly called Thanksgiving cactus by some and Christmas cactus by others. The more proper common name probably is Thanksgiving cactus because for a given set of conditions, it does flower earlier than *S. bridgesii*. It is the cultivars of *S. truncata* that are more common in the trade, however, and they are forced for the Christmas market.

The remarks here are specifically about *Schlumbergera truncata* cultivars, and they will be referred to by the common name of Christmas cactus.

Flowering in Christmas cactus is affected by temperature as well as photoperiod. At night temperatures below 13°C, flowers can develop in either long or short photoperiods. At temperatures above 16°C, flower formation will occur only in short photoperiods. In night temperatures of 21°C and above, flowers may not form regardless of length of photoperiod.

Flowering should occur earlier in the fall in natural conditions in the northern United States than it would in Florida because of the prevailing temperatures. Northern greenhouse operators can give their plants an 18°C temperature and long photoperiods until early October to time flowering more closely with the Christmas market.

It is possible that Christmas cactus can be forced for other periods of the year if temperature and photoperiod are regulated suitably.

Chrysanthemum *(Chrysanthemum* X *morifolium—Compositae)*

Within recent years no other potted plant has increased in demand as much as the potted chrysanthemum. It is comparatively easy to grow compact, graceful specimens economically and, in addition, the chrysanthemum keeps exceptionally well in the home and is available in a comparatively wide range of colors.

Chrysanthemums are grown the year-round in carefully controlled temperature and day-length conditions to produce vegetative growth or flowering as desired. Rooted stem-tip cuttings are potted directly into the pot in which they are going to be finished—either four or five cuttings per 16-centimeter pot. The plants may be grown in long days for several days to

Figure 6-6 Pot mums should be started in warm temperatures (18 to 21°C) and high humidity. Using intermittent mist or plastic-film enclosure for several days after planting is good practice. *(Yoder Bros., Inc. photograph.)*

produce leaf growth and increase in stem length; they are then pinched and placed in short days until flower buds are well developed. From potting to flowering, the pot chrysanthemum is about a 3-month crop.

Chrysanthemum cultivars that are suitable for use as pot mums must flower on relatively short stems, branch readily, form a well-shaped plant, and have flowers of the size, shape, and color that are desired. It is mainly the large-flowered cultivars that are used, and the lateral flower buds usually are removed (disbudded), producing a lone, large flower per stem.

There is a good market demand for chrysanthemums the year-round as well as for some of the holidays. The best holiday markets for pot mums are Easter and Mother's Day, but some additional plants are produced for Valentine's Day, Thanksgiving, and Christmas. The 9-, 10-, and 11-week cultivars are used the year-round, and in addition the 7- and 8-week garden cultivars are grown as pot plants for Mother's Day and Decoration Day.

Potting, Pinching, and Spacing   Before potting, the rooted cuttings should be graded for size so that each pot will have cuttings of uniform size. The cuttings should be potted as shallowly as possible because that provides the best soil air-moisture relationship for rapid root growth. If the cuttings are planted at an angle, with the top of the cuttings extending over the edge of the pots, each cutting has a greater area in which to grow, more shoots develop per cutting, and the plant is larger and better formed. After potting they are set pot to pot, and if the plants are to be furnished long days artificially, it is most economical to do it at this close spacing. Growth and development of the young plants will be best in a warm (18°C minimum) and moist atmosphere. Uniformly moist air can be provided with an intermittent mist system or by enclosing the area in clear plastic film or a combination of the two. In such an environment root growth is rapid, the new leaves attain maximum size, and more shoots develop when the plant is pinched. The plants should be in this moist atmosphere for approximately 1 week and then given standard greenhouse conditions.

When the plants have been lighted as long as necessary (from 0 to 3 weeks depending on cultivar and time of the year), they should be spaced, at the final distance of about 1,125 square centimeters per pot. It is possible to space the pots several times, gradually giving them more space as the plants grow, but it is seldom that this spacing gets done on time. Gradual spacing may conserve some space, but it requires more labor. Since the closely spaced plants cast shade on adjacent plants, they do not develop as well. Actually, the amount of final spacing allowed the plants and the method of

Figure 6-7 Chrysanthemums flower sooner and more uniformly if they are supplied short photoperiods each day. Left: short photoperiods 5 days a week. Center: short photoperiods 6 days a week. Right: short photoperiods every day of the week. *(Yoder Bros., Inc. photograph.)*

Figure 6-8 Delay in disbudding causes delay in flowering in chrysanthemum. Right: plants disbudded as soon as the lateral buds could be handled. Left: plants disbudded about 1 week later. *(Yoder Bros., Inc. photograph.)*

spacing can be used to adjust the size of the finished plant. In some instances the plants are grown closer together so that a greater number of plants of smaller size may be produced per unit area to satisfy a market demand for plants of that quality.

Chrysanthemums are pinched to produce branched plants. The pinching is done in such a way that the maximum number of shoots develops following the pinch. The plants should be pinched after they have made enough growth so that the pinch can be made in the new growth. Just a small amount of stem tip should be removed in making the pinch, and this is called a "soft pinch" or "roll-out." If the plants have been grown properly and the pinch is well executed, there will be about 10 leaves below the place of pinch.

Growth Regulators Height control in pot mums is of constant concern because the finished height must be within certain limits above the top of the pot, and the cultivars of chrysanthemums that are grown differ in their height potential. The cultivars are classed as short, medium, or tall, and various procedures are used to finish all cultivars at the same height regardless of their growth characteristics.

Because chrysanthemums form leaves and increase in stem length in long days, and because flower buds form and stems terminate with flowers in short days, the day length that is provided can be used to influence the finished height of the plants. Before short-growing cultivars are provided with short days, they are grown for a sufficient number of long days to increase the length of the stems. Tall-growing cultivars may not be given any long days in an effort to terminate stem growth with a flower as soon as possible.

Height control by means of day length is a good standard practice, but additional control of height can be provided with some chemicals. B-Nine is an effective growth retardant, and it can be used to produce shorter pot mums. The plants are sprayed about 2 weeks after pinching, and in some instances a second spraying may be used 1 or 2 weeks later or at the time of disbudding.

Troubles New root growth should be evident 2 or 3 days after planting. Failure of new roots to develop rapidly may be due to heavy soil that drains poorly, too frequent irrigation, too much fertilizer in the soil, too deep planting, or too low temperature. When new roots develop slowly, stem growth will also be slow, and not as many shoots will develop after the pinch.

Plants can be too short due to several different causes. If the root growth is poor, it is not possible to have good stem growth because the plant will not obtain the water and fertilizer needed for growth. If the root growth is good

Figure 6-9 Some growth chemicals may be used to regulate the height of pot mums. The plant on the left was sprayed with B-Nine about 2 weeks after it was pinched. *(Uniroyal Chemical Division photograph.)*

but the stem growth is not, it is possible that the plants had insufficient nitrogen available in the early stages of growth. This can produce stunting from which the plants do not recover. Another possible cause of short plants is the failure to provide enough long days for the necessary increase in stem length.

Plants that are too tall can be caused by too many long days after the pinch, inadequate spacing of plants, growing the plants in shaded locations, and too high temperatures (above 32°C). If too high temperature is the cause, flowering will be delayed as chrysanthemum flower buds do not continue to develop at high temperatures.

Uneven flower bud development may be a problem during the winter, and it can be caused by too low night temperatures. Some cultivars flower uniformly at 18°C but develop unevenly at 16°C or below. Failure to form flower buds can occur at night temperatures below 16°C with some cultivars.

Crown buds form in hot weather (temperatures about 32°C), and they do not continue to develop into flowers until the temperatures become lower. During this delay in flower development the stem continues to elongate, the plants become too tall, and the stems have a stretched appearance. The temperatures may be reduced in chrysanthemum houses by use of fan and pad systems during the daytime. Night temperatures can be reduced by maximum ventilation, by air-circulation fans, by applying the black shade fabric later in the day (7 P.M. standard time), or by raising the sides of the black shade fabric after dark to increase air movement through the plants.

The development of too few shoots per plant after the pinch can be caused by unfavorable conditions in the first 2 weeks after the cuttings are potted. Some of these conditions are poor root growth, insufficient nitrogen in the soil, too cool night temperatures, dry air, and too hard a pinch.

Flower malformation usually is the result of poor control of day length or fluctuation of short days and long days.

For discussions of flower types, propagation, light, temperature, air, diseases, and pests, refer to the section on chrysanthemum in Chap. 5.

Cropping and Rotations Various schedules, designed to adjust the height of plants, are used for cropping pot mums. The height desired varies with the market area. Then, too, the plants do not reach the same height in every greenhouse in spite of being grown on the same schedule, because growing conditions or methods of handling may vary. Propagators or sellers of chrysanthemum cuttings suggest schedules which are suitable for average conditions, and each grower should adjust the schedule as needed for the particular situation. The schedule should allow enough time before pinching so that the pinch can be made in new growth and leave about 10 leaves below the pinch. For short- and medium-growing cultivars long days are always provided for this growing period before the pinch. Short-growing cultivars are given at least a week of long days after the pinch in order to give them additional stem length, but medium-growing cultivars are usually given short days immediately after the pinch as they then will finish at about the right height. Tall-growing cultivars may or may not be given any long days before the pinch, and they are seldom given long days after the pinch as that would make them taller than desired. Short days for tall-growing cultivars often are started about a week before the pinch in an effort to reduce the height at which the plants finish.

Chrysanthemums do not grow as rapidly in the cool and dark weather of the winter as they do in better light and warmer temperatures. The schedules that are used for pot mums must take this into consideration and provide for more long days before the start of short days for plants grown in the winter.

The time of flowering of chrysanthemums is determined by the time of starting short days. The different cultivar classes or response groups flower in a set length of time after the start of short days regardless of when they are planted or when they are pinched—10-week cultivars flower about 10 weeks after the start of short days. It is the 9-, 10-, and 11-week cultivars that are used mostly for year-round flowering. If crops are produced at regular intervals throughout the year, no adjustment needs to be made in time of planting of the various response classes or short-, medium-, or tall-growing cultivars, as there will be some of each kind of flower at all times no matter when they were planted or how long they take to flower after the start of short days. However, for holiday crops when all the plants are required to be in flower at the same time, the different response classes must be planted and handled so that all are in flower exactly for the holiday market. Scheduling pot mums for the holidays is an interesting problem in management, as the 10-week cultivars must be planted 1 week before the 9-week cultivars, and the short-growing cultivars have to be planted earlier than those that grow tall.

The keeping qualities of pot chrysanthemums are better in the flower shops and in the homes if the flowers are allowed to develop fully in the greenhouse before they are sold; however, this is not common knowledge to the people buying the plants. In some market areas the customers insist that the flowers be in tight bud at the time of sale, and in other areas various stages of flower development are requested. This may not be a problem for year-round sales, as flowers at all stages of development are available, but for holidays the grower must be able to have the entire crop at just the right stage of development for the particular sales area. At holidays there is generally a greater demand for plants with fully developed flowers than there is at other times, as the plants are used immediately for maximum display.

It is possible to grow pot chrysanthemums in the natural season in the fall without the use of either lights or black fabric, but this is seldom done, as exact scheduling is not possible, height control is variable, and the possible savings are slight.

In the spring, the garden cultivars (7- and 8-week response class) can be flowered in May in natural conditions without the use of either lights or black fabric. The garden cultivars make good Mother's Day items as the individual plants can be cut back and planted outdoors after the holiday, and they may flower again in the fall and for several years thereafter. Because many of the garden cultivars are not large-flowered types, the stems are not disbudded, resulting in a spray of flowers on each stem. Some garden cultivars are flowered in 8-centimeter pots and used in combination planters for Mother's Day or Memorial Day.

In some instances large-flowered mum cultivars are grown single-stem in pots—the plants are not pinched. This produces fewer but larger flowers per pot, and they make an entirely different quality of plant. The market demand for single-stem pot mums varies with the sales area, but in general it is greatest for the spring holidays.

In a year-round pot-mum program, the pot mums rotate with themselves, and a uniform quantity of pots is produced throughout the year. Many different methods of moving and spacing pot mums are used; and because of this, space requirements do vary. If it were desired to produce 500 sixteen-centimeter pot mums each week, the pots would be lighted in one area while spaced pot to pot, and then moved to another area and placed at the finish spacing of 1,125 square centimeters per pot until they flower. This would require about 28 square meters of bench space in lighted area and about 651 square meters of bench space for short days until the plants flowered. The potential production would be about 3.7 sixteen-centimeter pots per 900 square centimeters of bench space per year.

Pot mums produced for the spring holidays must be rotated with some other crop, and the most likely pot-plant crops with which to rotate are poinsettias and azaleas. The Easter pot mums would occupy the bench space shortly after it was vacated by the poinsettias in December, and the Mother's Day pot mums could use the bench space in which azaleas had been forced in January and February. It is possible to rotate the spring pot mums with cut-flower crops such as cut chrysanthemums or roses, but this might involve additional labor and less desirable growing conditions for the pot-mum crop.

Cineraria *(Senecio* X hybridus—*Compositae)*

The cineraria is an inexpensive flowering plant for sale from January to May. Seed sown in June will produce flowering plants in January, a July 15 to August 1 sowing will flower in February, and a September sowing will flower for Easter. A number of compact strains with numerous flowers are available. Since the seeds are small, care should be exercised in selecting a suitable soil for sowing and preventing the seed flat from drying out.

The seedlings are transplanted to flats when large enough to handle and are grown there until large enough for 6-centimeter pots. Seedlings may be planted 8 centimeters apart in the transplant flat. When they become crowded, they are shifted directly to the finishing pot, saving considerable labor, though additional space is needed in the early stages.

All soil, flats, and pots should be steamed to prevent verticillium disease, which causes the plants to wilt, from which they never recover and eventually die. The disease becomes apparent between the time the plants are half grown and maturity. A mixture of three parts soil and one part peat can be used. Azalea pots of the 13- to 15-centimeter sizes are preferable to standard pots.

Fertilizer should be applied every 2 or 3 weeks when the plants are established to obtain large, dark-green specimens. Spacing is necessary to prevent the plants from becoming leggy. Because cinerarias develop a large leaf area, they must be watered frequently, and in the spring when the sunlight is intense, the plants may wilt even if the soil is moist. A night temperature of 7 to 10°C is best.

Since the plants grow rapidly, the cost of production is comparatively low. This makes cinerarias suitable for reasonably priced sales.

Cinerarias are subject to aphids, red spider, leaf rollers, whitefly, and thrips. Stem rot is often caused by too deep planting.

Clerodendrum *(Clerodendrum thomsonae—Verbenaceae)*

The red flower petals and white calyx make a very attractive and unusual flowering pot plant or hanging basket. Flower initiation is not affected by photoperiod, but flower initiation and development are promoted in high light intensity. Flower development may be promoted in short photoperiods.

Propagation is from stem cuttings—either stem-tip cuttings or stem-segment cuttings. When stem-segment cuttings are used, single-node cuttings are used and the leaf is removed before sticking the cutting in the propagation bench. The soil temperature in propagation should be 22°C.

One cutting may be used in a 10-centimeter pot and pinched, and three or more cuttings in a 15-centimeter pot and pinched. Vegetative growth is most favorable at 21°C and in high light intensity and long photoperiods. For flowering, the temperature can be reduced to 17°C and the plants treated with growth regulators. Flower development will be more rapid in photoperiods of about 12 hours.

Iron chlorosis may be a problem above pH 6.3.

Flower and/or lower leaf abscission may occur in low light intensity.

Crocus *(Crocus species—Iridaceae)*

The crocus corms are potted in October. They may be given vernalization temperatures either outdoors or indoors, but much better forcing can be done with plants that are in controlled temperature indoors. Crocus may be potted in regular pots, but the greatest market demand is for those that are potted in the ornamental, compartmented pots that are designed specifically for crocus. They may be brought into the greenhouse for forcing from mid-December to mid-February for flowering from early January to late February. Precooled corms are used for January flowering, and regular corms may be used for forcing from February on.

Cultivars that can be forced are Flower Record, Joan of Arc, King of the Striped, Peter Pan, Pickwick, Purpurea Grandiflorus, Remembrance, and Vanguard. The corms used are either 9/10 or 10/11 centimeters in circumference and are potted with the nose of the corm about at the soil surface.

After potting they should be thoroughly watered and placed in the storage operated at 9 to 10°C until root growth is adequate. This should be a period of 3 to 4 weeks. The temperature then should be controlled at 5°C until the first week in January or until the shoots are 3 centimeters long. The temperature then is changed to 1°C.

Crocus forcing temperature is 13°C. For January flowering, the forcing time is about 3 weeks. For February flowering, the forcing time is 2 weeks or less.

Cyclamen *(Cyclamen persicum—Primulaceae)*

Cyclamen is propagated from seed. It is large seed that is sowed individually at 3- to 6-centimeter squares, and the seedlings are grown in the seed flat until the leaves touch. Depending on the spacing used, the seedlings may be allowed to remain in the seed flats for several months before transplanting to pots.

The standard scheduling for cyclamen has been to sow the seed in the fall for finished plants to be marketed from December to February—18 months later. In the United States most cyclamen have been finished in about

16-centimeter pots on such a schedule. More recently procedures have been developed for growing cyclamen in about 8 to 9 months by sowing the seed in April for plants in flower from December to February in pots 16 centimeters and smaller. Such scheduling requires the use of early-flowering cultivars, good germinating procedures, higher forcing temperatures, the use of giberellins, and generally good environmental conditions. Both procedures will be referred to here.

The cyclamen develops a prominent hypocotyl that is similar in appearance to those developed in beets and radishes. Roots develop from the base of the hypocotyl and leaves and flowers from the top portion of it. The proper term for this structure is hypocotyl, but sometimes it is referred to as corm or tuber.

Cultivars   Most cyclamen cultivars originated in Europe. The greatest market demand is for salmon-pink to red flowers. For fast scheduling, early-flowering cultivars such as the Tas Series and Rosa von Zehlendorf are used.

Propagation   As indicated previously, propagation is by seed and for standard scheduling the seed is sown in the fall. For fast scheduling the seed can be sown in April. Both sowing dates are for cropping from December to February, but the standard schedule is for December to February of the next season.

The seed is sown about 0.5 centimeter deep, and germination is best in the dark at 20°C. Higher temperatures may inhibit germination.

If seed spacing is on 3-centimeter squares, transplanting probably should be done in 2 months. At 6-centimeter spacing, transplanting should be done in about 4 months. For standard scheduling, transplanting usually will be to 8-centimeter pots, and with fast scheduling transplanting might be directly to the final pots.

Light   From fall to spring, cyclamen should have the maximum light intensity available. Partial shade should be provided during the summer with maximum light intensity of about 4,000 foot-candles.

Temperature   Standard-schedule cyclamen usually are grown at 13°C night temperature, but 20°C is recommended for those grown on fast schedule with gradual reduction about November 1 to 17°C.

Gibberellic Acid   A single spraying of the fast-schedule cyclamen with gibberellic acid in the fall about 2 months before flowering has been reported to promote flowering and increase the number of flowers that are open at one time. If too much spray is applied, however, the flower stems may be weakened.

Pests and Pathogens   As the name implies, cyclamen are susceptible to cyclamen mite. Dwarfing and cupping of the young leaves are the symptoms of a mite infestation. A specific miticide is needed to control this. Other pests are controlled with routine programs.

Most of the cyclamen diseases can be prevented with good growing procedures. Steamed soil should be used, and in potting just the base of the hypocotyl should be below the soil line. Irrigation should be done in such a way that the top of the hypocotyl and the crown of the plant dry rapidly.

Daffodil (*Narcissus pseudonarcissus—Amaryllidaceae*)

The daffodil bulbs are potted in October and given vernalization temperatures either outdoors or in cool storage. They then may be brought into the greenhouse for forcing from December to February for flowering from January to April. Precooled bulbs must be used for flowering in January and early February. Regular bulbs can be used for flowering mid-February and later.

Cultivars that are suitable for forcing in pots are Covent Garden, Dutch Master, Explorer, Gold Medal, Mount Hood, President Le Brun, Rembrandt, Triandrus Thalia, and Trocadero. Double nose #1 (DN#1) bulbs should be used, and they are potted bulb to bulb with the nose of the bulb about even with the top edge of the pot.

After potting, they should be thoroughly watered; the first objective is root growth. At temperatures of 10°C or higher, there should be adequate root growth within 3 weeks. For bulbs started outdoors, the natural temperatures should be satisfactory for root growth. For bulbs that are started indoors, the storage temperature should be regulated at 10°C or above until there is sufficient root growth, and then the temperature can be reduced below 10°C.

Daffodil forcing temperature should be 16°C. Some of the pots may be brought into the greenhouse for forcing about mid-December. At this time the flower buds should be at the top of the bulb. From 3 to 4 weeks is required for early-season flowering. For late-season flowering, the forcing time may be about 1 week.

Exacum (Exacum affine—Gentianaceae)   This is an interesting addition to the pot plants being marketed because of the flower color and the flowering season. The blue flower color is unusual, and the best flowering time from spring to fall provides a needed pot plant at that time of the year.

Exacum is propagated from seed. The seed is very small, and it must be sown on the soil surface and lighted. It germinates in about $2^{1}/_{2}$ weeks at 21°C. When the seedlings can be handled they should be planted in flats on 5-centimeter squares.

This plant can be finished in small pots planted one per pot in 8- to 10-centimeter pots or in larger pots planted three to five per pot in 13- to 16-centimeter pots. Exacum is about a 6-month crop from seed sowing to flowering.

Fuchsia *(Fuchsia* X *hybrida—Onagraceae)*

The fuchsia is used as a specimen plant, in hanging baskets, and in combination pots in the spring.

Plants that are not sold in the spring and stock plants reserved especially for propagation are grown during the summer in a shaded greenhouse or lath house. In late summer they may be carried on the dry side or dried off to rest them for 1 month. In September or October they may be started by removing some of the old soil and repotting them in a mixture of three parts soil and one part peat, placing them in the same size of pot. The plants should be cut back, and if possible some foliage allowed to remain. If the shoots are free of insects, the severed portion may be used as cuttings for an early propagation. A complete fertilizer should be applied each month to the stock plants when they have become established. The night temperature should be maintained at 16°C for stock plants.

Cuttings are taken from November through March and may be rooted in sand, sand and peat, or vermiculite. When rooted, the cuttings are placed in 6-centimeter pots at a night temperature of 13°C. In January or early February, three plants in the 6-centimeter pots are placed in a 16-centimeter pot, and if they are pinched, these will make bushy specimens for spring sale. Single-plant specimens are obtained from plants propagated early and shifted to a 10-centimeter pot in December or January and then to a 13-centimer pot in March.

Bushiness and compact growth on pot specimens are obtained by pinching. For Mother's Day the plants should be pinched 8 to 9 weeks before they are wanted in flower, and for Memorial Day a pinch is necessary 6 to 7 weeks prior to the date. Fuchsias may be rooted as late as March and will make satisfactory unpinched plants for combination pots.

There is good demand for hanging baskets. In January, three to four plants of suitable cultivars are placed in a 25-centimeter basket, and they are pinched as previously described to induce branching.

Fuchsia cultivars have either an upright or a trailing type of growth. The upright types are used for specimen pots and combination pots. The trailing types are used in hanging baskets. Cultivars must be selected carefully to satisfy local market preferences.

Fuchsias can be infested by red spiders, mealybugs, aphids, and whitefly.

Gloxinia *(Sinningia speciosa—Gesneriaceae)*

Gloxinias may be started from seed or tubers. Usually seed is sown in December, January, and February for flowering plants in spring and summer, but recently the gloxinia has been popularized as a suitable plant for any season, so that seed is sown any time. About 6 to 8 months from sowing, the plants will be in flower, if conditions have been provided for rapid growth.

Since the seeds are extremely small, they should be sown on the surface of a screened soil and watered from below. The seed flat or pan should be placed where the night temperature is 21°C for most rapid germination and early growth. Direct sunlight is injurious, and the seed flat and seedlings should be protected with a moderately heavy shade. Steaming of flats or pans and soils is helpful in preventing damping-off, and subirrigation is advised to prevent disturbing the small plants.

When the seedlings are large enough to handle, they should be pricked off to transplant flats, spaced about 3 centimeters apart each way, using a well-sharpened pencil. A mixture of two parts soil, one part sand, and two parts peat, passed through a fine mesh wire screen, is suitable. Care must be exercised in watering and in the regulation of light intensity at this stage of their growth.

When the leaves touch each other, the plants can be placed in pots. For shipping purposes the 6-centimeter size is used; otherwise 8-centimeter pots are recommended because the larger volume of soil does not dry out as quickly. The soil mixture suggested for the seedlings can be used throughout the entire life of the plants.

When the root system is well developed, the plants can be shifted to the finishing pot, which could be a 13- or 16-centimeter size, depending on the vigor of the specimen. Since gloxinias are not tall, azalea pots are much more in proportion than standard pots. The young plants grow rapidly and must be fertilized frequently to obtain dark green leaves. Any complete fertilizer is satisfactory, but the solution should not be allowed to remain in the crown of the plant because it will burn the leaves.

Watering is an important factor in the culture of gloxinias because if water is allowed to remain on the crown of the plant overnight, losses from stem or crown rot will occur. Light intensity must be regulated in the same manner as for African violets, except that 2,400 foot-candles of light at noon is optimum.

Gloxinias develop large, ungainly leaves which necessitate spacing the plants to prevent them from stretching or becoming leggy. These leaves are rather brittle, which makes shipping a difficult procedure, but brittleness can be reduced somewhat by keeping a high relative humidity and a night temperature of 21°C. At temperatures lower than 16°C, growth practically ceases.

Lighting gloxinias often results in earlier flowering if the plants are grown at 16°C. This is apparently the effect of light and heat on food manufacture rather than any photoperiodic effect on the plant. Either 100-watt incandescent lamps 120 centimeters apart and 60 centimeters above the plants or standard cool-white fluorescent lamps may be used. They should be turned on after sundown and continued for 4 or 5 hours. Light is most effective if it is started as soon as the seeds germinate.

Gloxinias grow well in an opaque structure, using fluorescent lights as the sole source of light, as described for African violets. Because the gloxinia takes so much space it is doubtful whether the culture of these plants in an opaque structure would be practical, except for the production of small plants in flats since they are grown quite close together. Flowering specimens will grow quite easily from seed in as little as 4 months under fluorescent lights.

If the old plants are not sold at the end of summer, they can be dried off and rested by turning the pots on their sides. The plants may be left in the pots or shaken free of soil and placed in dry peat and stored at not less than 10°C. After January, they can be started in growth.

New or leftover tubers are best started by placing them in a flat of moist peat and keeping them at 21°C. As soon as a few leaves begin to unfold, the started tubers can be placed in the finishing pot and handled as described for seedlings. Tubers started in January will flower in spring; those started in March will flower throughout the summer.

Mite is the most serious pest, and crown or stem rot causes loss of plants.

Hyacinth *(Hyacinthus orientalis—Liliaceae)*

When hyacinths are received in the fall, those that have been treated for early flowering should be potted at once or placed in a 13°C storage until potting. Untreated bulbs should be unpacked and spread out in layers in flats or shallow boxes and kept at a temperature of 19°C. If bulbs are left in the shipping cases, any rot that may be present will spread very quickly.

Hyacinths are potted with one bulb in a 10-centimeter pot, two bulbs in a 13-centimeter pot, or three bulbs in a 15-centimeter pot in a soil that is porous for good drainage. The nose of the bulb is placed about 1 centimeter above the surface of the soil. If the soil is acid, some lime should be added.

Cultivars which produce large, heavy spikes will need staking, and green sticks may be inserted into the bulb, and the stems tied with green twine.

In "spitting," or "toppling," the flower spike appears to have been cut off; it is a rather common trouble with hyacinths being forced. It can be caused by too early planting (before October 15), too high a soil temperature outside, poor drainage in the area when the bulbs are buried outside, and exposure to cold when dug from outside beds or brought out of storage for forcing.

Christmas Only the 19-centimeter, or larger "special" or "prepared," bulbs are suitable for this early forcing. The special bulbs are grown in Holland in soil over heating pipes. This extra heat hastens maturity of the plant and causes earlier formation of the flower parts. Prepared bulbs have been stored at 27°C for several weeks after digging, which also accelerates the formation of the flowers.

The bulbs should be potted in late October and placed in a 10°C storage. An outside storage is recommended only for early forcing when bulbs can be covered with a deep mulch or put in a shady location where temperature variations can be kept at a minimum.

Between November 25 and December 1 the bulbs should be brought into a 16°C greenhouse for 1 week and then raised to a temperature of 18°C if desired when sufficient roots have developed and the tops are at least 3 centimeters long. The pots may be placed under a bench where there are heating pipes, or on top of a bench where they may be shaded with black fabric or newspapers until the shoots are 3 centimeters long, and then exposed to full sunlight. The plants should be kept at 16°C with some bottom heat, and after flowers show color, the temperature should be reduced to 10°C, which hardens the plants before sale.

Midseason Bulbs to be flowered from late January until mid-March need not be planted until late October or early November. Prepared bulbs are not necessary for this forcing period, but large bulbs produce the best plants. The bulbs are potted and handled as described above, but they are not brought into the greenhouse until very late December or early January, and at intervals thereafter. From 3 to 4 weeks should be allowed for maturity at 16°C early in the season, but later in the forcing period, at 18 to 21°C, this may be reduced to 2 weeks.

Late Bulbs to be forced for late March and April can be stored at 18 to 21°C and then planted the first 2 weeks of December. After planting, the temperature is maintained at 16°C for about 2 weeks and then at 10°C or below until time for forcing. Without cold-storage facilities it is difficult to hold hyacinths for a late Easter since they force rapidly.

Cultivars   The list of hyacinth cultivars for forcing has not changed appreciably within the past few years. No plants should be forced unless they show well-developed roots and have at least 3 centimeters of top growth. The dates for bringing in hyacinths are as follows:

December 1, 15, and 25: Bismarck (blue), Pink Pearl (pink), L'Innocence (white), prepared or special bulbs

January 1: Bismarck (blue), Ostara (blue), Lady Derby (pink), L'Innocence (white), Pink Pearl (pink), and Anne Marie (pink)

January 15: Pink Pearl (pink), Ostara, Lady Derby, and Bismarck (blue)

February 1 and 15: Anne Marie (pink), Jan Bos (red), Marconi (rose), Colosseum, Ostara, and Delft Blue (blue)

March 1 and later: Delft Blue, Carnegie (white), Eros (pink)

Hydrangea *(Hydrangea macrophylla—Saxifragaceae)*

Hydrangeas are produced only for the spring pot-plant market. The plants are propagated in late spring from rooted stem cuttings, grown outdoors during the summer, and placed in cool temperatures in late fall until the flower buds mature and the leaves drop. The dormant (quiescent) plants are brought into the greenhouse to start forcing for Easter flowering in late December or early January, depending on the date of Easter. For Mother's Day, forcing is started in late January.

The production of hydrangea plants is limited to areas that have fairly cool summer temperatures, as the growth of the plants and the formation and development of the flower buds are best in a temperature range of 13 to 18°C. There is an advantage, too, in being able to use natural cooling in the fall for the cool-temperature treatment of the plants.

The hydrangea flower is a large, globular cluster of pink, blue, or white flowers. The sepals are the showy and colorful parts of the flower, and the petals are rather inconspicuous.

Propagation   Cuttings of hydrangeas are taken in February, March, April, and May from blind wood on Easter or Mother's Day plants or stock plants reserved especially for this purpose. The notion that cuttings of blind wood will not produce flowering plants is erroneous, and it is not necessary to sacrifice flowering wood for the sake of propagation. Where stock is scarce, leaf-bud cuttings will be found fully as satisfactory as stem-tip cuttings. With leaf buds the cuts should be made about 3 centimeters below the node and 1 centimeter above, splitting the stem in half, with each half bearing a leaf. Some trimming of leaves is necessary to conserve space and to prevent severe wilting. Steamed sand, or sand and peat, in an open bench with a bottom heat of 18°C and an air temperature of 13 to 16°C is recommended. For the first few days covering soft cuttings with cheesecloth or newspaper may be necessary to maintain high relative humidity and reduce wilting, unless a mist system is used. The cuttings should be ready to pot in 3 to 4 weeks. Cuttings taken in April or May can be placed directly in 13- or 16-centimeter pots.

When smaller plants are desired, propagation in June and July is feasible. Cuttings are made from the plants propagated earlier, which are pinched in June or July. When the plants are pinched, the portion of the plant removed is rooted rather than thrown away.

There are disadvantages in using the plants being forced into flower as the source of cuttings. It may not be possible to obtain the quantity of cuttings needed, and the cuttings must be taken earlier than the plants can be handled conveniently in the greenhouse. These problems can be overcome by using either softwood or hardwood cuttings from the West Coast. Unrooted softwood cuttings should be obtained in April or early May, rooted in about 3 weeks, and then potted in 13- or 16-centimeter pots. The cuttings should be lifted from the propagation bench promptly when the roots are 1 centimeter long, as cuttings that are left in the propagation bench too long are adversely affected by the lack of nitrogen and grow slowly after potting.

Unrooted hardwood canes obtained from the West Coast in January or February are cut into about 5-centimeter sections, each bearing a node or joint and stuck in the propagation bench for rooting. With this type of cutting it is possible to get too many shoots developed after potting, and the young plants should be pruned to one or two good shoots.

Light Hydrangeas are grown outdoors in the summer; and in most parts of the country best leaf size and plant growth occur in the partial shade of lath or plastic screen. However, this partial shade should be removed in August, and the plants should be finished in full sun for the best development of the flower buds.

When the plants are forced into flower in the winter and spring, they should be placed in the best available light. If bright and hot weather develops at the time of flowering, partial shade will improve the intensity of flower color and cause less wilting of the plants or burning of the leaves and flowers.

Flower bud formation in hydrangeas is not dependent on length of day, but buds do form faster in short days than in long ones. In natural conditions hydrangea flower buds form in September, and the day length is naturally short at that time.

If the plants are in long days during forcing, the internodes will be longer. This is one of the reasons why hydrangeas for Mother's Day are taller than those forced for Easter.

Temperature   Hydrangeas are grown outdoors during the summer and early fall without control of temperature other than some reduction given in summer by partial shade, or protection from frost in the fall by covering cold frames with sash. If the plants were grown in controlled temperature conditions, the night temperature should be 16°C with day temperatures about 6°C warmer. Growth of the plant and formation and development of the flower buds are best at these temperatures. Flower bud formation is slow and questionable at temperatures above 18°C or below 13°C. Because most hydrangeas are grown under natural conditions, the time of flower bud formation in the fall will vary depending on the weather and the resulting temperature.

By early November the hydrangea flower buds should be fully developed, and the plants should then be given 6 weeks of cool temperatures to mature the flower buds. This cool temperature should be uniform and below 10°C; a temperature range of 4 to 7°C is best. Cold frames, sheds, refrigerators, or cool greenhouses can be used for cool treatment of hydrangeas, but at least a portion of this period should be in the dark so that the plants will shed their leaves, which helps to mature the flower buds.

The plants must be given adequate protection from freezing temperatures in the fall, but slow cooling to temperatures well below freezing is not detrimental. In many areas of the country, killing frosts are possible any time after early September.

For forcing hydrangeas into flower, 16°C night temperatures should be used with day temperatures about 6°C warmer. The plants will flower in about 4 months at these temperatures. In some instances plants that are to be flowered for Mother's Day are started at 10°C night temperatures, but this is a questionable practice as the internodes increase in length and the plants are taller at this temperature than at 16°C.

Fertilizer and Flower Color   Except for white-flowered types, hydrangea flower color can be controlled by the amount of aluminum available in the plant. Aluminum is generally present in soils, but it will not be available to plants in alkaline soils or in soils that have an excess of phosphorus. Aluminum and other minerals cannot be taken into the plant even if they are available in the soil unless the roots are growing and functional.

Hydrangea cultivars differ in the effect of aluminum on flower color, but in general the flower is blue if aluminum is available in the plant, and pink if it is not available. The color potential of each cultivar is known, and the cultivars that develop the best colors are selected for treatment.

Flower color can be controlled with fertilizer treatments given during the forcing period; but for more reliable results, the plants should be treated in both the growing period in the summer and the forcing period in winter and spring. If the native soil that is used is definitely acid in reaction, the flowers will generally be blue unless the soil is made more alkaline or fertilizers high in phosphorus are used. In areas of alkaline soil, hydrangeas typically have pink flowers unless the soil is made more acid or some aluminum fertilizer is added to the soil.

For pink flowers, choose cultivars that have the potential for good, clear pink flowers, and use fertilizers that contain phosphorus for growing and forcing the plants. The soil pH should be maintained in the range of 6.0 to 6.5, and this may require the addition of limestone or hydrated lime to acid soils.

For blue hydrangea flowers, select the cultivars which produce the best blue colors. Some cultivars do not have good, blue flowers regardless of treatment. No phosphorus should be added to the soil or fertilizers very low in phosphorus should be used, and the pH of the soil should be maintained at about 5.0. In areas where the soil is alkaline, periodic applications of iron sulfate will be required at the rate of 1,300 grams per 380 liters of water or aluminum sulfate at the rate of 3 to 4.5 kilograms per 380 liters of water. If aluminum sulfate has to be supplied during the summer or if the native soil is acid, about three applications of aluminum sulfate will be sufficient during the forcing period; however, if no aluminum sulfate was used in the summer or the native soils are alkaline, at least six applications of aluminum sulfate should be made during forcing, starting as soon as new root growth is observed and at about 10-day intervals thereafter.

Potting and Spacing Various methods of potting and growing hydrangeas are used, but regardless of the methods, large enough pots should be used so that the plants can grow actively. From the propagation bench the rooted cuttings should be potted directly into 13- or 16-centimeter pots or started in 8-centimeter pots and then shifted to the larger pots as soon as they are established. There must be no delay in shifting to larger pots, and it should be done within 3 weeks after the cuttings are potted. The time of propagation must be scheduled so that the plants can be handled in the best possible way after propagation. Most pot-plant greenhouses are completely filled with plants being forced for the spring holidays until mid-May, and there just is no room for handling young plants until the finished plants are sold. If the hydrangea cuttings are stuck in the propagation bench the last week in April, the plants can be potted in 8-centimeter pots about the middle of May, shifted to 13- or 16-centimeter pots in early June, and moved outdoors later in June as soon as new root growth has been made following transplanting.

The plants can be spaced pot to pot in 8-centimeter pots as well as after shifting because in either instance they will not remain there long enough to require additional space. Outdoors the plants are spaced on about 30-centimeter centers, and the pots may be plunged or set on the ground. Hydrangeas require a great quantity of water, and growing the plants in large pots provides a more uniform moisture supply. If the plants are grown in 10-centimeter pots and an irrigation system is not available, or if the natural conditions in the locality are dry, it is better to plunge the pots. If the pots are plunged, it must be in a well-drained area so that the plants do not remain in saturated soil following heavy rains.

The plants must be protected from freezing temperatures in the fall by placing them in cold frames or in greenhouses. Whenever possible, this should be the same area in which the plants later will be given their cool-temperature storage. Pot-to-pot spacing is used, but the plants must be watered, fertilized, and given uniformly suitable temperatures, as they are in active growth and at an important stage in the formation of the flower buds.

From November to mid-December or later the hydrangeas must be in cool temperatures (below 10°C) to mature the plants, and during this period they are set pot to pot in cold frames, cool greenhouses, sheds, or refrigerators. In order for the plants to mature properly, the leaves must drop, and this is hastened by placing the plants in complete darkness. Because of the dormant condition of the plants and the cool temperatures, very little maintenance of the plants is required in storage. The fallen leaves must be removed to prevent disease infestations, 4°C temperature maintained as uniformly as possible, the plants watered sparingly, and continuous air circulation provided in order to prevent bud rot from *Botrytis Cinerea.* Leaves should not be induced to drop before late October or flowers may be poorly developed.

When the quiescent hydrangeas are removed from storage in preparation for forcing at 16°C night temperatures, they can be set pot to pot or at final spacing, whichever is better because of available space and labor. If the plants are to be shifted to larger pots for forcing, they should be started in the same size of pot they were grown in and then shifted when new root growth has started. If irrigations are well spaced, new roots should be evident about 1 week after the plants are started. Root growth starts slowly when the plants are shifted to larger pots immediately from storage. The final spacing for three-cane hydrangeas in 16-centimeter pots is approximately 1,350 square centimeters per plant, but this differs with varieties as some make larger plants than others.

Troubles Blindness is the failure of flower buds to form in the stems, and this can be caused by any conditions that are unfavorable for flower bud formation. The most common causes of blindness are not enough active leaf area (too few leaves, not large enough leaves, or damaged leaves), too cool or too warm temperatures in late summer and early fall, generally poor growing conditions including inadequate supply of minerals, and too late pinching.

Summer flowers develop in some stems, and this usually is related to the stage of development of the stems used for cuttings. In some instances summer flowers form in stems that are pinched early.

Burned leaves can occur in plants at any stage of growth if the plants wilt in the bright sunlight, and this can be prevented by adequate irrigation and syringing plus the use of shade over the plants. In most areas of the country the outdoor growing area in the summer should be equipped with a good nozzle system so that the plants can be misted or syringed frequently. Burned leaves should not be a problem during the forcing period in winter and spring if the plants are not allowed to dry out and are protected from the direct rays of the sun when near maturity.

Chlorosis of the leaves is generally considered to be caused by a lack of available iron in the plant. However, it may be caused by poor root growth, insufficient iron in the soil, too alkaline soil, or an inadequate supply of nitrogen. Most soils should receive a few applications of iron sulfate (ferrous sulfate) at the rate of 1,350 grams per 380 liters of water during the summer. Chlorosis, common in plants at the start of forcing, is invariably due to poor root growth. At this time there is a temptation to make an application of iron, but no fertilizer should be applied until root growth is good.

Poor root growth can be caused by soils that are waterlogged or have too much fertilizer in the soil. The problem is most common just after the dormant plants are brought in for forcing and usually is caused by too frequent irrigation.

Slow development of the plants in forcing and short stems with small flowers are caused by an insufficient length of time in cool temperatures before forcing. The most common reasons for too short a cool period are (1) abnormally warm falls during which it is impossible to keep the storage area cool enough and (2) an early Easter date for which the plants are removed too soon from storage.

Hydrangeas often are too tall for Mother's Day, and there may be several reasons for this: (1) The plants may be forced slowly at temperatures below 16°C, which causes increase in stem length. (2) Hydrangea stem length is greater in the long days of later spring. (3) The plants may not be adequately spaced because of the large number of Easter plants being grown. (4) Some cultivars of hydrangeas grow tall even in the best-regulated conditions, and the height of these plants can be reduced with growth chemicals. For shorter growth in the summer, the plants should be sprayed with B-Nine in late July when the shoots are 4 centimeters long following the pinch. For shorter growth during the forcing period, the plants can be sprayed with B-Nine about 2 weeks after forcing starts, when four or five pairs of leaves are visible.

Diseases Botrytis blight or bud rot can occur in cool storages, and this is a particular problem with the cultivar Merveille. The control of bud rot includes the removal of fallen leaves promptly as they are sure to become badly infected with *Botrytis Cinerea* and therefore a source of inoculum for infection of the buds, the careful use of water so that the area does not remain wet, and provision of continuous air movement with air-circulation fans.

Powdery mildew is more common in the fall with the combination of cooler night temperatures and reduced air movement because the plants have been set closer together. Some heat and increased air movement provide the best control. The plants may be sprayed or dusted with sulfur, or other powdery mildew controls may be used. Septoria leaf spot is caused by a fungus, and purplish blotches appear on the leaves usually in the late summer and fall. Spraying or dusting with fungicides that control leaf-spot diseases will be effective.

Pests Two-spotted mites and aphids are the principal pests, and they are easily controlled with ordinary precautions. Particular care should be taken to assure that the plants are entirely free of pests before they are placed in frames or greenhouses in the fall as an infestation will spread rapidly in warm temperatures and among the closely spaced plants. The cyclamen mite may also infest the shoot tops, causing malformed growth.

Pinching and Cropping Plants propagated very early must be pinched twice to prevent them from becoming too tall. The first pinch is made sometime in April or May, and the second pinch in June or early July.

It is erroneously believed that late pinching causes blindness of shoots; in reality it is not the pinching itself but rather the failure of the plants to develop shoots properly following the pinch. It may be desirable to pinch late-propagated plants in late August or early September to make them branch and reduce their overall height. Provided the plants have been fertilized properly and growth is satisfactory, blindness will not result because of a pinch made at such a late date.

When shoots are pinched, at least two pairs of good leaves should remain on the stem. If the foliage is small or injured, additional pairs of leaves should remain or shoot development may be slow and blindness may be troublesome.

On vigorous plants a number of shoots will develop after pinching. As soon as these are convenient to handle, all unwanted stems should be removed. The demand is greatest for specimens with two or three flowers, and limiting the number of stems on each plant can be done at this time.

If there were a market demand for hydrangeas at any time of the year other than in the spring, the plants probably could be produced for flowering at any time by using controlled temperatures in greenhouses and refrigerators, but this would increase the costs of production considerably. Because of the relatively poor keeping quality of hydrangeas in the home unless careful attention is given to watering, it is doubtful whether there would be much demand for out-of-season plants. The cropping schedule that is used for hydrangeas is based on using natural conditions for producing the plants and controlled greenhouse conditions for forcing the plants into flower. At 16°C temperature approximately 13 weeks is required for flowering after the quiescent plants are brought into the greenhouse; however, longer periods are commonly used, as the plants often are started at 16°C but finished at 10°C. The plants develop more slowly at the cooler temperature, but they are of better quality. Depending on the date of Easter and the temperatures that will be used, the quiescent plants must be brought into the greenhouse forcing temperatures between late December and the

Figure 6-10 Hydrangea flower buds should be about the size of a nickel 6 weeks before Easter.

middle of January. For Mother's Day flowering, forcing of the quiescent plants will have to be started between late January and early February.

If the quiescent plants are to be available and ready for forcing from late December on, the cuttings must be rooted by April, the plants pinched by July, and the plants with well-developed flower buds placed in cool storage in early November. This is the minimum length of time required when light, temperature, moisture, minerals, and other conditions are suitable. If optimum environmental conditions are lacking, additional time may be required.

Kalanchoe *(Kalanchoe blossfeldiana—Crassulaceae)*

Kalanchoe and some other plants that have thick, fleshy stems and/or leaves are referred to as succulents. Many of the succulents are known as foliage plants. Some of the kalanchoe species are used as foliage plants; *Kalanchoe blossfeldiana* cultivars, however, are grown as flowering pot plants. Because of increased activity in selection and hybridization in this species, it has become more prominent in the pot-plant market. The inflorescences are terminal cymes with color ranging from yellow to orange to red. Here, although the name kalanchoe is used, the reference will be to cultivars of *K. blossfeldiana.*

Propagation   Kalanchoe can be propagated from seed, leaf, and stem-tip cuttings, but now stem-tip cuttings usually are used. Much of the propagation is done by specialists, and they supply the plants to growers in 5- to 6-centimeter pots.

Light   The maximum amount of sunlight should be provided from fall through spring. During the summer, growth will be best if partial shade is used.

Kalanchoe is a short-day plant and very sensitive to light. During naturally short days, the plants must be lighted when vegetative growth is desired. The same type of lighting that is used for mums is satisfactory. In northern United States, use light for 1 hour in September and March, 2 hours in October and February, 3 hours in November and February, and 4 hours in December. In other latitudes the length of lighting needs to be adjusted so that the length of the daily dark period is less than 13 hours.

Short photoperiods will cause flowers to form in kalanchoe if other conditions are suitable also. From October 15 to February 15 the natural day length in northern United States is short enough to initiate flowering in kalanchoe. However, from February 15 to October 15 at this latitude black fabric should be placed over the plants daily so that they receive a minimum of 14 continuous hours without light each day. Because of the sensitivity of kalanchoe to light, the black fabric must be very effective in eliminating light, and the cover must be placed over the plants each day. If other factors have been suitable for induction of flowering, flower development will proceed to maturity if the short-day treatment has been continued for 6 weeks.

In some kalanchoe cultivars flower formation is inhibited in temperatures above 24°C. This must be considered for summer flowering. Because of increased temperatures under black fabric, the best time to place the cover over the plants at that time of the year is from about 7 P.M. to 10 A.M.

Temperature Night temperatures of 17°C should be used with kalanchoe.

Pinching The size of the finished plant can be adjusted by the use of pinching and long days. Plants to be finished in small pots should be given short days when they are potted. Plants to be finished in larger pots should be given long days after potting and then pinched before the start of short days. The length of the long-day period is increased to produce larger plants.

Pests and Pathogens Aphids and caterpillars are the most common pests, but they are controlled with ordinary methods.

Some of the kalanchoe cultivars are susceptible to powdery mildew, but regulation of water, temperature, and air should control the pathogen responsible for this disease.

Lily *(Lilium longiflorum—Liliaceae)*

The pot lily is flowered only for Easter. The plants are started from bulbs that are produced on the West Coast, in the southern United States, or in Japan. The bulbs are dug in the fall and either are shipped to the growers directly from the fields or are given temperature treatments before being shipped to the pot-plant growers in late November.

Propagation The propagation of lilies is an operation for specialists. Lilies are propagated primarily from scales separated from the parent bulb or stem bulblets produced underground. The scales are planted in the fall in rows about 15 centimeters apart. Bulblets are formed in the first growing season, and they are dug and replanted in the field. The mature bulbs are dug the following fall and graded by size in circumference from the smallest size of 16 to 17.5 centimeters, to the largest, 25 to 27.5 centimeters. The smaller bulbs produce smaller plants with fewer flowers than do the larger bulbs.

Digging of the bulbs is done about the first week in October on the West Coast. Earlier digging is not done by the bulb growers because the bulbs continue to develop and increase in size in the fall, and later digging cannot be done or there would not be time to plant the new crop of stem bulblets before the start of the general rains in late fall. In southern fields the bulbs are harvested as early as late August.

Light   In the greenhouse, lilies should be grown in the best available light. If the light intensity is too low because of weather conditions, overhead structure, or too close spacing, the plants will be tall and have few flowers, and the lower leaves may turn yellow and wither.

The length of day apparently has little or no effect on flower formation in lilies, but plants provided with long days will be taller than those in short days and will flower earlier. Commercially the day length is seldom adjusted to control height as the results that are obtained are not considered worth the cost of treatment; however, if the lilies are consistently too tall or too short, either black cloth treatment or artificial lighting could be used. The treatments, to be effective, must be provided from about the time the stem emerges from the soil until the flower buds are clearly visible. Lighting to hasten flowering is used, but it must be started at least 6 weeks before maturity if there is to be any marked effect.

Flowering in lilies is promoted by cool-temperature treatment (vernalization) of the bulbs for at least 6 weeks from the time of digging the bulbs until forcing is started. In some instances there is not enough time to complete vernalization by cool-temperature treatment, and it has been demonstrated that vernalization can be completed by providing long photoperiods later when the shoots emerge from the soil. If it is suspected or known that the bulbs did not receive enough cool temperature before forcing, the plants should be supplied light intensity of 15 foot-candles each night from 10 P.M. to 2 A.M. for about 2 weeks after emergence of the shoots. It can be expected that 1 day of lighting will substitute for 1 day of cold-temperature treatment. If the time deficiency in cold-temperature treatment is known, the plants may be lighted for that length of time.

Temperature   The lily bulbs grown on the West Coast are harvested in October. Because of naturally cool temperatures in the fields, the bulbs may be partially vernalized at the time of digging. After digging, the bulbs are placed in cool temperatures (below 10°C) for at least 6 weeks. This cool-temperature treatment may be provided while the bulbs are in packing cases or after the bulbs are potted.

The lily bulbs that are to be given cool-temperature treatment while in the case (precooled) are shipped from the lily fields to cool storage facilities in the vicinity of the greenhouses where they will be forced.

The lily bulbs that will be given cool-temperature treatment after potting are shipped directly from the lily fields to the greenhouses where they will be forced. The greenhouse operator pots these lily bulbs as soon as they are received and maintains warm temperatures (16°C) for these potted bulbs until roots are well developed (about 2 weeks). The potted bulbs then may be supplied the cool-temperature treatment outdoors (natural cooling), or they may be placed in refrigerated storage (controlled temperature forcing—CTF).

All of these methods of vernalization can promote flowering in lily to the same degree. There are, however, other effects to be considered. Precooling the bulbs while in the packing case probably is the simplest method. Less storage space is required, and the grower avoids handling the potted bulbs for a period of 7 weeks or so. However, the other two methods have some beneficial effects on plant growth and development. Usually more flowers develops per plant, the stems are larger in diameter and shorter, there are a greater number of leaves, and the basal leaves are fully developed.

The natural-cooling method is somewhat less precise than the CTF method because of variable outdoor weather conditions.

Easter lilies usually are forced at 16°C night temperature and it is considered that about 100 days of forcing are required. When the precooled-bulb method is used, however, an additional 2 weeks should be allowed for root development after potting.

Precooled bulbs are shipped from storage in late November or early December after they have had at least 6 weeks of cool-temperature treatment. They should be potted soon after they are received.

The rate of flower development is faster with increase in temperature up to approximately 27°C. If it is apparent that flower development is behind schedule, the temperature may be raised above 16°C. Generally it is better to schedule flowering a few days early and then reduce temperatures as marketing time approaches. If flowers mature too early, it is possible to place the plants in cool storage (7°C) for several days, but this should be done just before the first flower opens.

Potting and Spacing Standard pots usually are used for lilies, the 14- to 16-centimeter sizes with one bulb per pot. The pot size is determined by the size of bulb that is used and the type of marketing.

Lily bulbs should be planted about 5 centimeters below the soil surface because the roots that develop on the shoot contribute to the development of the plant.

Lilies are very susceptible to root and stem diseases. The pathogens that cause the diseases develop more rapidly in soils that are constantly wet, and for this reason lily soils should be well drained—coarse and porous soil mixtures.

Lilies usually are set pot to pot at the start of forcing and then given a final spacing on about 20-centimeter centers. If there is any difference in height of the plants, the taller plants should be set at the center of the bench.

If lily pots are left in the same position on the bench, the stems will curve in the direction of the greatest light intensity (phototropism). In the northern hemisphere, this will be toward the south. Upright lily stems are more desirable than curved ones, and the stems will grow upright if the pots are rotated periodically.

Frequently the rate of flower development varies in the plants, and there is need to move the slow developers to warmer temperatures and the fast developers to cool temperatures. As the forcing season progresses, the lily grower must evaluate the need for pot moving daily and then move pots when necessary.

Timing Easter Lilies During the forcing period it is difficult to determine if the plants are on the right flowering schedule. When the flower buds can be observed it will be known if the flowering will be on time, but before the appearance of the flower buds some means other than judging the external features needs to be used. A leaf-counting technique can be used to evaluate timing. It is a reliable means of determining the rate of development in lily. The procedure is based on determining the average number of leaves that the lily cultivar has in the current year, observing the number of leaves that unfold each week, and estimating if that rate of leaf development will provide flowering on schedule.

The leaf-counting procedure needs to be used on each lot of lily bulbs because the total number of leaves and the rate of their development may vary with cultivar and the environmental conditions in which the bulb was grown or stored.

As the shoot grows in the lily bulb, stem and leaf tissues develop for several days to a few weeks, and then flower structures start to form in the shoot tip. About the time the shoot emerges from the soil surface, all of the leaves have been initiated and flower initiation has started. There is no external evidence of this other than the basal leaves that unfold and expand as the shoot emerges. However, if the shoot tip were dissected and observed by means of a lens, the initials of the leaves and flowers could be seen. For the leaf-counting procedure, stem samples are taken when the shoot tips are approximately 10 centimeters above the soil surface. About 10 stems that appear to be typical of the lot should be taken. They are severed at the soil surface and the number of leaves per stem determined. The leaf counting starts at the base and proceeds toward the tip. The tiny leaves near the tip may be dissected with a large needle and observed with a reading glass. The total number of leaves for all the stem samples is divided by the number of stems in order to get the average number of leaves per stem.

Then 10 typical plants are chosen for observation among the lot of lilies and identified with a stake. The leaves that are unfolded to a 45° angle are counted and averaged. The difference between this number and the total number of leaves is the number of leaves that have to unfold before flowering. The last leaf counted on each plant is marked, and the number of new leaves that unfold will be counted each week. This will determine the average number of leaves unfolding per week.

All of the leaves should be unfolded by 30 days before Palm Sunday. If it is determined that the average total number of leaves per plant is 80 leaves and there are 70 days from the time of shoot emergence from the soil to 30 days before Palm Sunday, an average of 1.15 leaves would have to unfold daily for flowering to be on schedule. If the weekly leaf counting indicates that the rate of leaf unfolding is not right, the temperature can be adjusted to increase or decrease the rate.

Troubles Environmental conditions on the West Coast sometimes cause the lily to sprout in the field, a stage of early growth of the stem that normally is dormant until forced by the florist. Sprouted bulbs, in general, are satisfactory, and they should be potted so that the sprout is buried in the soil, if possible.

The problem of too few flower buds may result from using too small bulbs, storing the bulbs too long before forcing, blasting the flower buds, or allowing the bulbs to become dry in storage. Blasting of the flower buds may be caused by lack of water in the plant because of poor roots or insufficient irrigation, low light intensity, and extremely high forcing temperatures.

Yellowing and eventual drying of the lower leaves may be due to insufficient light (very often the result of spacing the plants too closely together) or lack of nitrogen. This can be prevented by spacing the plants more promptly and supplying nitrogen fertilizer regularly after the tip of the plant emerges through the soil.

Diseases The most prevalent causes of root rot are *Rhizoctonia solani* and *Pythium* spp., but other pathogens are often found in diseased roots and may be associated with the trouble. The soil and all handling equipment must be thoroughly steamed before use with lilies. Coarse, porous soils will drain more readily, favoring active root growth and limiting the development of the root rot pathogens. If root growth is poor because the soil has been saturated, root growth will be promoted by knocking the plants from the pots and setting them back in the pot lightly to increase the air around the surface of the soil ball.

Botrytis blight is caused by *Botrytis elliptica*, and it produces circular or oval spots on leaves or flowers. In damp conditions the spots become covered with gray mold. The best control is to reduce the humidity of the air by heating while ventilating and by increasing air circulation. Moisture should be kept off leaves and flowers.

There are several virus diseases of lilies, but because of continuing efforts among the bulb growers to propagate from virus-free stock, and because of control of insects that transfer virus in the fields from plant to plant, severe effects of virus diseases are not common in bulbs used for forcing in greenhouses.

Pests Aphids are common pests of lilies. Aphid infestations occur primarily on the stem tips. If the flower buds are involved, splitting of the flower may result.

Nematodes can infest lily bulbs, and root rot is usually associated with

Figure 6-11 Lily root rot is evident in plants on right. Top: comparison of the plants as they are knocked out of pots. Bottom: roots after removal of the soil.

the nematode infestation. Excellent measures for control of nematodes are used in the lily fields with the result that the presence of nematodes in the bulbs is negligible.

Pepper *(Capsicum annuum conoides—Solanaceae)*

There is a limited demand for peppers at Christmas. The pepper plant is produced in a similar manner to the Jerusalem or Cleveland cherry except that it should be grown in pots. The plants are pinched in early July to make them bushy and compact. Seed sown in June will be ready by Christmas if three plants are placed in a 13- or 15-centimeter azalea pot and not pinched.

Poinsettia *(Euphorbia pulcherrima—Euphorbiaceae)*

The outward appearance of the other members of the *Euphorbia* genus that are produced in the greenhouse business is quite different from that of *E. pulcherrima*. They resemble cactus and may have common names that indicate this resemblance, such as good luck cactus (*Euphorbia trigona*) and candelabra cactus (*Euphorbia lactea*). Crown of thorns (*Euphorbia splendens*) also has a cactuslike appearance.

The poinsettia has the appearance of a landscape shrub with large green leaves, and in the fall terminal flowers form that are subtended by colorful bracts. The flowers are small and unisexual. A female flower and several male flowers are enclosed in a structure known as a cyathium, and the cyathia form in cymose fashion. Each cyathium is about pea-sized and yellow. The most common bract color is red, but there are cultivars that have pink, white, or varicolored bracts.

In mild climates, the poinsettia is used as a landscape plant. When procedures were first established for the production of poinsettia pot plants in the greenhouse, the greenhouse operator started plants from stem-tip cuttings taken from stock plants that had been field-grown in California. These were received as large, dormant (quiescent) plants in the spring, usually just after Easter. After the stem-tip cuttings were harvested from July to September, the stock plants were discarded. That stock plant procedure is no longer used. Greenhouse operators now establish their stock plants from stem-tip cuttings or small plants received from poinsettia progapators who produce the plants in greenhouses in California or other locations.

Propagation Poinsettias are reproduced from stem-tip cuttings. In order for the pot plants to be the right size for the Christmas market, propagation is done from late July to late September. The early propagation is for the plants to be forced in large containers and the late propagation for those that will be in small pots. Much of the poinsettia production is in 16-centimeter pots, and the cuttings for this size of plant will be stuck from the middle of August to the middle of September depending on whether the plants will be pinched or grown single stem.

The stock plants are started from cuttings or small plants received in the spring from poinsettia specialist propagators. Some greenhouse operators have the space to start their poinsettia stock plants as early as March, and others cannot start until June. A most popular time to start poinsettia stock plants is after Easter.

The stock plants may be grown in benches or in containers. When they are grown in benches, the plants must be spaced sufficiently to accommodate the full-grown stock plant. For planting the stock plants right after Easter, those grown in benches should be planted about 38 by 38 centimeters. If they are to be grown in containers, they should be in about a 25-centimeter pot. For planting after Mother's Day, those in the bench should be spaced about 30 by 30 centimeters, and those in containers need about a 20-centimeter pot.

Poinsettia stock plant stems are pinched throughout the summer so that the maximum number of stem-tip cuttings is available at the time of propagation. The plants are pinched about 2 weeks after planting, and then the stems that develop can be pinched about 4 weeks later. Most poinsettia growers figure back from the date they need the greatest number of cuttings and pinch at 4-week intervals before that time. If the greatest number of cuttings are to be stuck on August 22 and the stock plants were planted about April 18, the pinches would be made on about May 2, May 30, June 27, and July 25.

It could be expected that stock plants handled on that kind of schedule would produce a total of 40 stem-tip cuttings each. The actual number will vary considerably depending on the length of the propagation period. The grower that starts taking cuttings early and continues into late September will get more cuttings than the grower who takes cuttings only in a 2- or 3-week period in late August and early September.

Poinsettia cuttings may be stuck in benches, in small pots, or directly in large pots, but regardless of the method the soil must be porous so that it drains rapidly, the soil temperature needs to be 21°C, and the relative humidity must be high. The seasonal daytime temperatures are normally high at the time of sticking poinsettia cuttings, but the night temperature in most areas is variable. The poinsettia propagator needs a foolproof means of regulating soil temperature regardless of natural conditions. In many instances the best temperature control is with electric cable. The high relative humidity can be provided with properly controlled intermittent mist.

The growers who stick cuttings directly into the pot in which the plant will be grown save considerable time and handling, but their success in propagation will be directly related to the propagative conditions that they provide. The correct soil temperature must be maintained, and this soil must drain as well and the relative humidity control must be as good as they would be in a regular propagation area.

About 3 weeks is required for rooting poinsettia cuttings. The cuttings that are rooted in benches should be inspected regularly for degree of rooting so that they can be lifted and potted as soon as possible. It is better to remove the poinsettia cutting from the propagation bench when the roots are less than 2 centimeters long than it is to leave them in the bench until there is a mass of long roots.

Poinsettias are susceptible to several diseases, and the conditions provided in propagation also are suitable for the growth of pathogens if they are present. Every possible means need to be taken to exclude, eliminate, and control pathogens in the poinsettia propagation area. Some of the mistakes have been to fail to include the tools and handling equipment at the time the soil is steamed or to reuse without steaming or sterilizing trays or other supportive material for small pots.

Light Poinsettias should be grown in full sunlight, and this includes the stock plants grown in the summer as well as the potted plants produced in the fall. Shade from adjoining structures, gutters, and overhead obstacles should be avoided.

Flowering in the poinsettia is controlled by the length of day. In long days the plants develop leaves and increase in stem length, and in short days flower buds are formed, and the stems terminate in growth with flowers. Under natural conditions flower buds start to form in poinsettias late in September, and depending on weather conditions and the variety, the plants flower in late November and December.

Some cultivars in natural conditions flower too early for Christmas, and for these it is possible to provide long days artificially in the fall before flower buds form, and thereby to delay flowering as desired. The artificially long days should be started about September 20, and they may be continued until about October 5 to 10. There are several variables that must be taken into consideration in making the decision on how long to provide artificially long days. Plants propagated earlier flower earlier than those propagated later. If weather conditions in the fall provide much sunlight and warm temperatures, the plants will flower earlier than they would in less favorable weather conditions. Some cultivars of poinsettia flower earlier than others.

Many homeowners wonder why their poinsettia never flowers in the home after the first year. This is invariably because the plants are kept in rooms that are lighted artificially each night so that the poinsettia plant is never in the short days required for forming flower buds.

Temperature Poinsettias are generally considered to be a 16°C night temperature crop, but some temperature manipulation is used. The stock plant night temperatures are maintained at 18°C with the day temperatures about 6°C higher. In some areas of the country where the day temperatures in the greenhouses during the summer exceed 35°C consistently, fan and pad cooling systems will provide better growth of the poinsettia stock plants.

In the fall the poinsettia pot plants should be provided 17°C night temperatures, with daytime temperatures about 6°C higher. At lower temperatures growth and flowering are slower and at higher temperatures they are faster, so some adjustment of temperature is used, depending on the rate of development that is needed. At lower temperatures soils stay wet longer, and root and stem rot can be more prevalent. At temperatures above 18°C flower bud development will be delayed if the day length is not short enough, but it will be more rapid if day lengths of 9 hours are provided artificially. In the later stages of flower development (from the middle of November and on) flower development is faster with increase in temperature. Bract size of poinsettias can be increased markedly if the night temperature is maintained at 18°C from mid-October to late November. This causes earlier flowering, necessitating lighting of the plants until about October 10.

Potting and Spacing When the poinsettia cuttings are rooted directly in 6-centimeter pots, they are spaced on about 10-centimeter squares and remain at that spacing until they are panned, which should be from 4 to 6 weeks after they were stuck in the pots. Cuttings that are rooted in propagation benches should be placed in 6-centimeter pots when the roots are about 1 centimeter long, and the pots should be spaced on about 10-centimeter squares until they are panned from 2 to 4 weeks later.

Cuttings propagated earlier to be used for pinched plants or for larger specimens should be potted into 8-centimeter pots as they will remain in the pot for a longer time before panning.

Irrigation and fertilization must be provided regularly while the poinsettias are in the small pots so that growth will proceed without check. The plants may or may not be treated with a growth retardant, depending on how long they will be in the small pots, how early they were propagated, and the height of finished plant that is desired. Plants in 8-centimeter pots should be spaced on about 15-centimeter squares.

Poinsettias should be planted in the finishing pot early in October. This is called "panning" as the poinsettia pot is either a bulb pan or an azalea pot rather than the standard pot. Single-stem poinsettias are planted at the rate of three or four plants per 16-centimeter pan, four or five plants per 18-centimeter pan, and correspondingly larger numbers of plants in larger pans or tubs. In most instances rooted cuttings are grown in small pots until they are established and then they are panned; however, sometimes the rooted cuttings are planted directly in the pan. This does save some labor and time, and good results can be obtained with direct planting. However, it does require closer attention to the moisture requirements of the plants until they are established in the pans, and the finished pan may not be as uniform because of the different rates of growth of the cuttings in each pan. Grading the cuttings by size and planting cuttings of the same size in each pan is a good method of producing finished pans with plants of approximately the same height.

After panning they may be set pan to pan and then spaced gradually as the plants grow, or the pans may be set at the final spacing at once. Poinsettias in 16-centimeter pans should be given about 1,350 square centimeters each, and the larger pans will require more space accordingly.

Troubles Leaf drop is a characteristic of poinsettias and is more common in some cultivars than in others, but regardless of cultivar it can be controlled under proper cultural conditions. Several events or conditions are known to promote leaf drop, and these probably are responsible for the problem because of their effect on the minerals and/or water supplies in the plants. A deficiency of nitrogen in the plant is a common cause of leaf drop which may be due to an insufficient supply of nitrogen in the soil or to very little uptake into the plant because of poor root growth. The most common causes of poor root growth are too frequent irrigation, root diseases, and the application of too much fertilizer. If the irrigation practices are not changed as rapidly as the weather conditions change in the fall, the poinsettia soils will be kept too wet. Root growth will cease, root diseases may get started, and leaves will drop.

Plants which are too tall are the result of too early propagation, and this should be corrected in succeeding years by later propagation. If some early propagation still must be used, the plants can be treated with growth regulant chemicals for control of height.

Too early flowering can be controlled by later propagation, by providing long days artificially in late September and early October, and by supplying cooler temperatures during the forcing period.

Diseases Loss of cuttings or plants is a common trouble, and at least three fungus organisms are known to be responsible for stem rot, root rot, or both. They are *Rhizoctonia solani, Pythium* spp., and *Thielaviopsis basicola.* Isolations made from a number of diseased specimens showed that *Rhizoctonia solani* in Ohio caused more than 90 percent of the losses.

Rhizoctonia solani generally attacks the stem at the surface of the propagating medium or soil. Too frequent watering of the cuttings in the propagation bench or the plants in pots or pans causes rapid spread of the organism and widespread losses due to stem rot. In the cutting bench an ever-widening area of dying or dead cuttings is typical of rhizoctonia stem rot. In the panned specimens one plant may die, and this is often followed by death of the other plants, although the organism may not always spread. The leaves on an infected plant usually curl upward at the edges, gradually turn yellow, and then fall off, beginning with the oldest foliage. At potting or panning, too deep planting leads to stem rot because the stem at the newly established soil line is soft and easily invaded by the rhizoctonia fungus.

If drainage is poor or the medium is too fine in the propagation bench, rot of the basal end of the cutting can be caused by *Rhizoctonia solani*. Rhizoctonia root rot of the plants is associated with too heavy a soil, poor drainage, or overwatering.

Losses can be reduced by steam or chemical sterilization of the propagation medium and by taking care that the rooting medium is not kept too wet. Pots, pans, and all soil mixtures should be steamed, but losses can occur through reinfection and careless culture. Regulation of the moisture content of the surface of the soil is very important. This is accomplished by watering heavily enough to moisten the entire soil mass and then allowing the soil to dry normally before watering again. Frequent light waterings should be avoided.

Pythium spp. are fungi which often attack seedlings, causing the loss known as damping-off. They may attack poinsettias. Control is the same as outlined for *Rhizoctonia solani*.

Thielaviopsis basicola is a root rot fungus that grows best between 13 and 16°C. Roots on infected plants die and quickly turn black. Lower leaves on infected plants curl, turn yellow, and fall, as with rhizoctonia stem rot.

Steaming of soil, pots, and bench areas where plants are to be placed is the best method of control. *Thielaviopsis basicola* is often found on geraniums and may live over in the sand or gravel in the bench, so that trouble may be experienced where these crops are grown in the same house even though at different seasons.

Maintaining the night temperature at 17°C will usually reduce losses from *Thielaviopsis basicola* since it grows best at temperatures of 16°C or just below. Losses can be reduced by the warm temperature, but lights are usually necessary to delay flower bud formation and resultant maturity of the plants. In December, cooling the plants, which have been growing at normal night temperatures, may result in losses from thielaviopsis root rot.

Symptoms of a bacterial disease appear as water-soaked longitudinal streaks on the stem which crack open and reveal a yellow-colored ooze which is made up of masses of the bacteria. The stem usually dies. The disease organism may be transferred with a knife, and there is no control except the destruction of the infected plants and steaming of the pots and soil. It is not a common trouble.

Poinsettia scab is usually confined to the tropical areas, and it may appear at any time of the growing season on either the cuttings or the stock plants. At first the stem turns somewhat purplish, and a small elongated canker appears, with the long axis of the canker parallel to the stem. The canker gradually enlarges, and if it girdles the stem, the foliage turns yellow and drops off, and the stem dies back from the tip. The center of the canker in the later stages is depressed and often covered with velvety-gray to gray-brown spores. The depression in the canker often develops into a crack, and the stem may break. Leaf lesions, or cankers, are smaller than those on the stem and are confined to the petiole and the midrib and smaller veins of the leaf. The leaf cankers closely resemble cankers found on citrus leaves, which are called "citrus scab." The poinsettia leaves are distorted and wrinkled in the area of the canker. If the petiole is attacked, the leaf will usually fall. Unfortunately, no control is known, and the infected stems should be cut well below the area of infection and burned. If they are not burned, spores will form and may blow into the greenhouse, causing reinfection.

The lesions caused by scab somewhat resemble a blisterlike raised area found on many poinsettia stems in late November and December. This is apparently a normal growth phenomenon and is no cause for alarm.

Pests Relatively few insect or allied pests attack the poinsettia. Plants carried over the winter season in the greenhouse often become infested with mealybugs and scale. Mealybugs prove troublesome, especially after bracts show color, since most insecticides bleach the color of the bracts. Every effort must be made to clean up any infestation of mealybugs by the middle of November.

Scale is a nuisance, and the sugary secretions are an ideal medium for the sooty mold fungus. This dirty-black condition of the foliage is very objectionable. Insecticides for scale control must also be applied before color appears in the bracts because of the danger of bleaching.

Whitefly is a pest that must be controlled before the bracts appear. Root aphids occasionally may be found in the soil and are recognizable as white or gray woolly masses around the roots. Growth of the plants is stunted, and in severe cases the lower leaves will turn yellow and drop.

Cropping and Timing The period for marketing poinsettias has expanded. It still is a Christmas market, but there is an active demand for poinsettias for several weeks before Christmas. Most of the plants purchased in November and early December are used in store decorations and promotional work for other Christmas merchandise. The starting time for the poinsettia crop is determined by the marketing date, the size of the finished plant, marketing method, and whether it will be pinched or single stem.

For plants to be marketed in mid-December in 16-centimeter pots, the cuttings should be stuck about August 8 for pinched plants and August 22 for single-stem plants. For plants to be marketed right after Thanksgiving, the cuttings should be stuck about July 25 for pinched plants and August 8 for single-stem plants. The plants to be finished in larger pots need to be propagated earlier, and the plants to be finished in smaller pots should be propagated later than these dates.

The rate of growth and development of poinsettias is faster with increase in temperature. Vegetative growth is much better at 21°C night temperature than it is at 16°C. For this reason generally it is recommended that 21°C be used for the young plants in August and until late September. Flower initiation in poinsettia starts about September 20, and somewhat lower temperature is more favorable for this reproductive development. At that time the temperature should be maintained at 18°C. In November if flower development is ahead of schedule, the temperature may be reduced to 14 to 16°C. The bracts should be well developed before temperatures are reduced.

Because flower formation in poinsettia is controlled by photoperiod, the time of flowering can be regulated by lighting or shading. In natural conditions the day length is short enough in late September to cause initiation of flowers. If it is desired to delay the time of flowering for a crop, the plants may be lighted. The lighting needs to be started by September 20 and it may be continued into the first week in October depending on the amount of time delay wanted. If plants are going to be lighted, they should be propagated correspondingly later so that they will not be too tall at maturity.

If it is desired to have a poinsettia crop in flower in early November, this may be done by giving the plants short photoperiods in September. The shading would have to start in late August and continue to early October. These plants would need to be propagated correspondingly earlier so that they would be large enough at time of marketing.

Although mum lighting and shading procedures can be used in general for controlling photoperiod with poinsettia, it must be understood that poinsettia is much more sensitive to light than chrysanthemum. The black fabric needs to be in good condition and placed over the plants for a minimum of 14 hours each day.

There are many instances of delay in flowering or even nonflowering in poinsettia crops because of stray lighting from within or outside the greenhouse.

For plants that will be grown as a pinched crop, the pinch is made about 4 weeks after the cutting is stuck. It can be expected that a flowering shoot will eventually develop at each node below the place of pinch. If a plant with four flowering shoots is desired, the plant should be pinched above the fourth leaf above the soil.

When the correct propagation date is used the finished plant will be the right height for the size pot that it is in. If it appears that for some reason or other the plants are going to be taller than desired, they can be treated with a growth regulator that will limit the height of the plant. The regulator, however, should be applied by early October. In addition to being shorter, treated plants usually will have heavier stems and darker green leaves. Plants that are treated too late in the season may have smaller and deformed bracts.

Primula *(Primula* spp.—*Primulaceae)*

Primula malaciodes is suitable for flowering in pot sizes from 9 to 16 centimeters, but more frequently it is produced in pot sizes from 10 to 13 centimeters.

It is propagated by seed, and germination is in about 3½ weeks at 16°C. The seed should be sown on the surface, and light promotes germination. The seedlings should be planted on 5-centimeter squares when they can be handled.

Primula is a cool-temperature crop. Seed should be sown in August for flowering in February in 10-centimeter pots at 8°C night temperature.

Primula elatior and *Primula veris* are hardy primulas that are used in gardening but also make attractive pot plants for the spring market.

The same propagation and growing procedures are used as those given for *Primula malacoides* previously, but usually they are propagated later and are grown only in 8- to 10-centimeter pots for flowering in April and May. They then may be planted outdoors after a brief stay indoors as a house plant.

Rose *(Rosa* X *hybrida—Rosaceae)*

Pot roses are very satisfactory for spring sales because they can be planted in the garden, where additional flowers may be obtained the same season.

Polyanthas or baby ramblers, hybrid teas, hybrid perpetuals, and climbers are used, and XXX is the most desirable grade. Rose plants should be purchased from a reliable nursery which specializes in their culture. Upon receipt late in December, all but the climbers should be trimmed 30 centimeters above the crown, and only the weak canes should be removed from the climbers. Pruning varies with different cultivars in the same group, and low pruning produces a smaller number of flowering shoots but makes longer stems. Low pruning is advocated for hybrid teas for exhibition, but low pruning on polyanthas will make top-heavy plants. All weak stems are removed at pruning. The size of the roots determines the size of pot for potting, whether 13-, 15-, or 18-centimeter. A slightly acid, fibrous soil is desirable.

After potting, the plants should be stored in a cool location, such as a 4°C greenhouse, shed, or cold frame. In the latter, the canes are covered with straw to prevent drying, but periodic examinations of the plant are necessary because mice cause damage. In January the plants are brought into the greenhouse and placed close together. Frequent overhead syringing encourages growth of the buds, and covering the plants with burlap or straw is desirable to raise the relative humidity. The temperature and time of starting growth depend upon the Easter date. Plants started January 1 in a temperature of 8°C flower in late March; plants started January 15 will bloom in April. The temperature should be raised gradually to 13°C by 1 month after starting, and after 6 weeks the temperature should be up to 16°C. During the forcing period, especially at cool temperatures, mildew may become serious.

After the temperature reaches 16°C, a complete fertilizer should be applied regularly until the plants are sold.

On polyanthas that develop exceptionally heavy stems, a pinch 7 to 9 weeks before Easter is recommended. Buds should develop on the polyanthas 6 weeks before Easter and should show color about 2 weeks before the date required. On hybrid teas and hybrid perpetuals, the bud should appear 4 weeks before Easter and should show color 1 week to 10 days before the holiday.

Schizanthus *(Schizanthus pinnatus—Solanaceàe)*

The common name is butterfly flower. The flowers are brilliantly colored and abundant, but they shatter. It is an unusual plant that is best suited for local sales.

Schizanthus is propagated from seed, and the seed germinates in 2 weeks at 16°C. Sowings from August through January will flower from January through April.

It should be pinched to keep it a suitable height.

Streptocarpus *(Streptocarpus X hybridus—Gesneriaceae)*

Usually the Wiesmoor hybrids are used as flowering pot plants. They may be propagated by seed or from leaf sections. White and blue are the most popular flower colors, but other colors are available.

The night temperature should be 18°C, and cultural procedures are the same as those used for saintpaulia and gloxinia.

Streptocarpus seed germinates in 2 weeks at 21°C. It should be sown on the soil surface and not covered. Seed sown from April through December will produce flowering pot plants from November to June.

The plants started from leaf sections require about 5 months from sticking the cutting to the mature plant.

Tulip *(Tulipa* X *hybrida—Liliaceae)*

Perhaps no flower has been more closely allied with the economy of any country than has the tulip with Belgium and Holland. The tulip craze which ended in 1637 was historic in that the desire for the flower was so widespread.

Tulip popularity has suffered greatly in recent years because of its relatively short keeping quality. However, a good many tulips are forced both as cut flowers and for potted plants.

There are various kinds of tulips available for forcing. Single Early tulips generally lack substance, but some of the Double Early types are useful after Valentine's Day. Mendel tulips are hybrids between Duc Van Tol and Darwins and are suitable for forcing in January for Valentine's Day. Triumphs are crosses between the Early tulips and the Darwins. They have the strong stems of the Darwins but flower somewhat earlier and have good keeping qualities. Darwins are the aristocrats of all tulips, possessing strong straight stems, outstanding colors, and excellent substance and keeping quality. Breeder tulips flower with Darwins but have oval-shaped flowers of pastel color. The origin of Cottage tulips is uncertain, but they have oval flowers on medium stems with a wide range of colors. Lily-flowered tulips belong to the Cottage group and are so named because of their resemblance to lilies. Broken tulips have an irregular distribution of colors and may be found among the Breeder, Cottage, and Darwin types. Rembrandts are broken Darwins. Parrot tulips have fringed petals and bizarre colors but do not force satisfactorily. The species of tulips that are useful in rock gardens are not suitable for forcing.

Tulips are dug when leaf primordia are present but the flower bud has not been formed, and bulbs are stored at 19°C to hasten formation of flower parts. If tulips are heated at high tempeatures as iris are, the flower parts will be killed.

The bulbs generally arrive in early October. A limited number of cut flower cultivars can be precooled either in soil at 10°C or dry at the same temperature for 6 weeks, after which time they must be planted and placed in a cool location. Bulbs not to be precooled should be held at 18°C until planting about mid-October. The 12- to 13-centimeter size is best for forcing.

Manure should never be mixed in tulip soil, nor should it be used as a cover for the bulbs outside. Botrytis blight may develop as a result of the use of manure, and this disease is very destructive. Bulbs that show evidence of rot should not be planted.

A well-drained field soil is very satisfactory for tulips. If grown for cut flowers, tulips may be planted in ordinary greenhouse flats. The flat should be filled halfway with soil, and the bulbs set in, almost touching each other. Soil is then filled in around the bulbs, but their noses can be left uncovered.

For pot plants, six or seven bulbs are placed in a 15-centimeter pan, eight or nine in an 18-centimeter pan, and eleven or twelve in an 20-centimeter pan. The first leaf develops on the flat side of the bulb, and if it is desired to have leaves droop over the pot, this flat side is placed next to the pot rim. Soil is generally placed in the pots, and the bulbs are pushed down until their noses are barely visible.

The flats or pots are placed in a 10°C refrigerated storage with high relative humidity, or buried outside. Precooled bulbs are best in a cool storage since the outside soil temperature is often too warm. Do not pot or flat precooled bulbs outside on a warm sunny day because the high temperature may nullify the effect of the precooling treatment. As a precaution against botrytis blight, the pots or flats of tulips can be dusted with fungicide when they are placed in storage. Some tulips are suitable for early forcing, while others are best for late, and the development of the tops and roots should be used as a guide. No tulips should be forced which do not have 8 centimeters of top growth and a heavy root system. For pot plants forced early, American-grown or specially precooled Dutch tulips should be used. Precooled bulbs often can be brought in for forcing 2 weeks earlier than bulbs not precooled.

The flats or pots are generally brought into a 13°C house for 10 days, then transferred to a 16°C location where they will force in 4 to 6 weeks. They can be forced in 4 to 5 weeks if brought directly to a 16°C house, but higher night temperatures soften the flowers. Bottom heat is beneficial provided it is not too intense. The shoots should be covered with black fabric or newspapers for several days if brought in when the sunlight is bright. This helps to stretch the stem in addition to preventing sunburn. When the growth is 8 centimeters high, it is advisable to spray with a solution of fungicide with a suitable spreader for prevention and control of botrytis blight, or tulip "fire." This disease can be recognized by the minute yellowish spots surrounded by water-soaked areas that appear on the leaves, stems, and flowers. A gray fungus growth may be visible in the center of these areas during periods of high relative humidity. If this occurs, give more air, spray as directed above, and keep water off the foliage and flowers. It is a good practice to water early in the day so that the foliage will be dry by night. The ventilators must be opened wider to dissipate the high relative humidity which is instrumental in promoting growth of the botrytis organism. Sometimes botrytis blight is troublesome in storage. Little can be done until the following year when sulfur or sulfur candles can be burned to kill fungus organisms before the bulbs are put in storage. Sulfur dioxide fumes are lethal to plants.

Recent experimental work on forcing tulips indicates that the bulbs may be stored dry at 4°C for 6 weeks, then flatted and kept for 6 weeks at 9°C, and then brought into a 16°C greenhouse. An even more radical, yet successful, procedure consists of storing the bulbs dry for 12 weeks at 7°C, then planting and forcing at 16°C. These procedures are experimental and are recommended on a trial basis only.

For pot plants there are only a few cultivars that force easily before Valentine's Day, but after this date some of the Mendel, Triumph, Cottage, and Darwin types force satisfactorily and can be brought in as needed beginning in mid-January.

Zinnia *(Zinnia elegans—Compositae)*

Zinnia is used primarily as a garden plant, but some of the shorter, large-flowered cultivars may be used as pot plants from spring through summer. Their best period of marketing probably is in early spring.

They are propagated from seed. The seed is sown directly in the pot in which it will be flowered. Germination is in 1 week at 21°C. One seed is used per 8-centimeter pot, and two or three seeds are used in 10-centimeter pots. Sowings from November through March will produce crops in flower from February through May at 16°C.

In addition to using short-growing cultivars, the plants may be treated with growth regulator when the flower buds are about the size of a dime.

FOLIAGE PLANTS

The most critical environmental factor for plants to be used in indoor landscaping is light quantity. Light intensities in homes, offices, and institutions are much lower than natural light outdoors or available light in greenhouses. Only plants with low light requirements can survive in these indoor conditions. Listed here are some of the genera that have species or cultivars that can be used as foliage plants indoors. The genera are grouped by family. A common means of propagation is indicated for the genus or family: seed (SD), leaf (L), stem tip (ST), stem segment (SS), air layer (AL), spore (SP), and offset (OS).

Acanthaceae
  Aphelandra (ST)
  Fittonia (ST)
  Hemigraphis (ST)
Agavaceae
  Agave (OS)
  Cordyline (ST, SS)
  Dracaena (ST)
Aizoaceae **(SD)**
  Faucaria
  Lithops
  Pleispilos
Amaranthaceae
  Iresine (ST)
Apocynaceae
  Carissa (SD)
  Nerium (ST)
  Pachypodium (SD)
Araceae
  Aglaonema (ST, SS)
  Anthurium (SD)
  Dieffenbachia (SS, ST)
  Epipremnum (SS, ST)
  Monstera (SD, SS, AL)
  Philodendron (SD, SS, ST)
  Spathiphyllum (SD)
  Syngonium (SD, SS)
Araliaceae
  Brassaia (SD, ST)
  Dizygotheca (SD)
  X *Fatshedera* (ST)
  Fatsia (SD, ST)
  Hedera (ST, SS)
  Polyscias (SD, ST, AL)
  Schefflera (SD, ST)
Araucariaceae **(SD)**
  Araucaria
Asclepiadaceae
  Ceropegia (ST, SS)
  Hoya (ST, SS)
  Huernia (OS)
  Stapelia (SD)
Begoniaceae
  Begonia (L, ST)
Bromeliaceae **(OS, SD)**
  Aechmea

Ananas
Billbergia
Cryptanthus
Neoregelia
Vriesia
Buxaceae
  Buxus (ST)
Cactaceae **(SD,ST)**
  Astrophytum
  Borzicactus
  Cephalocereus
  Cereus
  Chamaecereus
  Cleistocactus
  Echinocactus
  Echinocereus
  Echinopsis
  Espostoa
  Ferocactus
  Gymnocalycium
  Lemaireocereus
  Mammillaria
  Myrtilocactus
  Notocactus
  Opuntia
  Pachycereus
  Parodia
  Rebutia
  Trichocereus
Celastraceae
  Euonymus (ST)
Commelinaceae **(ST)**
  Cyanotis
  Dichorisandra
  Gibasis
  Rhoeo
  Tradescantia
  Zebrina
Compositae **(ST, SS)**
  Gynura
  Senecio
Cornaceae
  Aucuba (ST)
Crassulaceae
  Aeonium (OS)
  Crassula (ST)

Echeveria (OS)
Kalanchoe (ST, L)
Sedum (ST, OS)
Sempervivum (OS)
Cycadaceae
  Cycas (SD, OS)
Euphorbiaceae
  Acalypha (ST)
  Codiaeum (ST, AL)
  Euphorbia (ST)
Gesneriaceae
  Aeschynanthus (ST, SS)
  Columnea (ST)
  Episcia (ST)
  Nautilocalyx (ST)
  Sinningia (SD, L)
  Streptocarpus (SD, ST)
Guttiferae
  Clusia (ST)
Labiatae
  Plectranthus (ST)
Leeaceae
  Leea (ST)
Liliaceae
  Aloe (OS, SD)
  Asparagus (SD)
  Beaucarnia (SD)
  Chlorophytum (OS)
  Gasteria (OS, SD)
  Haworthia (OS)
  Sansevieria (L)
  Yucca (SS)
Marantaceae **(ST)**
  Calathea
  Maranta
Moraceae
  Ficus (ST, AL)
Musaceae
  Musa (OS)
  Strelitzia (SD, OS)
Myrsinaceae
  Ardisia (SD)
Palmaceae **(SD)**
  Caryota
  Chamaedorea
  Chamaerops

Chrysalidocarpus
Howea
Livistona
Phoenix
Rhapis
Pandaceae
Pandanus (OS)
Piperaceae
Peperomia (ST, L)
Pittosporaceae
Pittosporum (ST)
Podocarpaceae
Podocarpus (ST)
Polypodiaceae (SP, OS)

Adiantum
Asplenium
Cyrtomium
Davallia
Nephrolepis
Pellaea
Platycerium
Polypodium
Pteris
Portulacaceae
Portulacaria (ST)
Rubinaceae
Coffea (SD)
Rutaceae (ST)

X Citrofortunella
Citrus
Saxifragaceae (OS)
Saxifraga
Tolmiea
Urticaceae (ST)
Pellionia
Pilea
Soleirola
Vitaceae
Cissus (SS, ST)

There are definite size limitations in the use of foliage plants. For the plants to be used in dish gardens and terrariums, the ultimate height must not be greater than a few centimeters. Some of the plants in this category are from the following genera or families: *Philodendron, Dracaena, Ardisia, Peperomia, Syngonium, Cactaceae, Crassulaceae,* and *Gesneriaceae.*

Foliage plants that make medium-sized specimen plants commonly come from some of the following genera: *Ficus, Philodendron, Dracaena, Pittosporum, Araucaria, Brassaia, Yucca, Sansevieria, Euphorbia, Cereus, Aphelandra, Aglaonema, Dieffenbachia,* and *Chamaedorea.*

Some of the better large foliage plants are from the following genera or families: *Ficus, Philodendron, Araucaria, Cycas, Cereus, Brassaia, Yucca,* and *Palmaceae.*

Foliage-Plant Production Areas

It is possible for foliage plants to be produced in any part of the country, but because of the kind of customer who will be served, the kind of plants that will be produced, and the need for propagative material, production can be handled in some areas better than in others. There is quite a difference in production and marketing procedures for small plants (plants in 10-centimeter pots and smaller) and large plants (plants in 16-centimeter pots and larger). It usually is best to start with either size group of plants, and then add the other size group as plans and arrangements can be made.

The foliage-plant production business often is more complex than the flowering-plant production business. There are so many variables, and these need to be limited as much as possible so that the work can be better organized and handled. The large number of different kinds of plants and

Figure 6-12 A slat shed used for growing monstera totem poles in southern Florida.

the different sizes that are involved make it difficult to operate efficiently.

Several years ago some northern greenhouse operators established foliage-plant production areas in the South. These were largely for small

Figure 6-13 Croton stock plants in a plastic screen house. *(South Florida Nurseries, Inc. photograph.)*

plants and developed generally on the basis of providing a slat shed area for stock plants together with a greenhouse propagation area. The rather large stock-plant area could be operated more reasonably down there than it could in the North. It did not take too many years of operation, however, to learn that even though the stock plants could be kept from freezing during the brief cold periods, there was so much cool weather during the winter that stock-plant growth was very slow. Since then the foliage-plant growers in the southern United States have added heating systems and covering to their stock-plant areas, and the increased production usually is sufficient to make the business profitable in spite of the increased costs.

In the southern part of Florida much of the foliage-plant production is of large plants. Depending on the kind of plant and the stage of growth, the plants are grown either in full sunlight or under screen shade. During the winter they are given some temperature protection by covering the structures with polyethylene film, but they do not have heating systems for other than emergency purposes. Some of these nurseries have greenhouses for propagation, but many of them handle propagation right in the screen houses.

Other growers have established production areas in even warmer climates in Puerto Rico and in Central America where natural temperatures are suitable the year-round for good stock-plant growth. The primary business of these producers is to supply propagative material to growers in the continental United States and other countries. They market unrooted cuttings, cane, and to a limited extent rooted cuttings, seedlings, and some plants in small pots—about 5 centimeters.

Northern foliage-plant growers may propagate some plants at their greenhouses from seed or cuttings, but these usually are sold as small

Figure 6-14 Slat sheds commonly are covered with plastic film during the winter to provide warmer temperatures. *(South Florida Nurseries, Inc. photograph.)*

Figure 6-15 Emergency means of heating slat sheds or plastic-screen houses are required in Florida to protect foliage plants from freezing during occasional cold weather.

plants—sometimes as seedlings or rooted cuttings and in other instances grown-on in 6- to 10-centimeter pots. If northern growers want to market larger plants, usually they will buy them from southern growers in the approximate size that is needed and then market them a few weeks after they are received. Some of the plants that may be propagated very well in the North are cacti, hedera, ferns, grape ivy, peperomia, epipremnum, and brassaia.

Foliage-Plant Marketing

There are various channels of distribution of foliage plants to the ultimate consumer. The home owner generally buys foliage plants from flower shops, garden or plant stores, various types of retail stores, and in some instances through interior decorators.

Foliage plants for offices, shopping plazas, and institutions may be marketed by wholesale growers, retail growers, interior landscapers, or distributors. Usually the plants are purchased, and sometimes a maintenance contract is included. In some instances plants are leased. This kind of marketing is handled best when there is good communication and understanding between the customer and the supplier, the plant seller is capable of handling the job, and there is good provision for assessment of plant suitability for several weeks after planting. Frequently these customers or their advisers have envisioned plants or plantings that are not practical, and the good supplier will somehow guide them into the purchase that will give them the most satisfactory service.

These various marketers of foliage plants to the ultimate consumer, if they do not have plant production facilities, buy the plants from producers. The retailers who require large quantities of plants frequently do contract buying with larger foliage-plant producers in the South. In too many instances this sort of arrangement has satisfied pricing requirements at the expense of quality of plants. This may be because of poorly grown plants or because of too long a time in shipping, storage, and marketing. The successful merchandiser of cabbage, corn, and cough drops may need some real help in the successful marketing of foliage plants.

Some of the wholesale marketers of foliage plants, who may be called distributors, have good knowledge of the product and a bona fide business, but there are some whose extent of knowledge goes no further than the operation of the truck. Foliage-plant producers need to realize that with that type of marketing they have aided and abetted the demise of the foliage-plant business.

Regardless of where the plants originated, there must be a reliable report on the condition of the plants during and after marketing. If the plants came from local sources, the grower should be available. If the plants came from a distant source there should be a local individual qualified to evaluate the marketing.

Foliage-Plant Growing Environments and Holding Environments

Foliage-plant producers need to provide areas where they are trying to actively grow plants and other areas where they can hold plants of mature size for marketing. The light, temperature, water, and fertilizer supply should be regulated differently in these two areas.

The two most common faults in growing foliage plants are temperatures that are too low and soils that have poor water drainage. There is no excuse for poor regulation of temperature, but the soil situation is a problem sometimes because of the different kinds of soils that have been used for the plants that are shipped in. The irrigation of these plants will have to be varied according to the soil. Most foliage plants do best in coarse and porous soils.

Pest control must be a regular program in both growing and holding areas. Two-spotted mite, mealybugs, and scales are some of the most

	Growing area	*Holding area*
Light intensity	1,500 foot-candles	1,000 foot-candles
Temperature	21°C	17°C
Water	75% relative humidity	50% relative humidity
Fertilizer	Regular amount	Half amount

persistent pests of foliage plants. The foliage-plant grower needs to keep active a good, current source of information on the best pest controls for foliage plants.

Foliage Plants Listed by Genus

Some plants are well known by botanical names that have been used for years. But many of the foliage plants are most frequently referred to by their common name or by outdated botanical names. It is believed that the botanical names used here are in accordance with either or both *Hortus Third*, Macmillan Publishing Company, Inc., and *Exotic Plant Manual*, Roehrs Company. In order to determine the botanical name for plants known by sight only, the *Exotic Plant Manual* is most helpful.

It was indicated earlier that the foliage-plant business separates naturally into work with small, medium-sized, and large plants. In this listing the size grouping for the plant has been indicated. Some of the plants have the potential of being used in any size, and a few are actually used in this way. The sizes indicated are the one or ones that are most common in the trade for the plant. In addition, the plants that vine are indicated with a "v." The size classifications used here are: small—bare root, rooted cuttings, or in 5- to 10-centimeter pots and up to 30 centimeters tall; medium—in 15- to 20-centimeter pots and 45 to 90 centimeters tall; and large—in pots 25 centimeters or larger and 120 centimeters or more tall.

Plant	*Small*	*Medium*	*Large*
Acalypha wilkesiana		x	
Aeschyanthus pulcher	xv		
Aeschyanthus speciosus	xv		
Aglaonema commutatum	x	x	
Aglaonema commutatum 'Pseudobrachteatum'		x	

Plant	Small	Medium	Large
Aglaonema commutatum 'Treubii'		x	
Aglaonema marantifolium		x	
Aglaonema X Silver King		x	
Aglaonema X Silver Queen		x	
Aglaonema X Snow Queen		x	
Anthurium scherzeranum	x	x	
Aphelandra squarrosa 'Apollo'	x	x	
Aphelandra squarrosa 'Dania'	x	x	
Aralias			
Dizygotheca elegantissima	x	x	x
Polyscias balfouriana	x	x	
Polyscias balfouriana 'Marginata'	x	x	
Polyscias balfouriana 'Penockii'	x	x	
Polyscias fruticosa		x	x
Polyscias fruticosa 'Elegans'		x	x
Polyscias paniculata 'Variegata'		x	x
Araucaria heterophylla	x	x	x
Ardisia crispa	x	x	
Asparagus densiflorus 'Meyers'	x	x	
Asparagus densiflorus 'Sprengeri'	x	x	
Asparagus plumosus (see *Asparagus setaceus*)			
Asparagus setaceus	x	x	
Aucuba japonica 'Variegata'		x	
Beaucarnia recurvata	x	x	
Begonia rex	x	x	
Brassaia actinophylla	x	x	x
Bromeliads			
Aechmea chantinii		x	
Aechmea fasciata		x	
Aechmea X *maginalii*		x	
Ananas comosus		x	
Ananas comosus 'Variegatus'		x	
Billbergia nutans		x	
Cryptanthus bivittatus 'Minor'	x		
Neorgelia carolinae		x	
Neorgelia carolinae 'Tricolor'		x	
Neorgelia marmorata		x	

Plant	Small	Medium	Large
Neorgelia spectabilis		x	
Vriesia **X** *mariae*		x	
Vriesia splendens		x	
Vriesia splendens 'Favorite'		x	
Buxus microphylla var. *japonica*	x		
Cacti and Succulents			
Aeonium arboreum	x	x	
Aeonium arboreum 'Atropurpureum'	x	x	
Agave victoriae-reginae	x	x	
Aloe ferox	x	x	
Aloe barbadensis	x	x	
Aloe variegata	x	x	
Aloe vera (see *Aloe barbadensis*)			
Astrophytum asterias	x		
Astrophytum myriostigma	x		
Astrophytum ornatum	x		
Borzicactus celsianus	x		
Borzicactus trollii	x		
Cephalocereus palmeri	x	x	
Cephalocereus senilis	x		
Cereus peruvianus		x	x
Ceropegia woodii	xv		
Chamaecereus silvestri	x		
Cleistocactus strausii	x	x	
Crassula argentea	x	x	
Echeveria agavoides	x		
Echeveria **X** 'Doris Taylor'	x		
Echeveria pulvinata	x		
Echinocactus grusonii	x	x	
Echinocactus ingens	x		
Echinocereus fitchii	x		
Echinocereus luteus	x		
Echinocereus pectinatus var. *neomexicanus*	x		
Echinopsis rhodotricha	x		
Espostoa lanata	x	x	
Espostoa melanostele	x	x	
Euphorbia canariensis	x	x	x

Plant	Small	Medium	Large
Euphorbia lactea		x	x
Euphorbia millii var. *splendens*		x	
Euphorbia trigona		x	x
Faucaria tigrina	x		
Ferocactus acanthodes	x		
Ferocactus hamatacanthus	x		
Ferocactus histrix	x		
Ferocactus latispinus	x		
Ferocactus setispinus	x		
Ferocactus wislizenii	x		
Gasteria verucosa	x		
Gymnocalycium mihanovichii var. *friedrichii*	x		
Gymnocalycium saglione	x		
Haworthia species	x	x	
Huernia pillansi	x		
Kalanchoe tomentosa	x		
Lemaireocereus dumortieri	x	x	
Lemaireocereus marginatus	x	x	
Lemaireocereus thurberi	x	x	
Lithops species	x		
Mammillaria bocasana	x		
Mammillaria celsiana	x		
Mammillaria elongata	x	x	
Mammillaria hahniana	x		
Mammillaria magnimamma	x		
Mammillaria zeilmanniana	x		
Myrtilocactus geometrizans		x	x
Notocactus leninghausii	x		
Notocactus ottonis	x		
Notocactus scopa	x		
Notocactus submammulosus	x		
Opuntia basilaris		x	x
Opuntia microdasys	x		
Oreocactus (see *Borzicactus*)			
Pachycereus pecten-arboriginum		x	x
Pachycereus pringlei		x	x
Pachypodium lamieri	x	x	

Plant	Small	Medium	Large
Parodia aureispina	x		
Parodia chrysacanthion	x		
Parodia maassii	x		
Parodia mutabilis	x		
Parodia sanguiniflora	x		
Pleispilos species	x		
Portulacaria afra	x	x	
Portulacaria afra 'Variegata'	x		
Rebutia minuscula	x		
Sedum blue	x		
Sedum guatemalense	x		
Sedum morganianum	xv		
Sedum pachyphyllum	x		
Sedum spectabile 'Variegatum'	x		
Sempervivum species	x		
Senecio species	x		
Stapelia species	x		
Trichocereus spachianus		x	x
Calathea insignis		x	
Calathea makoyana		x	
Carissa grandiflora 'Bonsai'	x	x	
Chlorophytum comosum 'Variegatum'	x	xv	
Cissus antarctica	x	xv	
Cissus rhombifolia	x	xv	
Cissus rhombifolia 'Mandaianum'	x	xv	
X *Citrofortunella mitis*		x	x
Citrus limon 'Meyer'		x	x
Citrus limon 'Ponderosa'		x	x
Clusia rosea		x	x
Codiaeum variegatum 'Aureo-maculatum'	x	x	
Codiaeum variegatum cultivars		x	x
Codiaeum variegatum 'Punctatum Aureum'	x	x	
Coffea arabica	x	x	x
Columnea cultivars and species	x	xv	
Columnea X 'Stavanger'	x	xv	
Cordyline terminalis	x	x	
Cordyline terminalis 'Baby Doll'	x	x	

Plant	Small	Medium	Large
Cyanotis kewensis	x	xv	
Cycas revoluta		x	x
Dichorisandra thyrsiflora 'Variegata'	x		
Dieffenbachia amoena		x	x
Dieffenbachia X Bausei		x	
Dieffenbachia 'Exotica'	x	x	
Dieffenbachia 'Exotica Perfection'	x	x	
Dieffenbachia picta 'Rudolph Roehrs'		x	
Dieffenbachia picta 'Superba'		x	
Dieffenbachia 'Tropic Snow'		x	x
Dracaena angustifolia 'Honoriae'		x	
Dracaena deremensis 'Janet Craig'		x	x
Dracaena deremensis 'Warneckii'		x	x
Dracaena fragrans		x	x
Dracaena fragrans 'Massangeana'		x	x
Dracaena godseffiana (see *Dracaena surculosa*)			
Dracaena goldieana		x	
Dracaena marginata	x	x	x
Dracaena marginata 'Tricolor'	x	x	
Dracaena reflexa		x	
Dracaena sanderana	x	x	
Dracaena surculosa	x	x	
Dracaena surculosa 'Florida Beauty'	x	x	
Dracaena thalioides		x	
Epipremnum aureus	xv	xv	
Episcia cupreata cultivars	x		
Euonymus japonica	x		
Euonymus japonica 'Mediopicta'	x		
Euonymus japonica 'Argento-variegata'	x		
X *Fatshedera lizei*	x	xv	
Fatsia japonica		x	
Ferns			
Adiantum raddianum	x	x	
Adiantum tenerum	x	x	
Asplenium nidus	x	x	
Cyrtomium falcatum		x	
Davallia species	x	x	

Plant	Small	Medium	Large
Nephrolepis exaltata 'Bostoniensis'		x	
Nephrolepis exaltata 'Bostoniensis Compacta'		x	
Nephrolepis exaltata 'Fluffy Duffy'	x	x	
Nephrolepis exaltata 'Fluffy Ruffles'	x .	x	
Nephrolepis exaltata 'Gold Coast'	x	x	
Nephrolepis exalta 'Norwoodii'		x	
Nephrolepis exaltata 'Plymouth Ruffles'	x	x	
Nephrolepis exaltata 'Rooseveltii'		x	
Nephrolepis exaltata 'Splendida'		x	
Nephrolepis exaltata 'Whitmanii'		x	
Pellaea rotundifolia	x	x	
Platycerium bifurcatum		x	
Polypodium aureum 'Mandaianum'		x	
Pteris ensiformis 'Victoriae'	x	x	
Pteris species	x	x	
Ficus benjamina	x	x	x
Ficus benjamina 'Exotica'		x	x
Ficus benjamina var. *nuda*		x	x
Ficus deltoidea	x	x	
Ficus diversifolia (see *Ficus deltoidea*)			
Ficus elastica 'Decora'		x	x
Ficus elastica 'Doescheri'		x	x
Ficus elastica 'Honduras'		x	x
Ficus elastica 'Robusta'		x	x
Ficus lyrata		x	x
Ficus pandurata (see *Ficus lyrata*)			
Ficus pumila	xv	xv	
Ficus retusa 'Nitida'		x	x
Ficus rubiginosa		x	x
Ficus triangularis		x	x
Fittonia verschaffelti	x	x	
Fittonia verschaffelti var. *argyroneura*	x	x	
Gibasis geniculata	xv	xv	
Gynura aurantiaca 'Purple Passion'	x		
Hedera helix cultivars	xv	xv	
Helxine soleirolii (see *Soleirolia soleirolii*)			
Hemigraphis 'Exotica'	x		

Plant	Small	Medium	Large
Hoya carnosa	xv		
Hoya carnosa 'Argentea Picta'	xv		
Hoya carnosa 'Compacta'	xv		
Hoya carnosa 'Compacta Regalis'	xv		
Hoya carnosa 'Krinkle 8'	xv		
Hoya carnosa 'Compacta Mauna Loa'	xv		
Hoya carnosa 'Rubra'	xv		
Hoya carnosa 'Tricolor'	xv		
Hoya carnosa 'Variegata'	xv		
Hoya purpurea-fusca 'Silver Pink'	xv		
Iresine herbstii cultivars	x		
Iresine lindenii cultivars	x		
Leea coccinea		x	x
Maranta leuconeura var. *erythroneura*	x	x	
Maranta leuconeura var. *kerchoveana*	x	x	
Monstera deliciosa		x	xv
Musa X *paradisiaca*			x
Nautilocalyx lynchii	x		
Nephthytis (see *Syngonium*)		x	x
Nerium oleander			
Palms			
Areca lutescens (see *Chrysalidocarpus lutescens*)			
Caryota mitis		x	x
Chamaedorea elegans		x	x
Chamaedorea erumpens		x	x
Chamaedorea seifritzii		x	x
Chamaerops humilis		x	x
Chrysalidocarpus lutescens		x	x
Howea forsterana		x	x
Livistona chinensis		x	x
Neanthe bella (see *Chamaedorea elegans*)			
Phoenix roebelini		x	x
Rhapis excelsa		x	x
Pandanus veitchii		x	
Pellionia daveauana	x		
Pellionia puchra	xv		
Peperomia caperata	x		

Plant	Small	Medium	Large
Peperomia obtusifolia	x		
Peperomia obtusifolia 'Marble'	x		
Peperomia obtusifolia 'Variegata'	x		
Peperomia scandens	xv		
Peperomia scandens 'Variegata'	xv		
Philodendron bipennifolium	x	x	x
Philodendron cordatum (see *P. scandens* subsp. *oxycardium*)			
Philodendron X 'Emerald Duke'		xv	xv
Philodendron X 'Emerald King'		xv	xv
Philodendron X 'Emeral Queen'		xv	xv
Philodendron domesticum		xv	xv
Philodendron hastatum (see *P. domesticum*)			
Philodendron X 'Majesty'		xv	xv
Philodendron micans (see *P. scandens* subsp. *scandens*)			
Philodendron panduraeforme (see *P. bipennifolium*)			
Philoddendron pertusum (see *Monstera deliciosa*)			
Philodendron X 'Prince Dubonnet'		xv	xv
Philodendron X 'Red Duchess'		xv	xv
Philodendron X 'Red Emerald'		xv	xv
Philodendron X 'Red Princess'		xv	xv
Philodendron X 'Royal King'		xv	xv
Philodendron scandens subsp. *oxycardium*	xv	xv	
Philodendron scandens subsp. *scandens*	xv	xv	
Philodendron selloum		x	x
Pilea cadieri	x	x	
Pilea cadieri 'Minima'	x		
Pilea involucrata	x		
Pilea microphylla	x	x	
Pilea 'Silver Tree'	x		
Pilea spruceana	x		
Pittosporum tobira	x	x	
Pittosporum tobira 'Variegata'	x	x	
Pittosporum tobira 'Wheeleri'	x	x	
Plectranthus australis	xv		
Plectranthus oertendahlii	xv		
Pleomele (see *Dracaena*)			
Podocarpus macrophyllus	x		

Plant	Small	Medium	Large
Pothos (see *Epipremnum*)			
Rhoeo spathaceae	x	x	
Sansevieria trifasciata	x	x	
Sansevieria trifasciata 'Hahnii'	x		
Sansevieria trifasciata 'Laurentii'	x	x	
Sansevieria trifasciata 'Silver Hahnii'	x		
Sansevieria zeylanica	x	x	
Saxifraga stolonifera	xv	xv	
Saxifraga stolonifera 'Tricolor'	xv	xv	
Schefflera actinophylla (see *Brassaia actinophylla*)			
Schefflera arboricola	x	x	x
Scindapsus (see *Epipremnum*)			
Senecio herreianus	xv	xv	
Senecio macroglossus 'Variegatum'	xv	xv	
Senecio mikanioides	xv	xv	
Soleirola soleirolii	x		
Spathiphyllum 'Clevelandii'	x	x	
Spathiphyllum 'Mauna Loa'		x	
Strelitzia reginae		x	x
Syngonium podophyllum 'Albovirens'	xv	xv	
Syngonium podophyllum 'Atrovirens'	xv	xv	
Syngonium podophyllum 'Emerald Gem'	xv	xv	
Syngonium wendlandii	xv	xv	
Syngonium xanthophilum	xv	xv	
Tolmiea menziesii	x	x	
Tradescantia albaflora cultivars	xv	xv	
Tradescantia fulminensis cultivars	xv	xv	
Yucca elephantipes		x	x
Zebrina pendula cultivars	xv	xv	

BEDDING PLANTS

The bedding plants are those that are used for flower gardens in the landscape. Some of the plants are perennial and continue to grow year after year. The production of perennial plants is largely an outdoor operation, and is not involved in this discussion. Bedding plants as discussed in this chapter are those handled as annuals. Most of them do not live through the winter, and new plants are set out each spring. The planting time may be February or earlier in the South and as late as June in the North, and the bedding plants must be scheduled carefully so that they are at the right stage of growth and size for planting. Actually the time of planting is based primarily on the last date that frost can be expected for the area; however, if the spring is cooler or warmer than usual, planting is delayed or advanced accordingly.

Many of the bedding plants are propagated by seed. This is an economical method of propagation if proper conditions are provided. The bedding plants propagated by seed that are used in the greatest quantities are petunias. Geraniums and a few of the other bedding plants must be propagated by cuttings in order to produce the desired plants.

Light The growth of most bedding plants will be best in full sunlight. Plants grown in shaded locations, closely spaced, or in poor light will be too tall with weak stems and will flower more slowly.

Most bedding plants can be started and grown for a few weeks solely in artificial light. Fluorescent light should be used at about 1,000 foot-candles, and this can be obtained by placing the tubes about 10 centimeters apart and about 15 centimeters above the plants. The light should be provided for a minimum of 16 hours daily. Excellent plant growth results in the early stages, but as the plants become larger, they are more easily managed in sunlight.

The length of day affects the kind of growth and the rate of flower formation of some bedding plants. The effects of length of day on the growth and flowering of petunias are covered in the discussion of that crop.

Temperature The production of bedding plants is known generally as a cool-temperature operation. In some instances cool temperatures are used simply because the physical facilities will not provide warmer temperatures. Warm temperatures and accurate control of them must be provided for the propagation of bedding plants, but only a relatively small area is involved, because the seed flats and cuttings do not occupy much space. Rigid temperature control during propagation is indispensable. After propagation the plants should be grown in cooler temperatures, and the more closely these temperatures are regulated, the better the growth and timing of flowering.

Usually bedding plants are grown at 10°C night temperatures with day temperatures about 6°C warmer. At these cool temperatures growth and flowering are slow, and stems are short, compact, and of good diameter. Geraniums and some of the other plants must be grown at 13°C night temperatures or warmer in order to produce satisfactory growth.

More recently there has been interest in growing many bedding plants at 16°C night temperatures in order to produce them in a shorter period of time.

Soil, Fertilizer, and Water   A reliable source of soil is required for bedding plants because the soil is sold with the plants. The soil must be well prepared so that it is porous and drains well. The bedding plants that are propagated by seed should be transplanted when the seedlings are very small, and for good contact between soil and the small root systems, the soil must be finely shredded. To compensate for the fineness of the soil, a sufficient amount of peat moss should be added so that the soil remains porous after shredding.

Artificial soil mixtures of peat moss with perlite, vermiculite, or fine sand may be used. These have the advantage of being uniform from season to season, and they can be handled in the same fashion, but fertilizer must be incorporated uniformly in these mixtures.

Soils which have not been used previously in the greenhouse will usually benefit by additions of phosphorus and calcium fertilizers at the time of mixing. Superphosphate should be used as the source of phosphorus and dolomite limestone as the source of calcium if the soil is somewhat acid in reaction, or gypsum if the soil is neutral or alkaline. Applications of nitrogen and potassium fertilizers then must be made regularly after planting. If some nitrogen fertilizer cannot be supplied shortly after planting, a small amount should be incorporated into the soil at the time of mixing as some nitrogen is required by the plants at all stages of growth.

If soils have been used previously in the greenhouse, excess of fertilizer may be expected. This must be corrected before planting, or the young plants may be seriously damaged from the excess fertilizer.

Fertilizers are most efficiently applied in the liquid form to bedding plants, and this can be done by means of an injector with each irrigation or periodically by other means. Fertilizer should not be withheld in order to delay the growth of plants which are ahead of schedule. This produces poor-quality plants, and they grow and develop very slowly after they are planted in the garden.

Watering   Bedding plants are generally grown at a time of year when increasing light intensity and temperature cause rapid drying of the soil. Frequently, the plants are severely checked because they suffer periodically from lack of water. While it is true that dry soil will cause the growth to be compact, very often this is carried to excess, so that too much additional time is required to produce a salable plant. This is particularly true of geraniums.

Overwatering causes chlorosis on a great number of annuals used for bedding. When they are grown in flats, boards nailed too closely together may swell, to the extent that water will drain only at the edges of the flat.

Plants near the edge will be nearly normal, while those at the center will be dwarf or yellow.

Newly planted seedlings must be watered with nozzles that provide a fog or fine mist so that plants or soil are not washed from the containers. As the plants grow, coarser nozzles can be used. It is usually most satisfactory to use an irrigation system with nozzles that provide a uniform spray of water for the entire area. The small-diameter plastic-tube irrigation systems can be used to advantage for geraniums in 10-centimeter or larger pots.

Growth-Regulant Chemicals Some chemical treatments can be used to produce shorter, more compact plants.

Diseases Geraniums are troubled with several diseases not common to the other bedding plants, and for that reason geranium diseases are included in the discussion of that crop.

The disease known as damping-off is most common with bedding plants. The pathogens involved may be *Rhizoctonia solani, Pythium* spp., or *Phytophthora* spp. They may produce seed decay, stem rot, or root rot, and in extreme instances they may invade the upper portions of the plants. Usually stem rot occurs at the soil line, and the plants topple and wither. The pathogens grow rapidly in the warm and moist environment provided for the seedlings, and as long as the conditions are favorable the plants become infested and die in an ever-increasing circle from the point of infestation. Control of damping-off results from eliminating the pathogens, providing environmental conditions less suitable for the growth of the organisms, and treating with chemicals that limit the growth of the organisms.

If steam is available, it should be used to eliminate these pathogens in the soil, containers, benches, and handling equipment before they are used for bedding plants. Chemicals such as methyl bromide or Vapam may be used for treating the soil and the surroundings in place of steam, but steaming is the most satisfactory treatment when it is available. After treatment, care must be taken not to reinfest the area. Some of the most common ways in which pathogens are reintroduced are bringing in infested plants, putting feet on benches or containers, and using contaminated tools, irrigation equipment, or containers.

The growth of the damping-off pathogens is favored in constantly moist conditions. It is possible to control damping-off by less frequent irrigation, better drained soils or containers, or more air circulation. Depending on the situation, improved air circulation may be obtained by sowing the seed more sparsely or spacing the plants farther apart, removing obstacles from around the plants, increasing ventilation, or using air-circulation fans.

If damping-off does occur, in addition to limiting the moisture and increasing the air circulation, the soil should be drenched with suitable chemicals.

Botrytis blight caused by *Botrytis cinerea* is common in bedding plants, but in contrast to damping-off, the infestation starts in the upper portions of the plants and grows downward. This pathogen develops most rapidly in moist areas on aging or injured tissues. It is commonly called "gray mold," because in the advanced stages the affected portions are covered with a mass of gray spores. The best means of control are the elimination of trash in the greenhouse such as old stems, leaves, and flowers, as the source of *Botrytis cinerea*, and the prevention of moisture from forming on the leaves and stems of the bedding plants. Irrigation earlier in the day and more ventilation and air circulation coupled with better spacing of plants are the best means of keeping them dry and less susceptible to a botrytis blight infestation.

Pests Bedding-plant pests are slugs, aphids, two-spotted mite, thrips, and whitefly, and a regular control program is needed.

Rotation and Structures Depending on the crops, how they are handled, and the area of the country, structures of some kind will be required for the production of bedding plants from about January to June. The greatest requirement for space in northern greenhouses comes from the middle of March to June. Because of this, bedding plants do not rotate well with pot-plant crops as most greenhouses are filled to overflowing with spring pot-plant crops at that time of the year. A pot-plant grower, who also desires to produce bedding plants, generally uses temporary structures for the bedding plants. Cold frames were used earlier, but they have been largely replaced with plastic-film houses because temperature and moisture are more easily controlled and less labor is required for handling the crops. Although these may be temporary structures or used for only a portion of the year, they should provide adequate means for controlling temperature and ventilation for the best results.

It is possible that year-round structures could be used by rotating Christmas crops such as poinsettias and azaleas with bedding plants; however, cut-flower crops such as chrysanthemums and snapdragons make a better rotation.

Geraniums should not be grown in cold frames as a greater degree of control is needed than can be provided in such structures.

Marketing Many improvements have been made in the marketing of bedding plants. The quality of the bedding plants has increased, the plants are grown in the size and units that the customers desire and can use conveniently, more information is available on how to use bedding plants and what the effect of each type of plant will be, and the sales areas have become more numerous, accessible, and attractive.

Acalypha *(Acalypha wilkesiana—Euphorbiaceae)*

Acalypha wilkesiana 'Marginata' is a free-growing handsome cultivar which has a leaf with a reddish-brown center and a carmine edge.

Acalypha wilkesiana 'Obovata' has green leaves in the early stages, edged with creamy white and with age the edge assumes a crimson hue.

Stock plants can be lifted in the fall and kept cool until January when the plants may be cut back and placed in a temperature of 16°C with high humidity. They produce a crop of cuttings which will root readily with bottom heat, and satisfactory plants can be produced by bedding time in May.

Ageratum *(Ageratum houstonianum—Compositae)*

This plant is a blue-, pink-, or white-flowered tropical American herb used extensively for outdoor flowering and to some extent as a pot plant for spring sales. The plants may be grown from seed or stem-tip cuttings. Seed sown in February will produce marketable plants in 10-centimeter pots in May, if grown in a temperature of 10°C. Cuttings may be taken in January from stock plants, lifted in the fall before frost, and carried in a cold house. Only 2 to 3 weeks is necessary in the propagation bench. After they are placed in 6-centimeter pots the plants should be pinched to obtain bushiness, and they will be flowering and ready for sale in about 4 to 5 weeks. Aphids, red spider, and thrips are serious pests.

Alternanthera *(Alternanthera ficoidea—Amarantaceae)*

The alternanthera is a very dwarf South American plant, with long lanceolate leaves, sometimes elliptic, acuminate, and colored green, yellow, and red. Alternantheras are used largely for ribbon bedding because of their compact growth, ease of shearing, and high coloration. They should be propagated in the fall by cuttings or division of plants. By either method they may be set in shallow flats and grown in a temperature of 16°C with reduced moisture at the roots. They should be potted in April for planting outside in late May.

Alyssum *(Lobularia maritima—Cruciferae)*

This annual alyssum is used frequently as an edging plant. The most common flower color is white, but the cultivars with lavender or purple flowers are also used.

A common name is sweet alyssum, a fitting description of the fragrance of this plant.

The seed should be sown about March 1; it germinates in 1 week at 21°C.

Asparagus *(Asparagus setaceus* and *A. densiflorus* 'Sprengeri'*—Liliaceae)*

These graceful plants, natives of South Africa, are used in hanging baskets, as fillers for window boxes and plant baskets, and as individual specimens.

Seed should be sown early in the spring, after soaking for 24 hours. Germination takes from 30 to 50 days. Seedlings should be planted in light but fertile soil and grown in a temperature of 16°C. Satisfactory plants are produced in about 12 months. The use of nitrogenous fertilizer is recommended during the summer. These plants should have partial shade during the hot months to prevent yellowing of the foliage.

Begonia *(Begonia* spp.*—Begoniaceae)*

Begonia* X *semperflorens-cultorum   The ever-flowering, or wax, begonia is used in combination pots or bedding in spring and as a reasonably priced specimen plant at any season. Propagation is by seed or stem cuttings. Seed sown in June will make 8-centimeter plants for Christmas or 10-centimeter plants for Valentine's Day. September sowings finish as 10-centimeter plants for spring. Late December and January sowings will make 8-centimeter plants in spring. The same soil mixture suggested for tuberous-rooted begonias is ideal, although the semperflorens type will grow well in three parts soil and one part peat.

The plants are pinched to make them bushy and compact. Fertilizers applied every 3 to 4 weeks keep the foliage lustrous. The temperature should be 10 to 13°C.

Red spider, aphids, mealybugs, whitefly, and leaf roller are common pests. Mites cause cupping of the young growth and browning and withering of the unopened flower cluster. Root-knot nematodes are a serious pest, and steaming soil, pots, and bench areas is the best control. The semperflorens withstand sprays, dusts, and aerosols and are not as tender as other types.

Begonia X *tuberhybrida*   These are sold as specimens or for bedding plants in shaded areas. The flowers of the large types may be used for corsages. Seed is sown in January, and since it is fine, the soil should be screened and the seed flat or pot watered from below. The germination temperature should be 21°C. As soon as the seedlings are large enough to be handled conveniently, they are pricked off 2 centimeters apart each way to flats. When crowded, they should be shifted to 6-centimeter pots, then later to 13- and 16-centimeter pots, where they are fertilized regularly and kept under a moderate shade. The plants stop growing in the fall because they are a long-day type, and they can be ripened by reducing the moisture. The pots may be placed in a 7 to 10°C house, and in winter the tubers are removed, cleaned, and started in growth again in 16-centimeter pots. A mixture of equal parts of soil, peat, leaf mold, and sand should be used.

Because seedlings are so difficult to handle, most florists buy tubers grown in California under lath. When started in January, flowering plants may be expected in early spring; and tubers started in March flower in summer.

The best way to handle tubers is to bury them upright in flats of moist peat at 21 to 27°C. As soon as several leaves are unfolding, place them in 13- or 16-centimeter azalea pots, using equal parts of soil, peat, or leaf mold, and sand. When established, apply fertilizer every 3 to 4 weeks. Tuberous-rooted begonias do best at 13°C with high relative humidity. Spacing will prevent undue elongation. A light to moderate shade will be necessary to prevent burn of the foliage and flowers. The tuberous-rooted begonia is a long-day plant and can be lighted to extend the flowering season if desired.

Browallia *(Browallia speciosa—Solanaceae)*

This is a good plant for shady locations in the garden and in hanging baskets. The cultivars with blue to purple flowers are best known, but the white-flowered cultivars are used also.

The seed should be sown about February 1, and it germinates in 2 weeks at 21°C. The plants should be grown at 16°C.

Caladium *(Caladium* X *hortulanum—Araceae)*

This South American perennial has beautifully marked leaves rising from large tubers. The tubers are usually potted in March in 10-centimeter pots in coarse loam and one-half peat and are grown in a temperature of 18°C with bottom heat. Watering should be done sparingly until good roots develop. Later shifting to 15-centimeter pots will produce brilliant plants during summer, provided that slight shade, high humidity, and sufficient moisture at the roots are maintained.

Canna *(Canna* X *generalis—Cannaceae)*

Rhizomes may be lifted in the fall with soil adhering and stored at a temperature of 7 to 10°C until January or February. At that time the rhizomes are separated, and each piece should have at least one eye and 8 to 10 centimeters of thickened root. These are placed in sand at a temperature of 18 to 21°C, with the eyes about 3 centimeters below the surface. The sand should be kept moist, and when the leaves are 10 centimeters long and the roots well developed, the pieces may be placed in 10-centimeter pots for later sale.

Celosia *(Celosia cristata—Amaranthaceae)*

Celosias either have cockscomb-type or plume-type red or yellow flowers. They should be placed in a sunny location in the garden. The celosias are showy and attractive in the landscape and as cut flowers indoors.

The seed is sown about April 1 and germinates in $1\frac{1}{2}$ weeks at 21°C. The seedlings should be grown at 18°C.

Chrysanthemum *(Chrysanthemum* X *morifolium—Compositae)*

The chrysanthemum is being used extensively as an item for mixed or combination pots and also as a spring flowering plant to enjoy in the home and then plant in the garden to flower in the fall. The production of flowering specimens of both garden and greenhouse cultivars in small pots is covered earlier in the chapter.

Coleus *(Coleus blumei* and *Coleus* X *hybridus—Labiatae)*

Coleus are propagated by seed or stem-tip cuttings. Vegetative reproduction by means of cuttings was the primary method of producing coleus plants for many years. Either stock was maintained by individual growers so they could propagate the desired cultivars as needed, or rooted stem-tip cuttings were purchased from specialist propagators.

Plant breeders eventually developed many excellent cultivars that are reproduced by seed, and much of the coleus propagation is by means of seed obtained from specialists. The seed is germinated at 21°C and lighted.

Coleus are grown at 16°C night temperature, and about 3 months is required from sowing to marketing in small pots in the spring. Cuttings should be stuck about 1 month before time of marketing.

Cordyline *(Cordyline indivisa—Agavaceae)*

Cordyline indivisa thrives at a temperature of 10°C and is raised from seed sown in the spring. During the first season the seedlings should be grown entirely under glass, but the following summer they will make satisfactory plants if set out in the field. They should be lifted in September and potted in 10-centimeter pots. *C. indivisa* is especially valuable for points of emphasis in window boxes, hanging baskets, and urns.

Croton *(Codiaeum variegatum—Euphorbiaceae)*

These very attractive South American tropical plants are used as specimens and in combination with other plants in boxes and baskets. They are not very satisfactory house plants unless a sufficiently humid atmosphere and a high temperature are provided.

Two methods of propagation are used. Stem-tip cuttings may be taken in February and March and rooted in soil at 21°C. A fibrous soil of one-fourth sand mixed with peat is a satisfactory potting medium, if drainage is provided.

A second method of propagation consists of mossing the top growths (air-layering) and potting the plants as soon as a mass of roots forms in the moss.

High humidity and a 21°C temperature are necessary. Unless these conditions are provided, the lower leaves will drop, and unsightly specimens will result. Fluctuations in temperature are also detrimental. Shade is necessary during the summer, as well as constant care in the control of red spider and mealybugs, which are serious pests.

Dahlia *(Dahlia pinnata—Compositae)*

The small-flowered types that grow to a height of 45 to 60 centimeters are used for bedding purposes. Seed sown in early March will make plants large enough to bed out in May. In the extreme heat of summer the dahlia flowers may not develop, a condition similar to "heat delay" of chrysanthemums.

Dianthus *(Dianthus spp.—Caryophyllaceae)*

The dianthus cultivars used in the garden commonly are called pinks. Several species of dianthus can be used, but the most common ones are cultivars of *D. barbatus,* sweet william, and *D. chinensis,* rainbow pinks.

The seed germinates in 1½ weeks at 21°C. The rainbow pinks seed should be sown about February 1 for spring sales. Sweet william is a biennial, and it usually is sown in late summer for marketing the following spring.

Dusty Miller *(Senecio cineraria—Compositae)*

Various kinds of plants have been known as dusty millers through the years. They all have silvery-white leaves, and they are used as edging plants. *S. cineraria* also has been classified as *Centaurea maritima* 'Diamond' and *Cineraria maritima.*

Centaurea candissima sometimes is listed for dusty miller, but apparently the classification of that cultivar should be *S. vira-vira.*

Some dusty millers are *Chrysanthemum ptarmiciflorum,* and they also are listed as *Pyrethrum ptarmiciflorum.*

S. cineraria seed should be sown about February 1, and the seed will germinate in about 2 weeks at 24°C in long photoperiods.

Echeveria *(Echeveria secunda var. glauca—Crassulaceae)*

These succulent, glabrous, dwarf plants, native to Mexico, form compact rosettes and are used for ribbon bedding and edging.

Old plants should be lifted in the fall for stock, planted closely in deep boxes, and kept fairly dry and cool. Leaf cuttings are taken in November and December. Each leaf should be taken individually with an axillary bud and inserted in sand, which should be kept rather dry until the roots develop and the new shoot begins to show. Rooting will occur in about 4 weeks at 16°C, and the young plants will be of satisfactory size for bedding in the spring.

Echeverias often stool, forming small rosettes at the base of each stem. These may be separated from the parent plant in the fall and grown in flats in a warm house; they will be bedding size in the spring.

Flowering Maple *(Abutilon hybridum—Malvaceae)*

The flowering maple is a shrubby plant, a native of warm regions, with drooping, bell-shaped flowers ranging in color from white to crimson. Abutilons have a limited sale, but make satisfactory plants for combination boxes in the spring. Either seed or cuttings are used for propagation. Cuttings may be taken in the spring from plants lifted in September, cut back, and grown on in a temperature of 13°C. Fall propagation may also be practiced. Seed may be sown in the spring. Bottom heat is necessary for both the cuttings and the seed. Porous soil of comparatively low fertility is the most satisfactory. High nitrogen content may cause failure to flower. Pinching is necessary to secure compactness of growth.

Mealybugs, red spider, thrips, and aphids are serious pests.

Fuchsia *(Fuchsia X hybrida—Onagraceae)*

The fuchsia is often used in combination pots or porch boxes. Cuttings taken in early February will make nice 6-centimeter plants for use in May if grown at 13 to 16°C. Culture of the plants as larger specimens is covered earlier in the chapter.

Geranium *(Pelargonium X hortorum—Geraniaceae)*

The primary market for geranium plants is in the spring, and they are used for planting in the gardens. In some instances geraniums are forced at other times of the year and used as flowering plants in the home or as gifts for hospital patients, and the market demand for them has been increasing, especially in the South.

Geraniums can be propagated by seed, and this is a common method of reproduction. Geranium hybridizers have developed several cultivars which can be reproduced from seed. This has added a new dimension to the geranium-production business. The length of plant-production time is approximately the same with both methods of reproduction. However, for the plants reproduced from seed there is no need for stock plants, and this expense and work is eliminated. The area needed for propagating geraniums from seed also is much smaller than that required for propagating them from cuttings.

The geraniums grown from seed do require a more exact forcing program in order to have them in flower for the spring market: The forcing temperature must be 17°C, the plants should be treated with a growth retardant, and apparently flowering will be promoted if they are supplied long photoperiods.

There may be more shattering of florets with the geraniums grown from seed, but they flower profusely in landscape plantings. In some ways they are more satisfactory in landscape plantings than the geranium cultivars started from cuttings.

The geraniums started from seed are produced for spring sales as flowering plants in 10-centimeter pots or as smaller plants, not in flower, in packs.

Vegetative propagation by means of rooted stem cuttings is used in order to reproduce the cultivars that have the most desired growth and flowering characteristics. The majority of the plants are finished in 10-centimeter pots, though there is demand for smaller sizes. Depending on temperature and other conditions, the 10-centimeter plant will be in flower and ready for sale from 3 to 4 months after the rooted cuttings or seedlings are potted; and since most of the plants are needed from the middle of May until early June, the rooted cuttings and seedlings should be potted in January and early February. Actually, because of conditions that exist or methods that are used, some growers start their geranium plants earlier than this, particularly when they are to be used as specimens for Mother's Day.

Propagation   For propagation by rooted cuttings geranium growers must have a source of supply of cuttings, and most of these are needed in December and January. In order to supply their needs at that time, growers either maintain their own stock or get the cuttings from outside sources. Southern California weather conditions are suitable for the growth of geranium plants outdoors the year-round, and many of the geranium cuttings originate from this area. These are largely outdoor operations although the cuttings may be rooted in structures. California geranium cuttings may be furnished as unrooted, callused, or rooted cuttings, but the majority of them are shipped as unrooted or callused cuttings. Unrooted cuttings are used because of the lower cost or because growers want to root the cuttings themselves. Callused cuttings are used because there may be less loss than with unrooted cuttings, and they may become established and grow as fast as or faster than rooted cuttings.

Geranium cuttings from any source must be handled promptly to avoid leaf drop and the start of some diseases. California geranium cuttings are shipped to all parts of the country via air freight satisfactorily, but on arrival they must be unpacked and handled promptly.

Because the California geranium stock is grown outdoors, weather conditions sometimes cause delays in shipping or affect the quality of the stock. In spite of the usually ideal southern California weather, there may be periods of extreme heat in the fall which affect the growth of the plants, there is danger of frost in the winter, and cuttings cannot be shipped during rainy weather since they deteriorate rapidly in the confines of the shipping container. Disease control in outdoor areas is not as easy as in greenhouses—and disease control in geraniums is a problem even in the best conditions. The best-regulated operations treat the fields before planting, select the stock carefully, and take all possible measures to maintain disease-free stock.

A greenhouse operator in areas of the country where frosts are expected in early fall who has geranium stock plants outdoors must harvest all the cuttings from the plants before frost. This might require that the cuttings be taken as early as September in many localities. Since this is much too early to start 10-centimeter geraniums for most purposes, it is not possible to produce geraniums economically from stock grown outdoors in the North.

When geranium stock plants are grown in greenhouses, they usually are started in early summer, and the best stock is selected for this purpose. The grower who uses discarded and rejected plants from spring sales as the source for geranium stock plants invariably has poor results. The selected stock should have the best flower and growth characteristics for the cultivar and should be free from disease. The finest source for geranium stock plants is the specialist propagator who can supply cuttings from culture-indexed stock of carefully selected plants. With this source of stock, the plants usually are started in early fall.

Several methods of growing geranium stock plants in greenhouses are used, but basically they are variations of two procedures. In the first, only stem-tip cuttings are used and these are harvested periodically from fall through spring. The other procedure calls for both stem-tip and stem-section or leaf-bud cuttings (stem-section cuttings), which are harvested from late December to March. Each method has its advantages. Considerably more cuttings may be obtained per plant from the second procedure, by using about half of each type of cutting. Stem sections require a somewhat longer growing period than stem-tip cuttings to develop the same size of plants, and this may be a problem in some instances. There is a definite advantage, however, in having cuttings available in quantity at the proper time to start plants for finishing in 10-centimeter pots. The procedure used is to allow the terminal stem to continue in growth after the initial pinch, with continuous pinching of lateral stems. This produces upright growth of the plant with numerous short, lateral stems. The plants are staked to keep them erect. Approximately the first of December, the terminal stem is pinched for the first harvest of stem-tip cuttings about the middle of January. Stem tips and stem sections then are taken in February. If earlier cuttings are desired, the terminal stem is pinched correspondingly earlier. Stem-section cuttings should not be taken until there is new growth in the axils of the leaves to provide more uniform shoot development after rooting.

Geranium stock plants may be planted directly in the ground or placed in large cans or baskets. If planted in the ground, they should be spaced about 30 centimeters apart each way. The soil for the stock plants must be coarse and well drained whether the plants are in the ground or in containers. After the plants are established, they should be regularly supplied with nitrogen and potassium fertilizers.

Geranium stock plants should be given 13°C night temperatures, with day temperatures about 6°C warmer. The plants should be allowed to produce a flower after planting to verify the cultivar, but following that, the flower buds should be removed as they form. As the plants grow, large leaves form toward the base of the plants, and some of these should be removed periodically in order to improve the air movement and light for the stems in that area.

A geranium cutting should be about 10 centimeters long, but shorter cuttings can be used when stock is scarce. The cuttings may be allowed to wilt without injuring them, and if they are soft, drying the cut end by exposure to air for 6 to 12 hours reduces loss from damping-off. Only the lower leaves should be removed, to facilitate sticking. Removal of too many leaves reduces the speed of rooting and the vigor of the root system, though some space in the propagation bench may be gained. To ensure that the stock plants have sufficient leaf area to develop food for new stems, no fewer than three perfect leaves should remain on a shoot from which a cutting is taken. Not allowing enough leaf area to remain on the stock plant reduces its vitality, and cuttings taken from hard wood do not root readily. Leaf-bud cuttings are very satisfactory, but more time is required to produce a plant.

Treatment with a growth substance decreases the time required for rooting, which is usually 4 weeks. Sand is an ideal rooting soil, and it should be steamed to prevent troubles from damping-off. Vermiculite is an excellent rooting soil but can be easily overwatered. Perlite is a satisfactory soil. After the cuttings are stuck, they should be given a heavy watering and then carried somewhat on the dry side. Further watering may not be necessary for as long as 2 to 3 weeks, depending on the fineness of sand and the season; however, the cuttings should not be allowed to become so dry that they wilt severely. Cuttings can be rooted under intermittent mist, provided there are no foliage diseases and the rooting medium drains well.

Geraniums can be rooted very well directly in pots if a well-drained soil is used. Commonly, 6-centimeter peat pots are used; and after the plants are well rooted, they can be shifted directly to 10-centimeter pots.

Geranium seed is large enough so that individual seeds can be sown. It should be sown in rows about 3 centimeters apart with the seeds spaced 0.5 centimeter apart in the row. The seed should be lightly covered with soil.

The soil temperature should be 22°C, and the soil should be kept moist. A misting system can be used successfully. Germination takes place in 1 week.

The seedlings should be transplanted about 2 weeks after sowing the seed, and the forcing temperature for seedling geraniums should be 17°C. Treatment with growth regulator should be made about 2 weeks after the seedlings are transplanted.

Light Geraniums should be grown in full light and without shade of any kind, with the possible exception of bright and hot periods in late spring when the plants are in flower. A light shade at that time will maintain good flower color or prevent burning of flowers of the softer varieties.

It has been demonstrated that flowering in geraniums grown from seed is promoted in long photoperiods.

Temperature   A night temperature of 13°C with day temperatures about 6°C higher should be used for geraniums grown from cuttings, and if faster growth and flowering are desired, 16°C night temperatures may be used to good advantage. Geraniums from seed are grown at 17°C. Growers who attempt to produce geraniums at the 10°C or lower night temperatures which may be used for other bedding plants find that the flowering and growth of geraniums are very slow at that temperature, and the leaves may be bronzed or edged with red.

Soil, Moisture, and Fertilizer   A porous, well-drained soil should be used for geraniums, and this is usually best supplied by adding chopped straw or peat moss. The soil should be tested before use, and if phosphorus or calcium is low, it should be incorporated into the soil before potting by adding superphosphate and dolomitic limestone or calcium sulfate.

When geraniums are irrigated and fertilized properly and regularly as required, growth and development of the plants are rapid and of good quality. Irrigation can be done with the small-plastic-tube system, which saves much labor and also keeps moisture off leaves and flowers, thus reducing the possibilities of disease. When phosphorus and calcium are incorporated into the soil before potting, fertilizers containing nitrogen and potassium should be used regularly after the plants are established in the small pots. Supplying fertilizer by means of an injector with each irrigation is an excellent method for maintaining the required quantities of minerals in the soil. Some florists believe use of nitrogenous fertilizers prevents flowering, but failure to flower in winter is generally due to poor light conditions.

Air   Apparently the quantity of carbon dioxide in the greenhouse air in the winter and early spring is not enough for the best growth and development of geraniums. The maintainance of carbon dioxide at 500 to 750 ppm has produced faster growth and flowering of 10-centimeter plants and a greater number of cuttings from stock plants. The amount of benefit from the additional amounts of carbon dioxide will depend on the amount of light, minerals, and water that are available to the plants.

Geraniums also benefit from adequate ventilation and air movement. This helps to limit infestations of *Botrytis cinerea* and the occurrence of edema by decreasing the air moisture (humidity) in the vicinity of the plants.

Figure 6-16 Geraniums appear to be one of the most responsive plants to increased quantities of carbon dioxide in the atmosphere, resulting in faster growth and earlier flowering. *(Yoder Bros., Inc. photograph.)*

Potting and Spacing Geraniums may be rooted directly in pots; and when this is done, it is usually in 6-centimeter peat pots set pot to pot. Within 1 month after the cuttings are stuck, either the pots should be spaced or the plants repotted.

Geraniums in 6-centimeter pots are set pot to pot until they are established. They should then be shifted to 10-centimeter pots within 1 month. It is also possible to place rooted cuttings and seedlings directly into 10-centimeter pots, but care must be exercised in watering in the early stages while the plant is becoming established.

Plants in 10-centimeter pots may be set for final spacing after potting, or they may be set pot to pot and then spaced out as the plants grow. If the space is available, the advantages in setting them at the final spacing immediately are that the plants are assured of good light conditions (no shading from adjoining plants) and that the labor of spacing the pots is eliminated. The finish spacing of 10-centimeter pots should be about 15 centimeters, which is four pots per 900 square centimeters of bench. Some adjustment must be made for bench widths that do not accommodate the correct number of pots across the bench for that spacing.

Troubles Edema is a common problem in geraniums, and it is identified by the corky areas that develop on the undersides of leaves and occasionally on leaf petioles or the stems of plants. The cause of edema is a surplus of water in plants which are in humid conditions and do not transpire enough moisture to the surrounding air. The development of edema will cease with lower humidity, and this usually can be accomplished simply by providing more ventilation and better air circulation. Irrigating in the morning rather than in the afternoon will help also.

Diseases The most prevalent disease of geraniums throughout the country is botrytis blight caused by *Botrytis cinerea.* This pathogen exists primarily on older plant tissues such as older florets at the center of the flower, lower leaves, and fallen or discarded portions of plants. The most common symptoms are petal or leaf spots or rots that are brown in color and often irregularly shaped. The botrytis organism also may produce stem rot in geraniums. Usually this starts in a cut or damaged area or at the place on stems where leaves or flowers are removed. In a moist atmosphere the involved area may be covered with a mass of gray spores. Spores of *Botrytis cinerea* are very common in greenhouse environments; however, their incidence is reduced considerably if plant refuse and trash are not allowed to accumulate in the greenhouse or around it. The spores germinate and grow rapidly on moist surfaces of the plants; thus, keeping moisture from the leaves and flowers by careful irrigation practices, good ventilation, and adequate spacing is an essential means of control.

The stem rot disease of geraniums caused by *Pythium* spp. is called blackleg, and this is appropriate as the involved area typically is coal-black in color. The propagation area, soil, containers, tools, and handling equipment must be thoroughly sterilized if this pathogen is to be controlled, and cuttings must not be taken from infected plants as the disease organism may accompany the cuttings.

Bacterial stem rot and leaf spot are caused by *Xanthomonas pelargonii,* and it may produce dark-brown, rotted areas on the stem or circular spots on the leaves which enlarge into irregularly shaped areas followed by the wilting and death of the leaf or the entire plant. Because this pathogen can be transmitted with the cuttings, it is very important to know that the source of cuttings is not infected. The best method for making this determination is a detailed laboratory procedure known as culture-indexing. Not every cutting is cultured, but the stock from which the cuttings are taken is cultured and then handled in such a way that the cuttings are free of this pathogen. The use of cuttings from culture-indexed stock must be coupled with strict sanitary measures to keep the cuttings from being infected subsequently with disease organisms of any kind.

Although possibly less common than other stem rot diseases of geraniums, stem rot produced by *Rhizoctonia solani* does occur. It is a soil-borne organism, and thorough steaming of soil, benches, tools, and handling equipment is essential for control. Typically a brown rotted area develops on the stem at the soil line, followed by wilting of the plant and death.

There are several virus diseases of geraniums, and their control lies primarily in the selection of virus-free stock for cuttings. This can be done quite successfully by careful and systematic observation of the visual symptoms of the plants to be used for stock. Virus-free stock can be produced by means of tissue culture.

Pests Ordinary control measures usually are sufficient to keep pests in check on geraniums. Geraniums are infested with some of the pests that are common on other crops, and in addition they are sometimes troubled by two pests that are rather rare. Termites may tunnel in the stems, causing wilting and possibly toppling of the stems. Because termites may inhabit wooden structures and then transfer to the geraniums, replacing wooden benches with concrete or transite can remove the source of this trouble.

The geranium plume moth is a pest of more recent origin. The adult is a small, tan-colored moth, and it lays its eggs on the undersides of leaves. The young caterpillars burrow into flower buds, leaves, and stems.

Pinching and Cropping In many marketing areas the customers demand that geranium plants have at least one flower on them at the time of sale; therefore, the plants must be started and handled in such a way that they are not only large enough and well-shaped but also in flower when they are marketed. The rate of growth and flowering of geraniums is dependent on many factors. Aside from the cultivars that are used, the temperature in which the plants are grown and the amount of sunlight that is available are responsible for their rate of growth and flowering. Because of the variability of the weather, many growers start their geraniums earlier than required for average weather conditions so that the plants will be in flower in time if the light and temperatures are below normal. If the weather conditions are above average, rapid development and flowering of the plants may not be a problem, as the first flower can be removed when it is too old and the second flower may be at the right stage of development at the time of sale.

Geraniums may or may not be pinched, depending on the cultivar and the type of desired growth. Some cultivars branch well without pinching if they are given sufficient space. Geraniums from seed usually are not pinched. Generally a branched plant is most desirable, and if the cultivar does not branch readily, it should be pinched. If just the tip of the plant is removed (soft pinch), the plants may be pinched as late as March 1 for flowering before Memorial Day. In some instances it may be worthwhile to remove enough of the stem tip in making the pinch so that the tip can be used for a cutting (hard pinch). When this is done, approximately 8 centimeters of the tip is removed, allowing at least two leaves to remain on the stem. Geraniums to be flowered before Memorial Day should be hard-pinched by February 1 as shoot development is not as fast after a hard pinch as after a soft pinch.

Globe Amaranth *(Gomphrena globosa—Amarantaceae)*

Gomphrena grows rather slowly as a small plant; hence seed should be sown in late January or early February for sales in May as well-developed plants. The night temperature should never be less than 13°C. Gomphrena does well in hot weather.

Impatiens *(Impatiens wallerana—Balsaminaceae)*

This is a revised classification for the garden impatiens. Formerly they were classed as *Impatiens sultani,* and they commonly were known as sultanas.

These impatiens grow and flower very well in shady locations in the garden, and for that reason their use in landscape plantings has increased. Also, many excellent cultivars have been developed by hybridization. The species impatiens were commonly propagated by means of stem-tip cuttings, but most of the hybrid cultivars are reproduced from seed.

Impatiens seed is sown about mid-February, and it germinates in 3 weeks at 21°C in long photoperiod. The seedlings should be grown at 16°C.

More recently some cultivars of *I. hawkeri* (commonly called New Guinea impatiens) have been introduced for use as landscape plantings. These cultivars have been selected for leaf color or variegation as well as flower color, and several cultivars have been developed by hybridization. These impatiens are reproduced by means of stem-tip cuttings.

The New Guinea impatiens may be used in sunny locations in the garden.

Iresine *(Iresine herbstii* and *I. lindenii—Amarantaceae)*

Iresines are South American herbs with red foliage, used largely for borders and ribbon bedding. Their culture is similar to that of coleus.

Lantana *(Lantana camara—Verbenaceae)*

This native of southern United States is a very showy shrubby plant, useful for spring sales and for bedding. The stock plants should be lifted and potted in September, pruned back, and carried in a cool house of 4°C. Specimen plants will be produced, and they will bloom in May. Ordinarily, cuttings are taken early in the fall from outdoor plants or from the potted stock plants grown in a warm house. Softwood cuttings root easily in sand or sand and peat, provided bottom heat of 18°C is supplied and transpiration is reduced to a minimum. Cuttings usually root in 3 to 4 weeks. They are generally pinched and will be flowering in 6-centimeter pots approximately 6 to 8 weeks after pinching. The plants do best in medium-heavy soil and a temperature of not less than 16°C. Red spider, mealybugs, thrips, and whitefly are troublesome pests.

Lobelia *(Lobelia erinus—Lobeliaceae)*

The lobelias are used mainly in edgings but also in hanging baskets. They are known primarily for their intense blue or purple flowers, but cultivars with white flowers also are available.

The seed is sown February 1 and germinates in 3 weeks at 21°C. The seedlings should be grown at 10°C.

Marigold *(Tagetes X hybridus—Compositae)*

The French, or dwarf, marigold is especially useful for bedding purposes or combination pots. The tall African kinds are cut-flower types. Seed of the French marigold cultivars sown in early January will be in flower in 6-centimeter pots in April, while sowings made February 1 will flower in early May in 6-centimeter pots. For Memorial Day, an early March sowing is satisfactory.

Most French marigolds do not flower well during extremely warm days, and as a result they often stop flowering in late July and early August. This is probably similar to heat delay with chrysanthemums. Flowers appear in profusion in cooler weather and continue until frost.

Nicotiana *(Nicotiana alata—Solanaceae)*

Flowering tobacco makes an attractive background plant in the garden. In addition, hummingbirds are attracted to them. Flowers are either pink or white.

It is marketed not in flower in small pots or packs. The seed is sown in mid-March and germinates in 2 weeks in long photoperiods.

Pansy *(Viola X wittrockiana—Violaceae)*

Pansies are very useful for early bedding. Seed is sown in August, and the seedlings are transplanted to cold frames about 15 centimeters apart each way in September. An application of a complete fertilizer is desirable after the plants are established. The plants can be mulched with straw after cold weather begins and a cold-frame sash can be placed over them, but it should be covered to prevent winter sun from heating the frame and causing the plants to start growing too early. The mulch may be removed in March, and the plants will be in flower in early spring.

Petunia *(Petunia* X *hybrida—Solanaceae)*

Petunias are one of the most popular bedding plants grown from seed. There are good reasons for this, as they are available in a wide range of colors and they make a maximum show with a minimum of care in the garden.

Significant advances have been made in recent years in breeding petunias, and excellent F₁ hybrids have been produced in all colors and classes. The F₁ hybrids are used almost exclusively, as the flower and growth characteristics are much better than those of the selfed cultivars. Petunias are classed by some of their flower characteristics. The grandifloras are the large-flowered cultivars and the multifloras have smaller flowers but a greater number of them. There are single and double forms of both these classes. The California giants have huge flowers, and they are single only. It is the single grandifloras and the single multifloras which are used in quantity in landscape plantings.

Propagation Petunias are propagated by seed. Because the seed is tiny, it must be sown on the surface of the propagating soil, which should be finely screened to assure good contact with the seed. At 21°C, petunias will germinate in about 1 week. Some petunia cultivars must receive light before they will germinate, but this usually is not a problem as the seed should be sown on the surface of the medium where light is available. Uniform moisture conditions must be provided for the germination of petunia seed; and since the seed is on the surface, the seed flat must be misted regularly or covered. After germination the temperature should be maintained at 16°C, and the seedlings should be transplanted promptly when the first true leaves develop.

Light Petunias are affected by day length as well as by the quantity of light they receive. After the plants are pricked off from the seed flats, they should be grown in full sunlight. Petunias in shaded locations will be tall and have stems of small diameter.

Petunias in short day lengths—10 hours or less—produce short, compact, branched plants that do not flower rapidly. In long days—13 hours or longer—they develop a single elongated stem and flower early. The temperatures at which the plants are grown also affect the nature of the growth. The petunias that are sown early in the spring—January and February—are in naturally short day lengths in their early stages of growth and can be expected to develop as compact, well-branched plants. Plants that are started in March and later in natural conditions may be elongated, single-stem plants which flower early because of the long day lengths at that time. If tall, single-stem petunias have been a problem, consideration should be given to providing short days (10 hours or less) artificially for about 1 month after the plants are pricked off, or the plants can be soft-pinched to induce branching.

Temperature Growth and development of petunias will be best if they are in 16°C night temperatures for about 1 month after transplanting, followed by 10°C night temperatures until they are sold. Many petunias are grown at 10°C with cooler night temperatures after transplanting. This produces short, compact, well-branched plants, but flowering is delayed and the plants develop slowly after they are planted in the garden.

It is possible to grow petunias in a shorter period of time if 16°C night temperatures are used continuously; but if this is done, artificially short days and growth substances may need to be used in order to produce short and well-branched plants.

Cropping Petunias may be grown in pots for use individually or in packs or flats for general bedding purposes. The potted petunias are used more commonly in early May for Mother's Day gifts, either alone or in combination planters with other garden plants. The doubles, the California giants, and the larger grandifloras are most popular for these purposes. They may be finished in 6- or 8-centimeter pots depending on how they will be used. If the plants are grown in 10°C night temperatures, the seed should be sown about December 15 to have the plants in flower for early May. When warmer temperatures are used, the seed may be sown later. The petunia seedlings may be transplanted directly from the seed flats to the pots in which they will be finished, but if they are to be finished in 8-centimeter pots, they may be pricked off to flats first and then transplanted to the pots.

Petunias that are to be sold in packs or from flats should be sown from mid-February to mid-March if they are grown at 10°C night temperatures. If they are grown at warmer temperatures, they may be sown later, and cooler temperatures require earlier sowing.

Phlox *(Phlox drummondii—Polemoniaceae)*

Several different species of phlox can be used in the garden, but it is this annual kind that is of concern with greenhouse bedding plants.

Phlox seed is sown mid-March and germinates in $1\frac{1}{2}$ weeks at 18°C.

Salvia *(Salvia splendens—Labiatae)*

Scarlet sage is the common name for salvia. Several cultivars are available in various shades of red. There also are height variations.

The seed is sown March 1 and germinates in 2 weeks in long photoperiods. The seedlings should be grown at 13°C.

Santolina *(Santolina chamaecyparissus—Compositae)*

Santolina is a half-hardy, silver-foliaged plant, a native of Mediterranean regions. It is very useful for edging, enduring much shearing and withstanding dry conditions. Cuttings made in the fall will produce excellent plants in 6-centimeter pots by spring if grown at 10°C.

Snapdragon *(Antirrhinus majus—Scophulariaceae)*

Several snapdragon cultivars have been developed by hybridization for use in garden plantings. They can be enjoyed as cut flowers indoors as well as in the landscape outdoors.

The seed should be sown February 15; it germinates in $1\frac{1}{2}$ weeks at 21°C.

Verbena *(Verbena X hybrida—Verbenaceae)*

Though verbenas can be sown in early March for spring sales, better plants with several flowers may be had by sowing in early February and carrying at 13°C. Pinching will make compact, bushy plants of the taller grandiflora types, although naturally dwarf cultivars are available.

Vinca *(Catharanthus roseus and Vinca major—Apocynaceae)*

The common periwinkle *Catharanthus roseus (Vinca rosea)* is an annual with white, pink, or red flowers, a very useful bedding plant which withstands extremes of heat and dryness well. Since the plant grows slowly when small, seed should be sown along with gomphrena.

V. major is a common vine, or trailing plant, which is used for window boxes and hanging baskets. The plants are propagated by cuttings with two buds, made in September; when rooted, they are potted in light soil in 6-centimeter pots and shifted to 8-centimeter pots in January. As they grow, they are usually placed on the edge of the bench so that the pendulous growths can hang down. A temperature of 10°C is desirable. Plants propagated in the spring may be lined out in the field, then lifted in the fall and potted in 8- or 10-centimeter pots, producing bushy specimens by May.

Zinnia *(Zinnia elegans—Compositae)*

Zinnias are very popular plants for use in the garden. They develop rapidly, however, from seed sown directly in the garden, and for that reason the number of zinnia plants produced as bedding plants in the greenhouse is relatively small.

The seed should be sown April 1; it germinates in 1 week at 21°C. The seedlings should be grown at 10°C.

7 Marketing

Flowers and plants are purchased by the public in various types of retail outlets: flower stores which handle only flowers, plants, and accessories; retail greenhouses; and general retail stores which handle flowers and plants in addition to many other types of merchandise. The flower store is the most common retail outlet for flowers and plants. Flower stores vary considerably in size and capabilities, but they should be able to take care of any request from selling a single flower to handling the largest wedding. They produce nothing, and all their merchandise is therefore purchased for resale. Flowers and plants are purchased from wholesale commission florists or directly from wholesale greenhouse operators. Flower shop proprietors may visit the wholesale store or the greenhouse in order to obtain supplies, they may order by telephone, or they may purchase from trucks operated on regular routes by the wholesalers. Most retailers use all methods of procurement at various times. In many instances the holiday pot plants are bought directly from the grower.

It is possible to get into the retail flower business with a minimum amount of capital, information, and ability. That many do get into it is illustrated by the fact that in most market areas approximately 50 percent of the entire retail business is done by about 10 percent of the retail florists. The ill-prepared and the lazy do not stand a chance of success in the flower business. This is a dynamic affair in which the manager must not only like to smell the flowers and work with them but must have real ability in presenting them for sale, as well as being a shrewd purchasing agent, a clever advertiser, a good manager of personnel and money, a sound merchandiser, and an adept credit manager. There are many opportunities in the retail flower business for industrious individuals who are well schooled in business principles as well as in some of the arts of handling flowers.

Retail greenhouses operate in much the same way as retail shops, except that they produce a portion of their own merchandise. The retail greenhouse is probably even more useful in the display of plants, particularly for the holidays, and in the perpetuation of the belief that all the flowers are "greenhouse fresh" even though they may have been purchased through the same wholesale channels as the retail store operator uses. Most retail florists, whether they have only a shop or a shop and a greenhouse, are associated with one of the national or international services through which flowers and plants can be supplied readily to any part of the country or world. A considerable portion of the retail florist's business is a result of the flowers-by-wire services.

Most of the flowers and plants sold by retail florists are special-occasion flowers—for holidays, funerals, weddings, anniversaries, and special events. Only a very small share of the florist's total sales are flowers for the home for everyday uses.

The general stores which commonly handle flowers and plants in addition to other items are either grocery stores or variety stores. Usually they do not have a complete florist's service. They do not design funeral pieces or install decorations, but they may have pot plants or packaged flowers which can be carried conveniently by the customer. The flowers and plants purchased in these outlets are largely used in the customers' homes rather than for gifts. These stores may carry a general line of foliage plants most of the time with special promotions periodically in packaged flowers or pot plants, or they may have pot plants primarily for the holidays. They usually buy directly from the wholesale growers. The local growers may service individual stores in the vicinity, or, in the case of chain stores, the grower may deliver only to the warehouse for distribution from that point.

Producers are vitally concerned with flower and plant sales. It is not being too practical to acknowledge that producers are in business to make a profit. In order to do this, they must not only produce the right product in quantity, but must make sure that it is marketed in such a way that they get the best return. Various methods may be used successfully, but regardless of the method growers must spend as much time on the sales portion of the business as on the production end, if not more.

Retail growers are in a difficult position. They wear two hats, and very often the head under the producer's hat is too generous to the head under the store operator's hat. Somehow procedures must be established so that the produce from the greenhouses is "sold" to the store. Usually the retail greenhouse production should be scheduled so that small quantities of a large selection of flowers are produced continuously. This makes sensible marketing possible as the retail shop may be expected to "buy" the entire production each day and supplement its needs with plants and cut flowers from wholesale florists. The retail grower who schedules large quantities of a single crop periodically not only makes profitable marketing impossible for the crop but may ruin sales for wholesale growers who supply that item regularly. Some retail growers try squeeze-play marketing in which they insist that unless the wholesaler can move some of their excess crop, they may transfer future purchases for their shop to another wholesaler. No one gains by this sort of merchandising, and responsible wholesalers will not become involved in it.

Some retail growers have developed single crops which they produce well and market profitably. This is possible only because the grower carefully surveyed the market and knew that there would be a ready demand for the crop at the time of maturity.

Wholesale growers may elect to sell their produce directly to retail florists or other retail outlets, or they may use a sales agency. There are several variations of each type of marketing. Throughout the country pot plants are more generally marketed directly than are cut flowers. Because of the difficulty in packaging and the weight, it usually is considered that pot plants must be marketed locally. Notable exceptions to this are the direct marketing of pot mums from Florida and California to several areas of the country.

The sales agencies generally used by the growers are wholesale commission houses to which the produce is consigned. The flowers are offered for sale together with flowers consigned from other growers, and periodically the commission house submits report of sales and dumpage to the grower together with payment for the flowers sold, less the commission. Some wholesale commission houses operate separately and have no direct connection with any producer. Several large producers of flowers and plants have established wholesale commission houses in which they sell their own produce as well as stock consigned from other greenhouses.

Some of the exceptions to the standard marketing patterns are the Boston and San Francisco markets and the cooperatives in Colorado. In

Consignment Report

PHONE 585-5365

A. RASMUSSEN & SON, Inc.

715 S. SEVENTH STREET
LOUISVILLE, KENTUCKY 40203

TOTAL SALES	1929 10
COMMISSION 20	385 82
NET SALES	1543 28
EXPRESS	—
	—
ALLIED	15 43
REMITTANCE	1527 85

SOLD FOR

John Doe Co.,
250 E.Main St.,
Anywhere,U.S.A.

REPORT ANY ERRORS IMMEDIATELY

DATE	Pomps	Mums	Fuji Mums	Snaps	EXPRESS
CARRIED OVER	73	25			
10-4	162 bu	600	7 dz	28 dz	
10-5		150			
10-6	119	600	10	21	
10-7	173	700	9		
10-10	176	800	9	26	
TOTAL RECEIPTS	703	2875	35	75	
SALES	578	2848	35	67	
THROWN OUT	16	5	0	0	
ON HAND	109	22	0	8	

10-4	107	134 75	558	195 30	7	24 50	25	50 00
10-5	32	40 00	192	67 20			3	6 00
10-6	144	177 25	619	216 65	10	35 00	21	41 75
10-7	96	114 75	688	240 80	8	28 00		
10-8	35	41 75	2 no chg		1	3 50		
10-10	164	169 00	789	276 15	9	31 50	18	35 25
	578	677 50	2848	996 10	35	122 50	67	133 00

CARRIED FORWARD

GROWER NO.	REPORT FOR PERIOD ENDING
51	10-10-66

Figure 7-1 **Consignment report from wholesale commission house to grower. Usually the report and the remittance are made weekly.**

Boston the growers cooperate to the extent of establishing a market area which all use and of providing the general management of the building, but individual growers lease the stall space they desire and maintain sales representatives for their own crops. In San Francisco many of the growers sell their own flowers from stalls in a common marketplace frequented by wholesale as well as retail sellers. Some of the growers in the Denver area formed cooperatives primarily for marketing flowers, although they do some purchasing through the cooperative and also obtain some other services. These were primarily one-crop sale organizations which sold carnations, but they now have diversified. They may sell to various wholesale commission houses, but much of their effort is geared to making sales directly to retail florists throughout the country.

The auction type of marketing used in some areas of Europe appears to have some advantages for the producer—advantages which are lacking in marketing methods used in the United States. It is at the auctions that the wholesale merchants obtain the stock which they will sell to the retailers. The growers bring their flowers and plants to the market early in the morning, the grade is verified by an official, and the stock is identified by lot number and placed on display. The auction proceeds rapidly; the flowers are brought in by lot, the clock is started at a price known to be too high, the wholesalers watch from tiered seats, and the first wholesaler to press a button, stopping the progress of the clock, purchases the lot. The clock indicates the price and buyer, and the auction starts on the next lot. Because the wholesale merchants can view all the flowers and then compete with all the other merchants in buying, the price is readily established by supply and demand, and the best-quality flowers receive the top price. The psychology of going from the high price down is good. There is no second chance to buy that lot of flowers; the first merchant to press the button makes the purchase. The clock moves rapidly, leaving little time for contemplation. Merchants know very well that if they want a specific lot of flowers, they must have fast button-fingers or go without. There are, no doubt, some undesirable features of marketing by auction, but it does appear to be an excellent method for selling flowers to wholesalers. After the buyers have purchased the flowers which they need at the auction, they sell them to retailers in much the same way as is done in this country.

Growers who specialize in the production of certain types of plants may sell their product to other growers through companies variously termed brokers, jobbers, or dealers. Such items as rooted cuttings of a wide variety of plants (chrysanthemums, carnations, poinsettias, foliage, and many others), quiescent plants (roses, azaleas, hydrangeas, etc.), and other kinds of plant material can be sold and distributed from one grower to another. Jobbers have sales representatives soliciting the growers, and the plant material is shipped direct from producer to grower without passing through the hands of the jobber who collects a commission for acting as sales agent. A few items—bulb stock and flower and vegetable seeds—may be purchased by jobbers for distribution, and jobbers may also handle supplies needed by growers in production of floral crops. These include pest-control materials, fertilizers and injectors for their application, tools, shading fabric, and a host of other items which are generally purchased directly by the jobber.

MARKETING THROUGH WHOLESALE COMMISSION HOUSES

Some growers have the time, ability, and facilities to sell flowers as well as produce them, but many need the marketing help which is available in the wholesale commission houses throughout the country. The wholesale commission houses receive flowers and plants from growers on consignment, sell them to retail florists, and then periodically pay the grower, subtracting a commission for their services.

All the wholesale commission houses carry a complete line of cut flowers, and in addition some of them also have pot plants and retail shop supplies. Very often some of the wholesalers in a locality specialize in certain items. One house may be best known for roses, another for greens, and another for supplies. Most wholesale houses carry as complete a line as possible in order to take care of all the needs of each retailer.

The earliest wholesale commission houses obtained flowers only from local growers for sale to local retailers, but as shipping facilities improved, flowers came to be shipped in from various areas of the country. The development of railroads throughout the country made it possible to ship flowers successfully for several hundred miles. Later, as air freight service became available and refrigerated and insulated truck shipping was started, it became possible to ship anywhere in the United States rapidly and economically. Transportation of flowers via air freight has become more commonplace and is likely to increase from South America, Central America, Israel and Holland. In addition to the general line of flowers the wholesale house may obtain from local growers, they may ship in from other areas of the United States: spray chrysanthemums and gladiolus from Florida; carnations from New England, Colorado, or California; roses from California, the East Coast, or various locations in the Midwest; greens from Oregon and Washington; and orchids from a few widely separated growers in various parts of the country. Orchids may also be shipped from as far away as Australia.

Usually the commission house managers attempt to procure the best local stock and supplement it with flowers obtained from other sources. In order to do this they must successfully market all the crops from the best growers so that the growers will continue to consign to the same commission house. Close cooperation is required between grower and wholesale house manager so that crops will be produced at the right times. The grower must know the market demands for the flowers, and the manager must be advised regularly of the kind and amount of flowers which the grower will have available. Only under pure happenstance will grower and wholesaler be able to work together successfully on any other basis. Actually the grower in planning the production in the greenhouse must base it on the market demand for those crops, and the best source of this information is the manager of the wholesale house. If there is no apparent market for the crops, other flowers in greater demand should be grown or a plan for development of the market should be in hand.

Consignment of flowers has good and bad features. Wholesalers probably stock more flowers than they would if they had to purchase them outright for resale—and having them on hand may cause greater quantities to be sold. Sometimes more flowers are sent to the market than can possibly be sold, and this usually depresses the price. There probably would not be too many flowers on hand if they were purchased by rather than consigned to the wholesaler. The consignment system is a bit too cozy for many individuals. It can produce a false feeling of well-being for both grower and wholesaler, with the unfortunate result that neither really works at selling flowers. This does not occur among alert, aggressive, or ambitious growers or sellers.

A grower who consigns flowers to a wholesale commission house really is hiring the wholesaler to be the sales agent for the crops. This relationship must be understood by both parties, and the grower must hold the wholesaler responsible for the desired results. In practice, some wholesalers become retailers' purchasing agents, and the growers must be close enough to the marketing situation to know whether they are being fairly served.

Some of the most successful growers use controlled consignment in which they set the minimum price for which their flowers can be sold, and request that all unsold lots be returned to them rather than dumped. This system may work well if the grower has top-quality stock and keeps well informed on market conditions.

There is a trend away from the consignment system and toward the purchase of flowers by wholesalers. This has good features for both producers and sellers. When the flowers are purchased, the producer becomes directly involved in the transaction. The relationship between producer and wholesaler is more clear-cut and generally better understood by both parties. Producers sell their own flowers, and their customers are wholesalers. The producers set the price, and the wholesalers either buy or decline, depending on the need, quality, and price. Having purchased the flowers, the wholesalers then establish a resale price based on purchase price and attempt to sell them to their retail store customers. This is a business procedure that places price setting and responsibility for sales in the hands of the producers. The wholesalers actually are customers in this procedure, rather than sales agents as is in consignment selling.

The practice of selling flowers to wholesalers arose among many of the California and Florida producers when they started in business, and it has since spread to some other areas. It is possible that some wholesalers do not stock as many flowers obtained by purchase as they would if the flowers were obtained by consignment, and prices may be higher. Of course, if all flowers were sold to wholesalers, the indiscriminate and blind shipping that some large producers practice in consignment selling would be eliminated.

Flowers are sold at wholesale commission houses directly to retailers visiting the market, by means of the telephone, or via truck routes which bring the stock to the retail shop. The methods used vary considerably in different areas. There was a time when the retailers made all their purchases while visiting the market early each morning. With improvements in communication and transportation, however, the retailers' buying procedures have changed. Some retailers make all their flower purchases by telephone or from trucks which stop at their shops two or three times a week. This places much responsibility on the salespeople using the telephone, as they must be the eyes and nose of the customers and cause them to be as stimulated as they would be by a trip to the market. In most wholesale houses each sales representative maintains a list of his or her customers and calls them several times a week to keep them advised of market conditions and incidentally make some sales. Depending on the size of the operation, the telephone company may be able to suggest improvements in telephone equipment and the use of it.

Whenever possible, the wholesaler establishes the truck route so that most of the load is sold before the truck starts on its trip. Some additional stock may be carried on the truck in anticipation of additional sales, but truck routes cannot be operated successfully on speculative sales. Some of the trucks bring flowers back to the market from greenhouses along their route for sale the next day.

When the flowers arrive at the wholesale commission house in the morning, they are unpacked and identified with the grower's number. (The grower is assigned a number when starting consignment to a particular wholesale store which is used for any stock brought in.) When a sale is made, the grower's number, as well as a description of the flowers and the price, appears on the sales slip; thus a record is maintained for each grower's stock. Various methods of display are used, depending on the type of flowers and the customs of the area. Since most of the stock should be sold within a few hours after it is received by the wholesaler, the flowers may be laid on tables, except that roses are commonly placed in vases of water in refrigerators. By late morning the flowers which remain unsold are placed in vases of water in refrigerators. The refrigerator is an integral part of the wholesale house. It makes it possible to keep flowers in much better condition. The walk-in refrigerator has been a big aid to proper handling of flowers, and more recently see-in refrigerators make it possible for salespeople stationed at telephones outside the refrigerators to see and describe the flowers within the refrigerators to their customers. Most of the refrigerators are operated at

4 to 7°C, but for longer-term storage some of them may be kept at 1 to 2°C. The minimum temperature for orchids is 10°C, to prevent chilling damage.

A minimum amount of wrapping and boxing is required for flowers which are purchased and taken from the market by the retailer. Flowers which are to be shipped require better protection. They must be packed well enough so that they can be stacked with other cartons and not damaged if weight is placed on them or if they are tossed about. They must be given adequate protection from extreme temperatures. In warm weather, if refrigerated transportation is not available, crushed ice should be packed with the flowers, and the carton should be insulated to retain the cool temperatures around the flowers. In cold weather the cartons must be well insulated to prevent freezing. In spite of the best packing, the flowers will be safe from freezing for only a few minutes if the carton is placed in low temperatures. Great care must be taken in selecting the best means of transportation. Many times the temperatures on the vehicle are satisfactory, but the carton may be left too long in extreme temperatures on a loading dock.

Local deliveries are usually adequately controlled by the wholesaler's own personnel, so that damage in transportation is negligible. Shipping to neighboring towns is best handled by bus as this service is available in communities of any size and is rapid. Long-distance shipping may be done with good results via either air freight or insulated and refrigerated and heated truck.

Truck routes operated by wholesale commission houses use insulated and refrigerated and heated trucks so that the flowers are protected from temperature extremes at all times of the year. Some of the flowers are transported in vases of water, and all of them must be packed in such a way that they will remain in good condition yet be available for delivery along the route.

Some wholesale commission houses sell supplies as well as flowers, others handle no supplies, and a few sell only staple supplies such as ribbon and wire. It is possible that a good line of supplies increases the potential customers for flowers. If the supplies can be handled at a profit, there is a definite advantage in having them for sale. Actually the supply business is quite different from the flower business. The merchandise is purchased rather than consigned, and for a complete line of supplies a few hundred thousand dollars may be tied up in supply inventory. These are nonperishable items with an unlimited shelf life, but many of them remain on the shelf too long because fashions or fads change rapidly. Some wholesalers believe the supply stock must be turned over three times a year in order to have a sound business. Thus an inventory of $100,000 should develop at least $300,000 worth of supply business a year.

The rate of commission on consigned flowers is 20 to 25 percent of the selling price. Most wholesalers report to their growers once a week, declaring the amount of flowers sold and dumped, the amount of commission being withheld, and the net return to the grower.

SELLING DIRECTLY FROM THE WHOLESALE GREENHOUSE TO THE RETAIL SHOP

At the local level direct selling is practiced more often with pot plants than it is with cut flowers. Some pot-plant growers deliver plants as they are ordered within a 80-kilometer distance of their greenhouse. Others operate regularly scheduled truck routes within about 160 kilometers of their greenhouse. In some instances the retailers come to the greenhouse to select their plants and transport them to their shop.

It has been considered generally that pot plants are too heavy and difficult to package for long-distance shipping; however, larger trucks, better roads, and insulated and refrigerated and heated truck facilties have made it possible to ship pot plants very nearly across the country economically.

Locally, cut flowers are not sold directly as a standard practice, but large quantities of flowers are sold directly from several areas of the country, such as spray mums and gladiolus from Florida, carnations and roses from Denver, and standard mums, carnations, and roses from the San Francisco area. The selling is handled by long-distance telephone, and transportation is by air freight or insulated and refrigerated and heated truck.

PREPARATION OF FLOWERS FOR MARKET

The sales potential for some of the best-grown crops can be ruined simply by the way the flowers are presented for marketing. The most successful growers prepare the flowers for market very carefully in order to realize the best possible price. This starts with cutting the flowers at the right stage of maturity. Keeping quality and the general display value of the flower may be greatly affected by the stage of development at which it is cut. The right time to cut varies with the kind of flower; some are cut in tight bud, and others when they are fully developed. The time of cutting must be determined by the effect on the usefulness of the flower. There is a common tendency to cut flowers too soon when the market demand is good, and too late when the demand is low.

Flowers must be graded so that those of the same kind and quality are bunched together. Various grading procedures have been used or proposed, and there has been some acceptance of standard grades as proposed by the Society of American Florists. Any grading procedure is only as good as the integrity of the individuals using it. Many growers have developed their own grading procedures and standards through the years and used them successfully in presenting their flowers for marketing. Such growers will use standard grades successfully, too, when they are adopted. Growers who use standard grade labeling in name but not actually in practice will not benefit the industry or themselves. The standards must be established for each kind of flower because of the different qualities involved, but regardless of kind, the flowers must be fresh, not diseased or malformed, and cut at the right stage of development. Then grading standards are based on size of flower, length of stem, strength of stem, and other qualities which may pertain to specific kinds of flowers.

Methods of bunching flowers vary with the growers and the market areas. Generally the wholesale bunch contains either 12 or 25 units depending on the flower. Roses are placed in bunches of 13 or 25, carnations are bunched 25 in a pack, and snapdragons and standard mums may be bunched by the dozen. More recently some kinds of cut flowers have been bunched in units of 10. Spray chrysanthemums are bunched by weight, as this is a more practical method of designating quantity than the number of flowers.

The wrapping for the bunch of flowers should provide maximum protection and display. Usually, clear plastic film is used since the same degree of protection may be provided as with paper, and in addition the flowers are attractively displayed. The grade designation should be on each bunch, and if the grower's name or trademark is used, the retailer may readily identify stock of the same quality in future purchases.

Figure 7-2   A flower order packed at a wholesale commission house for shipment to a retail shop.

Before the flowers are marketed, they should be "hardened" by placing them in vases of water in cool storage (4 to 7°C) for a few hours. The usual routine is to cut, grade, and bunch the flowers, and then place them in vases of water in the refrigerator overnight.

Packaging of the flowers for shipment to the market depends on the distance from the market and the method of shipment. Flowers taken to the local market often are trucked in vases of water. Flowers to be shipped any distance must be well packed so they are not damaged in transit. The bunches of flowers are placed in the carton with stem and head ends alternating, and paper rolls or pillows are used to support and cushion the flowers. If each bunch of flowers is not protected by a wrapping, waxed tissue paper is placed around the flowers for protection. The packaging material must not absorb water from the flowers; waxed cartons must be provided, and parchment or waxed paper used for direct contact with flowers. The packaging used and the method of shipment must assure protection from temperature extremes. Refrigerated or iced facilities must be used in warm weather, and insulated or heated ones in cold weather. Some protection can be provided by insulating materials used in packaging, but this is very limited, short-term protection if the package is exposed to extreme temperatures.

KEEPING QUALITIES OF CUT FLOWERS

In spite of having been separated from the plant, cut flowers have life. True enough, the termination of that life is inevitably a few days to a few weeks after the flower is cut, but during this period the flower is living and may continue to develop and increase in size. The death of the flower occurs when its food or water supplies are exhausted. Anything done to increase the keeping qualities (life) of the cut flower is based on adequately maintaining its food and water supply.

The potential length of life after cutting varies with the different kinds of flowers. Under a given set of conditions roses might remain in good condition 5 days, carnations 7 days, chrysanthemums 14 days, and cymbidium orchids 28 days after they are cut. The flower does not necessarily distinguish among times spent with wholesaler, retailer, or consumer. Its potential life is the same regardless of ownership, but the ultimate consumer will not enjoy enough of that life if the flower has dallied too long en route. The keeping quality in the hands of the consumer is of most concern, and shortening the time from greenhouse to consumer is an excellent method of increasing the keeping quality of any flower. This is generally well understood by the individuals in the industry, and efforts are made to handle cut flowers rapidly.

The flower contains food and water at the time it is cut, but these will become depleted if new supplies are not added. The food supply varies considerably in the flower, depending on the conditions in which it was produced. Flowers grown in insufficient light, dark cloudy weather, or temperatures which are too high have a lower food supply and do not keep as long as those produced in more favorable conditions.

After the flower is cut, it should be placed in cool temperatures to reduce respiration and transpiration and to conserve the food and water in the flower. Flowers live longer in cool temperatures. A dramatic difference in keeping qualities may be demonstrated between room temperature (21°C) and a 4°C refrigerator. Some further benefits in keeping qualities are possible with some cut flowers when they are kept at temperatures just above freezing. The proper and continuous use of temperatures must become something of a religion if the best job is going to be done to conserve the keeping qualities of cut flowers. Of course it is not possible for consumers to exercise rigid temperature control, but they should be guided and counseled to display the flowers in as cool a location as possible. Some consumers do not realize that placing cut flowers in front of hot air registers or in direct sunlight will reduce their keeping qualities.

Cut flowers require a continuous supply of water. This may be approached from two directions: supplying adequate water to the flowers regardless of other environmental conditions, and reducing water loss from the flowers by cool temperatures or high humidity. Both approaches should be used. High humidity around the flowers is best provided by wrapping them in a moisture-proof film. The use of transparent plastic film around bunches of flowers protects them from physical damage, reduces moisture loss, and improves the display value of the flowers.

Water may be supplied adequately to cut flowers only if the stem is able to absorb water and there is sufficient water available. The stems should be recut before they are placed in a vase of water. Water can enter the stem where leaves or thorns have been removed or the stem sliced or lightly crushed; hence the vase must be deep enough so that the stems are immersed deeply in water to cover these areas. Warm water (43°C) should be used as it is absorbed more readily than cooler water. Clean water and vases must be used. Water and containers that are used repeatedly for cut flowers become fouled with bacterial growth, and when this occurs, the stems also become infected and plugged so that water is not absorbed effectively. Cut-flower containers should be cleaned regularly and treated with sodium hypochlorite or LF-10 solutions, and fresh water should be supplied each time the containers are used. Plugging of water-conducting tissue can also occur from breakdown of cells near the cut or wound on the stem.

Unfortunately, many retailers make flower arrangements without concern for the water requirements of the cut flowers. Apparently they have no conception of or concern about the effects of water on the keeping quality of flowers. Flowers placed in small vials of water or stuck into blocks of absorbent material in shallow containers are doomed to death from desiccation within a few hours. There is no possible way for even the informed and interested consumer to add water often enough to such containers to keep the flowers in good condition.

Some excellent commercially prepared cut-flower preservative mixtures are available, and no doubt improvements will continue to be made in these products. Most of these provide food for flowers plus an acidifier and possibly some growth regulators. These preservatives should not be used instead of proper temperature and moisture control but in addition to it. Keeping cut flowers in preservative solutions at all stages—wholesale, retail, and consumer—is helpful.

Ethylene gas has an aging effect on flowers. It may produce sleepiness in carnations, petal drop in roses, leaf drop in many flowers, and floret drop in snapdragons. The most common sources of ethylene are imperfect combustion of fuel, decaying plant material, florists' greens, and some fruits and vegetables. Flowers must not be stored in the same areas as fruits, vegetables, and florists' greens. Old flowers and plants must be eliminated from flower storage areas as they may produce ethylene. Combustion products from vehicle exhausts or the boiler may have harmful effects on flowers.

Costs of Production

There are many concepts of costs of production—not only of actual values per product but of methods for deriving them. The methods vary all the way from elementary ones that assume that the costs of production equal the amount of money disbursed currently to highly sophisticated and involved methods that project, prorate, and assign costs in the finest details. Actually many growers are willing to assume that the costs of production for the crops which they grow are the same as cost figures reported by some other grower. The only good method is the one which provides each individual grower with the complete costs involved in producing each crop.

Through the years it has become necessary to keep more detailed business records and make more voluminous reports to the government. It is necessary in most instances to employ an accountant to make the reports in an acceptable form. It is essential that the manager or owner of the business understand and fully appreciate that many of the accountants may do an acceptable job of making governmental reports but may have only slight interest in or knowledge about keeping some business records or analyzing them. The government, the accountant, and the owner of the business have their individual interests in the business. The primary interest of the government is in analyzing each business to determine whether it pays its proportionate share of the tax. It is possible that the accountant who is used will become involved only in the part of the business which requires governmental reports. The owner of the business may be highly interested in all phases of the business, and usually this will require keeping some records not required by the government. The analysis of these records leads to management decisions which affect the welfare of the business. The case in point here is costs of production. This is not the responsibility of the government or of accountants, but it is essential information which management personnel must develop so that decisions may be made which will lead to the profitable operation of the business—and incidentally the ability to pay taxes and accountants. Managers must choose the method of determining the complete costs of production for each crop.

COSTS VARY WITH THE EXPENDITURES AND THE QUANTITY PRODUCED

The cost of production per unit is the total cost for the crop divided by the number of units produced for sale. Because expenditures and yield both may vary with each crop, it is necessary to keep continuous records of both so that an accurate production cost figure will be available to compare with the income on the crop. This is the only way in which it can be determined whether the crop in question produces a profit.

Production or yield records are rather easily taken, but it is necessary to establish the exact manner in which they are to be kept. The yields of the various kinds of crops must be recorded separately, and in some instances it will be desirable to segregate the yield by cultivar. This record should be the number of units offered for sale rather than the number of flowers cut or the number of pot plants grown per bench. The methods of reporting yield and income must be made in the same manner so that meaningful comparisons may be made readily.

It is difficult to establish a workable method for keeping accurate cost records. The system must be foolproof enough that all the costs are assigned and to the right crops, but it must be simple enough to operate so that only the minimum amount of labor and time is required to maintain it. There is no one system of keeping cost records which will be suitable for all greenhouses. Each owner or manager must devise the system which best suits the purposes of the individual business. Some of the costs for a crop are the proportionate shares of the costs of conducting the entire business. Other costs can be charged directly to the crop, as they pertain solely to it.

The specific costs which can be assigned directly to each crop are labor, plants, seeds, bulbs, soil, pots, special equipment or power, packaging or wrapping, and transportation. With some crops the amount of labor is static, and the same labor costs are incurred each week. With most of the crops, however, the amount of labor which is used varies, and a system must be designed for charging the labor to the proper crop. In some instances each worker may be required to list the amount of time worked on each crop per pay period, and in other situations the supervisor may keep this record. Once the routine is established, it is not difficult to maintain the labor-crop record.

The general costs for the entire business may be prorated to each individual crop based on the area occupied per crop. This may be either the area under glass (which includes walks as well as bench area), or it may be bench area. Both methods have merit. In the discussions in this book, bench area per crop is used. Keeping records of the space occupied is easy for long-term crops such as roses and difficult for pot-plant crops which are continually moved and spaced. The best plan seems to be to take inventory of the entire range once a month and charge the area to the crops according to the space used at that time. All the area must be accounted for and charged to some crop each month. If any idle area cannot be charged properly to a specific crop, it then must be prorated to all the crops. Some of the general costs for the entire business which must be prorated to each crop are heating system, labor, irrigation system, taxes, structure, cooling system, vehicles, communication, repair and maintenance, fuel, power, night and weekend personnel, bad debts, insurance, office and storage buildings, refrigeration, handling equipment, general labor, administration including the owner's salary, interest on invested as well as operating capital, fertilizer, and pesticides.

Most greenhouses will have all these cost items, and some have others. All costs must be included. Either by design or through error some costs are commonly omitted. These are structure, owner's salary, and interest on invested and operating capital. Depending on governmental regulations, the cost of structure is depreciated over a period of years rather than assuming it all in a single year. Permanent structures are usually depreciated in 20 years and temporary structures in a shorter period of time. If the business has been operating within costs, at the end of the depreciation period funds will be available for replacing the structure. In the minds of some, the owner's salary is part of the profit. Actually, however, it is a definite cost of the business, and any residue which may remain after the total costs are subtracted from the total income is the profit which may go to the owner in addition to his salary.

In order to start and operate a business, a certain amount of capital is required. It is generally realized that capital is required to provide structures and some equipment, but too often the requirement of operating capital is forgotten or ignored. Supplies and equipment must be purchased, payrolls met, and credit extended. For a greenhouse range of 2,990 square meters (1,860 square meters of bench space), it is possible that the capital invested in land, structures, and equipment might be approximately $200,000. Depending on the crops and other factors, the potential gross income from such a greenhouse might be about $80,000 per year. Most of this gross income would be paid out in various costs—including the owner's salary. It is to be hoped that all costs would be met, and there would be a remainder left known as profit. The operating capital required for such a business might be approximately $20,000. This is money that is tied up constantly in current expenses and extended credit. Depending on how the products are sold, the capital involved in credit might be about $10,000 on the total amount of business. These are not bad debts but current accounts. For the 1,860 square meters of bench space, it might then be possible to need about $220,000 to provide the necessary structures, equipment, and operating capital. At 8 percent interest this would be $17,600 yearly to be included in the costs of production.

LABOR IS THE LARGEST ITEM IN COST OF PRODUCTION

The expenditure of funds varies with each greenhouse, but invariably the single item contributing the most to the cost of production is labor. Usually pot-plant crops require more labor than cut flowers. In areas of higher wage scales, the labor cost is higher. In some large greenhouse ranges, where the owner actually functions solely as an executive, it is possible that the expenditure for labor in proportion to the total cost will be higher and the administrative and owner's salary expenditure corresponding-ingly lower, whereas in smaller greenhouses the owner works as a laborer as well as an administrator. On the other hand, larger ranges may have more labor-saving equipment which reduces the expenditure for labor. For the greenhouse of 1,860 square meters of bench space referred to above, the distribution of costs might be as follows:

MEANS OF REDUCING COSTS OF PRODUCTION

Unfortunately, the means used commonly for reducing costs is simply to ignore some of the costs. This produces a false cost figure, creating the impression that the business is operating at a profit when in fact it may be losing money on each sale.

It is no more possible to operate a business without invested and operating capital than without structures or labor. The owner using personal

Item	Percentage of total costs
Labor	37
Administration and owner's salary	15
Interest on invested and operating capital	13
Structures and equipment (depreciation)	10
Fuel	10
Plants	5
Repairs	5
Other items	5
Total	100

funds to operate the business must charge to costs a fair rate of interest on this money. To some individuals it is clear that the interest on money borrowed to finance the business is a cost of production, but they see the use of the owner's own funds as a convenience which does not enter into the costs. The owner who operates on that basis is not getting the proper return on these funds.

Structures and equipment must be charged to costs on a depreciation schedule so that at the end of the depreciation period funds are on hand to replace them. Repairs must be made continually so that the best use and life are obtained from structures and equipment. Individuals who ignore these costs are commonly referred to as "living off the greenhouse." It is possible to operate a greenhouse on this basis for a limited time, but eventually structures and equipment become unusable and there is no money for repair or replacement.

There are really only two ways in which costs of production may be reduced. One is to produce more units of equal quality in the same space, and the other is to reduce expenditures. Both routes should be explored in the attempt to reduce costs of production. The discussions on various crops throughout this book include methods of producing more units of equal quality per given area; and if some of these suggestions can be used without increasing expenditures, costs per unit may be decreased.

Discussions of methods of reducing costs often get no further than saving labor. Since this may be the largest single item of expense, savings in this category certainly should be investigated—but not to the exclusion of the other costs. The analysis of labor costs is a complex subject which must consider more than the hourly rate paid and the total hours worked. Labor hired at a low rate may be less productive per dollar than higher priced help. Equipment and machines may replace some labor but may actually save labor only if managers make sure that the replaced individuals are either released or placed on other productive work. In some instances the high cost of labor is a direct result of lack of planning or instructions by the owner or manager. There are possibilities of saving labor costs if management personnel will expend the thought and time required for planning.

In the example used earlier in this chapter, the capital investment was based on the erection of the most durable structures and permanent equipment. This requires the maximum invested dollar, but usually the repair and depreciation rates are lower. It is possible to save some interest on invested capital by building on more reasonably priced land and erecting semipermanent structures. Young people interested in an "operation boot strap" venture may be able to get into business with a plastic film range to be replaced later with more permanent structures as funds become available. This is possible because not as much capital is required for a plastic house, and the costs of production may be lower because of savings in interest on the money invested.

An even bigger "savings" is effected by an individual starting in business who works extremely long hours for a very low salary. This may reduce the costs of production sufficiently so that there is money available to put back into the business for improvement of facilities or expansion. It must be recognized, however, that this is only a temporary expedient, and if the business is to flourish, a more realistic view of costs of production will have to be taken.

Index